SOCIAL JUSTICE, MULTICULTURAL COUNSELING, AND PRACTICE

*To my students, clients, and sons, Gabriel and Eliot, who led me
and lead me to grow emotionally, intellectually, and spiritually*

SOCIAL JUSTICE, MULTICULTURAL COUNSELING, AND PRACTICE
BEYOND A CONVENTIONAL APPROACH

HEESOON JUN
Evergreen State College

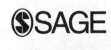

Los Angeles | London | New Delhi
Singapore | Washington DC

For information:

SAGE Publications, Inc.
2455 Teller Road
Thousand Oaks,
   California 91320
E-mail: order@sagepub.com

SAGE Publications India Pvt. Ltd.
B 1/I 1 Mohan Cooperative
   Industrial Area
Mathura Road, New Delhi 110 044
India

SAGE Publications Ltd.
1 Oliver's Yard
55 City Road
London EC1Y 1SP
United Kingdom

SAGE Publications Asia-Pacific Pte. Ltd.
33 Pekin Street #02-01
Far East Square
Singapore 048763

Printed in the United States of America.

Library of Congress Cataloging-in-Publication Data

Jun, Heesoon.
Social justice, multicultural counseling, and practice: Beyond a conventional approach / Heesoon Jun.
     p. cm.
Includes bibliographical references and index.
ISBN 978-1-4129-6056-4 (cloth)
ISBN 978-1-4129-6057-1 (pbk.)
   1. Cross-cultural counseling—United States.   2.   Counselors—Training of—United States.   3.   Multiculturalism—United States.   I. Title.

BF636.7.C76J86 2009
158´.3—dc22   2008053519

12   13   10   9   8   7   6   5   4   3   2

Acquiring Editor:	Kassie Graves
Editorial Assistant:	Veronica Novak
Production Editor:	Sarah K. Quesenberry
Copy Editor:	Melinda Masson
Proofreader:	Jenifer Kooiman
Indexer:	Michael Ferreira
Typesetter:	C&M Digitals (P) Ltd.
Cover Designer:	Gail Buschman
Marketing Manager:	Carmel Schrire

Contents

Preface

I initially had no intention of writing a book. I had been getting great satisfaction from teaching psychology, including multicultural counseling, and maintaining a part-time private practice. I was satisfied with my small part in facilitating a path of empowerment for my students and clients. However, I started to struggle with a question: What is my responsibility for a broader social change in the areas of diversity, multiculturalism, and pluralism? I have been successful on a small scale of social change, since the majority of my students have been implementing multicultural counseling theories into practice. Some of my former students had encouraged me to write a book about the multicultural program model to share with others who also want to make a small difference in the area of multicultural counseling. However, I was hesitant to enter the arena where other authors had promoted inclusiveness and a holistic perspective yet implemented these concepts according to a model of hierarchy and one-upmanship, negating the very perspective they were championing.

Reports on the substantial increase in multiracial and biracial people and people with diverse social identities, the increasing amount of thorough and well-done research in multicultural counseling, and frustration from not finding ways to bridge multicultural theories into practice set me free from my excuse. I no longer wanted to spend time struggling with my responsibility in areas of diversity, multiculturalism, and pluralism. My answer to the nagging question was to write a book on multicultural counseling and share what has worked in my multicultural counseling programs since 1996. What I would like to share is that practitioner-trainees can learn to view others from a holistic perspective by transcending inappropriate dichotomous, linear, and hierarchical thinking and transforming these thinking styles/patterns to holistic thinking. They can also learn multicultural issues through transformative learning, which facilitates compassion, resilience, collaboration, and understanding, and implementing social justice not only for the self but for others.

The book's proposals of shifting thinking and learning styles are basic foundations of dealing with multicultural issues locally, nationally, or internationally (globally). Once a practitioner-trainee learns to shift both thinking and learning styles, he/she/ze can work with individuals with complex demographic identities and dynamic and complex sociocultural contexts.

Heesoon Jun, PhD
Evergreen State College
Olympia, WA

Acknowledgments

This book is a product of several people's contributions. It was born as a result of their talents, gifts, and generosity. I am grateful to all of them.

Former senior editor at SAGE Dr. Art Pomponio's suggestion to include my students', my clients', and my own stories as examples was especially valuable, as was the willingness of Ms. Kassie Graves, acquisitions editor at SAGE, to finish someone else's project. Not only was she supportive of my ideas on including multiple identities and their intersections for accurate assessment and treatment, but her support extended to being flexible in allowing my vision and recruiting other scholars to review my drafts. Much appreciation goes to those scholars, especially to Dr. Judith Durham for her thoughtful suggestions for the final draft and Dr. Paul Pedersen, one of the leading pioneers in the field, for his generous and reassuring feedback on the final draft. Ms. Veronica Novak at SAGE linked all of us together.

My son, Gabriel Aust, and my dear friend, Earle McNeil, cannot be thanked enough for reading the entire manuscript for critique and encouragement. Their input was invaluable due to their passion and practice for social justice and equity. After 30 years of teaching sociology and psychology at the University of Puget Sound and Evergreen State College, Earle continues his social justice work by volunteering at a food bank and senior citizens' center. Gabriel works as a social worker to prevent injustice against children and marginalized families. Their generosity and dedication to social justice and their willingness to assist were instrumental to maintaining my energy level throughout the process. My sincere appreciation goes to my former students and clients for their permission to share their stories. All stated they wanted to contribute to the important work of social justice and equity for all people.

I am grateful to Ms. Sarah Quesenberry, production editor at SAGE, who let me know detailed schedules of the copyediting stages. She was open, flexible, and resourceful. Ms. Melinda Masson, a freelance copy-editor, was thorough with detailed observation for each sentence and brilliant in facilitating what I wanted to express. Her thoroughness and insightful suggestions were invaluable.

Each one's talent, gift, expertise, or generosity led me to reflect and reprocess my way of thinking, feeling, and writing. The process provided me with my own transformative learning experience.

1

Introduction

⫻ THE MILLENNIUM AND TWO ESSENTIAL INGREDIENTS FOR MULTICULTURAL COMPETENCIES

The new millennium was entered with the sociocultural context of increasingly diversified populations in the United States (Jons & Smith, 2001; United States Census Bureau, 2003, 2004). Various helping professional organizations responded to this change by updating their ethics codes or existing multicultural competencies to emphasize practitioners' cultural sensitivity to human diversity (American Counseling Association [ACA], 2005; American Psychological Association [APA], 2002, 2003; National Association of Social Workers [NASW], 1999; Roysircar, Arredondo, Fuertes, Ponterotto, & Toporek, 2003).

The National Association of Social Workers' mission statement includes the following:

Social workers are sensitive to cultural and ethnic diversity and strive to end discrimination, oppression, poverty, and other forms of social injustice. (NASW, 1999, Preamble, ¶ 2)

The American Psychological Association's unfair discrimination section states:

In their work-related activities, psychologists do not engage in unfair discrimination based on age, gender, gender identity, race, ethnicity, culture, national origin, religion, sexual orientation, disability, socioeconomic status, or any basis proscribed by law. (APA, 2002, Section 3.01)

1

The American Counseling Association's code of ethics includes the following:

> Association members recognize diversity and embrace a cross-cultural approach in support of the worth, dignity, potential, and uniqueness of people within their social and cultural contexts. (ACA, 2005, Preamble, ¶ 1)

These conceptual frameworks to serve the multicultural population have been well postulated with good intentions. Numerous scholars and multicultural counseling theorists have also responded to this need by emphasizing how to be culturally sensitive to certain groups or how to understand the complexities involved in multicultural counseling (Atkinson & Hackett, 2004; Axelson, 1999; Constantine & Sue, 2005: Harper & McFadden, 2003; Pedersen, Lonner, Draguns, & Trimble, 2007; Ponterotto, Casas, Suzuki, & Alexander, 2001; Robinson-Wood, 2008; Sue & Sue, 2007). They have contributed substantially to raising consciousness of understanding multicultural counseling, as well as expanded the concept of counseling beyond traditional models. D'Andrea and Heckman (2008), who have been reviewing multicultural counseling outcome research for the past 40 years, state:

> The multicultural counseling movement is clearly transforming the thinking and practices of many counselor educators, practitioners, researchers, and students in training. . . . After almost 40 years of scholarly work, multicultural theorists have greatly extended counselors' thinking about the impact that racial/ethnic/cultural factors have on counseling endeavors aimed at stimulating healthy human development. (p. 356)

D'Andrea and Heckman (2008) conclude that the multicultural counseling movement has expanded the importance of examining the differences among racial/ethnic/cultural groups because human development and appropriate psychological intervention vary according to different cultural perspectives. The movement has also extended the importance of understanding within-group differences for accurate assessment and treatment. The authors' findings indicate the importance of not stereotyping culturally different groups.

In an attempt to understand racially different groups, most existing multicultural counseling textbooks categorize people according to convention. Conventional categorization of ethnic groups provides basic information about each. However, identifying a counseling approach for each racial group increases the tendency for it to be stereotyped, and such an approach provides no instructions for counseling individuals from the racial group who do not fit the stereotype. This approach also minimizes individuals who do not fit into these categories, including those who claim bicultural (e.g., race) or multicultural (e.g., race, gender, class) identities. Racial categorization is not realistic because it is impossible to accurately describe the characteristics of each ethnic and racial group partly due to the fact that variations within one group are as diverse as variations among separate groups and partly due to the fact that a person's identity construction is a result of not a single factor but intersections of race, ethnicity, gender, sexual orientation, age, language, class, disability, religion, and so on. Racial categorization not only strengthens stereotypes; it also perpetuates inappropriate dichotomous thinking. The challenge for a multicultural practitioner is how to obtain and accurately apply knowledge about a particular racial group without minimizing or missing idiosyncrasies of an individual within it.

Emphasis on racial issues has been predominant in multicultural counseling textbooks. They focus on race as if racial issues—such as racial identity, racial discrimination and prejudice, systematic and internalized racial oppression, and racism—represent other diversities related to gender, sexual orientation, class, age, language, religion, region, and so on. Hays's (2008) review of multicultural competence assessment indicates that the current definition of multicultural counseling "fails to directly apply to the needs of other disenfranchised groups" (p. 97). Numerous scholars and researchers have suggested that understanding a client's relevant social and demographic identities is necessary to understand a client's worldview (Berry & Sam, 1997; Cross, 1995; Croteau & Constantine, 2005; Douce, 2005; Paniagua, 2005; Ponterotto et al., 2001). The following represents the common theme of need for understanding a client's multiple identities by most scholars and researchers:

> An individual can be fully understood only in a holistic manner that includes understanding the influences and interactions of the individual's multiple sociodemographic groups, some or all of which may be salient "identities" for the individual. (Croteau & Constantine, 2005, p. 162)

If the complexities of multiple identities, intersections of multiple identities, and sociocultural contexts are simplified into static, dichotomous, and hierarchical categories, the individual is totally missed.

Equating a person with a single identity as if it alone represents him or her is creating superficiality and illusion (Collins, 1991; Katz-Gerro, 2006; Markus, 1977). Several researchers have examined the intersections of some multiple identities, and their studies are discussed throughout this book in relevant sections. Despite the need for them, there are few books that address other areas of social and demographic identities in relation to race. Pope-Davis and Coleman (2001) emphasize the intersection of race, class, and gender in constructing the identity of an individual. Croteau, Lark, Lidderdale, and Chung (2005) address heterosexism in counseling. Robinson-Wood (2008) discusses race, gender, socioeconomic class, sexual orientation, and physical ability and disability. Bieschke, Croteau, Lark, and Vandiver (2005) explain the difficulty of integrating all of a client's social identities:

> While we strongly believe that the counterdiscourse needs to more fully integrate multiple social identities and cultural contexts, such a shift toward complexity and inclusiveness will be painful, giving rise to unexplored conflicts and necessitating difficult exploration and dialogues. (p. 203)

Bieschke et al.'s (2005) statement is a crucially important point that needs to be addressed by scholars, practitioners, and researchers of multicultural counseling competencies. Such professionals need to consider whether they are truly interested in multicultural counseling competencies or whether they are only interested in promoting their salient identities under the name of multicultural competencies. If they are interested in only their own importance, they need to examine how they differ from members of the dominant groups who have oppressed and marginalized them. Multicultural counseling competencies require tolerance for ambiguity; assigning equal importance to others' cultural values, beliefs, and ways of making meaning; and respect for the ways of being and traditions of others. It is important to have counterdiscourse no matter how painful it is. In order to do so, various factors that have prevented practitioners and scholars from addressing unexplored conflicts need to be examined.

It may be valuable to reflect on barriers to implementing conceptual theories of multicultural counseling by exploring whether there are some parallels between the difficulty of having counterdiscourse of integration of multiple identities and contexts and the difficulty of incorporating conceptual theories into practice. Research has indicated several barriers to implementing conceptual theories, including the fact that Western ideology is embedded in the practices of counseling and development (Daniels, 2007; Gladding, 2006; Ivey, D'Andrea, Ivery, & Simek-Morgan, 2007). Western ideology emphasizes the rational over the relational, logic over emotion, competition over cooperation, and independence over interdependence. That practitioners have pathologized people of color and women may be a result of misunderstanding behaviors that stem from a non-Western ideology (Rapley, 2004; Robb, 2006; Stubblefield, 2007). Western ideology is based on individualism, which often leads to self-focused behavior. Research findings with regard to social projection, attribution error, asymmetric perception, introspection, and ingroup favoritism have indicated individuals' tendency toward high self-appraisal and low appraisal of others. Participants in a number of studies (Epley & Dunning, 2000; Pronin, Gilovich, & Ross, 2004; Pronin, Lin, & Ross, 2002; Steele, 1988; Taylor & Brown, 1988) believed that they were *less* biased than their peers and thus that their peers were *more* biased than they. Implications of high self-appraisal and low appraisal of others are indications of ethnocentric bias.

Another barrier to incorporating conceptual theories of multicultural counseling into practice is the inability to be aware of inconsistencies between walk and talk. Inconsistencies between behavior and knowledge have appeared in studies of implicit learning, aversive racism, and attribution error (Banaji & Bhaskar, 2001; Blair & Banaji, 1996; Chen & Bargh, 1997; Dovidio, Gaertner, Kawakami, & Hodson, 2002). It is possible that some scholars, practitioners, and researchers are not aware of their ethnocentric biases or of inconsistencies between their behavior and their knowledge. Recent cognitive and social psychology research has revitalized the role of the unconscious process in learning. Dovidio and colleagues' work on aversive racism and Banaji and colleagues' work on implicit attitudes and learning in particular demonstrate its importance. Banaji and Bhaskar (2001) state:

> In contrast to the first hundred years of research, which conveyed a view of memory and beliefs as operating exclusively in a conscious mode, the past two decades have shown increasingly that both memory and belief also operate implicitly in powerful yet unconscious ways, outside the actor's awareness. (p. 140)

The discovery of the role of the unconscious process in learning explains the challenges involved in dismantling prejudice and stereotypes and integrating multiple identities. It suggests the need to develop strategies for dealing with the unconscious learning process in order to transcend racism, sexism, classism, heterosexism, ableism, ageism, and other "isms."

Just intending to deconstruct or transcend prejudice and stereotypes is not an effective strategy. Just intending to integrate multiple identities will not lead to their integration without painful and uncomfortable counterdiscourse. Various studies that will be discussed in relevant chapters indicate that children learn and develop strong attachments to their worldviews, values, and beliefs at an early age through socialization. Transcending some of these values and beliefs must include processing the emotional attachment to them. Intellectual understanding alone does not activate automatic transcendence. Cognitive information processing research indicates the resistance of implicit attitudes to change.

There are parallels between the inability to implement theoretical conceptualization of multicultural counseling and the inability to have counterdiscourse for an integration of multiple identities and contexts. Embedment of Western ideology, ethnocentric bias, and unconscious learning may all play a part. It is the author's hope that the holistic model presented in this book makes a small contribution for counterdiscourse.

The recent social justice movement in multicultural counseling implies that practitioners no longer can hide behind conceptualization of multicultural competencies. They need to know how to implement competencies emotionally as well as intellectually to work toward equal access to justice and equity for marginalized individuals and groups (Constantine, Hage, Kindaichi, & Bryant, 2007). Constantine et al. identified nine specific social justice competencies for practitioners. They are (a) awareness of oppression and social inequities; (b) ongoing self-reflection with regard to race, ethnicity, oppression, power, and privilege; (c) the impact of a practitioner's power and privilege on clients, communities, and research participants; (d) questioning, challenging, and intervening in inappropriate or exploitative therapeutic or intervention practices to promote the well-being of an affected individual or group; (e) having and, when appropriate, sharing knowledge about indigenous healing practices; (f) awareness of ongoing international social injustice; (g) conceptualizing, implementing, and evaluating comprehensive mental health intervention programs for the multicultural population; (h) collaboration with community organizations to provide culturally relevant services; and (i) developing systematic intervention and advocacy skills for social change. Social justice–oriented programs include service-based learning through internships and volunteer work (Kenny & Gallagher, 2000; Mulvey et al., 2000). Social justice and equity is an essential component of multicultural counseling, in which a practitioner assists clients with rising above systematic oppression and works with them to deconstruct, transcend, and transform internalized and systematic oppression.

Collins and Pieterse (2007) examined the affective transformative process of Roysircar et al.'s (2003) multicultural counseling competencies, which were adopted by the American Psychological Association in 2003. This signifies APA's conceptual commitment to serving individuals who are culturally different. The multicultural counseling competencies are divided into three areas: (a) counselor awareness of her own cultural values and biases, (b) counselor awareness of the client's worldview, and (c) culturally appropriate intervention strategies. Each area is further divided into three sections: (a) attitudes and beliefs, (b) knowledge, and (c) skills. For example, a culturally skilled counselor's specific characteristics are described under (a) the attitude and belief section, (b) the knowledge section, and (c) the skill section of all three multicultural counseling competencies. Operationalized for clarity, these descriptions provide specific goals for practitioners to achieve in order to be multiculturally competent. Collins and Pieterse discuss the set of limitations to goal-oriented multicultural counseling competency description, including the possibility that counselors will focus on identifying and describing competency and just "saying the right things at the right time" without delivering what is said in practice. They suggest using the process perspective in conjunction with the "fixed goal" approach:

> We focus on competency as a process that involves engaging in an honest exploration of one's experience of racial and cultural reality. Such a process may not necessarily arrive at an end point; rather, it requires a daily choice to engage issues of race and culture internally and externally. . . . It requires mechanics of competence as a daily lived experience. The process perspective also emphasizes that competence involves ongoing effort and commitment. (p. 15)

Collins and Pieterse's (2007) suggestion to add a process component to multicultural counseling competencies is an attempt to facilitate affective processing of cognitive understanding of multicultural awareness. This is an important step since most training programs focus on cognitive aspects rather than integrating cognition and emotion (Adams, Bell, & Griffin, 1997; Holcomb-McCoy & Myers, 1999; Ponterotto, 1998). Training that uses such unconventional methods as "reaction papers, journal writing, role playing, videotaping, cross-cultural immersion experience, cross-cultural simulation experiences, experiential exercises, fishbowl exercises, small group processing and focus groups" (Collins & Pieterse, p. 16) seems to have some success in changing trainees' attitudes toward multicultural competencies (Helms et al., 2003).

This book attempts to bridge the gap between theoretical conceptualization and implementation of theories by providing a comprehensive multicultural counseling model that treats multiple identities of an individual and intersections of multiple identities equally. The model is similar to the multicultural counseling competencies in its integration of the goal and the process, cognition and emotion, and justice and equity for clients with nondominant cultural backgrounds. This book includes a chapter on accessing inner experience through unconventional methods, such as integrating subjective (personal) inquiry with objective (scientific) inquiry, in an attempt to balance the affective transformative process with the rational transformative process.

The purpose of this book is to provide practical strategies for increasing multicultural competencies from a holistic perspective, which allows practitioners to understand clients from their sociocultural historical contexts with multiple identities and truths. This requires being cautious of conventional racial categorizing and being aware of the effect of a practitioner's own culture, worldview, and thinking styles on assessing and treating clients. This book proposes (a) a shift from a single identity–based conceptual framework to one that is based on multiple identities and (b) a shift from talking about practical implementation to delivering it through transformative learning to increase multicultural competencies. The inclusion of multiple identities requires a holistic thinking style that comprises appropriate dichotomous, linear, and hierarchical thinking in addition to multilayered and multidimensional thinking. Shifting from inappropriate dichotomous, hierarchical, and linear thinking styles to a holistic thinking style is a challenging task since the former are embedded in the American psyche (Singer & Kimbles, 2004). Hierarchical and dichotomous thinking styles first emerged in the United States with the birth of the country by new White settlers from England (Jahoda, 1999; Takaki, 1993; Thompson 1977). Both Nash (1992) and Root (1992) discuss the impact of hierarchical social systems and simplifying (dichotomizing) complex relationships on oppression of people who are racially different. Dichotomous and hierarchical thinking styles are the basis of ethnocentrism (Bizumic & Duckitt, 2007; Brown, 1995). If children are socialized in a culture where linear, dichotomous, and hierarchical thinking styles are valued, they are more likely to internalize these values and become ethnocentric without being aware of it. If they are socialized in a culture that emphasizes either a multilayered perspective, a multidimensional perspective, or both (diunital) thinking styles, they are more likely to internalize these values and unconsciously develop a holistic perspective. Children from cultures that emphasize competition, superiority, and the importance of external images are likely to learn to see these values as core values, and these values foster hierarchical and dichotomous thinking styles in children (Black-Gutman & Hickson, 1996; Powlishta, Serbin, Doyle, & White, 1994). As a result, these children are likely to think in terms of winning, being right, and being correct (*dichotomous thinking*) and to believe that these are better than losing, being wrong, and being incorrect (*hierarchical thinking*). These types of thinking lead to unintentional racism, sexism, heterosexism, ableism, classism, and ageism (Brewer & Brown, 1998; Hewstone, Rubin, & Willis, 2002). This book postulates that deconstructing inappropriate dichotomous and hierarchical thinking is one way to shift to holistic thinking.

Multicultural counseling is just lip service as long as practitioners perpetuate inappropriate dichotomous and hierarchical thinking patterns in their assessment, diagnosis, and treatment of culturally diverse clients. These thinking styles/patterns hinder practitioners' ability to implement conceptually sound multicultural counseling theories. Practitioners are not likely to understand clients' worldviews or accurately assess their own worldviews without deconstructing inappropriate dichotomous, linear, and hierarchical thinking. Racism, sexism, classism, heterosexism, ableism, and other "isms" are based on such inappropriate thinking, and practitioners must understand the complexities of these "isms" and their intersections in order to provide effective assessment and treatment. Deconstructing inappropriate thinking styles and patterns requires diligent and mindful practice each day. Understanding the need to deconstruct is not the same as deconstructing.

The other proposed shift, delivering practical implementation through transformative learning, begins with the definition of transformative learning: learning to integrate intellectual understanding (knowledge) with emotional understanding (affect). The importance of emotional understanding in examining practitioners' values has been discussed in the past but not emphasized in connection to transforming the knowledge component of learning (Lee, 1997; Sue, Arredondo, & McDavis, 1992; Sue & Sue, 1990). This book considers transformative learning as an essential ingredient along with deconstructing inappropriate thinking styles/patterns because intellectual learning alone does not transcend egocentric and ethnocentric attitudes, values, and beliefs that are learned through socialization from early childhood. This is an enormously challenging task, primarily due to exclusion of emotion from academic contexts and the long-held belief that reacting emotionally to academic material is a sign of weakness. Such cultures as that of the United States in which intellectual understanding is valued throughout academic life have learned to equate intelligence and logical thinking with academic achievement. Often, parents and teachers unintentionally or intentionally devalue the emotional aspects of development in an attempt to encourage high academic achievement—a guarantee, they assume, that students will get into a "good college," receive "good scholarships," get a "good job," and/or be accepted by a "good graduate school." As a result, most children from this type of cultural context learn to disconnect their emotion from academic learning. Some parents and teachers punish children when they do not perform at their expected level on the assumption that they would do "better" next time to avoid punishment. It may appear to work for some children because they maintain expected academic achievement. Other children, however, may develop feelings of inferiority or low self-esteem as a result. For these children, it may contribute to long-lasting emotional scars. By the time these children become young adults, they believe that academic learning occurs within a rational, logical, and intellectual framework that seems like a fact and not a belief. Devaluation of emotion in academic settings is treated as if it is a core learning principle. For example, most students in psychology, counseling, social work, education, and communication intellectually understand that perception is the way people organize and interpret sensory input to make meaning. Such students are also likely to understand that perception is influenced by their own culture, gender, class, sexual orientation, birth order, religion, language, disability, motivation, education, socioeconomic status, age, race, ethnicity, expectations, and region. They also understand that people can make meaning only on the basis of the information they have in their mind (brain) and that people's different experiences influence how they process that information. Therefore, they intellectually understand the concept that 10 people can see the same object and interpret it in 10 different ways. For example, one simple picture shown to a college class may elicit various responses. If students are asked to describe a picture of two women with a single adjective, their responses may range from *beautiful* to *ugly*. If they are then asked why the same picture received such a broad range of interpretations (from *beautiful* to *ugly*), they may have no problem attributing it to individual differences in perception. However, these same students may express frustration and anger when others do not behave according to their expectations because they are not able to apply their conceptual (intellectual) understanding of "individual difference in perception" to their practice. They have a theoretical and conceptual understanding of perception without practical application to their situations. This is partly due to the fact that conventional learning of perception excludes the opportunity for students to integrate their intellectual understanding of perception with their emotional understanding of it. Conventional learning often does not provide the opportunity to assess whether students have learned through transformative learning. Transformative learning takes students to another level from conventional learning. It asks how they feel about their conceptual learning, as well as asks them to report their reactions when they integrate emotion into the concept. In order for learning to be transformative, it must reach the emotional core of an individual's values and beliefs so that it transforms the individual internally as well as externally and intellectually as well as emotionally. The emotional aspects of learning require learning through the heart with awareness of one's own culture, biases, thought patterns, and communication styles and the impact of one's own dominant (special or salient) identity. The emotional component of transformative learning means that it cannot be hurried. It takes time to process complex emotions, desires, wants, and "shoulds."

What is unique about this book is its emphasis on both a holistic thinking style and transformative learning as essential ingredients for increasing multicultural competencies. The book proposes devoting effort to deconstructing inappropriate thinking styles and allowing space for transformative learning. Shifting from conceptual to transformative learning will stir intense emotions in class because multicultural issues provoke strong emotions. Multicultural issues are about systematic inequity and injustice, which have been perpetuated for generations. They are about untold history, social injustice, systematic oppression/privilege, internalized oppression/privilege, and White guilt. For different reasons, emotions are stirred in both the privileged and the oppressed. These strong emotions need to be examined through transformative learning in an academic or organizational/institutional setting in order to prevent generational perpetuation of unintentional and intentional injustice and inequity. Conceptual and rational understanding has not been able to transcend injustice, inequity, and complex emotions around multicultural issues.

The book's broader conceptual framework on multicultural counseling competencies is based on the Association for Multicultural Counseling and Development (AMCD) model as described in *Multicultural Counseling Competencies* (Roysircar ct al., 2003). The model emphasizes a practitioner's awareness of her own cultural values, beliefs, and biases in order to be aware of the client's worldview and to provide culturally appropriate treatment. However, the AMCD model does not explain the process of achieving multicultural counseling competencies. The proposed model guides practitioner-trainees to become multiculturally competent practitioners. It focuses on the process of achieving the goal of multicultural counseling competencies through experiential and reflection-based learning activities. Personal narratives of marginalized individuals, excerpts from other books, case studies, centering, drawing, narrative- and reflection-based writing, small-group discussions, and so on are built into each chapter for affective processing of multicultural issues. Systematic oppression/privilege and internalized oppression/privilege are also discussed as necessary to expand practitioners' awareness, which assists in their attempt to understand clients' worldviews.

※ UNIQUE STRUCTURES

This is the first book that conceptualizes the identity of a person from a holistic perspective by simultaneously examining one's multiple identities and how they intersect. Most theorists have conceptualized each social identity of an individual as if it is independent of his/her/zir other identities (i.e., race, gender, sexual orientation, class, age, language, religion, region). Focusing on one identity whether it is race, gender, or class creates something that does not represent the person (Collins, 1991). The whole person's identity within a particular sociocultural context is represented by intersections of multiple identities and how they interrelate. Part II illustrates the complexities and interwoven characteristics of multiple identities as each chapter adds another identity and examines how it intersects with those previously mentioned. There are other unique structures of the book:

1. It provides practical application through concrete strategies immediately after each concept for transformative learning. These are mostly experiential learning activities, written in the first person, that facilitate affective transformation. Most of these activities are designed for individuals rather than groups. This is intentional as it allows for an individual's transformation in inner experiences and prevents ingroup influence.

2. It integrates conventional or traditional theories and techniques with unconventional theories and techniques to explore complexities of multicultural issues.

3. It shows how practitioners can be aware of their own inner dialogue and thought processes (intrapersonal communication) as they shift from inappropriate *dichotomous* and *hierarchical* thinking to a multilayered and multidimensional (*holistic*) thinking style. This shift in thinking will assist practitioner-trainees not only with helping their clients identify their thought styles/patterns and processes but also with understanding their own worldview as well as that of clients.

4. It shows how to incorporate scientific inquiry into clinical inquiry for accurate assessment, diagnosis, and effective treatment.

5. It uses case studies, the author's former students' writings or statements, excerpts from already published books, and the author's own experiences as a practitioner, a faculty member, and a bicultural and bilingual person as models for concrete examples or to facilitate emotional integration with intellectual understanding of a particular concept.

6. It explores effective strategies for using the *Diagnostic and Statistical Manual of Mental Disorders (DSM-IV-TR*; American Psychiatric Association, 2000) and current professional ethics codes of the multicultural population.

7. It does not include chapter summaries. This is to encourage readers to take a moment to center and observe their inner experience about each chapter.

8. It does not include conventional chapters on categorizing different racial groups and suggesting implications for practitioners for each racial group. That type of approach, though valuable in giving basic information, is dangerous because it has the potential to minimize variations within a particular group and may lead to stereotyping.

9. It is not written like a traditional textbook. The strong emphasis on writing is designed to get practitioner-trainees interested in learning and applying theories and practical strategies for being multiculturally competent.

Fictitious first names for individuals who gave both written and verbal permissions are used to protect their privacy. Real stories have the power to connect to an individual's emotion and intellect, and all of the case studies, students' writings and statements, and author's stories are real.

The term *practitioners* is used to imply counselors, psychologists, social workers, therapists, and other helping professionals. *Practitioner-trainees* is used for those who are in training to become professionals. *She* is used for a practitioner or practitioner-trainee. *He* is used for a client. On a few occasions, *ze* or *zir* is used in conjunction with *he* and *she* or *his* and *her* to include transgender populations.

＄＄ SUGGESTIONS FOR USING THE BOOK

It is imperative that practitioner-trainees read this book sequentially from the introduction to the last chapter since each chapter is a building block for the next. Each chapter is designed to provide the opportunity for practitioner-trainees to enhance their transformative learning skills and incorporate conceptual theories into practice. Certain concepts are designed for practitioner-trainees to learn through feeling before moving on to the next chapter. It is crucial for practitioner-trainees to complete each learning activity before reading the next section. Some may feel resistant to experiential learning activities due to their unfamiliarity and/or a habit of excluding emotion from academic learning. Only through acknowledging these feelings and completing the activities, however, will a new level of understanding come to the chapter material. Change happens gradually because it requires a new or different way of learning. As practitioner-trainees complete the learning activities diligently, mindfully, and consistently, the resentment or awkwardness will gradually disappear.

＄＄ OUTLINE OF THE CHAPTERS

Chapter 1 describes the thesis, unique characteristics, and function of the book in increasing multicultural competencies. The rest of the book is divided into three parts: Part I, "A Practitioner's Awareness of Her Own Worldview"; Part II, "A Practitioner's Awareness of Systematic Oppression/Privilege and Internalized Oppression/Privilege"; and: Part III, "A Practitioner's Awareness of the Client's Worldview." The first two parts prepare a practitioner-trainee for being able to be aware of a client's worldview. There are two chapters in Part I (Chapters 2 and 3), and they center on a practitioner's awareness of her own intrapersonal communication, thinking style or pattern, values, beliefs, and biases. The process of how thinking styles become automatic thought patterns, the role of intrapersonal communication in shaping automatic thinking patterns, and the role of socialization in meaning making are discussed. There are seven chapters in Part II. Six of these (Chapters 4–9) explore the practitioner's awareness of systematic oppression/privilege and internalized oppression/privilege, as well as the role of inappropriate linear, dichotomous, and hierarchical thinking in perpetuating "isms." Prejudice and intersections of multiple identities are examined from a multilayered and multidimensional perspective while providing an opportunity for transformative learning. Chapter 10 provides practical strategies for deconstructing inappropriate dichotomous, hierarchical, and linear thinking styles.

The first 10 chapters prepare practitioner-trainees for increasing their ability to access their own awareness of their cultural values, beliefs, and biases, and these are preparation for Part III. It is almost impossible to understand others' worldviews without being aware of one's own culture, beliefs, values, and biases. Chapter 11 discusses various models of identity development for nondominant monoracial groups, biracial and multiracial groups, the dominant (White) group, and the gay and lesbian group. The role of internalized privilege and oppression in constructing identity development is also explored. Chapter 12 discusses how identity development runs along a continuum and how multiple identities operate at multiple degrees and multiple dimensions simultaneously. It discusses how simplifying these complexities by using dichotomous and hierarchical thinking leads to inaccurate understanding of clients. Chapter 13 explores the importance of accurate assessment for developing culturally appropriate healing/treatment. The chapter discusses specific strategies for obtaining accurate information from clients who have multicultural backgrounds—for example, (a) exploring the relationship between intake and developing effective treatment strategy, (b) understanding the relationship between the type of verbal communication style and the type of listening style, (c) incorporating scientific inquiry into clinical inquiry, (d) discussing effective use of multiaxial assessment of *DSM-IV-TR* (American Psychiatric Association, 2000), and (e) applying the ethics code of ACA (2005), APA (2002), or NASW (1999) to provide a culturally sensitive and accurate assessment. Chapter 14 discusses the qualities of a multiculturally competent practitioner who can provide culturally appropriate treatment for clients with different cultural backgrounds.

Part I

A Practitioner's Awareness of Her Own Worldview

As indicated in the introduction, there have not been major changes in clinical practice despite numerous attempts to provide effective assessments and treatments for multicultural populations (Lee, 1997; Sue, Arredondo, & McDavis, 1992). Neither inventing nor adding more guidelines has assisted practitioners with being able to apply them in practice because how to implement them in practical settings is not explained. For example, the first principle of the American Psychological Association's guidelines states:

> Ethical conduct of psychologists is enhanced by knowledge of differences in beliefs and practices that emerge from socialization through racial and ethnic group affiliation and membership and how those beliefs and practices will necessarily affect the education, training, research, and practice of psychology. (APA, 2003, Principle 1)

APA's acknowledgment of the importance of the impact of racial and ethnic differences on the education, training, research, and practice of psychology is a substantial improvement compared with its historical position on racism (Guthrie, 1998; Ponterotto, Utsey, & Pedersen, 2006; Thomas & Sillen, 1972). However, having the knowledge alone does not necessarily enhance "ethical conduct." Psychologists may understand the concept, but conceptual understanding does not automatically lead to practical application. Various cognitive and social psychology research findings have shown inconsistencies between knowledge and behavior (Banaji & Bhaskar, 2001; Banaji & Hardin, 1996; Blair & Banaji, 1996; Chen & Bargh, 1997; Dovidio, Gaertner, Kawakami, & Hodson, 2002; Greenwald, McGhee, & Schwartz, 1998; Henderson-King & Nisbett, 1996). For knowledge to enhance "ethical conduct," practitioners need to take concrete steps to examine their own cultural values, beliefs, and biases because what they are required to do as ethical professionals may not be consistent with their worldview or because they may not be aware that their knowledge and behavior are inconsistent. Being aware of the inconsistencies between one's knowledge and one's behavior requires an ability to reflect on one's own values, beliefs, and biases and how they manifest through interpersonal communication and behavior. Chapter 2 explores the relationship between intrapersonal communication and values, beliefs, and biases. The chapter also explores the complex relationship among intrapersonal communication; thinking styles/patterns; and values, beliefs, and biases. Chapter 3 discusses the importance of a practitioner's ability to be aware of her inner experience because it is affected by her values, beliefs, and biases. Various unconventional strategies for accessing one's inner experience are included.

2

Intrapersonal
Communication
(Inner Dialogue)

C hapter 2 discusses the mechanisms involved in learning and
manifesting individuals' values, beliefs, and biases and their
relationship to intrapersonal communication. Interwoven and
complex relationships among socialization, internalized privilege and
oppression, the formation of thinking styles, the process of thinking patterns, and the formation of automation are explored. This chapter discusses the origin of inappropriate hierarchical, dichotomous, and linear
thinking styles in the United States and theories such as social learning,
attribution error, and social projection; the major U.S. cultural values;
and inappropriate generalizations in an attempt to illustrate the challenge
involved in deconstructing inappropriate hierarchical, dichotomous, and
linear thinking styles/patterns. The chapter concludes with the necessi-
ties of transformative learning in order to meet the challenge.

⧗ INTRAPERSONAL COMMUNICATION
AND VALUES, BELIEFS, AND BIASES

Intrapersonal communication is a mirror image of one's own cultural values, beliefs, and biases. All communication starts from intrapersonal
communication (Ruesch & Bateson, 1987). Interpersonal communication occurs when a communicator interacts with others. Intrapersonal

communication occurs when a communicator talks or thinks to himself/herself/zirself. In intrapersonal communication, a communicator (the self) is his/her/zir own message sender and receiver in an ongoing internal process. Intrapersonal communication is also known as self-talk, inner dialogue, inner monologue, self-dialogue, inner speech, and self-verbalization. It is an active internal process ranging from conscious to altered to unconscious states. The conscious part of intrapersonal communication ranges from thinking to interpreting the verbal and nonverbal communication of others. The altered states of intrapersonal communication range from daydreaming to nocturnal dreaming to body language, which can appear anywhere in the spectrum of conscious to unconscious intrapersonal communication. There is a dynamic relationship between intrapersonal communication and interpersonal communication (Vohs & Finkel, 2006). Intrapersonal communication is a foundation for all intercommunication and starts in early childhood as a result of external messages from parents, schools, churches, media, and culture. A practitioner's understanding of her intrapersonal communication is one of the important elements in understanding her values, beliefs, and biases. When a practitioner is not aware of the impact of her values, beliefs, and biases on her ability to help clients, she may unintentionally marginalize them. This point is well illustrated in the reality therapy section of Corey's (2001) casebook:

Ruth: It was really bad last night, all horrible feelings.

Therapist [interrupting]: The sweats, the palpitations, the fear of impending doom, the whole kit and kaboodle of your midnight misery. I will grant you this, if you've learned anything in your 39 years, it's how to panic. Don't you think it's time to learn something better to do at night?

Ruth: How can you talk like that? Do you really believe I'm choosing this panic, that I enjoy these attacks? How can I possibly be choosing them? They come on while I'm sleeping, and they wake me up.

Therapist: Tell me if you're not choosing them, who is? You've read about choice theory. You choose all you do, just as I do and just as everyone does. Of course, you're not enjoying this choice, but—I know this is hard to believe—to you it's better than anything else you could choose in the middle of the night. (p. 146)

In this case, the therapist assumes what Ruth is feeling without letting her finish her story. By interrupting Ruth and telling her about her feelings, the therapist is not only marginalizing the client but also assuming she knows the client's internal world (*hierarchical and patriarchal thinking*). This type of therapeutic process damages rather than helps the client despite being done in the name of "helping." Stating "if you've learned anything in your 39 years, it's how to panic" is belittling the client—a practice that does not ensure that "clients' interests are primary" (National Association of Social Workers, 1999, Section 1.01); nor does it demonstrate that the therapist is in support of the "worth, dignity, potential, and uniqueness" of the client (American Counseling Association, 2005, Preamble, ¶ 1). The therapist, it appears, is engaging in "unfair discrimination" (APA, 2002, Section 3.01). Another culturally insensitive remark in the above example, the therapist's comment about choice, indicates that she is generalizing her own beliefs about choice. The therapist's concept of choice is based on Euro American individualistic values. Most people from collectivism-oriented cultures are not socialized to value choice in the same way that Euro Americans are (see "Culture and the Meaning of Words: A Vietnamese Perspective on 'Choice' Versus 'Duty'" at the end of this section).

The therapist in the above example might know that a therapist-client relationship is a power differential relationship, and most clients believe that therapists are experts who have more knowledge with which to assist them. The therapist might have had every intention of assisting Ruth. The purpose of citing the above example is to address how difficult it is to incorporate theoretical knowledge into therapeutic practice due to various unintentional and/or unconscious factors such as implicit learning, ethnocentrism, social projection, and attribution theory, which are discussed in various chapters throughout the book.

One way to minimize an incident like the above is to develop strategies to increase multicultural competencies by exploring how a practitioner's cultural values, beliefs, and biases are reflected in her own interpersonal and intrapersonal communication. In intrapersonal communication, unlike interpersonal communication, there is no feedback loop for a reality check because the sender and the receiver are the same person, the self. Thus the process of intrapersonal communication is not visible to anyone else. It is a difficult process because the self is both sender and receiver, having the same values, beliefs, and biases; both are in agreement. Endless internal repetitions of a message lead to an illusion that the message is based on facts rather than based on the repeated self-talk (*intrapersonal communication*).

The author's clients and students have reported that their intrapersonal communication is mostly negative, especially toward themselves. They compare themselves to others and judge themselves by applying dichotomous and hierarchical thinking. According to them, their intrapersonal communication is restricted by their contextual values, beliefs, and biases. In other words, their intrapersonal communication is based on the values, beliefs, and biases of their outer world. Cognitive therapists assist clients with examining the effects of their negative intrapersonal communication and with changing it into positive intrapersonal communication. The goal of cognitive therapy is to assist clients with restructuring their cognitive schema. However, cognitive therapy, like most other therapies, does not deal with the impact of the practitioner's intrapersonal communication on the kinds of questions or issues she raises during the therapeutic process.

Intrapersonal communication reflects individuals' cultural values, beliefs, and biases, regardless of whether they are clients or practitioners. Nugent's (1994) study indicates the powerful relationship between culture and values. According to the study, individualism-oriented cultures like that of the United States emphasize competition over cooperation and personal achievement over group achievement throughout the socialization process. In contrast, collectivism-oriented cultures like that of Japan stress cooperation over competition and group achievement over individual achievement. Children who are socialized to value racial and ethnic cultural values that are different from the dominant cultural values in the United States experience inner and outer conflicts throughout the socialization process, and their ways of perceiving are different from those of children whose racial and ethnic cultural values are the same as the dominant cultural values. For example, children of Native American descent, Alaska natives, Latinos, children of African descent, children of Asian descent, native Hawaiians, Pacific Islanders, and White members of the lower socioeconomic class experience internal conflict due to inconsistencies between the values learned at home and the dominant cultural values. At home, these children learned such cultural values as inclusion of extended family, interdependence, and cooperation, which are not valued by the dominant culture (Dana, 1993; Garrett & Garrett, 1994; Gloria & Peregoy, 1995; Gunn Allen, 1994; Peregoy, 1993; Robinson, 2005; Sandhu, 1997b; Santiago-Rivera, Arredondo, & Gallardo-Cooper, 2002; Sue & Sue, 1990; Uba, 1994; Ying, 2002). Children who experience inner and outer conflicts throughout the socialization process due to a discrepancy between their home values and the dominant cultural values would have a very different intrapersonal communication style from that of their peers who have been socialized with the same cultural values in the home as in the dominant culture. As individuals modify or restructure their values, beliefs, and biases, their intrapersonal communication also changes. Intrapersonal communication can be dynamic, with multiple dimensions and layers, if individuals' values and beliefs are multidimensional and multifaceted. It takes time to process new ideas and concepts, and intrapersonal communication reflects this process. The following is an example of how an individual acquires a new concept.

PERSONAL STORY

Culture and the Meaning of Words: A Vietnamese Perspective on "Choice" Versus "Duty"

I have a Vietnamese friend who came to the United States at age 7 by boat with his family. Because he is an older brother, he paid for his younger brother's education from college to dental school. It was the right thing to do according to his culture, although he has lived in the United States for many years. It was not his choice to support his brother financially and emotionally. It was his duty, which he never questioned. We need to be careful in defining the word *duty* for this context. It may have a slightly different meaning from the dominant Euro American meaning. Even though I was also raised in Asia with collectivistic cultural values, I do not understand why an older brother would be totally responsible for a younger brother's college education. I think it is the parents' responsibility. From my cultural beliefs and values, I have no way to understand my Vietnamese friend's concept of "duty." However, if I were to understand his worldview, I would need to accept and honor his cultural concept of "duty" without looking through my cultural lens. I would need to ignore my intrapersonal communication, which is based on my cultural values and beliefs, and add a new concept: I have no right to interpret his "duty" from my cultural perspective. I just need to accept his cultural concept of "duty" and hope I may understand it someday.

Socialization, Internalized Privilege/Oppression, and Intrapersonal Communication

As children interact with their environment (family, teachers, media, church, temple, peers, etc.), they learn to formulate their own worldviews. There are various definitions of the term. According to Bufford (2007), *worldview* represents

> a set of beliefs about humans and the world. Worldviews answer basic questions about what exists, how we know it, how things work, what is good and bad or right and wrong, and who we are. (p. 293)

The construction of one's worldview starts in early childhood and shapes the self and others (Bufford, 1997, 2007). Brown and Bigler (2004) found children learned about gender and racial inequity through socialization at an early age. They studied children between the ages of 5 and 10, the majority of whom perceived discrimination or likely discrimination when contextual information was unambiguous. When contextual information was either ambiguous or unlikely, however, only the minority children perceived discrimination. This study also showed girls had a higher tendency to see girls as victims of discrimination than boys. Other studies also found children from marginalized groups were more aware of stereotypes and discrimination than children of dominant groups, and they were more context bound (Brown & Bigler, 2005; Garcia Coll, Crnic, Lamberty, & Wasik, 1996; McKown & Weinstein, 2004). The experience of ethnic and racial discrimination affects children's development negatively due to the normalization of Euro American standards (Altschul, Oyserman, & Bybee, 2006; Brody et al., 2006; Pahl & Way, 2006). The dominant cultural values are emphasized in most learning environments, and the effects of this on children from nondominant cultures are not considered. These studies imply that children from the dominant culture develop very different intrapersonal communication styles and worldviews than do children from the nondominant cultures because children at an early age learn the concept of privilege and oppression through implicit learning.

Jackson, Barth, Powell, and Lochman (2006) found the White children in their study experienced racial privilege but were not cognizant of it. Other research findings indicate that privilege holders' lack of awareness concerning their privilege often leads them to misunderstand the impact of systematic oppression on nondominant cultural groups. This will be discussed in detail in sections of Part II on systematic privilege/ oppression and internalized privilege/oppression. The Jackson et al. study showed how White children were perceived to have power by both Black and White children. White children were chosen as leaders by their peers even when they were the numerical minority, but Black children were chosen only when they were the substantial numerical majority and had a Black teacher. Black children were rated "less" than White children even when more of them were present, unless the authority figure (teacher) was also Black. Jackson et al.'s study suggests that children learn to internalize privilege and oppression at an early age and, despite conceptualization of racial equity, there has been little change toward it. The fact that both groups valued White children is indicative of their inappropriate hierarchical thinking. Repeated experiences of this type of learning add to one's intrapersonal communication, which is based on the way one is treated (*dichotomously and hierarchically*). Repeated inappropriate thinking styles become thinking patterns, and thinking patterns become automatic by internal repetition. The process of learning internalized privilege and oppression is gradual, subtle, and often unconscious. Thus, it is difficult to be aware of internalized privilege and oppression. The following reflection-based learning activities are designed to highlight a practitioner-trainee's intrapersonal communication by paying attention to her inner experiences.

CONCRETE STRATEGIES

Reflection-Based Learning Activities on Intrapersonal Communication

The purpose of this exercise is to be aware of your intrapersonal communication. Please do not judge your inner dialogue (intrapersonal communication) as "appropriate" or "inappropriate" or "good" or "bad." When you start to judge whether or not your intrapersonal communication fits into your ideal image of what you should be, you cannot reach self-awareness.

Learning Activities

Carry a small notebook with you for 7 days and jot down what you are thinking, feeling, and saying to yourself from the minute you wake up until

(Continued)

(Continued)

you go to bed. After a week, reread what you wrote and group your notes into similar categories.

1. List 10 frequently used thoughts, feelings, or statements to yourself (intrapersonal communication).

2. What did you learn about yourself by analyzing your intrapersonal communication?

The Formation of Automatic Thought Patterns

Solso (2001) defines thinking as a cognitive process, which means it occurs "internally" (p. 418) in the mind. Thinking is a complex, fluid, dynamic, private, and invisible process. Thinking processes start early in life internally when children are not able to differentiate between a parent's or teacher's opinion and fact. This is partly because of their cognitive developmental stage and partly due to the way adults communicate with them. Thinking can start with one piece of factual information or one opinion, but a thinker can fabricate, leap, generalize, and create new stories on the basis of that one fact or belief. The work of Beck, Rush, Shaw, and Emery (1979) and Beck and Weishaar (2000) on cognitive distortions such as arbitrary inferences, selective abstraction, magnification and minimization, personalization, and polarized thinking explains this process in detail. Because thinking is a private process, there is no internal feedback system that checks how much of a person's thinking is based on factual information, how much is from fabrication, and how much is from leaping to generalizations. This is why some people are not able to identify that their thought patterns are based on cognitive distortions (Beck et al.; Beck & Weishaar).

Intrapersonal communication reflects thinking. It is what individuals say to themselves (inner dialogue). Many of the author's clients' and students' daily recordings of their intrapersonal communication reveal that they make degrading and marginalizing remarks to themselves by focusing on the negatives. Such negative intrapersonal communication—not only focusing on the negatives but also magnifying them—often leads to cognitive distortions (Amsterlaw & Wellman, 2006; Beck et al., 1979;

Beck & Weishaar, 2000). Most of these negative messages are a result of what individuals derived as children from the messages of social agents such as parents, church, media, peers, school, or temple. Wellman (1990; Wellman & Cross, 2001; Wellman, Cross, & Watson 2001; Woolley & Wellman, 1992, 1993), one of the leading theory-of-mind researchers, indicates that children as young as 2 years have some understanding that people have desires. This implies that they know their social agents have desires when their social agents communicate to them. Kohlberg (1987) has theorized that preschool children behave according to their social agents' desires because they want to please them. According to Inhelder and Piaget (1958), the ability to think about one's own thoughts (second-order thinking) does not develop prior to the formal operational stage of cognitive development. Children repeat thoughts of culture, parents, church, temple, and so on, and this repeating not only becomes the foundation for autonomic thought formation but also is the basis of intrapersonal communication.

Individuals' automatic thought patterns and styles do not disappear simply because they have decided to become helping professionals. Most academic programs focus on helping clients rather than on helping practitioners deconstruct their own negative automatic thought patterns in order to help their clients. Even programs with an emphasis on counselors' awareness of their own worldview often do not provide concrete strategies or a structure for students to practice deconstructing inappropriate thinking styles/patterns. Structured spaces are needed to provide students with a way to learn how to observe and reflect on their thinking patterns and styles in order to turn automatic activation of inappropriate thinking into controlled processing.

One way to identify thought patterns is to examine intrapersonal communication (inner dialogue) without screening or judging.

Types of Thinking Styles

There are four types of thinking styles: (a) holistic, (b) linear, (c) hierarchical, and (d) dichotomous.

Holistic Thinking

Holistic thinking is nonjudgmental and is based on a multilayered and multidimensional perspective. Individuals with this thinking style are able to give equal weight to their opinions as well as those of others. They are able to think in terms of both "either/or" and "both/and" (diunital thinking). They know when it is appropriate to use linear, dichotomous or hierarchical thinking and when to use different degrees of multilayered and multidimensional thinking. An example of holistic thinking is "I see she is upset and has called me a racist. I understand her point from America's historical perspective." Holistic thinkers reflect on and examine their remarks from a multilayered and multidimensional perspective rather than being defensive of their position. After reflecting, a holistic thinker may say to himself/herself/zirself, "I do not think my remark was racist, but let me think further to see whether it could be interpreted as an unintentional racist remark." After further critical examination, he/she/ze may say, "I can see where both of us are coming from. I need to figure out my purpose for saying what I said."

Linear Thinking

According to a linear thinking perspective, a particular behavior or attitude of a group of people (e.g., a certain racial or ethnic group; women or men; lesbian, gay, bisexual, and transgender/transsexual [LGBT] people; blue-collar workers; the elderly, impaired, and disabled; people representing a certain religion; city people; farmers) at the moment stays constant. Linear thinking is attempting to predict the future on the basis of the moment. It is *projecting* and *generalizing* on the basis of the past. It is assuming that events, things, and people stay the same regardless of sociocultural contextual changes, time changes, and developmental stage changes. Some events in life are linear and others are not, but most human affairs do not happen linearly. Discriminating against, stereotyping, oppressing, minimizing, or marginalizing others on the basis of long-held cultural beliefs or a one-time experience with a certain group or person who represents a certain group is thinking *linearly*. Racial profiling and a woman calling a man sexist not on the basis of the man's behavior but on the basis of a past experience are due to *linear* thinking. This type of thinking is characterized by judging others or oneself as if a particular behavior or attitude at the moment is the same as it was at a past event and thus interpreting the moment or predicting the future by generalizing from the past. Some examples of linear thinking are "I will not do well on the test because I didn't do well last time"; "I am struggling with my life, and I know it will not get better"; "She dumped me, and I know no one will ever love me again"; "This happened because I am a lucky person, and I will always be lucky"; and "I know I am a loser—I know it." Not all linear thinking is inappropriate. There are appropriate situations for linear thinking—for example, "If I watch TV instead of studying, I won't be able to get the grade I want"; "If I spent $30 for dinner tonight, I will only have $20 left to spend until Thursday"; and "If I eat ice cream now, I will gain weight like before." Only inappropriate linear thinking hinders individuals' attempts to be aware of their own values, beliefs, and biases, which foster "isms."

Racialized socialization is also an example of linear thinking because it is motivated by parents' past pain and not due to children's experience interacting with children of another race. Children learn to stereotype and discriminate against individuals of another race on the basis of their parents' experience and not their own. Discrimination, prejudice, and "isms" related to race, gender, class, sexual orientation, impairment/disability, age, language, religion, and region are linear because they are based on the past experience or cultural myths that have been perpetuated generation after generation. Due to projecting past experience to the future, linear thinkers discriminate against a person or group of people without knowing anything about the person or group. For example, when a White practitioner stereotypes a person who is not White as "lazy" because she had an experience with one "lazy" person with the same racial background, she is not only thinking linearly but is also *generalizing*. She is thinking linearly because she is assuming that all individuals in a particular racial group are "lazy" and will be for the rest of their lives. She is *generalizing* from her experience with one "lazy" person that all people with the same racial background as that person are "lazy." *Generalizing* about all people in a racial group on the basis of one, two, or three negative experiences is detrimental not only to the practitioner but also to individuals from that racial group. It is detrimental to the practitioner because she has abandoned her opportunity to learn about the racial group's culture, language, traditions, and so on. It is detrimental to individuals from the racial group because the practitioner may share her experience with others, some of whom may also distance themselves from that racial group and in turn limit their own opportunity to learn about it. Inappropriate *linear thinking* blinds individuals' ability to learn new things, feel new things, and perceive old things in new ways. It hinders individuals' ability to create, discover, and enjoy life's mysteries as they unfold. It limits individuals' intellectual, emotional, and spiritual development. The following learning activities are designed for reflecting on inappropriate linear thinking styles and their impact on intrapersonal communication.

CONCRETE STRATEGIES

Inappropriate Linear Thinking and Intrapersonal Communication

The purpose of these activities is to gain conscious awareness of how you think and how your thinking style affects your interpersonal communication. It is important that you do not judge, censor, or minimize your inner dialogue (intrapersonal communication). You can only be aware of your values, beliefs, and biases by accepting your inner thoughts as they are.

Learning Activities

Record your inner dialogue (intrapersonal communication) on a daily basis for at least a week to 10 days. Then do the following:

1. Examine whether you used an inappropriate linear thinking style and what happened as a result. Draw a picture to symbolize the results or write them down.

2. If you used an inappropriate linear thinking style, do you recall the first time you were exposed to it?

3. Did your parents, siblings, and/or schoolteachers use inappropriate linear thinking while you were growing up? How did this shape your intrapersonal communication?

4. Close your eyes for about 5 min while breathing in and out slowly and evenly. Reflect on your answers to the previous questions. Open your eyes and write down your relationship to the inappropriate linear thinking style.

5. Think of one incident where you were frustrated with a client, boss, co-worker, or friend. What were your assumptions? What did you expect? Was your frustration related to inappropriate linear thinking? If so, explain.

6. Estimate the percentage of inappropriate linear thinking in your inner dialogue each day.

Hierarchical Thinking

When individuals put others or themselves into a superior or an inferior position, they are using hierarchical thinking. As stated earlier, cultures that value competitiveness and individual achievement over group achievement foster hierarchical thinking (Black-Gutman & Hickson, 1996; Nugent, 1994; Powlishta, Serbin, Doyle, & White, 1994). The long-held emphasis on the intellectual superiority (scientific racism) of White over other races is a prime example of inappropriate hierarchical thinking (Herrnstein & Murray, 1994; Jensen, 1969). Some White Americans tend to claim their superiority without being aware that they have this tendency, which makes it difficult to assess its impact on the oppression, marginalization, and minimization of people from different cultural backgrounds (Taylor & Brown, 1988). Examples of putting one group (race, sex, class, sexual orientation, age, disability, religion, language, region, etc.) or individual in a superior category are "We [Whites] are more intelligent than Blacks"; "Men are more intelligent than women"; and "School is boring because I am much more intelligent than the rest of the class." Examples of putting one group or individual in an inferior category are "My race is less intelligent than the White race"; "Women are weaker than men"; and "Heterosexuals are better." The author once had a client who, upon hearing his friend say, "I finished my homework," interpreted it as "She thinks she is better than me." Then the client generalized, "She thinks she is smarter than me." When the author asked him how he knew that his friend thought she was better than him on the basis of one comment, "I finished my homework," it took awhile for the client to realize that his assumptions came from his own hierarchical thinking. When he understood his thought patterns, he said that it was possible for his friend to have stated that she completed her homework out of relief and not out of wanting to put him down.

People can favor ingroups, but discriminating against intergroups in order to favor ingroups is based on inappropriate *hierarchical* and *dichotomous* thinking. Studies of asymmetric perceptions and introspections have shown that participants believed they were *less* biased than their peers. They believed that their peers were *more* biased (Andersen, 1984; Andersen & Ross, 1984; Baumeister, 1998; Dunning, Meyerowits, & Holzber, 1989; Epley & Dunning, 2000; Heath, 1999; Pronin, Gilovich, & Ross, 2004; Pronin, Kruger, Savitsky, & Ross, 2001; Pronin, Lin, & Ross, 2002; Steele, 1988; Taylor & Brown, 1988). The concept of *less* or *more* is based on hierarchical thinking.

Asking a client for specific information rather than going by the client's interpretation of the situation provides the practitioner with more information about the client. When the client says, "She thinks she is better than me," the practitioner may ask, "What did your friend say and do to make you think that?" or "How do you know that?" If the practitioner says this with empathy, the client is likely to ponder the question without being defensive. The practitioner may decide to psychoeducate the client about the process of perception in general and how to distinguish his own thought process (i.e., inner dialogue) from that of others. The practitioner may want to facilitate an idea that there is no way an individual can know exactly what another is thinking because he is not the other. The practitioner can explore the client's thinking style and whether he has made the generalization on the basis of his thinking style or whether it is evidence based. This may gradually assist the client with differentiating between his beliefs from his intrapersonal communication and others' beliefs and attitudes. The following learning activities are designed for reflecting on an individual's inappropriate hierarchical thinking style and its impact on intrapersonal communication.

CONCRETE STRATEGIES

Inappropriate Hierarchical Thinking and Intrapersonal Communication

The purpose of these activities is to gain conscious awareness of how you think and how your thinking style affects your interpersonal communication. It is important that you do not judge, censor, or minimize your inner dialogue (intrapersonal communication).

Experiential Learning Activities

Reread your recorded inner dialogue (intrapersonal communication) and do the following:

1. Examine whether you used inappropriate hierarchical thinking and what happened as a result. Draw a picture to symbolize the results or describe the results in writing.

2. If you used an inappropriate hierarchical thinking style, describe the first time you were exposed to it.

3. Did your parents, siblings, and/or schoolteachers use inappropriate hierarchical thinking styles while you were growing up? What did they say? How did these statements shape your intrapersonal communication?

4. Close your eyes for about 5 min while breathing in and out slowly and evenly. Reflect on your answers to the previous questions. Open your eyes and write down your relationship to the inappropriate hierarchical thinking style.

5. Think of one incident where you were frustrated with a client, a coworker, a family member, or a friend. What were your assumptions? What did you expect? Was your frustration related to inappropriate hierarchical thinking? If so, explain.

6. Estimate the percentage of inappropriate hierarchical thinking in your inner dialogue each day.

Dichotomous Thinking

Dichotomous thinking is conceptualizing within an "either/or" mindset, which leads to only two extremes: I am either "good" or "bad" and either "right" or "wrong." Most individuals do not want to be on the negative side ("bad" or "wrong"), so they put themselves on the positive side ("good" or "right"). This results in others being put on the negative side by default since there are only two choices (good vs. bad, right vs. wrong) in a dichotomous mindset. The logic behind this thinking may be explained by statements such as "If I am good, you must be bad" and "If I am right, you must be wrong." This type of thinking does not facilitate "both/and" (diunital) thinking. It does not lead to "We can both be right even though our opinions are very different from each other." Dichotomous thinking divides "us" from "them," and it often operates in tandem with hierarchical thinking. This type of thinking leads to classifying the values of the dominant group as superior or the norm rather than classifying the values of both dominant and nondominant groups equally. Frankenberg (1993), McIntyre (1997), and Perry (2002) have indicated that White identity is often experienced and socialized as the norm. Knowles and Peng (2005) have indicated that participants who scored high on the White Identity Centrality Implicit Association Test (WICIAT) excluded racially ambiguous faces. Racialized socialization is also based on dichotomous thinking (Caughy, Nettles, O'Campo, & Lohrfink, 2006; McHale et al., 2006). Parents may intend to protect their children, but by doing so they may teach their children—before they have a chance to find out for themselves—that there is a division between the dominant culture and their own. Numerous studies have demonstrated a high correlation among dichotomous thinking and discrimination, internal and external oppression or privilege, and marginalization. Hierarchical and dichotomous thinking are the basis for ethnocentrism and ethnocentric biases. The following learning activities are designed for reflecting on inappropriate dichotomous thinking styles and their impact on intrapersonal communication through narrative writing, imagery, drawing, and centering.

CONCRETE STRATEGIES

Inappropriate Dichotomous Thinking and Intrapersonal Communication

The purpose of these activities is to gain conscious awareness of how you think and how your thinking style affects your interpersonal communication. It is important that you do not judge, censor, or minimize your inner dialogue (intrapersonal communication).

Reflection-Based Learning Activities

Record your inner dialogue (intrapersonal communication) on a daily basis for at least a week to 10 days and then do the following:

1. Examine whether you used an inappropriate dichotomous thinking style and what happened as a result. Draw a picture to symbolize the results or write them down.

2. If you used an inappropriate dichotomous thinking style, do you recall the first time you were exposed to it?

3. Did your parents, siblings, and/or schoolteachers use inappropriate dichotomous thinking while you were growing up? How did this shape your intrapersonal communication?

4. Close your eyes for about 5 min while breathing in and out slowly and evenly. Reflect on your answers to the previous questions. Open your eyes and write down your relationship to the inappropriate dichotomous thinking style.

5. Think of one incident where you were frustrated with a client, boss, or friend. What were your assumptions? What did you expect? Was your frustration related to inappropriate dichotomous thinking? If so, explain.

6. Estimate the percentage of inappropriate dichotomous thinking in your inner dialogue each day.

If practitioner-trainees have not been censoring their feelings while doing the *Concrete Strategies* activities, they probably have found that their thinking patterns are linear, hierarchical, and dichotomous, and these patterns probably have assisted and still assist them with succeeding in certain situations. As a result, they may feel ambivalent and defensive about giving up the inappropriate dichotomous and hierarchical thinking style and resist the learning activities. They may resist because dichotomy and hierarchy are important cultural values, or they may resist because they have been using inappropriate thinking styles that became automatic through repetition. They may be uncomfortable with the fact that these automatic thinking styles became their thought patterns and operate unconsciously (Banaji & Hardin, 1996; Devine, 1989; Perdue & Gurtman, 1990). Completing the activities is difficult because linear, dichotomous, and hierarchical thinking styles, thought patterns, and generalizations operate simultaneously and have been important parts of many cultural values. It is difficult because practitioner-trainees may not want to admit or may not be aware that they are using inappropriate thinking styles that are inconsistent with their self-image. Their ideal self-image, such as believing in equity and social justice for all people and working for underprivileged populations, interferes with their ability to examine what Jung called shadow (Campbell, 1976; Jung, 1985).

Aversive racists hold implicit racism with explicit antiracism (Dovidio, Evans, & Tyler, 1986; Dovidio & Gaertner, 1998, 2000, 2004, 2005; Dovidio, Gaertner, et al., 2002; Dovidio, Kawakami, & Gaertner, 2002; Dovidio, Kawakami, Johnson, Johnson, & Howard, 1997; Fazio, Jackson, Dunton, & Williams, 1995; Gaertner, 1973; Gaertner & Dovidio, 1977, 1986; Gaertner & McLaughlin, 1983; Hodson, Dovidio, & Gaertner, 2002). Campbell (1976) describes Jung's concept of shadow as follows:

> Closer examination of the dark characteristics—that is, the inferiorities constituting the shadow—reveals that they have an emotional nature, a kind of autonomy. . . . Affects occur usually where adaptation is weakest. (p. 145)

What may assist practitioner-trainees with seeing their blind side is reflecting on their own behavior, thoughts, and feelings without screening and judging. In *Meeting the Shadow*, a collection of short essays on the Jungian concept of shadow, people who represent such diverse areas as psychology, literature, and spiritual work depict the power of shadow in a spectrum for facilitating individuation if individuals are willing to face it (Zweig & Abrams, 1991). More than 50 years ago, Allport (1954) was concerned about individuals' inability to deal with human relationships despite their advanced capabilities in other areas, but so little progress has been made in "human relationships" (Allport, 1954, p. xiii) for people who are different from the dominant group (Knowles & Peng, 2005; Ponterotto et al., 2006: Robbins & Krueger, 2005). Aversive racism, the concept of shadow, implicit learning, and ethnocentrism seem to explain the challenges involved in incorporating multicultural counseling theories into practice.

For example, many White North Americans resist acknowledging the long-standing history of ethnocentrism in the United States. Ethnocentrism started with White newcomers' strong desire to secure their economic status. Thus they created racial separation on the basis of hierarchy ("Whites are superior to Blacks") and dichotomy ("us" vs. "them"). Hierarchical thinking and dichotomous thinking have been embedded in the North American people's psyche and have been perpetuated as a desirable goal to reach through the socialization process (Singer & Kimbles, 2004). As a result, these thought patterns are common in the United States, and accomplishments made by using these thinking styles are often considered a success in both the academic and the business world. Rapley (2004) and Stubblefield (2007) have described the dangers involved in practitioners assessing clients by applying dichotomous thinking.

Teaching the impact of dichotomous and hierarchical thinking on multicultural competencies is one of the most challenging tasks. The author once had a student whose thinking pattern was dichotomous and unknown to him. During counseling skill practice, he kept interpreting a client's comments in a dichotomous way when he was role-playing as a counselor. For example, when another student, playing a client, said, "My feelings toward my sister are ambivalent. I love her, but I don't want to spend too much time with her," the first student said, "If you don't like her, do you need to spend time with her?" His dichotomous thinking did not allow him to hear the client's complex emotion toward her sister. Even though the client said, "I love her," he was not able to hear that because he interpreted "ambivalent" as "dislike" and there was no room for him to understand the client's multilayered emotions toward her sister. If he thought she could feel "ambivalent" and "love" simultaneously, his comments or questions would focus on exploring the client's complex feelings, and he might assist her with exploring her feelings about spending too much time with her sister and how she knows when she has spent too much. Instead, his dichotomous thinking silenced the client. She could have learned how to deal with her sister if she was listened to and guided to explore her complex feelings. When practitioners use inappropriate thinking styles with their clients, they cannot assess their clients from the clients' worldview. Practitioners may know about multicultural counseling competencies, but their inappropriate thinking styles may prevent them from putting their knowledge into practice. If a practitioner's thinking style is *dichotomous* and she considers herself an expert, she automatically classifies the client as a nonexpert due to this "either/or" thinking. If a practitioner's thinking style is also hierarchical, she will think she knows better about what the client needs to do than the client himself. Such practitioners unintentionally put themselves in the power position.

Unintentional marginalization or minimization stems from practitioners' inappropriate thinking styles and not from their lack of care. For example, a practitioner who was raised with dominant American values that emphasize individualism over collectivism may think that her role as a practitioner is to make sure the client does what is best for the client. If she sees a Mexican American female client who says, "I feel selfish for doing stuff for myself because I was raised to consider my family first," she may interpret the client's concern for her family as a sign of dysfunction. She may not be aware that her assessment of the client is inaccurate because it is based on her cultural values and not those of the client. Inaccurate assessment may occur not as a result of the practitioner's desire to marginalize or minimize the client but as a result of her inability to distinguish the cultural differences between her and the client (countertransference). The practitioner may care and want to develop an effective assessment and treatment for the client. However, caring alone does not automatically ensure multicultural competencies.

Seeing a client through his worldview requires the practitioner to see her blind side. Seeing the blind side is a complex and difficult process, which the practitioner may start by reflecting on her own behavior, thoughts, and feelings without screening or judging. Identifying her own thinking style or pattern without judgment may lead the practitioner to assess whether she is applying inappropriate linear, hierarchical, or dichotomous thinking. When the practitioner identifies her own inappropriate linear, hierarchical, or dichotomous thinking style or pattern without judgment, she may be able to start working on deconstructing it. Deconstructing an inappropriate thought pattern requires diligent and mindful practice on a daily basis. The more the practitioner works on deconstructing the inappropriate thought pattern, the clearer her understanding of her cultural values, beliefs, and biases. This expands her ability to understand the client from the client's worldview. In 2001, after playing the role of counselor, receiving feedback from his peers, and videotaping for a quarter, one of the author's multicultural counseling students, Allen, wrote:

> I did not think myself to have a pattern of hierarchical and dichotomous thinking. I did not think I had hidden prejudices and biases. I thought of myself as a liberal and open-minded person. . . .

> These biases interfere with my ability to hear. . . . My assumptions tell me that I know what someone means before they tell me what they mean. I realized that I have often confused insight with assumptions.

If a practitioner's intrapersonal communication is based on inappropriate dichotomous, linear, and hierarchical thinking, she might interpret the client's statements in dichotomous, linear, and hierarchical ways. All practitioners need to assess whether they use inappropriate dichotomous, linear, and hierarchical thinking styles to interpret clients' statements. The following experiential learning activities are designed to illustrate the impact a practitioner's misinterpretation may have on the effectiveness of therapy.

CONCRETE STRATEGIES

Misunderstanding Clients Due to a Practitioner's Hierarchical and Dichotomous Thinking Style

Please participate in the following experiential learning activities without screening your inner thoughts.

Experiential Learning Activities

1. Provide an example of a counselor interpreting a client's statement in a dichotomous and hierarchical way.
   a. Record the client's statement.
   b. Record the counselor's hierarchical interpretation of the client's statement.
   c. Record the counselor's dichotomous interpretation of the client's statement.

2. Provide an example of a counselor interpreting a client's statement in a linear way.

   a. Record the client's statement.
   b. Record the counselor's linear interpretation of the client's statement.

   For practitioner-trainees who are completing these exercises in class, please do the following additional activity:

3. Divide into groups with four or five members.

   a. Role-play counselor and client roles by using your answers to Questions 1 and 2.
   b. Each group member must play the role of a counselor and that of a client.
   c. Discuss how you felt as a client and as a counselor.

4. As a class, discuss how you felt as a client and then discuss any lessons learned from the exercise.

⚟ INTRAPERSONAL COMMUNICATION AND ETHNOCENTRISM

The Historical Understanding of Hierarchical, Dichotomous, and Linear Thinking

Takaki (1993) chronicles an American history that is not taught in public schools. In his book, *A Different Mirror: A History of Multicultural America*, he reminds us that America's foundation was multicultural. He concludes:

> As Americans, we originally came from many different shores, and our diversity has been at the center of the making of America. Filled with what Walt Whitman celebrated as the "varied carols" of America, our history generously gives all of us our "mystic chords of memory." Throughout our past of oppressions and struggles for equality, Americans of different races and ethnicities have been "singing with open mouths their strong melodious songs." . . . Our denied history "bursts with telling." As we hear America singing, we find ourselves invited to bring our rich cultural diversity on deck, to accept ourselves. (p. 428)

Takaki's (1993) book is an emotionally challenging read for most White students, but it (a) illustrates why it is difficult to transcend inappropriate thinking patterns and (b) provides the opportunity to reframe coexistence among culturally different people through understanding the history of White ethnocentrism. He suggests that justice and equity are possible for all people if we embrace each other's differences; only then can we "hear America singing," share "our rich cultural diversity," and "accept ourselves."

According to Takaki (1993), the first English colonizers in the United States brought their old country's hierarchical and dichotomous thinking patterns with them. They treated the American Indians as the Irish had been treated in England; the English viewed the Irish as "other" and therefore inferior (*hierarchical thinking*), and the English colonizers likewise viewed the American Indians as "other." Dichotomous and hierarchical thinking led "other" to be less (lower on the hierarchy) than they, and if they were good, "other" must be bad (*dichotomous thinking*). Initially, the American Indians, whose cultural values emphasized collectivism, shared their food and resources with the English settlers. However, the English settlers were not satisfied with being helped. They wanted to secure their economic status on the American Indians' land, so they started to attack the American Indians to take their food and land instead of appreciating them for their generosity. This was the beginning of racialization by the White English settlers. These newcomers brought inappropriate hierarchical and dichotomous thinking patterns with them, although they left their country because they did not want to be the victims of marginalization and oppression. Understanding this history of the origin of inappropriate dichotomous and hierarchical thinking is crucial in understanding why there have not been major changes in multicultural counseling.

As stated earlier, ideas about claiming White racial superiority came with White settlers to the United States (Jahoda, 1999; Thompson, 1977), and some of these ideas are still persistent, partially because they are embedded in Americans' consciousness (Singer & Kimbles, 2004). There is a great body of evidence to support the embedded nature of White racial superiority. Ideas from the eugenics movement, which branched off from Darwin's theory of evolution, and ideals about treating Africans as if they were subhuman continued under the disguise of scientific racism. Psychologists like Lewis Madison Terman, Arthur Jensen, and Richard J. Herrnstein and Charles Murray perpetuated Whites' intellectual superiority (Guthrie, 1998; Herrnstein & Murray, 1994; Thomas & Sillen, 1972). The dominant value emphasis on socialization practices; the dominant value placed on advertisements, education, and living standards; and the higher value put on light skin tone by people of color are examples of the dominant value superiority (Brown, Ward, Lightbourn, & Jackson, 1999; Thompson & Keith, 2001). Personal narratives depict the marginalization and oppression of counselors and therapists who do not fit into the dominant value categories of race, gender, class, sexual orientation, ethnicity, and religion (Thomas & Schwarzbaum, 2006). There must be untold stories of many whose sense of self has been shattered by unfair treatment and socially constructed systematic oppression. These people may be too traumatized to take care of themselves physically, psychologically, and emotionally.

Understanding the origin of inappropriate dichotomous and hierarchical thinking and that it persists will assist practitioners who want to examine multicultural issues from a holistic perspective.

FEEDBACK

MY STUDENTS ON TAKAKI'S (1993) BOOK

My students gave me permission to share the following selections from their weekly seminar reading responses. Their reactions to learning a different North American history and their new perspectives on racism may help other Takaki readers who respond to the book with uncomfortable and complex feelings that range from resistance to anger to guilt to sorrow. Takaki's book is a catalyst for transformative learning, and my students expressed a wide range of emotions. Despite the difficulty of processing information in the book, both White students and students of color bonded. Students of color felt that they really had allies who showed their emotions (anger, shame, guilt, rage, sorrow) as a gesture of understanding how people of color had been oppressed, marginalized, and victimized throughout history due to systematic oppression.

Looking back at the last week of reading brings up many feelings. Frustration, anger, and sadness were prevalent while I read Takaki. This book brings to light internalized national scars that have been buried by decades of lies. The words of this book are hard to swallow in the same way that horror movies based on real-life events are the scariest because they actually happened. The reality is shockingly surreal.

—Jane, 2004

(Continued)

(Continued)

A Different Mirror by Ronald Takaki is the story of multicultural America that was not taught to me while I was growing up. To read that the English conquerors came to this country and stole the land from indigenous people, enacted harsh slavery, and established systematic racism created a mixture of anger, sadness, and shame within me. I learned a great deal about immigration and the discriminatory policies of the United States used throughout history.

—May, 2004

I relate to others' expressions of frustration regarding the history presented in A Different Mirror *and frustration that this text is not implemented into the school system. I had not realized those same feelings within myself until I went to seminar both times and heard the class' feedback.*

—Nan, 2004

I am so mad for being lied to at such a young age. I have now seen and experienced the pain of my life. TRUTH, my truth is nothing. It's a lie. Others will never know and never have the opportunity to relearn or see that their truths are based on this same lie! History—our history told from one perspective, is what children are taught to be truth. These truths of colonization, immigration, and seeing racism so deeply ingrained in society, I feel hopeless. I feel free, but at the same time I'm having a really hard time knowing what has happened to me happened to almost all others and is continuing to happen and will continue until our country as a whole puts an end to this blind life. The whites with privilege need to stop. Relearn, be open enough to really look at their beliefs and see what has shaped them.

—Amy, 2004

Understanding Inappropriate Thinking Styles From a Social Learning Perspective

For the last 30 years, Bandura (1977) and his followers (Comstock, 1993; Eisenberg, 1988; Huesmann, Lagerspetz, & Eron, 1984; Huston, Watkins, & Kunkel, 1989; Strassberg, Dodge, Pettit, & Bates, 1994) have researched and demonstrated the power of learning through observation. In addition, research on violence and sexual abuse has shown repeatedly that people have a tendency to model the behavior of the oppressor even when they disagree with or despise that behavior (Gilligan, 1997).

Learning through modeling was evident when White settlers, who were outcasts in their own society, treated the American Indians who were kind to them exactly the same way they were treated in their own country (Takaki, 1993). If we examine the ethnocentrism practiced by settlers at the beginning of American history from Bandura's learning-through-modeling perspective, we may come to understand the complexities of modeling despised behavior (Huesmann, 1998).

The media generally use stereotypical images to portray people who are culturally different from the dominant culture. Carter and Steiner (2004) examined the media portrayal of gender. Their content analysis of popular films (*Gladiator*, the *Lord of the Rings* series, *Men in Black*, and *Spider-Man*) and children's television programs, movies, and books (*Digimon: Digital Monsters, Yu-Gi-Oh!, Cinderella, Sleeping Beauty*, and *Rapunzel*) suggests how the media have been participating in the preservation of the American cultural complex. A cultural complex is defined as "unquestioned assumptions, underlying beliefs held to be true by most of the members of the group, certainly by the group's power elite" (Meador, 2004, p. 172). It is in the personal and collective psyche of a culture. People may talk about equity and social justice while modeling and reinforcing the very behavior that would hinder equity and social justice for people who are culturally different. Consciously, people may really want to empower those who are the targets of prejudice, discrimination, and oppression; unconsciously, however, they may not have had the opportunity to sort out the complexities involved in their own emotions, values, beliefs, and thinking styles and the impact of cultural conditioning. Research on implicit learning, aversive racism, and attribution error has repeatedly found inconsistencies between behavior and knowledge (Banaji & Bhaskar, 2001; Banaji & Hardin, 1996; Blair & Banaji, 1996; Chen & Bargh, 1997; Dovidio et al., 2002; Greenwald, McGhee, & Schwartz, 1998; Henderson-King & Nisbett, 1996). As long as people intentionally and/or unintentionally reinforce and model the dominant culture's assigned gender, race, class, sexual orientation, age roles, attitudes, beliefs, and values that are based on inappropriate dichotomous and hierarchical thinking, they will perpetuate racism, sexism, classism, ableism, heterosexism, ageism, and other "isms."

The media are not the only model that promotes stereotypical images of people whose culture is different from the dominant culture. There is an abundance of role models that perpetuate discrimination, stereotypes, and biases that are often the result of inappropriate thinking. Throughout the socialization process, children grow up being rewarded for following the dominant cultural values. In 2007, one of the author's gender and media students, Tina, wrote:

> In a culture that values having the biggest, the newest, and the best, dichotomous thinking is required to keep the status quo alive. The sad thing is that most people do not notice that they have been programmed to think a certain way.

Dichotomous gender roles by which men are symbolized as powerful, strong, aggressive, and independent and women are symbolized as fragile, weak, kind, compassionate, and dependent are still portrayed as appropriate and reinforced by family, peers, schools and other social organizations to which children belong, and society (Kimmel, 2000; Lorber & Moore, 2002; Weinstein & D'Amico, 1999).

Ethnocentric bias will continue as long as media, institutional, peer, and family models portray dominant group values as better, superior, powerful, right, and normal. According to the social learning perspective, however, children will internalize the privilege of human diversity if they are socialized and exposed to media, institutional, peer, and family models that celebrate human diversity; if they treat each other with respect; and if equal access to education, housing, jobs, and justice is provided for all people. The social learning perspective implies that it is up to individuals and institutions to create equality- and justice-based role models for children to learn from. Following are the findings of a spring 2007 survey conducted by gender and media students at The Evergreen State College.

PERSONAL FEEDBACK

MEDIA PORTRAYAL OF GENDER IN 2007

I taught a gender and media course with my colleague, Dr. Sally Cloninger, in spring 2007. On April 30, all the students in the course were divided into 10 groups who watched 10 news broadcasts and analyzed the content by using the Global Media Monitoring Project (Gallagher, 2005), which combined media monitoring and content analysis techniques. The overall result was that 9 out of 10 groups reported gender inequity. Men reporters talked for a longer time and covered "real" news, and women reporters talked for a considerably shorter time than their male counter-parts and covered "soft" news. Each of the same 10 groups chose one TV program to study how gender roles operate in a contemporary media genre, series, or time slot. The 10 TV programs they analyzed were *Law & Order: Special Victims Unit*, *The L Word*, *Heroes*, *The Simpsons*, *Nip/Tuck*, *Gilmore Girls*, *Curb Your Enthusiasm*, contemporary music videos, *Sex and the City*, and *South Park*. The results indicated that most of the TV programs perpetuated gender stereotypes. Students also reported there was only one movie in which a woman had the first billing among the last year's (2006) top 10 blockbuster movie hits.

Attribution Error and Social Projection

Attribution error theory and social projection theory are products of ethnocentrism and often lay the foundation for stereotyping, discrimination, prejudice, racism, sexism, classism, heterosexism, ableism, ageism, and other "isms" (Park & Judd, 2005; Robbins & Krueger, 2005). It is favoring the ingroup over the outgroup to suggest positive behaviors as the internal traits of the ingroup and negative behaviors as the internal traits of the outgroup (Allport, 1954; Gilbert, 1998; Livingston & Brewer, 2002; Maddox, 2004; Pettigrew, 1979; Tajfel, 1981; Tajfel & Turner, 1979, 1986). Both social projection and attribution error distort reality in order to support an ingroup. Robbins and Krueger define social projection as "a process or set of processes, by which individuals come to expect others to be similar to themselves" (p. 32). In other words, individuals assume that their view ($N = 1$) is or should be the same as that of others ($N = 1$ is the same as that of others). They are assuming that their perception (sample size one, $N = 1$) is the representation of many ($N = 1 = $ many). Robbins and Krueger's review and meta-analysis of social projection indicates that there is ingroup favoritism. Both attribution error and social projection divide "us" and "them" and contribute more positive aspects to the ingroup ("us") than to the outgroup ("them"). The behavioral expression of ingroup favoritism is intergroup discrimination, and the term *intergroup* can be defined in terms of race, gender, class, sexual orientation, disability, age, religion, region, language, size, and so on. Severe forms of intergroup discrimination lead to "isms" such as racism, sexism, classism, heterosexism, ableism, and ageism. Often, intergroup discriminations are perpetuated by generalizations of attribution error and social projection and become a part of people's automatic thinking patterns due to repetitions in their intrapersonal communication. Studies indicate that from early on children are socialized to believe their own cultural values and rituals are right or correct. For example, Friedlmeier and Trommsdorff's (1999) study of 2-year-olds and their mothers indicated the toddlers were socialized to exhibit culture-specific behaviors; Japanese toddlers were socialized to feel and express their feelings in order to comfort another toddler while German toddlers were socialized to control their feelings in order to comfort another toddler. Farver, Kim, and Lee's (1995) study indicated the extent to which culture-specific ingroup values could be ingrained in people. Korean American teachers in a Korean American preschool applied a traditional Korean teaching style that put a heavy emphasis on academics with a structured curriculum even though they were born in the United States and were educated in American colleges and universities. The importance of ingroup values is also supported by extensive cross-cultural studies by Stetsenko, Little, Gordeeva, Grasshof, and Oettingen (2000). Equal gender representations of 3,000 school-aged children (second to sixth graders) from seven different regions of the world (East Berlin, West Berlin, Moscow, Tokyo, Berne, Los Angeles, and Prague) indicated the importance of culture-specific socialization with regard to school-aged children's beliefs about the effects of gender on school performance.

Attribution error and social projection theories may explain why some people often are frustrated, confused, angry, and enraged and feel abandoned. They may expect others to behave, think, and feel the same way they do. When people's expectations are not met, some of them may blame others or themselves for their unmet expectations, which may lead to various assumptions and emotions. The following story shows that overall frustration is due to attribution error and social projection and not to a particular event or person.

PERSONAL STORY

Frustration With Life in the United States and Social Projection and Attribution Error

The attribution error and social projection theories explain my frustration with life in the United States when I came to this country to study psychology. I tried to make meaning by using the way I knew—the old way, the Korean way—even though the cultural context had changed.

Even though I knew intellectually I was in a different culture, I was not able to apply my intellectual understanding to developing a new way of making meaning. My perception was based on my ($N = 1$) very limited life experience in Korea, and I was projecting my Korean experiences to my new culture in the United States. I used to think North Americans were dirty because they wore shoes in the house, which is not a Korean custom (ingroup favoritism). I used to think American students had no manners because of the way they interacted with their professors. When I was in Korea, Korean students bowed to their teachers to show respect if they saw them in the hallway or on the street. The American students waved at their professors or called them by their first or last names ("Mr. _____"). In Korea, calling someone "Mr." does not show him respect as it does in the United States. When Koreans call someone "Mr.," it means his status is somewhat equal to theirs. If Koreans want to show respect, they use professional titles like *shunsaingnim* ("teacher"), *sajangnim* ("president," "business owner"), or *gukjangnim* ("director," "manager"). Again I was judging an outgroup on the basis of my ingroup values and customs. I did not know I was judging.

Please complete the following narrative writing and experiential learning activities before reading the next section. They are designed to help practitioner-trainees reflect on individuals' value formation by significant others.

CONCRETE STRATEGIES

Experiential Learning Activities on Values

Have colored crayons, colored pencils, or watercolors; pens; drawing pads; and paper to write on. Find a quiet place and make sure you will not be distracted by the radio, the TV, the phone, or music. Sit as comfortably as you can and close your eyes for about 5 min while breathing in and out slowly and evenly. Reflect on what you have read about attribution error and social projection. Capture the image—whether a word or words, a phrase or phrases, or a sentence or sentences—of whatever comes to your mind. Slowly open your eyes while still breathing in and out evenly and slowly.

(Continued)

(Continued)

1. Write down the word or words, phrase or phrases, or sentence or sentences that came to your mind. You may also choose to draw a picture.

2. Look at your response to Question 1. Expand on what you have written or draw a picture to represent what came to your mind.

3. What values did your father (or a person who played the father's role for you) emphasize?

4. What values did your mother (or a person who played the mother's role for you) emphasize?

5. What type of interpersonal communication style did your father or father figure use in terms of social projection to communicate his values? For example, was he more likely to say, "This is the right way" or "This is the only way" than "This is one of the ways"?

6. What type of interpersonal communication style did your mother or mother figure use in terms of social projection to communicate her values?

7. What types of values were emphasized by your siblings, if any, and your schoolteachers while you were growing up?

8. Which values do you still practice?

9. What are your prejudices, and what role do the values you listed in response to Question 8 play in your prejudice?

10. Do you seek approval from others? If so, compare the most important person's approval to the least important person's approval. If you think it is equally important to get approval from everyone, write that down.

11. How are your parents' communication styles and your approval seeking related?

12. Rate the importance of your ingroups and describe your relationship to them.

13. Describe your relationship to social projection (e.g., if you are upset because no one seems to understand you, you may be implying that you want others to agree with you or perceive something the same way you do).

Reread your answers to Questions 1–13. Close your eyes for about 5 min and think about your answers. Write about or draw a picture of what you have learned through these experiential activities.

Inappropriate Generalizations

Attribution error, social projection, bias, stereotyping, and discrimination, inappropriate thinking styles that result from ethnocentrism, are based on inappropriate generalizations. Generalization starts with one specific event—for example, a single display of less-than-intelligent behavior by X ("X must not be intelligent"). However, if an individual talks about the particular incident as an indication of X's overall intelligence without gathering further evidence ("Since X did not show intelligent behavior in this particular situation, X must not show intelligent behavior in all other situations"), he/she/ze is inappropriately generalizing. The individual in this situation often generalizes further about the intelligence of X's family and race ("X's family must not be intelligent"; "X's race must not be intelligent"). This generalization influences the individual's perception. By repeating generalizations frequently but unconsciously, generalizing becomes a habit, and this habit forms the person's thinking or thought pattern. The process is similar to Beck et al.'s (1979) cognitive distortion discussed earlier. In other words, $N = 1$ (a behavior in a specific situation) becomes $N =$ many (a behavior in a specific situation becomes a behavior in all situations) through generalization. Generalization takes place inside the individual (internally) without an adequate feedback system, so it is difficult to stop and analyze the process critically. Inappropriate generalizations, whether they are inter- or intrapersonal communications, often lead to prejudice, discrimination, systematic oppression, and internalized oppression.

Some individuals are constantly busy in their mind, thinking in linear, hierarchical, and dichotomous ways while adding generalizations. Thinking styles and generalizations about these thinking styles often work simultaneously with other generalizations such as individuals' believing that other people think the same way they do (*social projection*). The author has discovered through private practice and teaching that some individuals whose thinking styles are dichotomous, hierarchical, and linear have a tendency to perceive others as thinking in the same way regardless of what others say or do (*social projection*). Statements including "never," "always," "everybody," "everyone," nobody," "no one," and "all the time" often lead to generalization. Henderson-King and Nisbett (1996) note that generalizations about members of a particular group are based on one's experience with single individuals, and the process is unconscious. What happens when $N = 1$ becomes $N =$ everyone is these generalizations often lead to stereotypes, prejudice, and oppression. Generalizing in inappropriate dichotomous and hierarchical thinking leads to an egocentric perspective (or the inability to see from someone else's perspective) when individuals are thinking and expressing their thoughts verbally about their ideas, beliefs, and values as if they are universal ideas, beliefs, and values for all people. If the dominant cultural group members intentionally or unintentionally think, believe, or express that people from nondominant cultural backgrounds should have the same values and beliefs as they do, they are ethnocentric.

One way to minimize generalizations, which hinder gathering information from a client for effective assessment and treatment, is to acquire specific information by applying quantitative research skills. How to incorporate learning from research methods and critiquing primary research articles into specific assessment and treatment inquiry will be discussed in Chapters 13 and 14. The following reflection activities are designed to facilitate transformative learning on generalizations. Please respond without censoring.

CONCRETE STRATEGIES

Reflection Activities on Generalizations

Remember not to screen or judge your thoughts and feelings.

1. Jot down your intrapersonal communication during a single day. Then examine whether you used generalizations.

2. If you used generalizations, do you remember the first time you were exposed to them? If you don't, try to reflect on your life until you do.

3. Did your parents, siblings, and/or schoolteachers use generalizations while you were growing up? Write down as many as you can remember.

4. Reflect on your answers to the previous questions. Close your eyes for about 5 min. Open your eyes and write down your relationship to generalizations.

5. Think of one incident where you were frustrated with a client. What were your assumptions? What did you expect? Was your frustration due to generalizations?

6. How much of your inner dialogue is related to generalizations?

There are various situations to which generalizations apply. For example, practitioners become practitioners because they are able to successfully complete the necessary academic and training standards. They must apply linear, dichotomous, and hierarchical thinking and generalizations appropriately in order to achieve their success. Such decisions as whether to stay home and study or go out with friends to have fun are based on dichotomous and linear thinking (e.g., "If I do not study now, I might not reach my goal"). When students generalize the fact that the more they study, the more likely they will be to earn high scores on their exams, generalization is beneficial for them. Applying linear, dichotomous, and hierarchical thinking and generalizations appropriately helps individuals achieve their desired goals and plan effectively. These thinking styles/patterns and generalizations become problems when they are used inappropriately to marginalize other people in an attempt to promote or protect their ingroup memberships with regard to race, gender, ethnicity, class, sexual orientation, age, impairment/disability, religion, region, language, and so on. If inappropriate generalizations are used by practitioners to assess and treat clients, the assessment and treatment will be ineffective because they are based on the practitioner's inappropriate generalizations and not on the client's worldview.

In addition, inappropriate generalizations and thinking styles often create interpersonal conflicts. The author has been in several situations where students were angry or behaved inappropriately in multicultural counseling classes. In one situation, a White female student believed that a Black student was "humiliating" her in front of "everybody." The alleged incident happened on the last class day of the quarter, and the White student agreed to process the incident with the author when the new quarter began. However, prior to the first day of the new quarter, she went to the dean instead. The author brought the covenant she signed and the class syllabus, which stated the learning objectives and students' responsibilities as colearners in the learning community, to the meeting. The author was warm, and her focus was how to facilitate the student's learning by allowing her to reflect on her behavior in a nonthreatening atmosphere. It was a difficult task since the author felt the student's way of resolving the conflict was based on a hierarchical power structure (*hierarchical thinking*) rather than the multicultural competency skills she had learned in class. At the meeting, the student said she went to the dean because the author was "siding" with the Black student, and by this she meant that the author did not perceive the Black student the same way she did (*dichotomous thinking and social projection*). The author did not agree to remove the Black student from the class, as the White student demanded. Asking her specific questions with a warm and caring attitude led her to realize her accusation was based not on evidence but on her interpretation of the Black student's statement during his presentation. Through processing her interpretation and reading the covenant, the syllabus, the course learning objectives, and her responsibilities as a student, she was able to understand that her reaction to the situation came from her ethnocentric socialization, which emphasized that White is better than Black (*dominant value and hierarchical thinking*). Her reaction also was due partially to racial tension in the particular region from which both students came (*contextual generalization*). The author was glad both students were able to tolerate each other enough to continue for two more quarters and complete the program. In the way that both students brought their outside-the-class experiences, their thinking styles, and their way of making meaning to the class, most people take their whole self to work, school, and other social situations.

The United States is not the only country exhibiting ethnocentrism. Numerous studies have indicated that ethnocentrism is common in other cultures (Bizumic & Duckitt, 2007; Friedlmeier & Trommsdorff, 1999). The author's sabbatical projects in 2001 and 2008, as well as a psychological conference in Russia in 2003, indicated that ethnocentrism is common in 14 European countries, Russia, Australia, and New Zealand. Being proud of one's own country will not lead to ethnocentrism if holistic thinking is the dominant thinking pattern of the country. From a holistic perspective, individuals can be proud of their own culture, traditions, values, and beliefs and understand that others are also proud of their own culture, traditions, values, and beliefs. Adopting a holistic thinking style can be accomplished by deconstructing dichotomous, hierarchical, and linear thinking and generalizations through transformative learning. The following reflection activities are an attempt to facilitate mindful internal observation on issues surrounding generalization.

CONCRETE STRATEGIES

Learning Through Reflection on Generalization

1. List some appropriate generalizations.

2. Describe a situation in which generalization is beneficial.

3. Describe a situation in which generalization is inappropriate or harmful.

4. How do you know when to generalize and when to discriminate?

5. Close your eyes for about 5 min and think of an instance when you were stereotyped and how you felt. Open your eyes and write down or draw a picture of your feelings.

Transformative Learning

Chapter 1 described transformative learning as one of two essential ingredients for multicultural competencies. As pointed out, transcending ethnocentrism by deconstructing inappropriate hierarchical and dichotomous thinking styles/patterns is one way to shift to a holistic thinking style/pattern. This process is almost impossible without transformative learning. The emotional aspects of learning are a necessary component of transformative learning. There are various kinds of emotions from the positive to the negative. Plutchik's (1980) emotion wheel indicates eight primary emotions (joy, acceptance, fear, surprise, sadness, disgust, anger, and anticipation). More complex emotions are created by combining adjacent primaries such as love (joy and acceptance), submission (acceptance and fear), awe (fear and surprise), disappointment (sadness and surprise), remorse (disgust and sadness), contempt (anger and disgust), aggressiveness (anticipation and anger), and optimism (joy and anticipation). Combinations of additional primary emotions, once removed from the wheel, produce despair (fear and sadness) and pride (anger and joy). The expression of emotion and the values put on a particular emotion are determined by a culture's traditions, customs, and beliefs. For instance, some individuals are socialized that expression of anger is not appropriate, and when they see a person whose cultural values encourage expressing anger as culturally appropriate, they interpret it from their own cultural frame of reference. It is important to consider culture-specific expression of emotions while allowing variations within a particular culture. Transformative learning occurs by integrating emotion, which is culture specific. All emotions must be integrated, even though learning to accept what is culturally labeled as "undesirable" or "negative" is a challenging task (Jackson, 1999; Reynolds, 1995; Steward, Wright, Jackson, & Jo, 1998). Due to the lack of emphasis on emotional aspects of learning, most individuals are not aware of inconsistencies between their inter- and intrapersonal communication and their emotional reactions. For instance, an individual may raise his/her/zir voice at another person while uttering, "I don't care what you do. You can do whatever you want!" If the individual does not care, there is no need for him/her/zir to be emotionally charged (raise his/her/zir voice). If an individual who yells, "I don't care what you do. You can do whatever you want!" could observe his/her/zir own body language for about 5 min, he/she/ze would be able to feel his/her/zir emotions in various parts of his/her/zir body. An individual may say he/she/ze is "fine"; however, one's body language and tone of voice may show something different from "fine." Part of the contradiction between verbal and nonverbal communication is a result of the devaluation of emotional awareness in learning by socialization practice. Miller and Miller (1997) summarize the importance of emotion in both verbal and nonverbal communication. They state that feelings "give you a reliable reading—positive to negative, and strong to weak—of a situation" (p. 47) if emotions are not distorted by substance abuse or organic disease. The following reflection activity is designed to assess practitioner-trainees' emotional state.

CONCRETE STRATEGIES

Reflection on Emotion

1. Rate your ability to be aware of your intrapersonal emotional state on a scale of 1 (very low) to 10 (very high).

2. What factors contributed to your rating in Question 1?

Kindlon and Thompson (2000) propose an alternative socialization practice that will facilitate the emotional aspect of learning. They write:

What boys need, first and foremost, is to be seen through a different lens than tradition prescribes. . . . Give boys permission to have an internal life, approval for the full range of human emotions, and help in developing an emotional vocabulary so that they may better understand themselves and communicate more effectively with others. (pp. 240–241)

Studies indicate that girls are encouraged to articulate their feelings in the early years of the socialization process but are discouraged from expressing their range of emotions as they enter adulthood. The powerful images of women in the media (TV, movies, magazines, and music for adults and children) nowadays portray them as acting more like traditional men (Carter & Steiner, 2004). This type of change is instrumental in perpetuating sexism and internalized oppression for girls.

One of the valuable tools for facilitating transformative learning is analysis of individuals' defense mechanisms. Individuals use defense mechanisms (e.g., regression, displacement, rationalization, reaction formation, projection, intellectualization, and identification) to cope with their stress and anxiety. Understanding the relationship between the conscious and the unconscious is also important in understanding their intra- and interpersonal relationships and the dynamics involved in defense mechanisms. Jung's pioneer work on the concept of the interrelationship of the conscious and the unconscious is well portrayed in *The Portable Jung* (Campbell, 1976). Whenever the author assigns defense mechanism awareness homework to students, they initially resist, but once they make themselves do it, they are fascinated by their inner world's dynamics of defense mechanisms, values, beliefs, expectations, and sense of self. They become aware of the fact that they often use more than one defense mechanism simultaneously to deal with a particular situation. By tallying their targets of defense mechanisms, they also find they are upset more often with family members or people they live with. Such defense mechanisms as regression, displacement, projection, rationalization, intellectualization, reaction formation, and denial are evident in their journal entries. However, it is hard to detect repression.

Being aware of when and with whom individuals use defense mechanisms can assist them with paying more attention to the emotional aspects of their meaning-making process. Recent research by Banaji and Bhaskar (2001), Banaji and Greenwald (1994), Dovidio and Gaertner (1998, 2000, 2004, 2005), Greenwald and Banaji (1995), and Schacter (1987) has contributed to dispelling the negative connotation attached to the unconscious. Banaji and Bhaskar write:

> In contrast to the first hundred years of research, which conveyed a view of memory and beliefs as operating exclusively in a conscious mode, the past two decades have shown increasingly that both memory and belief also operate implicitly in powerful yet unconscious ways, outside the actor's awareness of control. (p. 140)

Individuals need to observe their emotional inner dialogue (intrapersonal communication) without judgment or censoring in order to assess their emotional characteristics. An ideal self-image that is carved out by an individual's rational (intellectual) side through conventional learning may interfere with the individual's attempt not to censor. For example, when an individual's ideal self-image takes over and his/her/zir self-talk (intrapersonal communication) says that it is a waste of time to pay attention to "undesirable" emotions, he/she/ze needs to have an inner dialogue emphasizing that no emotions are "undesirable" as long as they do not harm anyone. Feelings are what they are. They need to be observed by an individual who is feeling them. Feelings do not need to be justified, denied, or avoided for transformative learning to occur. "If you do not attend to your emotions, you miss important self information that is essential for making good decisions or resolving conflicts" (Miller & Miller, 1997, p. 47).

Transformative learning has a long history beginning with Dewey (2004), who emphasized experiential application of knowledge. His educational philosophy is that learning should be process oriented and learners should be given the opportunity to develop the relationship between their experiences and their knowledge. As a learner interacts with intellectual information (knowledge) as a whole person, he/she/ze comes to his/her/zir own conclusion about the information through active participation in the process. Transformative learning brings life-changing behaviors because it requires students' active involvement, deep-level processing, and reflection (Ferrer, Romero, & Albareda, 2005; Karp, 2005; Moore, 2005; Pugh & Bergin, 2005; Salomon & Perkins, 1989). Flumerfelt, Ingram, Brockberg, and Smith (2007) conducted a study with graduate students who were enrolled in a graduate leadership program that used the Interstate School Leaders Licensure Consortium (ISLLC) standards (1996). The ISLLC standards were based on a taxonomy that emphasized process orientation, holistic thinking, and transformative learning. The results of Flumerfelt et al.'s study showed that more transformative learning occurred for students who were given more opportunities to practice; the knowledge and performance levels of these students showed more depth as well. The researchers recommended providing a more practical experience for students who were not in the practice group: "more role playing, simulation activities, mentorships, job shadowing, job sharing and internships" (p. 117).

In counseling, practitioners facilitate the transformative learning process of clients since the goal of therapy is for clients to change their thinking, feeling, and/or behavior so that they can accept, cope, adjust, function, and/or maximize their potential. When practitioners increase multicultural counseling competencies through transformative learning, they are likely able to assist clients with transcending their old ways of thinking, feeling, and behaving and adapting a modified or new way of thinking, feeling, and behaving. The transformative learning process for practitioners is similar to the therapeutic process for clients. A practitioner may resist transformative learning in the same way that clients may resist when a practitioner introduces new ideas or asks specific questions for reframing. Some clients resist with intense emotion when they perceive that their long-held myths need to be changed, even though they understand intellectually that changing is for the better. Learning to change one's ways of thinking, feeling, and behaving is a difficult task but a transformative process. The following experiential learning activities are designed to promote self-awareness by examining patterns in practitioner-trainees' defense mechanisms.

CONCRETE STRATEGIES

Experiential Learning Activities on Defense Mechanisms

1. Keep an emotional diary for at least 14 days without analyzing the content. Focus on how you felt about your inter- and intrapersonal relationships throughout the day. Do not describe simply what you did each day but how you felt about doing whatever you did. For example, let's say that today you got up late because you didn't set the alarm clock last night, and you were speeding to get to work. You got a speeding ticket, which upset you. To make matters worse, you found out you forgot to bring important papers to work for a meeting. Your emotional diary would be something like this:

   > I can't believe that I didn't set the alarm last night. I am so stupid. I got a speeding ticket because I wasn't lucky. It always happens to me. I saw lots of people who were going faster than me, but it was me who had to get the ticket. I felt that the world is against me. $200 for speeding? I don't have that kind of money. I'll never get out of the slum I'm in. Maybe I am not cut out for my job. Can't believe I would forget the papers I worked hard on last night. I don't know why I am so stupid. I am sure everyone knew I was stupid. I could tell they were laughing at me. I know I shouldn't yell at Brian. It wasn't his fault. I don't know why I always blame him whenever I don't feel good. But then, he does the same to me, so I shouldn't feel bad about that.

   Your emotional diary is a forum for writing about your intrapersonal communication with regard to your feelings about an event or a situation.

2. After at least 14 days of keeping the diary, go back to each entry and critically examine what type of defense mechanisms you used each day.

(Continued)

(Continued)

3. Tally the types of defense mechanisms and see whether you can learn something about your inner world: Who or what is your target of defense mechanisms? Which defense mechanisms do you use the most, and when do you most often use them? Do you feel better or worse about yourself after using defense mechanisms?

4. Summarize your general intrapersonal communication on the basis of the 14 days.

5. Did your parents, siblings, and/or schoolteachers use defense mechanisms when you were growing up? What kind of defense mechanisms did they use?

6. Reflect on your answers to the previous questions while closing your eyes for about 5 min. Open your eyes and write down your relationship to defense mechanisms.

7. Think of a recent incident where you were frustrated with a coworker, a friend, a family member, or a client. If you used defense mechanisms to cope with your frustration, what kind of defense mechanisms did you use?

3

Assessment of a Practitioner's Values, Beliefs, and Biases

This chapter explores barriers to an individual's self-assessment of values, beliefs, and biases. It proposes unconventional strategies to transcend these barriers to gain inner experience, which facilitates self-awareness of one's own values, beliefs, and biases. Unconventional strategies such as narrative and reflective writing, consciousness-raising activities, and listening to one's own body are discussed. Progoff's (1992) writing to gain inner experience, Blackmore's (2004) consciousness-raising questions, and Olsen's (1998) body awareness and communication are explored in depth.

Experiential and reflection-based learning activities are provided to increase practitioner-trainees' awareness of their inner experiences. The chapter illustrates the importance of a practitioner-trainee knowing her own values, beliefs, and biases and her thinking style with regard to assessment and treatment of clients by providing concrete examples.

※ BARRIERS TO AN INDIVIDUAL'S SELF-ASSESSMENT OF HER OWN VALUES, BELIEFS, AND BIASES

Self-assessment of one's own values, beliefs, and biases is a challenging task because awareness of inner self has not been an important component of socialization practice in the United States and other cultures that value extrinsic valuation, which puts greater emphasis on the conscious, intellect, and rational and logical reasoning than on the unconscious, emotion, intuition, and creativity. Self-awareness is one aspect of human consciousness, and individuals are not born with culture-specific awareness. Individuals learn to value the culture-specific values and beliefs they are born into before they are capable of examining the impact of these culture-specific values and beliefs on the formation of their own understanding of self (Blackmore, 2004). Self-assessment requires self-reflection, and it is difficult to learn to self-reflect if the dominant culture emphasizes extrinsic valuation rather than intrinsic valuation. In addition, self exists inside the person (Shotter, 1989), and it is almost impossible to be aware of what's inside a person without the ability to self-reflect.

Self-assessment of an individual's own values, beliefs, and biases is challenging in extrinsic valuation–oriented cultures because individuals are rewarded for carrying out culturally expected behaviors rather than searching for behaviors that are meaningful to them. Markus, Kitayama, and Heiman (1996) raised the question of whether or not high self-appraisal is a culture-specific characteristic. They suggested that the tendency to appraise oneself higher than others is a characteristic of individualistic cultures such as those of Europe and North America since studies have not found these characteristics in collective cultures. Taylor and Brown's (1988) study supported the finding that Americans in the United States tend to think of themselves as superior to their peers in terms of their abilities and personality traits (*hierarchical thinking*). This implies that hierarchical thinking is embedded as a culture-specific character, and it is hard to deconstruct culture-specific characteristics. Simply suggesting a new idea does not lead to transcendence of culture-specific characteristics. The new idea has to be accompanied by concrete strategies to transcend culture-specific characteristics.

Some culture-specific characteristics like high self-appraisal are due to asymmetric perception, which is a tendency to praise oneself highly compared with others and to detect others' biases readily but deny these biases within oneself (Pronin, Gilovich, & Ross, 2004). Pronin et al. reviewed the literature concerning differential perceptions of self versus others from 1949 to 2004. All reviewed studies showed that individuals regard themselves as more favorable than others. For example, study participants overestimated their ability to judge objectively compared with others and underestimated others' ability to judge objectively (Epley & Dunning, 2000; Kruger & Gilovich, 1999; van Boven, Dunning, & Loewenstein, 2000). Participants were in denial about being biased but readily pointed out others being biased. Similar studies indicated that individuals tend to assess themselves much more positively compared with others (Baumeister, 1998; Pronin, Lin, & Ross, 2002; Steele, 1988; Taylor & Brown, 1988). When participants were led to believe that they did not do well on a test but that others did well on the same test, they reported that the test was not valid. When participants were led to believe that they performed well, they reported that the test was valid. They also believed that their assessment was objective and that others' assessment was biased (Pronin et al., 2002). This type of asymmetric perception was also shown in participants' assessment of introspection. Participants reported the value of introspection in self-assessment for themselves but did not perceive the same value of introspection for others' self-assessment (Pronin et al., 2004). The above findings in high self-appraisal and asymmetric perception shed light not only on individuals' difficulty with self-assessment but also on understanding the reasons for the lack of major changes in multicultural counseling despite various attempts. Accurate self-assessment of their own cultural values, beliefs, and biases is not possible as long as individuals operate from high self-appraisal and asymmetry. As a result, unintentional racism, sexism, heterosexism, ableism, classism, and ageism will continue even if individuals develop theories to deconstruct them (Brewer & Brown, 1998; Hewstone, Rubin, & Willis, 2002).

Another reason for the challenge is the role of unconscious and implicit learning (DeCoster, Banner, Smith, & Semin, 2006; Rydell, McConnell, Mackie, & Strain, 2006; Rydell, McConnell, Strain, Claypool, & Hugenberg, 2007). A desire to hold onto an ideal self-image may interfere with individuals' ability to assess their cultural values, beliefs, and biases when there is conflict between their ideal image of self and what they value and believe (Banaji, 1997; Banaji & Greenwald, 1994; Banaji & Hardin, 1996; Chen & Bargh, 1997; Devine, 1989; Fazio, Jackson, Dunton, & Williams, 1995; Greenwald & Banaji, 1995). Researchers have found that stereotypes often unconsciously activate implicit expressions of beliefs and attitudes, and these are often unrelated to explicit expressions of the same beliefs and attitudes. Extensive research (Dovidio, Evans, & Tyler, 1986; Dovidio & Gaertner, 1998, 2000, 2004, 2005; Dovidio, Gaertner, Kawakami, & Hodson, 2002; Dovidio, Kawakami, & Gaertner, 2002; Dovidio, Kawakami, Johnson, Johnson, & Howard, 1997; Fazio et al., 1995; Gaertner, 1973; Gaertner & Dovidio, 1977, 1986; Gaertner & McLaughlin, 1983; Hodson, Dovidio, & Gaertner, 2002) has demonstrated the difficulty of self-awareness due to aversive racism. Aversive racists show explicit behavior of caring for marginalized people by believing consciously in equity and justice but implicitly and unconsciously having negative attitudes toward marginalized people. According to Dovidio and Gaertner (2005), aversive racism is "more subtle and is presumed to characterize the racial attitudes of most well-educated and liberal Whites in the United States" (p. 618).

In addition, attribution error and social projection, as discussed in Chapter 2, lead to ingroup favoritism and create barriers to assessing individuals' own values, beliefs, and biases because individuals' perception is shaped by their own cultural context (Brewer & Brown, 1998; Fiske, 1998; Hornsey & Hogg, 2000; Swim, Hyers, Cohen, Fitzgerald, & Bylsma, 2003). Furthermore, individuals' values, beliefs, and biases have been automated through internal repetition since childhood, and this automatic thinking process influences individuals' perception and judgment (Banaji & Hardin, 1996; Devine, 1989; Perdue & Gurtman, 1990). This private process gives an impression that these values, beliefs, and biases are based on facts due to the absence of an external feedback loop.

It is understandable how and why these barriers contribute to challenges not only in self-assessment of one's own values, beliefs, and biases but also in walking the talk of multicultural competencies. This section discussed barriers to self-assessment of one's own cultural values, beliefs, and biases. These barriers explain that multicultural competencies need to consider the multiple and complex factors discussed in this section to assess the feasibility of implementation of multicultural counseling theories or concepts. Strategies of implementing conceptual theories in practice need to consider how to be cognizant of these barriers and include concrete plans to reduce or eliminate these barriers. Implementation is not feasible without examining the barriers that stem from inner experience. Barriers from inner experience interfere with the implementation phase without an individual's awareness.

⟋ AWARENESS OF INNER EXPERIENCE

The purpose of this section is to increase individuals' awareness of their inner experience. This task is enormous because it takes a lifetime to become conscious of inner experience and unconscious processes and learn to integrate body and mind. Personal inquiry (first person), which has been considered trivial in academic settings, is essential to gain awareness of inner experience. Inner experiences have been accumulated through both subjective, first-person inquiry (personal inquiry) and objective, third-person inquiry (scientific inquiry). Searle's (1997) explanation about pain clearly demonstrates that an individual's inner experience is the result of interaction between subjective and objective experience; the pain an individual feels when he is pinched is the pain only he would know since it is a subjective experience. When a person is pinched, neurons begin to fire at the receptors, and the individual feels pain as soon as it reaches the brain. Degree and intensity of perceived pain vary from individual to individual because each individual has a different experience with pain. The neurological pathway from the receptors to the brain is an objective (third-person) phenomenon, and perceived pain is a subjective experience. Distinguishing between the subjective and objective experiences of an individual as if they are different entities is artificial creation and prevents the individual from understanding his/her/zir own inner experience. Psychotherapy and counseling must emphasize both personal inquiry and scientific inquiry to obtain accurate assessment, diagnosis, and treatment. Changing feelings, thoughts, and behaviors requires examining a client's whole self. The whole person consists of the physical, psychological, emotional, sociocultural, and spiritual selves, which include both subjective and objective experiences. Considering only observable behavior through scientific inquiry and ignoring systematic and thorough inquiry of subjective experience allows practitioners to gather only partial information about a client. In order to assess, diagnose, and treat a client, practitioners need to have as much information about the client as possible. Both subjective (personal) and objective (scientific) inquiries are necessary to gather information about a whole person. Various therapeutic techniques have been developed without focusing on raising practitioners' awareness of their own inner experiences even though many practitioners explore clients' inner experiences in order to assist them with changing thinking, feeling, and behavior. If practitioners are more aware of their inner experiences through writing, centering, paying attention to their body language, paying attention to their dreams, or doing consciousness-raising activities, they are more likely to accurately assess clients' inner experiences without countertransference.

Practitioner-trainees can learn to notice their inner experiences through actually doing activities.

Thinking about what you would write is not the same as actually writing it. . . . Thinking about it and figuring it out is not enough, because that gives us the illusion that we understand it conceptually when we cannot in fact understand how the dynamic of its principles operates without working with it over a period of time. (Progoff, 1992, p. 11)

This section provides experiential learning activities that allow practitioners to get in touch with their inner experiences. These learning activities are not written in the third person (scientific inquiry) in order to provide an opportunity for fully engaging in subjective experience (first-person inquiry). Four different kinds of experiential learning activities or learning through reflection are discussed in this chapter: (a) writing, (b) consciousness raising, (c) listening to the body, and (d) paying attention to dreams. These activities can be effective if practitioner-trainees are able to fully engage in them by creating a peaceful inner space by centering without censoring or screening. Individuals cannot rush the process of learning to be aware of their inner experiences, just like transformative learning. It takes time.

Awareness of Inner Experience Through Writing

Writing without censoring or screening, like journal writing, allows for self-reflection, which facilitates self-discovery of rich resources within oneself. It allows for discovering inner wisdom. It takes time to write without automatic censoring, but practicing writing on a regular basis may gradually reduce this tendency. An individual's values, beliefs, biases, and access to unconscious materials are revealed in the process of this type of writing and self-reflecting. This type of writing can be practiced individually, as a group, or both. Start with centering regardless of the format of practicing. Each writing activity needs to begin with centering to focus on the task. Centering and breathing are emphasized for clarity and calmness throughout each writing activity. Then how to focus on inner experience in the moment and every day is introduced. The writing activities explore four dimensions of inner experience: time, dialogue, depth, and meaning (Progoff, 1992). Each dimension is explained briefly prior to the corresponding experiential learning activity. The following is a centering exercise. Centering quiets the mind so one can focus on a learning task.

CONCRETE STRATEGIES

Experiential Learning Activity on Centering

Close your eyes and imagine you are sitting in a cozy place. Practice three-dimensional breathing by moving your chest, rib cage, and stomach. Breathe slowly and evenly. Breathe in relaxation and see what is in your mind. If your mind is not with your body, ask your mind to be with your body. Breathe out tension and resistance. Breathe in relaxation and see what is in your mind. If your mind is with yesterday or tomorrow, inform your mind that the only reality you have is in this moment. Ask your mind to embrace your body and be still. Breathe out resistance and tension. Breathe in relaxation and appreciate your mind for trying. Breathe out tension and resistance and slowly open your eyes.

Some practitioner-trainees may find writing to gain access to inner experiences difficult and the process slow. The process is like learning a foreign language for the first time. One of the best ways to learn a foreign language is to practice through repetition. It is one thing to understand how to pronounce a word, but understanding does not help with pronunciation. Pronouncing well only comes by practicing the pronunciation over and over again. The following exercise is designed to help practitioner-trainees practice not judging or screening.

CONCRETE STRATEGIES

Experiential Learning Activity

After centering, repeat to yourself the following: "I understand why I judge myself and screen automatically. I was conditioned to do what is proper according to my cultural, institutional, and family values. This exercise in not judging or screening is for me to really know myself. I want to know aspects of myself that I don't have access to. It is my understanding that I will have access to them only if I don't judge or screen what I think, feel, and do. I would like to try. I am interested in transcending the talk of multicultural competencies and transforming it into the walk of multicultural competencies." Read each sentence and then close your eyes and repeat the sentence silently while breathing slowly and evenly.

One of the effective ways to know an individual's inner experience is "just simply stating the fact of our experience" (Progoff, 1992, p. 244). Below is an experiential learning activity to state the fact about the present and today.

CONCRETE STRATEGIES

Experiential Learning Activities

1. Inner experience of specifics of the present

   a. Write down whatever comes to you spontaneously.

   b. When (e.g., a year ago, a week ago) did you start to feel or think this way?

   c. Was there an event or a series of events that led to this? If so, describe the event or events in detail including feelings you felt at the time.

   d. Describe your inner-world experience, your outer-world experience, and the intersection of your inner- and outer-world experiences at this time in detail.

      (1) Inner world: feelings, thoughts, sense of self, mental health, relationships with ingroups, and so on.

      (2) Outer world: physical health, sociopolitical issues, relationships to ingroups and outgroups, and so on.

      (3) How mental health affects physical health and vice versa; how the way you are treated by outgroups/ingroups affects your sense of self, identity, and belief systems; and so on.

2. Inner experience of a day

   a. What was your physical condition when you started the day, and what is it now?

   b. What were your emotional conditions and wishes as you began the day?

      (1) Describe the details of your emotions (e.g., joy, anxiety, depression, frustration, anger).

      (2) Describe your wishes in detail.

   c. How did you begin your work (or schoolwork) of the day?

   d. Describe the types of relationships you had throughout the day.

Practitioner-trainees will discover many differences between their inner and outer worlds as they continue the writing activities. One difference is the Time Dimension between the inner and outer worlds. The inner experience of time is qualitative time, and outer-world time is chronological time. Qualitative time is "the subjective perception of objective events in terms of the meaning and value they have to the person" (Progoff, 1992, p. 74). For example, an individual may be 30 years old chronologically (by outer-world time) but still may be 5 years old according to inner experience and perceive the world according to a 5-year-old's beliefs and values. The inner experience of qualitative time of individuals who are systematically oppressed due to race, gender, class, sexual orientation, age, disability, region, language, or religion is dramatically different from that of those who are systematically privileged. The following reflection-based learning activities are designed to facilitate consciousness of inner-world time.

CONCRETE STRATEGIES

Reflection-Based Learning Activities on Inner-World Time

Close your eyes. Breathe in relaxation and breathe out tension. As you breathe deeply and slowly, travel back to your early childhood and see what events stand out. Feel the movement of your life. Observe these events with your mind's eye and sit still. Slowly open your eyes.

1. Record the first set of events (8–10) that stood out in your mind.

   a. Read your list silently to yourself. Write down any emotions you feel as you read the list. If you are doing this as a group, the group leader/instructor may ask someone to read, and the group may listen quietly. It may be a powerful experience for the person to read out loud. You may also read aloud into an audio- or a videotape recorder. You may have different feelings about the events as you listen to yourself and/or watch your own verbal and nonverbal expressions on a videotape. Write down your feelings about listening to and viewing yourself. Regardless of the format, it is important for you to hear your own narratives and allow yourself to feel any emotions without judgment.

(Continued)

(Continued)

  b. Choose one event that stirs the most emotion and elaborate on it in detail.

  c. Specifics of the event:

    (1) Describe your feelings about yourself then.

    (2) Describe the kind of person you were then.

    (3) Describe your attitude about life then.

    (4) Describe your beliefs about your destiny then.

    (5) Describe any religious beliefs you had then.

The Dialogue Dimension of inner experience involves the relationships among separate aspects of an individual's inner life. These separate aspects often operate without awareness of each other. The writing process allows practitioner-trainees to build an inner relationship with all the significant areas of their lives. Mindful and devoted work in this dimension may lead to awareness of deeper inner direction than is available at a conscious level. The following are experiential learning activities on the Dialogue Dimension that involve reflection, imagery, and centering.

CONCRETE STRATEGIES

Experiential Learning Activities on the Dialogue Dimension

It is extremely important not to judge your emotions, behaviors, or thoughts but to simply report. If judgment and censoring come automatically, close your eyes and breathe in and out slowly at least three times (or however many times it takes to create calmness and stillness within you). Open your eyes slowly.

Dialoguing with:

  1. People who have inner importance to you

    a. Listing the people: Close your eyes as you breathe deeply and evenly. Travel from the present time to your early childhood and think about those who were important to you and those with whom you have unfinished business. Include individuals you have not seen in years and individuals who have died. Sit still in silence and breathe evenly and slowly while thinking and feeling about these people. Slowly open your eyes and write down their names.

b. Write each person's name at the top of a page. Start with the first person on the first page. Close your eyes and imagine the person. What feelings come to you when you are thinking of him/her/zir?

   (1) Describe the history of your relationship with this person and different stages of the relationship from the beginning.

   (2) Describe the present status of the relationship.

2. Work

   a. Close your eyes and imagine your work. What feelings come to you when you are thinking of your work?

   (1) Describe your work history and different stages of your relationship to work from the beginning.

   (2) Describe the present status of your relationship to work.

3. Body

   a. Close your eyes and imagine your body. What feelings come to you when you are thinking of your body?

   (1) Describe your relationship to your body throughout its different developmental stages.

   (2) Describe the present status of your relationship to your body.

4. Society

   a. Close your eyes and imagine society. What feelings come to you when you are thinking of society?

   (1) Describe society and different stages of your relationship to it from the beginning.

   (2) Describe the present status of your relationship to society.

When you have finished writing, close your eyes and breathe slowly and evenly for about 2 min. Sit in stillness and let your body and mind absorb the feelings you have been describing without judgment.

Being the other:

1. Close your eyes and breathe deeply and slowly while being aware of your emotions. Imagine one of the people who have inner importance

(Continued)

(Continued)

to you and see whether you can take his/her/zir role for a moment. Imagine placing yourself inside the other's life. Breathe deeply and slowly and sit still. When you feel you can take the role, slowly open your eyes.

a. List the other's events (8–10) in the first person as you did yours. Begin with the phrase, "I was born. Then . . ."
b. Describe details of the events if you desire.

2. Starting the dialogue: Close your eyes, breathe deeply and evenly, and sit in silence thinking and feeling about yourself and the other person. Imagine you are sitting across from each other. Begin to have a conversation in your mind's eye and record this inner dialogue.

a. When you have finished writing, close your eyes again, breathe evenly and slowly, and feel your emotions without judgment or censoring. Then read the dialogue to yourself and take notes of any emotions as you feel them. Observe whether these emotions are the same as those you had before reading the dialogue to yourself. Record your emotional status.

When you have finished writing, close your eyes and breathe slowly and evenly for about 2 min. Sit in stillness and let your body and mind absorb the feelings you have been describing without judgment.

The Depth Dimension leads individuals beneath the conscious level of the Dialogue Dimension and symbolizes the root of an individual's problems and potential that lie under the conscious level. "The Depth Dimension is a primary means by which we can discover what our life is trying to become" (Progoff, 1992, p. 197). The symbols represented in an individual's dreams need to be recorded by the individual as he/she/ze observes and experiences them. The purpose of recording dreams is not to interpret, analyze, and understand dreams but to place the individual "back into the movement of our dream process as a whole so that the process can now freely extend itself" (Progoff, p. 200). The following experiential learning activities are designed to help practitioner-trainees gain access to the unconscious through dreams.

CONCRETE STRATEGIES

Experiential Learning Activities on the Depth Dimension

Close your eyes. Breathe in and out slowly for at least 3 min (or however long it takes to create calmness and stillness within yourself).

Dreams

1. Record your dreams as you observe and experience them.
   a. Record the earliest dreams that you remember.
   b. Record any dreams you remember from childhood.
   c. Record recurrent dreams (pleasant and unpleasant, including nightmares).
   d. Record fragmented dreams.
   e. Record recent dreams.

2. To reach the Depth Dimension, close your eyes. Breathe in and out evenly and slowly until you feel calm and still.
   a. Observe which dreams stand out to you. Experience the quality and tone of the dreams without judgment or censoring.
   b. Pick a dream and see whether you dreamed other dreams that stood out to you around the same time. If you did, group dreams according to chronological points in your dream sequence.
   c. Read the series of dreams loudly to yourself several times. Record yourself reading so you can listen to your dreams at any time or draw images from your dreams that represent them symbolically.

The Meaning Dimension of inner experience is the process of integrating inner and outer life by combining subjective and objective experiences. Report all experiences, new and old, without judging or interpreting them because "their significance for your life may not be apparent at that time" (Progoff, 1992, p. 220). These experiences provide valuable feedback in life. Integration of inner and outer life needs to be practiced until an individual feels oneness and whole. The following experiential learning activity provides the opportunity to experience integration of inner and outer life through imagery. This activity needs to be repeated until practitioner-trainees feel unity among their inner and outer experiences.

CONCRETE STRATEGIES

Experiential Learning Activity: Integration of Inner and Outer Life

Close your eyes as you breathe slowly and evenly. Reflect on your life and the inner experiences you have recorded so far. Feel the ongoing movement of your life up to the present. Embrace all of your experiences. Let this moment become an experience of total unity of your inner and outer life. Sit still in silence as you breathe and feel the oneness of your life. Open your eyes when you feel unity.

"The Meaning Dimension covers the aspect of life that we experience in terms of beliefs about the meaning of life. It deals with beliefs about fundamentals" (Progoff, 1992, p. 224). Beliefs, values, and biases are based on learning from the outer world and made a part of the inner world. For example, some individuals have learned to be dichotomous thinkers, and inappropriate applications of dichotomous thinking hinder individuals' ability to embrace opposites. Thus it is difficult for these individuals to balance and integrate their inner and outer experiences. "The integral movement of the whole process of our inner life requires both of the opposites" (Progoff, p. 227). These individuals may feel frustration and resistance to the integration process of the Meaning Dimension of inner experience. The following learning activities are designed to explore the Meaning Dimension of an individual's values and beliefs through reflection and centering.

CONCRETE STRATEGIES

Experiential Learning Activities on the Meaning Dimension: Values and Beliefs

1. Observe and attend to your inner voice: Close your eyes and sit still while focusing on breathing. Breathe in slowly and evenly and breathe out slowly and evenly. Think about your values and beliefs without judgment. As they come to you as images, words, or phrases, just observe them and pay attention to your feelings as you breathe. Slowly open your eyes.

    a. Write down your feelings and list your values and beliefs.
    b. How did you arrive at these values and beliefs?

2. Whose (or what) influence did you value in your inner experience, and are your values and beliefs related to it?

3. Critical inquiry: Examine your beliefs and values without censoring.

    a. What are your primary beliefs (without considering political correctness) about race, gender, ethnicity, class, sexual orientation, disability, religion, region, age, and size?

    b. How are your beliefs about the above areas similar to or different from those of your ingroups (e.g., family, work, friends, church)?

    c. What doubts did you have about your beliefs when you were a child, a teenager, and a young adult, and how did you resolve them?

    d. Describe the history of the inner movement of your core values and beliefs.

    e. How do you define fear? Describe your relationship history with fear.

    f. How do you define anxiety? Describe your relationship history with anxiety.

    g. How do you define loneliness? Describe your relationship history with loneliness.

    h. Have you accepted others' values and beliefs (e.g., those of your culture, family, or religious organization) because of your fear, anxiety, or loneliness?

The function of the Meaning Dimension is for individuals to collect the data from their inner experiences and make strong inner connections. Censoring or denying one's inner experiences is not only deceiving and marginalizing oneself but also preventing oneself from integration and connection. Strong inner connections enable individuals to understand others who appear to act indifferently toward them or to reject them. Instead of reacting negatively to indifference and rejection, individuals may be more compassionate toward others even though at the moment they do not know others' inner experiences. Individuals do not judge or project their feelings onto others, as they do not judge their own inner experiences. Writing for awareness of the four dimensions of inner experience allows individuals to explore the possibilities of their infinite inner wisdom.

Consciousness Studies

Another way to examine one's inner experience is through consciousness studies. Most researchers of consciousness studies agree that consciousness encompasses everything there is; it includes both subjective and objective experiences, although there are variations in researchers' definition of consciousness. Most consciousness studies suggest that first-person experience and third-person experience do not operate as separate entities. They do not operate linearly and sequentially. They interact simultaneously in consciousness (Blackmore, 2004; Metzinger, 2003; Searle, 1997). This point is well illustrated by Searle's study on pain perception. According to Searle, the pain felt when one is pinched is only experienced by the pinched individual (it is a personal and subjective experience) even though the individual goes through the same neurological pathway from the receptors to the brain as other individuals. The neurological mechanics are an objective (scientific pathway) phenomenon while perception is a subjective phenomenon, and the individual cannot feel the pain until a stimulus is delivered to the brain by the neurological mechanics. This explains variations in perceived pain by different individuals. Being aware of inner experience in consciousness is the result of both objective and subjective experience.

Consciousness studies reveal characteristics about inner experience that are similar to those of Progoff's (1992) four dimensions of writing. This section discusses these similarities between Progoff's four dimensions of writing and the consciousness perspective. Consciousness studies support the notion that individuals can reach a meditative state through no self-judgment, which is emphasized in Progoff's journal writing. Progoff's journal writing combines reflective narrative writing with meditation and imagery. Common to all forms of meditation is a goal to reach change in an individual's state of consciousness by paying attention and not thinking. The emphasis on not censoring and not screening in Progoff's narrative writing is an attempt to create a mental space similar to that created by not thinking. Achieving a meditative state through not censoring/not screening or not thinking leads to changes in consciousness. Recent attention to Buddhism by researchers of consciousness studies is partly due to the role of meditation in changing one's state of consciousness (Kabat-Zinn, 1999; Kapleau, 1980; Sheng-Yen, Crook, Child, Kalin, & Andricevic, 2002).

Both Progoff (1992) and researchers of consciousness studies have shown interest in dreams. For Progoff, it is dreams' ability to bring a deeper level of inner experience from the unconscious, and for consciousness researchers, it is the nature of the conscious in the dream stage. Most individuals who study dreams agree that dreaming is a form of consciousness that is different from the waking stage of consciousness

(Atkinson, Atkinson, Smith, Bem, & Nolen-Hoeksema, 2000; Carlson, 1999; Dennett, 1976; Hobson, 1999; Searle, 1997). There are various definitions of consciousness, and they range from altered states of consciousness to the unconscious. Some define consciousness as everything there is, including the unconscious, and others differentiate consciousness from the unconscious. There are also various theories about different kinds of dreams. Regardless of how they define consciousness, most dream theorists relate dreams to inner experiences such as fears, hopes, creativity, and insight (Blackmore, 2004; van de Castle, 1994).

Consciousness researchers support Progoff's (1992) distinction between inner-world and outer-world experiences. Consciousness studies also reveal there is a difference between one's inner experience and the outer world. Several consciousness researchers have found that there is a difference between experienced time and chronological time (Blackmore, 2004). Events experienced in the outer world can be clocked, but events experienced in the inner world cannot be clocked in the same way. Individuals do not experience outer events sequentially in their inner world. For example, events of systematic oppression are past incidents according to chronological time but are alive in the inner world of individuals who have been oppressed and discriminated against. Statements like "Let's move on," "Forget about the past," "Don't dwell on the past," and "It's a waste of time" are based on external clock time. All these statements are intended to assist individuals with functioning more effectively and becoming healthier and more peaceful. What these statements are ignoring is the fact that there are differences between inner- and outer-world time. It is not that individuals do not want to transcend their past; it is that they are not able to due to their inner experience. Understanding the difference between outer and inner time is critical in practitioners' awareness of their own values, beliefs, and biases; having accurate empathy; understanding the impact of systematic oppression on internalized privilege/oppression; and seeing clients from their worldviews. Inner experience affects both clients and practitioners. If practitioners are or have been victims of oppression, their inner experience may facilitate an inaccurate perception and interpretation of clients' verbal and nonverbal communication. If practitioners are unearned privilege holders in relation to race, gender, sexual orientation, age, class, and so on, their inner experience is dramatically different from that of clients who have been systematically oppressed because of who they are (e.g., a member of a nondominant race or class, someone with a nondominant sexual orientation) throughout their lives. Raising consciousness to be able to differentiate between their inner- and outer-world experiences will help practitioners observe their values, beliefs, and biases as they are, as well as those of clients.

Research on consciousness and cognitive neuroscience with regard to attitudes, stereotypes, and prejudice revitalized the role of the unconscious in shaping beliefs, values, prejudices, and stereotypes. The study of the unconscious had been neglected in psychology due to its emphasis on scientific inquiry (the third-person perspective) in an attempt to secure psychology's position as a science. Over the past 2 decades, numerous researchers have found that learning can take place without a learner's awareness (Banaji & Hardin, 1996; Devine, 1989; Dovidio et al., 1986; Dovidio & Gaertner, 1998, 2000, 2004, 2005; Dovidio et al., 1997; Dovidio, Gaertner, et al., 2002; Dovidio, Kawakami, et al., 2002; Perdue & Gurtman, 1990). Consciousness researchers have also found that individuals behave as if they are aware of stimuli even though they report no awareness consciously (Merikel, Smilek, & Eastwood, 2001; Sidis, 1898). Blackmore (2004) illustrates the role of the unconscious in perception:

> Suppose you are sitting at dinner, chatting with your friends, oblivious to the hum of the microwave in the corner—until it stops. Suddenly you realize that it was humming along all the time. Only in its silence are you conscious of the noise. This simple, everyday phenomenon seems odd because it suggests perception without consciousness. It suggest that all along, in some unconscious way, you must have been hearing the noise. . . . The crucial finding is that people deny consciously detecting something while their behavior shows that they have detected it. (p. 274)

Acknowledging perception without consciousness and the role of the unconscious in perception and learning from both psychology research and consciousness research is an important step toward understanding not only the difficulties of accessing inner experience but also the complexities involved in knowing one's own values, beliefs, and biases, as well as truly understanding those of others. Implicit learning in the formation of values, beliefs, and biases is an example of the role of unconscious perception in learning. Some individuals talk of justice and equity in human diversity (on the conscious level) but are against justice and equity for people who are culturally different from them (on the unconscious level).

Individuals' values, beliefs, and biases are formulated through both conscious and unconscious processing with fluidity. Blackmore (2004) summarizes the implications of unconscious perception:

> Perceptual thresholds are not fixed but depend on variable response criteria; there is no undisputed measure for deciding whether something has been consciously perceived or not; and there are many stimuli that are deemed to be consciously perceived by some measures and not by others. All this threatens the idea that any stimulus is unequivocally either "in" or "out" of consciousness. It suggests instead that sensory information is processed in a wide variety of ways, with different consequences for different kinds of behavior. Some of these behaviors are usually taken as indications of consciousness, such as verbal reports or choices between clearly perceptible stimuli, while others are usually considered to be unconscious, such as fast reflexes, guesses or certain measures of brain activity. In between lie many behaviors that are sometimes taken to indicate consciousness and sometimes not. But there is no right answer. (pp. 279–280)

The above statement indicates consciousness can be understood from a holistic perspective that includes dynamic fluidity as a process. Conventional dichotomous categorizations hinder the ability to understand a whole range of perception, making divisions between personal inquiry and scientific inquiry by claiming that scientific inquiry is the only acceptable path for academic studies or learning. Dichotomous and hierarchical thinking is no longer adequate in explaining inner and outer experiences. Postmodernity requires a holistic perspective that embraces inner and outer experiences, the conscious and the unconscious, personal inquiry and scientific inquiry, intellect and emotion, body and mind, self and community, and monocultural and multicultural values with equal emphasis. The focus of this section was awareness of inner experience by being conscious. Expanding one's conscious awareness takes mindful and diligent practice on a daily basis. Finding experience itself without thoughts, theories, and conceptualization is difficult and challenging, especially in academia. The following experiential learning activities are selected from Blackmore's (2004) book to raise awareness of inner experience.

CONCRETE STRATEGIES

Experiential Learning Activities

These are consciousness-raising exercises from Blackmore's (2004) book. Each question should be asked without judgment every day as many times as possible.

Inner experience through consciousness exercises:

1. "Am I conscious now?" (p. 10)

2. "What is it like being me now?" (p. 24)

3. "Did I do this consciously?" (p. 43)

4. "Am I conscious now?" And then "Where is this experience?" (p. 67)

5. "Am I the same 'me' as a moment ago?" (p. 112)

6. "Am I doing this?" (p. 124)

Listening to the Body

Listening to the body is another way to access inner experience. The body expresses inner experience much more adequately than does verbal communication. Without awareness, individuals often communicate with their body (body language). Some individuals state that they have "butterflies" in their stomach, have headaches, or are shaky when they are anxious or nervous. Some individuals complain about their physical symptoms without knowing why. Some individuals state that they feel "fine," but their body language contradicts their verbal expression. An individual may smile as tears roll down his/her/zir cheek and say, "I am sorry. I don't know why I am crying" or raise his/her/zir voice with shallow breathing. The inability to identify outer expression of body language as the inner expression of an individual is a result of cultural conditioning by which individuals have been conditioned to separate their body from their mind as if they are two separate entities. Historically speaking, Descartes considered the body a machine without considering its connection to mind, memory, and emotion (Radomsky, 1995). Radomsky discusses healing the body not by focusing on the correct diagnosis on the basis of symptoms but by paying attention to inner experiences expressed through bodily symptoms. As she shifted from a biomedical approach to a socio-cultural approach, she learned that her female patients' chronic pain was related to psychological, emotional, and mental abuse by their partner or cultural myths about their role as women rather than due to specific organic causes. Radomsky writes:

> My effort to put these women into tightly defined categories reg-ularly failed. In addition, I realized I was not connecting with them in a meaningful way. Eventually I stopped trying to make the correct diagnosis when it came to these chronic pain prob-lems that had no identifiable organic cause. I started listening and asked different questions. As I altered my obsession with cure for chronic pain, I began to notice some changes. Many of these women started to talk to me about their lives. Some told painful and disturbing stories. . . . I gradually realized the con-nection between chronic pain and powerlessness in women. (p. 3)

Radomsky (1995) addresses the importance of the mind-body connection and listening to patients' inner experiences for healing. Body and mind are an integrated whole. Radomsky's female clients expressed their powerlessness through their bodies. Body language and movement are important aspects of understanding individuals' inner experiences, even though individuals may not be aware of their body language. In order to understand how the mind and body are connected, individuals need to understand the fundamentals of the human nervous system (see Table 3.1). The activities of individuals' bodies are governed by the ner-vous system, which can be divided into two parts: central nervous system (CNS) and peripheral nervous system (PNS). The CNS has two parts: the brain and the spinal cord. The PNS has two parts: the autonomic nervous system (ANS) and the somatic nervous system (SNS). The ANS (visceral) deals with involuntary functions, is responsible for internal functioning, and affects such organs as the heart, the lungs, and the digestive and reproductive organs. The autonomic division has two parts: the sympa-thetic and parasympathetic nervous systems. The sympathetic nervous system is activated when the body needs to cope with emergency situa-tions such as a natural disaster, an accident, or a personal crisis. For

Table 3.1 The Nervous System

Nervous Systems			
Central Nervous System (CNS)		Peripheral Nervous System (PNS)	
Brain	Spinal Cord	Autonomic Nervous System (ANS)	Somatic Nervous System (SNS)

a) Forebrain
b) Midbrain
c) Hindbrain
	Reflex	Involuntary
		  a) Sympathetic system
		  b) Parasympathetic system
			Voluntary

example, if an individual feels that someone is following him in the middle of the night as he's walking, he will walk or run as fast as he can to get to his destination, and this results in increased activity of the heart and lungs and decreased activity of the digestive organs. He may be surprised by how fast he is able to run or walk to be secure. The parasympathetic nervous system acts opposite to the sympathetic nervous system to create wholeness within the body. It is activated when the body is relaxing and resting. It is what an individual feels after a big dinner. He may feel totally relaxed because of his decreased heart rate and slowed breathing while his digestive system is activated. Often, he may feel sleepy. The daily balance of the functions of the sympathetic and parasympathetic nervous systems determines the health of the body. However, if an individual is stressed, symptoms of dysfunctions of organs manifest, resulting in an imbalance of the functions of the sympathetic and parasympathetic nervous systems. For example, he may listen only to the sympathetic nervous system because he perceives that his life is a series of crises. This imbalance may lead to some type of sickness. The SNS deals with voluntary functions and is responsible for interaction with the external world. The individual is often aware of such activities of his SNS as smiling, frowning, and shaking hands. He feels sensation through messages carried on somatic sensory nerves. His body experience is from the dialogue between the ANS and the SNS.

Olsen (1998) has a set of exercises that are valuable for understanding the relationship between the somatic and autonomic nervous systems. The author's students have found them valuable in learning to understand their beliefs and values. The following experiential learning activities are taken directly from Olsen's book (p. 124). Olsen's questions have been modified and arranged with some explanations in an attempt to provide clear directions. Centering prior to doing these activities may improve your ability to focus.

CONCRETE STRATEGIES

Experiential Learning Activities

The following activities are designed to increase your awareness of listening to your body. Close your eyes and sit still while focusing on breathing. Breathe in slowly and evenly and breathe out slowly and evenly until you feel calm and centered.

1. Body need versus demand of others: There is no right or wrong way of responding, but there is a dialogue between the needs of the body and the outer demands of the world. Observe your interactions throughout a day.

    a. How often do you respond to your own body's needs? How often do you make choices based on your body's needs and wants, and how often do you make choices based on the demands of others?

    b. Write a dialogue between the needs of the body and the demands of others.

2. Observing your body's experience:

    a. In a standing or seated position, imagine yourself in the following situations and observe your body's responses:

        (1) You are feeling sick and would really rather stay home and rest, but you are going out to work/school.

        (2) You really don't feel like talking to anyone, but it is your turn to lead the group discussion.

        (3) You are in a class and have something very important to say, but the teacher interrupts you whenever you start to say it.

        (4) You go home and want to tell your family everything about your life, but no one is interested in listening.

        (5) You have something to say, and you get to tell it to your best friend.

        (6) You want to celebrate, and you are invited to a great party.

        (7) You need to rest, and you choose to stay home and sunbathe.

        (8) You are tired, and you take a vacation to go to your favorite beach.

Some individuals who have negative beliefs about themselves and/or their environment may never have known a safe state. Practicing breathing, yoga, visualization, and other types of centering exercises on a regular basis may lead to relaxation of the nervous system. Images help integrate multiple layers of an experience within a single body-awareness activity. When the body feels safe, it finds its own natural rhythm between activity and rest. The importance of body language in expressing an individual's inner experience is discussed by experts in mind-body work, health, narrative movement, and communication (Halprin, 2003; Miller & Miller, 1997; Olsen, 1998; Radomsky, 1995; Schure, Christopher, & Christopher, 2008). Yet there has been too little emphasis on this aspect and too much emphasis on appearance of the body in relation to meeting the cultural "norm" of beauty and attractiveness. Media (magazines, TV, music videos, movies) portray the body image as important even when they are trying to create strong female images. Tough women are still portrayed as physically attractive and therefore meeting the cultural norm of women's ideal body image (Carter & Steiner, 2004). Some cases of eating disorders, depression, and low self-esteem are a result of individuals' attempts to fit their bodies into an appearance-based cultural norm.

The author once had a client whose mother told her that she (the mother) had to make the author's client's clothes since she (the mother) could not find dresses that fit the author's client well. The mother often said, "You look just like your grandma—fat—and your torso is too short." The client learned to have a poor body image. She said she was fat all her life. She came to counseling because her physician recommended weight loss for her health. She had been encouraged to devalue her body throughout the socialization process by her family, academic institutions, and culture. Her beliefs about herself were distorted by what she was led to believe about her body image. Due to her distorted body image, she was not able to listen to her natural body rhythm. As Progoff (1992) and consciousness studies (Blackmore, 2004) indicate, lack of self-judgment is a key to reaching inner wisdom, and the author's client was unable to reach her own wisdom because of her critical intrapersonal communication on her body image. She accepted her mother's evaluation of her body before she was old enough to formulate her own opinion of her body. The following experiential learning activities are to facilitate transformative learning on having compassion for others through an affective role-taking perspective.

CONCRETE STRATEGIES

Experiential Learning Activities on Compassion

How would you feel if you were the following two individuals?

1. "Latinas in this country live in two worlds. People who don't know us may think we're fat. At home, we're called *bien cuidadas* (well cared for)" (Haubegger, 2000, p. 242).

2. "My self-hatred became fuel for the self-mutilating behaviors of the eating disorder" (Chernik, 2000, p. 244).

   What messages have you received about your body in relation to your race, gender, class, sexual orientation, age, religion, and region?

Individuals' bodies are their home as long as they live. Their inner experiences enrich their lives, as they become aware of the activities their bodies engage in on a moment-to-moment basis. Olsen's (1998) 31-day body exercises indicate that each body part—skeleton, head, joints, spine, vertebrae, ribs, lungs, shoulders, hands, forearms, bones, pelvis, hips, thighs, knees, tibia, fibula, feet, digestive tract, eyes, face, mouth, nose, ears, elbows, and so on—is active each moment and is engaged in a dynamic process. If individuals are able to listen to their bodies (their inner workings), they are able to know the inner states of their bodies. For example, Olsen writes, "Tension in any part of the body restricts cellular activity vital to healthy tissue. Through bodywork, we use responsiveness of the cell membranes and the skin to heat, vibration, and touch to bring awareness and affect change" (p. 20). The following experiential learning activities are designed to explore a practitioner-trainee's body history through memories, beliefs, and feelings.

CONCRETE STRATEGIES

Experiential Learning Activities on Knowing Oneself Through the Body

The purpose of the following activities is for you to know another aspect of yourself through your body history.

Prepare drawing pads and crayons, colored pencils, or paints. Find a quiet place and make sure you are not going to be distracted. Close your eyes as you breathe deeply, slowly, and evenly. Breathe in relaxation, let the relaxation go through your body from head to toe, and breathe out tension. Again breathe in relaxation and see what's in your mind. If your mind is not with your body, ask your mind to be with your body and breathe out tension and resistance. Breathe in relaxation, appreciate your mind for trying to be with your body, and let appreciation run through your body from head to toe. Breathe out tension and resistance. As you are breathing in and out, draw your body image in your mind and feel and listen to your body.

(Continued)

(Continued)

Be aware of your images, thoughts, and feelings. Count backward from 10 to 1 slowly and when you reach 1 slowly open your eyes.

1. Draw your body image and record any words or phrases that came to your mind.

2. Think and feel about where your body image came from and write them down.

3. Write down your feelings about your body image.

4. If your feelings about your body image are positive or neutral, accept them as they are. If they are negative:

   a. Assess your criteria for the negative image.
   b. Replace the negative image with a positive picture. Observe your body language (how did your body respond to this exercise?).
   c. Write down your body's reaction to this exercise.

5. What was your belief about your body image before, and what is your belief about your body image now?

6. Write your body's story.

   a. What do you know about your birth?
   b. What stories did you hear about your infancy about how you physically moved your body as an infant? What do you know about your activity level and your body movement when you are happy, contented, or crying?
   c. Write down your earliest movement memory (e.g., being rocked, first walking, swimming, falling, running).
   d. Write down your most significant movement memory.
   e. Write down your attitude toward movement throughout your life.
   f. Write down your relationship to your body size, weight, strength, and flexibility.
   g. How much of your assessment of your body is influenced by your cultural norm?
   h. If you have had trauma in your life, did it change your body image? Describe as much as you can.

7. Describe your feelings toward your body prior to and after completing the experiential learning activities.

8. What have you learned through the experiential learning activities?

Individuals gradually learn to listen to their bodies and increase their awareness of their inner experiences through their bodies by diligently practicing experiential learning activities. By listening to their bodies, individuals will expand their awareness of their own values, beliefs, and biases. The following experiential learning activity is designed to process the Depth and Meaning dimensions (Progoff, 1992) of a practitioner-trainee's own body.

CONCRETE STRATEGIES

Experiential Learning Activity on the Body

Close your eyes for 10 min and observe what your body is feeling. Open your eyes, sketch the area of your body where feeling was observed, and describe the feeling.

⁂ SELF-ASSESSMENT OF VALUES, BELIEFS, AND BIASES

The exploration of the various ways to access one's inner experience in the previous section suggests that to increase multicultural counseling competencies one needs to pay more attention to knowing the differences between inner experiences and outer events. Various theories emphasize a practitioner's need to understand a client from the client's worldview without providing concrete strategies as to how to explore the client's inner experience (Croteau & Constantine, 2005; Croteau, Lark, & Lance, 2005; Dana, 1998; Flaskerud & Liu, 1991; Lee, 1997; McGoldrick, Giordano, & Pearce, 1996; Paniagua, 2005; Ponterotto, Utsey, & Pedersen, 2006; Ridley, 2005; Robinson, 2005; Santiago-Rivera, Arredondo, & Gallardo-Cooper, 2002; Sue, Arredondo, & McDavis, 1992; Sue et al., 1998; Sue & Sue, 1999, 2003, 2007).

Jackson (1999) found that students were reluctant or resistant to learn because they were asked to think about issues or concepts they had never thought about and did not care to learn about. Transcending the talking about multicultural counseling competencies in order to walk the talk requires learning about concepts and ideas that individuals are not comfortable with. The following series of experiential learning activities is designed to increase awareness of inner experience. These experiential learning activities will assess a practitioner-trainee's values. It is imperative that these activities be carried out without censoring or screening, which creates superficiality. As indicated previously, inner wisdom comes from lack of self-judgment. Experiencing uncensored values and beliefs leads to inner experience and inner wisdom (Blackmore; 2004; Progoff, 1992).

CONCRETE STRATEGIES

Experiential Learning Activities

Sit in a quiet place without intrusion (e.g., phone, people, TV). Practice self-reflection by engaging in remembering your own early childhood. Close your eyes and breathe in and out slowly and evenly while recalling your family values. Start from the present and travel back to as far as you can remember in your childhood. When your images and/or words represent at least four family values, slowly open your eyes.

Values

1. Draw four pictures that represent your childhood values.

2. What are your relationships to these values now?
   a. Do you still have these values?
   b. Have you modified these values and still kept them as part of your core values?
   c. State reasons for discarding values if you discarded any.
   d. Do you want to discard a value but find yourself being influenced by it?

3. Which values were emphasized by your mother (or a mother figure), and which values were emphasized by your father (or a father figure)?

4. What were your feelings about yourself if your parents' values were contradictory to each other? How did you manage? Did you make up your own values, follow those of one of your parents, or ignore values altogether?

5. How did your parents or parent figures communicate their values to you (e.g., with anger, force, an attempt to induce your guilt, warmth, inductive reasoning)?

6. Describe the sociocultural and political context of your childhood. What cultural values were emphasized?

7. Reflect on your answers to the previous questions. Close your eyes for about 5 min. Open your eyes and write down the words or draw the images that came to your mind.

8. What is the significance of the words or images in Question 7?

9. What are your significant values now? State at least five core values. What are their relationships to your childhood values?

10. How do you deal with people who have different values from yours? Give a specific example of a value you have and how it is different from that of another person. Describe your thoughts, feelings, and behaviors about the other person.

11. How much of your intrapersonal communication is based on your values?

Expanding on your answer to Question 10 will allow for an in-depth understanding of the process of inner experience. The following exercises are intended to facilitate expansion on your answer to Question 10. Paying attention to each answer without censoring or judging will lead to multiple layers and multiple dimensions of inner experience.

CONCRETE STRATEGIES

Expansion of Question 10

Think about the last time you had negative feelings about someone, whether the feeling was frustration, anger, sadness, loneliness, or disgust.

1. What did the other person do or not do or say or not say that made you have the negative feeling?

2. What was your expectation of the person?

3. Where did your expectation come from?

4. Which of your values were applied in order to form your expectation?

Paying attention to details of inner experience can facilitate understanding oneself on a deeper level. For example, an individual is frustrated with her roommate for not doing dishes. She expected her roommate to do his dishes. She was raised with the value that she should be responsible for her actions. She remembers getting into trouble with her mother for not rinsing her dishes after dinner. The trouble ranged from a lecture by her mother about why it is necessary to do her own dishes to not being able to watch her favorite TV program. She resented getting into trouble when she was a child, but later on she realized the importance of taking responsibility. The roommate not doing dishes triggered her own unpleasant and complicated history about dishes and the family dynamics involved in her own story. By understanding her own history, she may project less and may be able to determine how much her frustration is due to the roommate's behavior and how much is due to her own history. By knowing the reason for her frustration, she may be able to divert her attention to negotiating a constructive solution with her roommate. This example is to illustrate how important it is to pay attention to the details of an individual's inner experience to gain access to one's inner mechanism of values. The following experiential learning activities are designed to assist practitioner-trainees with understanding how they constructed their own beliefs and biases. Centering prior to the activities may assist practitioner-trainees with not censoring.

CONCRETE STRATEGIES

Experiential Learning Activities

1. Think of one incident where you were frustrated with a client/person/peer. What were your assumptions? What did you expect? Was your frustration related to your values? If so, how?

2. What did you think your role as a practitioner/participant was last session/quarter/semester, and what did you think your role was in this particular situation?

3. How much of your inner dialogue was related to your cultural/family/individual values?

Beliefs

1. State what core beliefs you learned growing up from the following:
   a. Father (or father figure)
   b. Mother (or mother figure)
   c. Extended family (grandparents, uncle, aunt, etc.)
   d. Community
   e. Country

2. What are your relationships to these beliefs now?
   a. Do you still have these beliefs?
   b. Have you modified these beliefs?
   c. If you discarded all or some of them, state your reasons for having done so.
   d. Do you want to discard some core beliefs but find yourself being influenced by them? Describe your inner experience.
   e. How did your parents or parent figures communicate their beliefs to you (e.g., with anger, force, an attempt to induce your guilt, warmth, inductive reasoning)?
   f. How do you deal with people who have different beliefs from yours? Give a specific example of a belief you have and how it is different from that of another person. Describe your thoughts, feelings, and behaviors about the other person.
   g. How much of your intrapersonal communication is based on your beliefs?

Biases

1. What were the biases you grew up with, and when did you realize that they were biases?

2. What are your relationships to these biases now?
   a. Do you still have these biases?
   b. Have you modified these biases?
   c. If you discarded your biases, state your reasons for having done so.
   d. Do you want to discard a bias but find yourself being influenced by it? Describe your inner experience.

(Continued)

(Continued)

3. Which biases were emphasized by your mother (or mother figure), and which biases were emphasized by your father (or father figure)?

4. How did your parents (or parent figures) communicate their biases to you (e.g., with anger, force, an attempt to induce your guilt, warmth, inductive reasoning)?

5. Describe the sociocultural and political context of your childhood.

6. Reflect on your answers to the previous questions. Close your eyes for about 5 min. Open your eyes and write down the words or draw the images that came to your mind.

7. What is the significance of the words and images from Question 6?

8. What are your significant biases now? How do they relate to your childhood biases?

9. How do you deal with people who have different biases from yours? Give a specific example of a bias you have and how it is different from that of another person.

10. Describe your thoughts, feelings, and behaviors about the other person.

Some practitioner-trainees may notice that their intrapersonal communication reflects their values, beliefs, and biases. They may be able to observe their inner experience clearly and discover various things about themselves. They may discover that they like people who have similar values, beliefs, and biases and do not like people whose values and beliefs are different from theirs. They may feel uncomfortable with the process of discovering their own values, beliefs, and biases that do not fit their self-image. They may feel uncomfortable due to a gap between their real self and their ideal self. Some may be delighted to discover their values, beliefs, and biases; acknowledge their feelings; and let their feelings be felt. Some may be indifferent about the process of acknowledging their indifference without judgment. There are multitudes of reactions, and all of them are unique. The goal of self-assessment through experiential learning and reflective narrative activities is to be aware of one's inner experience with regard to one's values, beliefs, and biases.

⟡ THE IMPACT OF A PRACTITIONER'S VALUES, BELIEFS, AND BIASES ON ASSESSING AND TREATING CLIENTS

The following are a few examples of what happens when a practitioner is not able to perceive the verbal and nonverbal languages of clients. Practitioner-trainees are encouraged to put themselves in the client's position in each case and observe their feelings as the client. Then, they should draw or write a few phrases to symbolize their feelings before reading the next example. Second, quotes from Fadiman's (1997) book are presented, and practitioner-trainees are encouraged to imagine they are Hmong and observe their feelings, thoughts, and behaviors as they read and pay special attention to their intrapersonal communication. The following example illustrates the impact practitioners' unawareness of their values, beliefs, and biases may have on clients.

PERSONAL STORY

The following is an e-mail the author received in late October 2007 from an Asian American college student who went to the school counselor to get help:

In terms of the school population being mostly "Christian"—my frustration! Your story about your friends (one Christian, the other's behavior) is like a story I see all the time. I like some of the faculty, but I interviewed one before about how non-white students feel like they are not part of the "community"—and she told me I wasn't trying hard enough! Or another example is—Thursday, I went to talk to my advisor (who I like) and he told me I should consider going to the counseling office, so I went . . . and in 15 minutes 3 of the 4 people in the office are minority kids. That is 75% in a counseling office, when we make up less than 12% of the college population (actually less than that, they cushion their numbers somehow). When I talked to a counselor about my frustration with only Euro-American ethnocentric views on campus and not being included in the community, she said I need to try hard to reach out. Can you believe?

When a practitioner is not aware of her own values, beliefs, and biases, she is not aware of how they affect her clients. She may not know they lead to unintentional marginalization, discrimination, prejudice, stereotyping, racism, sexism, heterosexism, ableism, and classism, which devastate clients' mental, physical, emotional, and psychological welfare (Paniagua, 2005; Ridley, 2005). She may not be aware of the fact that her values, beliefs, and biases may compound the client's problem in the name of helping. There is no one who could intervene to minimize the harm by the practitioner because counseling or psychotherapy usually takes place in the privacy of an office. It is not that the practitioner is intentionally marginalizing, minimizing, or oppressing the client but that she does not know her own values, beliefs, and biases. Robinson (2005) writes, "Regardless of race, counselors who choose not to face their biases with courageous introspection are not appropriate candidates for the mental health profession" (p. 140). The following are two more examples of what happens when a practitioner is not able to hear a client due to her inability to perceive clients from the perspective of their cultural values.

PERSONAL STORY

Maria is a 27-year-old Mexican American who goes to see a counselor because she is torn between her desire to pursue her career and her obligation to do what is expected of her. Her counselor tells her to listen to herself and do what is "best for her." Maria tells her counselor that she doesn't know what's best for her, and the counselor asks her, "Didn't you say you want to pursue your career?" Maria feels that the counselor has no idea about her culture.

Peter's counselor encourages Peter to move out of his parents' home. The counselor asks, "Don't you think it will be healthy for you to move out of your parents' home?" The counselor continues, "You are 34 years old, and you have a good job." Peter, who is a Vietnamese American, feels he is not understood by his counselor. Peter came to counseling to sort out what he really wants to do for his career; however, the counselor is "fixated" on Peter's living condition. The practitioner does not understand that Peter has no problem living with his parents. Peter has explained to the counselor that it is his cultural custom and he has no problem with his living arrangement. Peter feels that the counselor is much more interested in honoring her values than she is in honoring Peter's. Peter wonders whether it is ethical for him to pay to fulfill the counselor's curiosity.

Native American culture, Afro American culture, Latino culture, and Asian American culture value extended family (Paniagua, 2005; Robinson, 2005). Individuals from these cultures and other cultures that value collectivism are influenced by collectivistic values regardless of their acculturation level. Therefore, doing their own thing creates intense internal conflict that cannot be understood by those who were raised in individualism-oriented cultures. Even though Maria wants to pursue her career, her desire to meet her obligation as a family member is equally strong due to her socialization practice where family is important and extended family members are as close as her immediate family members. It is easier for members of the dominant culture to focus on doing their own thing because they have been socialized to practice being individuals. It is difficult for individuals who have been socialized to value collectivism to do what is best for themselves, even though that is what they want. It is a complex process to sort out or to modify collective values and beliefs to adjust to a way of balancing one's desires and wants with collective values and beliefs. Maria needs a practitioner who can understand this complex process she is going through. A practitioner who can see Maria from Maria's cultural perspective will be able to provide empathy for her. Peter is normal from his cultural perspective. It is a common practice that grown-up children stay with parents until they get married in many cultures with collective value orientations. The sign of independence is not determined by whether grown-up children move out at a certain age in these cultures. These children save up their money while they are staying with their parents, and this money is used for their down payment on a house or condominium. The practitioner's value interferes with her ability to help Peter with his career decisions. She needs to critically examine her role in counseling and how she would feel, think, and behave if she were marginalized—especially by her own practitioner as a result of having different values and beliefs.

Fadiman (1997) portrays the difficulties involved in helping individuals from another culture when helping professionals do not understand the other culture and its way of defining illness and healing. In California, for example, helping professionals did their best to care for Lia, a Hmong child, according to what they knew about helping with regard to North American cultural values. The California court decided that Lia's parents were unfit to take care of their daughter because they were not compliant with medication administration that was determined by Western medical professionals who cared deeply for Lia but were not trained by their culture to consider the role of the soul in sickness and health. Taking a child away is hard from the perspective of a North American cultural value orientation, but it is even harder from a Hmong perspective because of its collectivistic value orientation. Hmong take care of each other. "I am Hmong. For the Hmong, it is never everyone for himself" (Fadiman, 1997, p. 247).

Fadiman (1997) writes in her book, *The Spirit Catches You and You Fall Down:*

> I do not know if Lia would be able to walk and talk today had she been treated by Arthur Kleinman instead of by Neil Ernst and Peggy Philip. However, I have come to believe that her life was ruined not by septic shock or noncompliant parents but by cross-cultural mis-understanding. (p. 262)

It is evident that Western doctors and other helping professionals did their best to help Lia. A language barrier and cultural differences with regard to beliefs, illness, and healing probably played a part in creating misunderstanding. For example, "the mind-body dichotomy does not exist in Hmong culture and because so much illness among Hmong refugees has a psychogenic element, the *txiv neeb* is an ideal collaborator in the healing process" (Fadiman, 1997, p. 267).

Fadiman (1997) continues:

> Sometimes the soul goes away but the doctors don't believe it. I would like you to tell the doctors to believe in our *neeb* (healing spirit). . . . The doctors can fix some sicknesses that involve the body and blood, but for us Hmong, some people get sick because of their soul, so they need spiritual things. With Lia it was good to do a little medicine and a little *neeb*, but not too much medicine because the medicine cuts the *neeb*'s effect. If we did a little of each she didn't get sick as much, but the doctors wouldn't let us give just a little med-icine because they didn't understand about the soul. (p. 100)

Lia's physician, who cared deeply about Lia, wrote to Child Protective Services in an attempt to help her:

> Because of poor parental compliance regarding the medication this case obviously would come under the realm of child abuse, specifically

child neglect. . . . It is my opinion that this child should be placed in foster placement so that compliance with medication could be assured. (pp. 58–59)

Lia was removed from her home.

The author's students in a multicultural counseling program learned to feel the pain for Lia's case. Fadiman's (1997) book provided transformative learning experiences for the students because they felt for Lia, Lia's parents, and North American helping professionals. They understood the importance of being aware of the client's worldview but did not know whether they were able to set aside their own values and beliefs in this particular case. Multicultural competencies require tolerance for ambiguity; assigning equal importance to others' cultural values, beliefs, and meaning making as one's own; and having respect for others' way of being and others' traditions. In order to acquire multicultural competencies, practitioner-trainees need to practice strategies to gain access to their inner experience.

CONCRETE STRATEGIES

Consciousness Practice

What is your inner experience right now?

Part II

A Practitioner's Awareness of Systematic Oppression/ Privilege and Internalized Oppression/Privilege

Understanding systematic oppression/privilege and internalized oppression/privilege is a precursor to understanding racism, sexism, heterosexism, classism, ableism, and other differences such as those with regard to language, religion, and region. Privilege—whether it is based on race, gender, sexual orientation, class, language, ability (learning, physical, mental), age, or religion—is invisible to privilege holders.

Privilege holders do not see that societal norms are socially constructed for their benefit while these norms discriminate against non–privilege holders. For example, White people in the United States are privileged because of their skin color while non-White people are oppressed because of their skin color. Skin color does not say anything about a person's character, socioeconomic status, education, sexual orientation, and so on. A statement by one of the author's students—"Discovering how I support racism through accepting the unearned privileges afforded me simply on the basis of my white skin has been especially profound" (Tammy, 2005)— is an example of unearned White privilege.

Contrary to privilege, oppression is very visible to those who are oppressed, whether it is due to their race, gender, class, sexual orientation, disability, age, religion, language, or region (Jackson, 2001; Mio & Awakuni, 2000; Swim, Hyers, Cohen, Fitzgerald, & Bylsma, 2003). However, it is invisible to oppressors. A Black student in one of the author's classes shared the following:

> This is 2004 and white people still judge me on the basis of my skin. I go to the Mall and some people grab their kids as if I would do something to their kids while putting a fake smile on their face. I love kids and I would never do anything to hurt them. . . . This is what I have to deal with on a daily basis. (George, 2004)

Injustice was done to him due to his skin color, not due to his past and/or present actions or behaviors. Young (2000) identifies exploitation, marginalization, powerlessness, and cultural imperialism as faces of oppression.

> Oppression refers to systematic constraints on groups and is structural, rather than the result of a few people's choices or policies . . . the vast and deep injustices some groups suffer as consequences of often unconscious assumptions and reactions of well meaning people in ordinary interactions, media and cultural stereotypes, and structural features of bureaucratic hierarchies and market mechanisms— in short, the normal processes of everyday life. We cannot eliminate this structural oppression by getting rid of the rulers or making some new laws, because oppressions are systematically reproduced in major economic, political, and cultural institutions. (pp. 36–37)

A concept that is crucial to understanding a practitioner's values, beliefs, and biases as well as a client's worldview is internalized privilege and oppression. Children are socialized by adults from birth on. Significant others in a child's life such as parents, relatives, siblings, teachers, and media influence the child's self-concept, values, beliefs, and biases. This process is both intrapersonal (how the child thinks about self) and interpersonal (how the child relates to others). Children of color have a higher probability of internalizing oppression (Jackson, Barth, Powell, & Lochman, 2006). Through internalized oppression, children become their own oppressors from within. George, the Black student mentioned above, expressed his anger and frustration about "White people" and

"White privilege," but he spent endless hours in the author's office questioning his scholastic ability and engaged in self-sabotaging behaviors such as not turning in homework assignments since he "already knew" (*generalization* from previous painful experiences) they were "not good enough." He would not show up for outside-class small-group discussions because he was convinced his classmates would not value his opinions. The following is some of the author's former students' feedback about learning about systematic oppression/privilege and internalized oppression/privilege.

STUDENT FEEDBACK

Systematic Oppression/Privilege and Internalized Oppression/Privilege

What impacted me the most was the realization of the difference between individuals as racist/elitist versus systematized racism/elitism and oppression of all kinds.... A huge part of learning about power and difference in privilege has been to see how hierarchical, dichotomous thinking is such a part of the privileged white culture that I have internalized. I have recognized the damage of this way of thinking and being to my own sense of self. It has colored all of my interactions. Most exciting learning has been recognizing how to begin to facilitate and to continue deconstructing the choices I made from invisible privilege, hierarchical, dichotomous ways of being and thinking.

—Anne, 2005

Discovering how I support racism through accepting the unearned privileges afforded me simply on the basis of my white skin has been especially profound. I am happy to have made this racist practice visible so that I can now begin to eradicate it from my life. My foundation as an advocate for oppressed people has been greatly strengthened through this work, and I am forever grateful for this opportunity to become more aware.

—Tammy, 2005

The concept of being an ally does not solely pertain to siding with a minority group to help expose oppression; one must commit to helping those within their own class of privilege come to an understanding of how that privilege impedes on others' freedoms and rights of life.

—Adam, 2005

Students like Tammy and Anne are excited about learning, submit their homework assignments on the due dates, and are proud of doing their best. They show up for small-group discussions, give and receive constructive criticisms, and enjoy learning from their peers. Their intra- and intersocialization processes allow them to seek justice and fair treatment from their environment. But students like George (see above) who have been socialized on "systematic constraints" (Adams et al., 2000, p. 36) are often the target of "deep injustice" (Adams et al., p. 36), unconscious marginalization, and discrimination because of their skin color and are likely to bring experiences of internalized and systematic oppression to class. Emotionally heated reactions in multicultural counseling classrooms are often a result of interactions between internalized oppression and privilege and reactions to one's unconscious systematic oppression and privilege.

A practitioner's ability to be aware of the self is determined partially by the quantity and quality of internalized oppression/privilege and partially by the degree of injustice/justice that she has experienced as a result of systematic oppression/privilege and its relationship to multiple identities (e.g., race, gender, sexual orientation, class, age, disability, religion, region, language). A dimension of these dynamic relationships is the practitioner's thinking patterns, which range from the holistic to the hierarchical, dichotomous, and linear. If a practitioner's thinking pattern is hierarchical and she puts herself in a superior position (*hierarchical*), she would have quite a different perception about the relationship between systematic and internalized oppression from that of a practitioner who puts herself in an inferior position (*hierarchical*). This dimension intersects with other identities (e.g., race, gender, ethnicity, sexual orientation, class, age, disability, religion, region, language) and creates multiple dimensions and layers for the practitioner as well as each client.

Complex relationships among systematic oppression/privilege, internalized oppression/privilege, intersections of multiple identities, sociocultural contexts, and a particular thinking pattern are examined in Chapters 4 through 9 (Chapter 4: racism; Chapter 5: sexism; Chapter 6: heterosexism; Chapter 7: classism; Chapter 8: ableism; Chapter 9: other "isms" due to age, language, religion, or regional differences; and Chapter 10: concrete strategies to deconstruct inappropriate dichotomous, hierarchical, and linear thinking styles).

4

Racism

This chapter discusses the issues of *race* as a biological term and racism as a product of social construction, as well as the social categorization theory. It explores systematic oppression/privilege and internalized oppression/privilege. The relationship between racism and inappropriate thinking styles/patterns is also explored. It concludes with strategies to dismantle racism, the importance of an accurate assessment of practitioners' standing with regard to these issues, and the impact of practitioners' accurate self-assessment on their relationship to internalized oppression/privilege. The chapter cites other authors', the author's former students', and the author's own writings in conjunction with experiential and/or reflection-based learning activities.

RACE AND RACISM

Some individuals argue that there is no racism, all people are 99.9% alike, and it is a proven fact by the Human Genome Project of the U.S. Department of Energy (Bonham, Warshauer-Baker, & Collins, 2005). The argument makes sense if the 0.1% biological difference between races is treated as only 0.1%, which indicates insignificant racial difference. According to this perspective, all racial groups should be treated equally in terms of their privileges. No racial group should be allowed to claim racial superiority, no governmental and institutional policies should be allowed to discriminate against nondominant racial groups, and no racial groups should be suffering from the results of internalized oppression. An examination of historical and current incidents of oppression as a result of race like slavery, lynching, racial profiling, systematic and institutional racism, and racial prejudice and oppression indicate that all racial groups have not been treated the same as the dominant group, and although the biological difference between races is 0.1%, society has reacted to this insignificant difference as though it is 99.9%, a significant difference. This clearly demonstrates that racial injustice and inequity have been the result of social construction by dominant racial group members to maintain their power and privilege as a group.

The original meaning of the term *race* frequently used by scholars of various disciplines is "human biogenetic variation," which focuses on phenotypes such as physical features (skin color, hair texture, eye shape, lip shape, and other facial features) and overt behavior (Smedley & Smedley, 2005). A biological definition of *race* is based on discrete biological differences among racial groups, each with its own social and cultural behaviors and beliefs. Several multicultural counseling books represent this school of thought by discussing cultural assumptions, acculturation processes, and assimilation processes of these groups. Such books usually categorize racial groups as Native American, Afro American, Asian American, and Hispanic American. Racial categories assist individuals with understanding how each race differs culturally; however, they have a tendency not only to stereotype racial groups but also to ignore variations within each racial group. They foster race-based societies, which are formulated on hierarchy and operate within a hierarchical social system. In these societies, racial differences are viewed as profound and unchangeable. Racialization is deeply embedded in the consciousness of people in race-based societies like those of North America (Brown, Ward, Lightbourn, & Jackson, 1999; Fredrickson, 1999; Smedley & Smedley).

Racialization often creates the emotional distance between Whites and people of color. Reactions to the film *The Color of Fear*[1] by students illustrate the impact of racialization on the ability to perceive individuals from their worldviews. Most White students become afraid of expressing their opinion of the film because they do not want to "hurt" the feelings of students of color. They also do not understand how the film is validating for students of color. In particular, White students whose thinking patterns are hierarchical, dichotomous, and linear assume the class in which they watch the film is for the students of color to vent. Students of color who are also examining their hierarchical, dichotomous, and linear thinking patterns express their accumulated pain throughout their lives and transfer their past pain and current pain to White students or generalize that their unfortunate experiences are due to the White students in the class. In this situation, most White students are often afraid or uncomfortable of students of color's anger, rage, or frustration because most White students are unable to understand that most students of color have been victims of systematic racial oppression throughout their lives. Most White students also do not understand that they have been White privilege holders and that they have been benefiting from unearned privilege without being aware of that privilege. Being born White gave them privilege (McIntyre, 1997; Oldmeadow & Fiske, 2007; Pack-Brown, 1999; Pope-Davis & Ottavi, 1994; Thompson & Keith, 2001). They did not have to do anything to earn that privilege.

The author once had a student of color who expressed hate toward the White students in the class. She openly called the White students in the class racists. She was filled with hatred to the extent that it was hindering her ability to learn. Often, she said that her race was "better" (*hierarchical*) than the White race. She had compassion for her own race and for other racial or multicultural groups but no compassion for White students. Seventy-five percent of the class was White, and some White students were fearful of her. Some felt White guilt, and some were frustrated because they signed up to learn about multicultural counseling and not to be accused of being racists.

The author spent many hours outside the class in order to assist this student with evaluating her behavior in relation to racism. The author listened to her pain with empathy and asked her how she could help so that all students would learn about not only her culture but also other cultures. The author asked her what she wanted the White students in the class to feel when she directed her anger toward them, and the author was also supportive of the White students who were the targets of her anger. The author encouraged honest dialogue among the students, even if it was painful and scary. At times, the student said that the author did not understand her culture because the author was not "bashing" Whites the way she wanted. She did not understand why the author, a person of color, was not angry toward White students. At times, she was angry at the author because she felt all the author wanted was "everyone" to be "nice" to each other. Explaining to her that the author's approach to racial issues was very different (not better) from hers, the author told her that she was interested in resolving the racial conflict through open and honest dialogue with compassion for all involved.

The author was concerned about the impact of the student's anger on her own learning. So the author shared Korea's history with Japan to see whether she could take a step aside from the classroom situation. The author told her that although she had no memory of Japan conquering Korea, the author was socialized through school textbooks in early grades to hate the Japanese. The author asked the student whether she should hate the Japanese students in the class since Japan conquered Korea and ruled it for 36 years. The author told her that Koreans were beaten and not permitted to wear their own clothes or speak their own language for 36 years. The author told her that the Koreans who were discovered using their own language were put into jail. Explaining that she did not intend to minimize the student's pain by sharing Korea's history, the author wanted her to think about racial issues from another perspective and always ended the conversation with genuine caring for her. The author often asked her what she would be teaching her racial group if she only stayed in hatred, as well as to let the author know how she could assist her so that she could focus on her learning. Toward the end of the quarter the student was able to differentiate between the White students in the class (individuals who belong to the White social group) and those White people (social group) who hurt her and her people. It was a difficult task for all parties (White students, the students of color, and the author), but all were able to transcend racial generalizations and to distinguish between reactions to systematic oppression and reactions to individuals who belong to a particular social group (ingroup vs. outgroup).

Everyone in the class took a risk by learning both intellectually and emotionally, and everyone was honest with him/her/zirself and with each other. It was very painful at times. It seemed easier just to blame one side (*dichotomous thinking*) or to pretend not to notice (*denial*). But everyone was committed to be open to new possibilities by transcending racism, denial, and White guilt. White students understood their White privilege comes at a cost to people of color and even to themselves. Although discussing White privilege was difficult after completing McIntosh's (1989) 26 White privilege statements, students really understood the difference between White privilege and systematic racial oppression as they were processing the student of color's questions. Transformative learning had occurred due to her courage to be honest and to challenge the whole class. Most students became close to her through this painful learning experience, and most were able to walk the talk of understanding White privilege and systematic oppression.

Racism is different from race in that it is socially constructed. It is systematic advantages given to a group on the basis of skin color (White), and it includes racial prejudice and racial discrimination (Brown et al., 1999; Carr, 1997; Sanchez-Hucles, 1998; Thompson & Keith, 2001; Utsey, Ponterotto, & Porter, 2008; Velasquez, 1997). Prejudice is prejudgment without any just ground, and discrimination occurs when prejudice is translated into behavior that denies individuals, or groups of individuals, equal treatment. Racism is much bigger than individual prejudice and discrimination. It is governmental and institutional policies, laws, and rules that favor Whites. Wise (2005) and Tatum (2000) both discuss the fact that racism hurts everyone, including White people. It is important for practitioners to understand how racism affects both people of color and Whites. The lack of understanding of racism by many North Americans is partially due to systematic unearned oppression and privilege. Much of racial privilege is just not seen, understood, or acknowledged. Throughout their entire socialization process, most Americans in the United States are led to believe that implementing White middle-class values and beliefs in governmental and private sector policies, laws, and educational goals is "normal," "correct," and "right." Probably most of them are not aware these policies, laws, and educational goals are based on socially constructed values that benefit White middle- and upper-class people. How racism is expressed has changed several times (dominative and aversive to colorblind) throughout history; however, it is still persistent. One challenge is that people can hide their racism more easily these days because it has changed from apparent, overt racism to subtle racism (Allport, 1954; Carr; Kovel, 1970). Some practitioners, whose worldviews are based on inappropriate hierarchical, dichotomous, and linear thinking patterns, also need to be mindful of the impact of their worldviews on clients (both people of color and Whites). Inappropriate thinking patterns perpetuate racism, White guilt, and blaming. Regardless of a practitioner's racial background, the practitioner needs to understand racism and racial issues from both an intellectual and an emotional perspective.

Takaki's (1993) book *A Different Mirror: A History of Multicultural America* is excellent for facilitating emotional and intellectual understanding of racism and understanding the origin of inappropriate hierarchical and dichotomous thinking patterns. The book is especially difficult for most White students because it triggers all sorts of emotions. As indicated earlier, multicultural issues are loaded with emotions. Students who want to be practitioners need to feel these emotions without judgment and without inappropriate dichotomous and hierarchical thinking. Reflective writing, narrative movement, or drawing what they feel without screening may assist them in dealing with these feelings. Feeling these difficult and complex emotions facilitates the path to transformative learning. Transformative learning can be enhanced when Takaki's book is used in conjunction with other books that address racial issues, allowing an individual's level of understanding racism and racial issues to deepen. The following are three examples of the writing of former students that represents the majority of students' reactions whenever the author uses two books together. These students were assigned to read Takaki's book and Rothenberg's (2005) *White Privilege: Essential Readings on the Other Side of Racism.*

STUDENT FEEDBACK

Understanding White Privilege

A Different Mirror *and* White Privilege *are two of the most influential books I have ever studied. I mourn that I never had access to the information and history with those pages in my Primary School education. . . . How race is a social construct, an illusion, one of the biggest lies—to ensure that one group always stays in power while the others remain oppressed. This has motivated me to continue building an awareness of the positions I hold privilege in and to use that privilege to become an ally for others.*

—Brit, 2005

This most recent cycle of inner agitation began with White Privilege. *I experienced a lot of internal resistance while I was reading this book. When I heard classmates talking about white guilt I couldn't relate. My initial line of reasoning was: "It's only natural for the dominant, majority population group to possess and defend the privileges they have—whether they are white or not. That's the way things are. Competition is universal and will always leave some groups disadvantaged. What's more, I like my privileges—I don't want to give them up!" It wasn't until I read Takaki's book that the first twinges of white guilt—more sadness than guilt, really—were activated. By reading the stories of different non-white groups' contributions to the creation of the U.S., I have seen exactly how my white privileges were paid for by the blood, sweat, and tears of those who were, and are, systematically denied the same privileges. In addition, I learned more history from reading Takaki's book than from any other source in my entire life! Somehow it all seemed more relevant the way Takaki framed it.*

—Todd, 2005

The book, A Different Mirror: A History of Multicultural America, *has had a profound effect upon my changing worldview and me. In the book,* White Privilege, *it mentions how there is a part in everyone's life where they feel racism in our country finally hits them. These books allowed the opportunity for me to explore my own racial biases while attending to the needs of society. Society needs people with privilege to fight against systematic oppression and to give up their privileges. Learning about the true history of America has opened my eyes and my heart to the pain that the oppressed people in our country experience on a daily basis. I am having a difficult time letting go of my anger and feelings of betrayal having been lied to for 21 years about the history of our nation and all its people.*

—Sonja, 2005

One of the most difficult concepts is that racism benefits Whites as a social group regardless of whether an individual within a White social group is racist. Racism is a system of advantages for Whites as a group. This is a very difficult concept for Whites. McIntosh (1989) lists 26 conditions about receiving benefits on a daily basis due to her White privilege in her article "White Privilege: Unpacking the Invisible Knapsack." Her work is a pioneer in addressing systematic oppression (racism). McIntosh was a White feminist scholar who spoke out for "the other" because she was no longer able to stand injustice. Her focus with regard to White privilege is that White people benefit from unearned White privileges because of their skin color. This is due to societal and cultural practices of making White middle-class values and beliefs a norm in the United States.

⧹⧹ SOCIAL CATEGORIZATION THEORY

It is interesting to note that the popular definition of race has been based on phenotypes of human biogenetic variation and that race is categorized by each racial group as if it is biologically discrete and exclusive (Maddox, 2004). The problem with this perspective is that biracial and multiracial groups do not fit into racial categories but neither do genetic, biological, and cultural variations within a racial group. Categorizing racial groups under the pretense of a biological concept of race has become a social categorization. On one level, this categorization may assist individuals with understanding each racial group's distinctive cultural characteristics. But on another level, it divides the dominant racial group from nondominant racial groups and prevents nondominant groups from having access to the dominant group's benefits. Thus the main complaint about the concept of race from a categorical perspective is inequality and perpetuating racial stereotypes under the name of scientific legitimacy (Helms, Jernigan, & Mascher, 2005; Omi, 2001). Social categorization divides and only perpetuates ethnocentrism. Research with regard to social categorization indicates that people favor ingroups (ingroup favoritism) over outgroups.

Ingroups Versus Outgroups

Meta-analysis on ingroups and outgroups by Robbins and Krueger (2005) indicates that people have a tendency to favor ingroups (ingroup favoritism) and to think they are similar to their ingroups on important issues. A behavioral indication of ingroup favoritism is intergroup discrimination, which is based on dichotomous thinking (Kowalski, 2003). Intergroup discrimination is also fostered by social projection (people's tendency to expect others are like them; $N = 1$ = other people) and attribution error. Ingroup favoritism, social projection, and attribution error are some contributing factors for persistent racial, gender, sexual orientation, class, disability, age, religion, language, and regional prejudices, biases, and discriminations. Studies show that ingroup members perceive outgroups as much more homogeneous than their ingroups (Gilbert, 1998; Linville, Fischer, & Salovey, 1989; Park & Rothbart, 1982; Simon & Brown, 1987), suggesting asymmetric perceptions.

Asymmetric perceptions and attribution errors regarding self versus others have been found in various studies, and they are the foundations of ingroup favoritism, which is based on ethnocentrism (Pronin, Gilovich, & Ross, 2004). Participants of studies on biases also report asymmetric perceptions. They believe that they are less biased than their peers because their judgments are more objective compared with those of their peers and believe their peers and other people are more biased due to their subjectivity. In other words, participants overestimate their own judgmental qualities as positive and objective and others' judgmental qualities as subjective and susceptible to external factors (Baumeister, 1998; Dunning, Meyerowits, & Holzber, 1989; Epley & Dunning, 2000; Heath, 1999; Pronin, Lin, & Ross, 2002; Steele, 1988; Taylor & Brown, 1988). Even studies about introspections show participants have asymmetric perceptions about self and others (Andersen, 1984; Pronin et al., 2002; Pronin et al., 2004).

Studies of asymmetric perceptions in introspection between self and others indicate participants have a tendency to value introspection in their own assessment of self but will not consider the value of introspection in others' assessment of self. Pronin et al. (2004) conclude that researchers' consistent findings with regard to introspection are based on an illusion: high self-appraisal on introspection and assumptions about the ability to know others from observing others' behaviors.

It is difficult to transcend inappropriate high self-appraisal, ingroup favoritisms, and asymmetric perceptions because of early childhood socialization. Some studies show that children 5 years and up dislike other children who do not conform to ingroup norms (Abrams, Rutland, & Cameron, 2004; Abrams, Rutland, Cameron, & Margues, 2003; Nesdale

& Brown, 2004). Children's explicit prejudice against an outgroup occurs when their identification with an ingroup is solid (Nesdale, Durkin, Maass, & Griffiths, 2005a). Children tend to display ingroup favoritism when an ingroup excludes an outgroup norm and perceives the outgroup as a threat (Nesdale, Durkin, Maass, & Griffiths, 2005b). Studies indicate that such socialization practices foster ingroup favoritism and asymmetric perceptions; stress and even overestimate the positive qualities of the ingroup (e.g., not biased, objective); and overestimate the negative qualities of outgroups (e.g., biased, subjective). All these lead to racial prejudice, discrimination, and racism.

Systematic Oppression/Privilege and Internalized Oppression/Privilege

Ingroup favoritism, asymmetric perception, social projection, and attribution error theories indicate racism is based on these types of ethnocentric biases, especially by the dominant racial group. Racism is systematic advantages for Whites on the basis of their skin color. This means governmental, institutional, and organizational policies, laws, and rules are written to favor Whites and unfairly discriminate against people of color. In other words, people of color have been oppressed by the system on the basis of their skin. The concept of White privilege, for some privileged individuals, is a difficult one to understand because some of them do not feel privileged. It is a difficult concept because privilege often is invisible to privilege holders and a person can be a privilege holder in one aspect of his/her/zir identity but be oppressed in another aspect or other aspects of his/her/zir identity. For instance, a White man who has been raised in poverty and is still living in poverty may feel frustrated, angry, alienated, and misunderstood when others say he has White privilege because he does not feel privileged. Johnson (2006) writes eloquently about the distinction between privilege and oppression. Both privilege and oppression result from socially constructed categories. Both racial privilege and racial oppression are determined by color of skin. Therefore, only White people have racial privilege because they belong to the White racial group, and people of color are targets of racial oppression because they belong to non-White racial groups, regardless of their class, sexual orientation, gender, disability, age, education, religion, and so on. "Whites can experience oppression for many reasons, but not because they're white" (Johnson, p. 40).

Some White individuals who are racially privileged do not feel privileged, but this does not mean they are not privileged in relation to a racial category. Being White means that they are systematically privileged in accessing or in relation to education, housing, health care, local and national laws, jobs, going through security systems at airports, religion, and so on compared with members of other racial groups. The following reflection and imagery activities are designed to provide a transformative learning opportunity with regard to oppression and privilege.

CONCRETE STRATEGIES

Experiential Learning Activities on Oppression and Privilege

1. Indicate whether you belong to a privileged group or an oppressed group in relation to your race. Remember that the task is not to determine whether you feel privileged or oppressed but to determine whether you belong to a privileged group or an oppressed group— and not according to your society.

2. Do you feel you are privileged or oppressed? Explain why.

3. Close your eyes and breathe in and out slowly and evenly for 5 min. Pay attention to your feelings and the images that come to your mind as you breathe. Slowly open your eyes and draw your feelings and/or images.

4. What have you learned from these activities?

5. What was your understanding about systematic privilege and oppression before completing these activities, and what is your understanding of them now?

6. Discuss your understanding of systematic oppression and privilege with others who have participated in the same experiential learning activities of this section.

7. What did you learn about yourself and others in your group?

Crucial factors in creating a society that treats everyone with respect, justice, and equity are understanding systematic oppression and privilege and acknowledging that an individual's personal experience may not be the same as that of his/her/zir group. The other crucial factors are understanding the role of inappropriate (dichotomous, hierarchical, and linear) thinking styles in shaping personal and systematic oppression and privilege and their impact on internalized oppression and privilege.

Internalized oppression and privilege affect interpersonal and intra-personal relationships on a daily basis. For instance, they affect how individuals relate to family members, friends, coworkers, institutions, governments, teachers, policymakers, managers, construction work-ers, and therapists. Reyna, Henry, Korfmacher, and Tucker (2005) show how racial policy decisions are made by the decision makers' cul-tural stereotypes and not by "the fundamental fairness of the policy" (p. 122). This is because systematic oppression and privilege are learned early on during socialization. Jackson et al.'s (2006) study shows how early children exhibit internalized oppression and privilege. Their research found that other children rate White children higher as leaders even when there are few Whites in a class compared with chil-dren of color. White children exert their power just by being White due to internalized privilege, and Black children cannot exert their power due to internalized oppression. Black children are not rated as leaders even when there are more Black students in a class unless Black chil-dren are the "overwhelming majority" and the teacher is Black. Probably both Black and White children are not aware that their behav-iors are the results of their internalized oppression and privilege. Some parents also perpetuate their own internalized oppression in an attempt to help their children with racial issues. For instance, parents who practice racialized socialization promote racial bias and racial mistrust in their children (Caughy, Nettles, O'Campo, & Lohrfink, 2006; McHale et al., 2006). These parents' intention is probably to minimize their children's pain as a result of racial discrimination, prej-udice, and racism. Even well-meaning researchers at times perpetuate internalized oppression or privilege by focusing on pathology with non-White children but not with White children, which is a direct expres-sion of an investigator's perpetuation of racial injustice and inequity (MacPhee, Kreutzer, & Fritz, 1994; McLoyd, 2006). A study of Afro American youth indicates that racial discrimination is much more per-vasive with youth in high-risk settings compared with youth in low-risk settings (Brody et al., 2006).

The following reflection-based learning activities are designed to facil-itate transformative learning related to race and oppression/privilege (Ferrer, Romero, & Albareda, 2005; Power & Dalgleish, 1997).

CONCRETE STRATEGIES

Reflection Activities on Race

After reading the research findings on the impact of internalized oppression/privilege and parental racialized socialization, close your eyes and breathe in and out slowly and deeply for 5 min. As you breathe, go back in your timeline as far as you can go to see whether you can recall a memory of racial issues in school from your childhood—for example, White privilege or racial oppression. Slowly open your eyes and then do the following:

1. Describe your memory of White privilege or racial discrimination, prejudice, or racism at school.

   a. How did you feel about it then, and how do you feel about it now?
   b. Did you share your experience with someone? If you did, with whom did you share it, and what was the person's response?
   c. If you did not tell it to anyone, what did you do with it?
   d. What was your feeling about your race and the other races represented in the class?
   e. What did you learn from your teachers about race?

2. What did you learn about race from your family when you were little? Be specific. If your parents applied racialized socialization practice, for example, what was the main message? How does that message affect you now?

3. Discuss concrete strategies to minimize internalized oppression for schoolchildren with individuals who have also participated in these experiential learning activities.

Much internalized oppression and privilege operates without an individual's awareness. Understanding one's own internalized oppression and privilege requires an ability to identify cognitive distortions and emotional attachments to these distortions. Observing an individual's body language and tone of voice as the individual listens to his/her/zir own interpersonal and intrapersonal communication may shed light on the individual's emotional attachment to these distortions.

Automatic Activation

Internalized privilege and oppression are sometimes manifested as prejudice and stereotypes. Prejudice and stereotypes are activated automatically and influence individuals' perception and judgment, and oftentimes individuals are not aware of this influence (Banaji & Hardin, 1996; Perdue & Gurtman, 1990). One of the most important discoveries of social psychology and cognitive and neuroscience research on memory in the past 2 decades has contributed to the recognition that unconscious processes are involved in stereotyping and prejudice (Banaji & Greenwald, 1994; Chen & Bargh, 1997; Greenwald & Banaji, 1995; Henderson-King & Nisbett, 1996). Banaji and Bhaskar (2001) discuss the role of unconscious processes in prejudice and stereotyping and how difficult it is to transcend racism, sexism, heterosexism, ableism, ageism, classism, biases, and prejudices. They conclude as follows:

> The best of intentions do not and cannot override the unfolding of unconscious processes, for the triggers of automatic thought, feeling, and behavior live and breathe outside conscious awareness and control. . . . Second, when stereotypes are unconsciously activated and used, two direct challenges to the implementation of fairness are posed: (a) perceivers and targets are often unaware of the steady and continuous rendering of judgments, and (b) judgments are based on beliefs about targets' social groups rather than on targets' actions. (pp. 142–144)

The author's clinical practice also suggests that internalized oppression and privilege are activated unconsciously and that implicit learning plays an important role in internalized oppression and privilege. Working with issues around internalized oppression and privilege is challenging because most clients have no awareness of being affected by internalized oppression and privilege. This is because of the role of the unconscious and automatic activation, in addition to ingroup favoritism, social projection and attribution error theories, and asymmetric perceptions toward self versus others. Banaji and Bhaskar (2001) found that implicit expressions of participants' beliefs about and attitudes toward stereotypes and prejudice have no correlation to their explicit versions of the same beliefs about and attitudes toward stereotypes and prejudice. Aversive racism is another example of an inconsistency between implicit and explicit attitudes on racism (Dovidio & Gaertner, 2000, 2004, 2005; Dovidio, Kawakami, & Gaertner, 2002; Gaertner & McLaughlin, 1983). Aversive racists "sympathize with victims of past injustice, support the principle of racial equality, and regard themselves as non-prejudiced but, at the same time, possess negative feelings and beliefs about Blacks, which may be unconscious" (Dovidio & Gaertner, 2005, p. 618). Most well-educated and liberal-minded Whites in North America hold this view. The racism they express is cautious and subtle. Not only is there no correlation between implicit and explicit beliefs and attitudes; in addition, people make generalizations about other members of the group on the basis of their limited experience or observation of a single individual (Henderson-King & Nisbett, 1996). Participants in another study reported that applying stereotypes is unjust and that they had no intention of doing so, but they still applied stereotypes implicitly (Chen & Bargh, 1997). These studies support Banaji and Bhaskar's (2001) notion that "the best of intentions do not and cannot override the unfolding of unconscious processes, for the triggers of automatic thought, feeling, and behavior live and breathe outside conscious awareness and control" (pp. 142–143). Automatic activation is a big barrier not only in transcending racism, sexism, heterosexism, classism, ageism, and other "isms" but also in transforming internalized oppression and privilege.

〰 VARIATIONS WITHIN AND AMONG RACES

There are variations within a racial group as well as among racial groups. People of color represent various racial groups (e.g., African Americans, American Indians, American Jews, Asian Americans, South Americans, Middle Eastern Americans, Central Americans, Caribbean Americans, biracial Americans, multiracial Americans), classes, ethnicities, sexual orientations, ages, disabilities, educational levels, regions, religions, and languages. Some of them are from a collective value orientation, some of them are from an individualistic value orientation, and some of them are from a mixture of the two. Some people of color who were born and raised in the United States have been oppressed, marginalized, discriminated against, and prejudiced against from childhood because of their skin color, facial features, or other physical features. There are biracial and multiracial people who were born and raised in the United States. Some people of color who were born in the United States or other countries have been adopted by Euro Americans. Some adoptees are satisfied with their adoption while others wonder about their biological parents. This is also true for those who have been adopted by members of their own racial group. Some adoptees may have unresolved adoption loss and abandonment issues. Some adoptees struggle with having skin color and facial features that are different from those of their adopted family (Cox, 1999) while others do not. Some adoptees of color feel marginalized when White children treat them as if they are not Americans (Koh, 1993) while others do not. Some adoptees are racially mixed, representing a mixture of diverse groups, while others are not. Some of them are born in the United States, and others became U.S. citizens through adoption or immigration. The racial identity of biracial and multiracial individuals varies greatly from individual to individual. Some enjoy their ability to appreciate more than one culture. Some frequently feel torn between two racial identities and feel disloyal to one parent's racial identity if they choose the other parent's racial identity. They may reverse their racial identity as they go through different developmental stages, and the degree of their identification with one race versus the other varies from individual to individual and with developmental stage. Some go through transitory periods where they feel they cannot identify with either race or they want to identify with both races simultaneously. For some, the transitory period becomes a struggle throughout their lives. Root (1992) states that a hierarchical social system and simplifying (dichotomizing) complex relationships become "vehicles of oppression" (p. 4). Nash (1992) also postulates that deconstructing inappropriate hierarchical and dichotomous thinking would likely lead to biracial and multiracial people being comfortable in their racial identity. He says (Nash, 1992, p. 331), "Rather than seeing myself as an Asian American or a European American, why can't I find strength and wisdom in each and both?" Biracial and multiracial individuals do not fit into existing racial classifications (Root, 1990). Insisting they fit their racial identity into a socially constructed either/or category is denying their right to be Americans. Some of them are immigrants, international students, or refugees (United Nations, 1995; United Nations High Commissioner for Refugees, Statistical Unit, 1998). There are variations among immigrants, international students, and refugees as well as variations among different racial groups of immigrants, international students, and refugees. Immigrants, international students, and refugees will be discussed in the language section of Chapter 9. Applying dichotomous (i.e., "either/or") thinking to racial groups excludes variations within and among racial groups. Applying concepts like "partly," "mostly," or "both/and" (diunital thinking) may lead the way to conceptualizing these variations (Salk, 1973; Teitelbaum, 1990).

※ RACISM AND RACIAL PREJUDICE AND INAPPROPRIATE THINKING STYLES/PATTERNS

Racism and racial prejudice are not possible without inappropriate thinking styles, which become patterns through repetition. Racism, racial prejudice, and discrimination involve seeing Whites as better than people of color (*hierarchical thinking*) and Whites as good (*dichotomous thinking*). Seeing Whites as good does not have to be interpreted dichotomously because one can say Afro Americans are good, Hispanics are good, and people of color are good as well. However, it has been interpreted that seeing Whites as good means seeing people of color as not good, due to applying an inappropriate dichotomous thinking style. The Human Genome Project by the U.S. Department of Energy has indicated that there is a 0.1% difference among racial groups (Bonham et al., 2005). This means people are 99.9% similar. Whites and people of color are equally good, and no people are superior, average, or inferior as a result of their race; 99.9% is almost 100% after all. Phenotypic characteristics distinguish individuals from each other. Skin color, facial features, type of hair, height, body size, and other physical features indicate individuals' uniqueness and authenticity. If being an American is not based on White standards as the norm, the beauty and wholeness of each individual can be seen and appreciated. However, the fact that racism and racial discrimination still persist indicates that the application of inappropriate dichotomous and hierarchical thinking to judge non-Whites on White standards as the norm for being an American is still pervasive. Takaki (1993) writes in *A Different Mirror: A History of Multicultural America*:

> The rearview mirror reflected a white man in his forties. "How long have you been in this country?" he asked. "All my life," I replied, wincing. "I was born in the United States." With a strong southern drawl, he remarked: "I was wondering because your English is excellent!" Then, as I had many times before, I explained: "My grandfather came here from Japan in the 1880s. My family has been here, in America, for over a hundred years." He glanced at me in the mirror. Somehow I did not look "American" to him; my eyes and complexion looked foreign. (p. 1)

At the spring 1997 conference of the American Counseling Association in Orlando, Florida, a Chinese American speaker who was born and raised in the United States spoke about his childhood experience with racial discrimination. His first language was English, and he said:

I didn't know what to say when my elementary school teacher asked me how certain things were in China. I told the teacher, "I don't know." I wondered why she did not ask the same question to the White children. My point is that this kind of unintentional racism leads children of color to think that somehow America is not their country and they do not have the rights of White American children.

The driver (in the excerpt from Takaki [1993]) and the teacher probably had no idea that they were stating that Americans are only White. The driver might have thought he was being friendly, and the teacher might have thought she was being inclusive by asking a Chinese student a question about China. Their comments reflect their belief about who can be Americans. White Americans need to think about how it would feel if they were treated as if they were not Americans by other Americans on a daily basis. This type of remark seems harmless to White people (privilege holders) but can lead to negative inner experiences for children and adults of color if they are treated repeatedly as outsiders in their own country.

The following experiential learning activities are designed to increase compassion for others.

CONCRETE STRATEGIES

Experiential Learning Activities: Role Play

1. Please do the following activities without screening or judgment:
   a. Close your eyes and put yourself in Takaki's position for about 10 min. Then, record your thoughts and feelings without screening.
   b. Close your eyes and put yourself in the Chinese American speaker's position for about 10 min. Then, record your thoughts and feelings without screening.

(Continued)

(Continued)

     c. What types of thinking style (hierarchical, dichotomous, and/or linear) did you find in your writing?

     d. Close your eyes to reflect. Stay still and feel and think without screening.

2. For those of you in a class, please do the following additional activity: Divide the class into groups of four or five and read aloud what you wrote. Listen to each other with respect and validate each other, regardless of whether you agree with each other. Students who do not feel comfortable sharing do not need to share but do need to be aware of their feelings and thoughts internally.

Experiential and Reflection Activities

1. Have you ever minimized, marginalized, or laughed at someone because of his/her/zir race?

     a. If you have, describe an incident.

     b. How did you feel about the incident then, and how do you feel about it now?

2. Have you ever been minimized, marginalized, or laughed at because of your race?

     a. If you have, describe an incident.

     b. How did you feel about the incident then, and how do you feel about it now?

STRATEGIES FOR AND BENEFITS OF DISMANTLING RACISM AND RACIAL PREJUDICE FOR WHITES

The first strategy for dismantling racism and racial prejudice at the personal, interpersonal, institutional, and cultural levels is eliminating inappropriate dichotomous and hierarchical thinking styles in evaluating racial issues. The second strategy at the personal, interpersonal, and institutional level is people of color taking more of an agent role than a victim role. People of color should not wait for Whites to understand systematic oppression and racial inequity since such understanding may take a long time to achieve due to the invisibility of privilege to privilege holders. Being an agent means being proactive rather than reactive. This means people of color should search every oppressed racial experience for an agent aspect. For example, if an individual is not included on the basis of his skin color, he needs to experience his feelings honestly and examine what he is learning from the experience. If his feelings are hurt and he is disappointed, he needs to feel his pain without being defensive or reactive. The other person (who is White) is not going to be able to understand him just because he is defensive or reactive. Instead of focusing on the other person changing for him, he can empower himself by focusing on his own feelings and what he can do about them. He needs to feel the hurt feelings without judgment as often as he is hurt and as long as it does not interfere with his life. He may have to feel the hurt once every 2 days for 30 min each time and focus on what he is learning through this painful experience. For example, he may learn to communicate more effectively when he is rejecting another person because he knows how painful it is to be rejected. For the same reason, he may become very supportive of people who have been rejected. He may learn it is better to suffer with the reality of rejection than be included for superficial reasons. Or he may learn he does not want to be friends with people who do not include him on the basis of his skin color. Through this process he not only gains knowledge about how to become an agent by focusing on the learning aspect of the experience but also learns to comprehend how others (people of color) feel when they are discriminated against on the basis of their skin color (e.g., Black). The following personal story is from one of the author's former students. It is the story of her own transformation to an agent from a victim.

PERSONAL STORY

So many of my old thoughts and habits have changed, so many things I took for granted have been wrong, and so many ways of thinking have changed in my life that I sometimes do not recognize the person who began this program. How many times have I told a male-bashing joke without a moment's pause to realize what I was doing? How many times have I said, "It's a man thing?" Or told a blonde joke? Now I think back and wonder how I could have believed I was a tolerant and fair person. I remember thinking on that first day of class, how I did not fit into the pattern of a sexist person, not me, how could I be like that. What a joke! . . . I wanted to stop being a victim and become an agent so I began to think differently. If I disagreed with an opinion, I refused to take it personal. My thought was to listen and learn instead of becoming defensive or blind.

—Barb, 2005

Some individuals resist processing their feelings and rationalize that it is better to leave it alone rather than "dig at the old wound." However, this statement does not acknowledge the fact that they are reacting strongly because the old wound is affecting their perception of the current reality. At the personal and interpersonal level, White individuals can engage in compassion- and empathy-raising activities by reexperiencing their own oppression. They can pick one dimension of one identity on the basis of which they have been oppressed. It could be, for example, gender, class, sexual orientation, impairment, religion, language, or region. If White individuals go through the same steps described previously for a person of color to become an agent, they may learn to communicate more effectively when they are rejecting another person. Through this process, they may learn how people of color feel about oppression, injustice, inequity, and racism. They may become advocates for people of color by owning their uncomfortable feelings and focusing on the learning aspect of their experience with oppression. They may want to work on dismantling systematic oppression as their social justice advocacy work.

Dismantling racism means that advocates do not take the path of least resistance. Taking the path of least resistance occurs when individuals say nothing despite feeling uncomfortable after hearing a racist joke. They do not have to react to the joker but can say that they are uncomfortable hearing the joke and share their reasons for the discomfort. They may respond to a statement such as "The ___ racial group is lazy" with "I feel uncomfortable hearing what you said. I feel uncomfortable because I think lazy people are in all racial groups, including White, and I am learning to show respect for all racial group members." They may also make an effort to get to know people from different racial groups. Research indicates that personal involvement decreases racial prejudice, discrimination, and racism (Heppner, Leong, & Chiao, 2008; Pettigrew & Tropp, 2006; Ponterotto & Austin, 2005). They may also monitor (without judgment) their tendency to favor the ingroup; their tendency toward social projection, attribution error, and asymmetric perception of self versus others; their tendency toward higher self-appraisal; and so on. They may be more willing to listen to people who have been or are targets of racial prejudice, discrimination, and racism. They may be aware of the impact of internalized oppression and privilege on their interpersonal relationships, as well as on institutional and governmental levels, and be mindful of their behavior toward people of color.

One of the strategies for dismantling institutional and governmental racism is to critically examine governmental, institutional, and organizational policies and regulations to see whether they are in compliance with Title VII of the Civil Rights Act of 1991. Title VII is the principal federal statute prohibiting unlawful employment discrimination based on race or color, gender, religion, and national origin. The Civil Rights Act of 1991 is "an act to amend the Civil Rights Act of 1964 to strengthen and improve Federal civil rights laws, to provide for damages in cases of intentional employment discrimination, to clarify provisions regarding disparate impact actions, and for other purposes" (U.S. Equal Employment Opportunity Commission, 2008). If institutions, governments, or organizations are not compliant, individuals can form a group to request their compliance.

Whites become allies of people of color at interpersonal, institutional, and governmental levels because racism, racial prejudice, and discrimination hurt Whites, too. Rothenberg (2005) lists 12 basic tactics for being an ally. In addition to the strategies described here, she advocates allying oneself with other people, noticing center of attention and power, taking a stand against injustice, and supporting the leadership of people of color.

Tatum (2000) summarizes Updegrave's (1989) description of benefits for Whites:

A *Money* magazine article called "Race and Money" chronicled the many ways the American economy was hindered by institutional racism. Whether one looks at productivity lowered by racial tensions in the workplace, or real estate equity lost through housing discrimination, or the tax revenue lost in underemployed communities of color, or the high cost of warehousing human talent in prison, the economic costs of racism are real and measurable. (p. 82)

Wise (2005) also writes about the benefits and losses of White privilege:

In the labor market, we benefit from racial discrimination in the relative sense, but in absolute terms this discrimination holds down most of our wages and living standards by keeping working people divided and creating a surplus labor pool of "others" to whom employers can turn when the labor market gets tight or workers demand too much in wages or benefits. We benefit in relative terms from discrimination against people of color in education, by receiving, on average, better resources and class offerings. But in absolute terms, can anyone deny that the creation and perpetuation of mis-educated persons of color harms us all? (p. 120)

There are other benefits besides economic benefits. White people will learn about history, art, cultural myths, customs, different styles of interpersonal communication, emphasis on extended family, different literature, and different healing practices, to state a few. White people will also learn different ways of problem solving and a different concept of time and place. Children will regain their openness to relate to each other and learn from each other. People of color and White people will expand their cognitive and emotional understanding of each other through interconnecting and relating. They will celebrate their culture, strengths, and beauty.

🞇 A PRACTITIONER'S ASSESSMENT OF SELF IN RELATION TO WHITE OPPRESSION/PRIVILEGE

It is one thing to assess clients with regard to degree of White oppression/ privilege and internalized oppression/privilege, but it is much more difficult for practitioners to admit that they are also affected by White oppression/privilege and internalized oppression/privilege. It is hard to imagine these are automatically activated and affect their ability to assess, diagnose, and treat clients.

How can practitioners access and change something that is automatic and has been implemented and reinforced for generations? One step is to gain access to inner experience as discussed in Chapter 3. As practitioner-trainees may have discovered from completing experiential learning activities in Chapter 3, when they do not judge or screen their emotions and thoughts, they are able to identify how they genuinely feel and think regardless of cultural expectations or conditioned norms. As they hear their voice within, they begin to identify their own thinking styles. The key to being aware of their thinking styles is to observe their internal dialogue. Banaji and Bhaskar (2001) illustrate this in their experiments and show how difficult it is for people to change their beliefs because what people say explicitly may have no relationship to their implicit expression of beliefs and attitudes. As Banaji and Bhaskar (2001) state, there is an "inevitability of unconscious stereotyping and prejudice" (p. 142). It is important for practitioners to know it is hard to be aware of their own biases and prejudices. All practitioners, regardless of their color, need to be mindful of the fact that ignoring "the other" and emphasizing mainstream values have been in existence since White European settlers started oppressing Native Americans in order to ensure their own economic security and are still alive and practiced today. A good example is illustrated by two pictures (see Kinney, 2005), which are almost identical, of individuals in chest-high water holding food items. One picture is of a person of color with a caption that reads, "A young man walks through chest-deep flood water after looting a grocery store in New Orleans on Tuesday, Aug. 30, 2005." The other picture is of two White individuals with a caption that reads, "Two residents wade through chest-deep water after finding bread and soda from a local grocery store after Hurricane Katrina came through the area in New Orleans, Louisiana." The article's subtle differences in language (*looting* vs. *finding*) illustrates internalized privilege in relation to race. The reporters probably had no intention of discriminating against the person of color. This is an excellent example of how the media (society) reinforce internalized privilege and systematic oppression. People who do not face discrimination, prejudice, or racism are likely not to comprehend that racial biases are alive today. This is also an excellent example of the impact of implicit learning about race through the media and different learning paths for people of color versus Whites. White people learned to internalize privilege, and people of color learned to internalize oppression. There are numerous implicit messages from the media. Practitioners can ask the following questions of themselves: How many TV programs' main characters are people of color? How can children of color feel equal to White children when they see mostly White role models portrayed as important by the mass media? How many chief executive officers are people of color? How many senators and members of the House of Representatives are people of color?

There are several steps that practitioners can take if they want to be open to clients' worldviews. There is a Web site on implicit learning that will assist practitioner-trainees with assessing their own prejudices in relation to race and other identities (http://implicit.harvard.edu/implicit/). What is important is not pointing the finger to blame Whites but understanding what has happened historically for them to be biased and identifying what can be done to promote change. This requires nondichotomous thinking. If practitioner-trainees would like to access their own unconscious in order to learn to stop automatic thoughts and feelings from manifesting in themselves, they can continuously practice the activities suggested in Chapter 3, including experiential as well as reflection-based learning activities such as narrative and reflective writing, raising consciousness, drawing, dream work, and raising body awareness (narrative movement, yoga) to gain access to their inner experience (Blackmore, 2004; Cameron, 1992; Olsen,

1998; Progoff, 1992; Schure, Christopher, & Christopher, 2008). McIntosh's (1989) list is another way to access White practitioner-trainees' systematic oppression/privilege and internalized oppression/privilege. When practitioner-trainees do these activities, they should complete them quickly in order to minimize the possibility of screening. If practitioner-trainees spend too much time with each list, they may rationalize and respond logically as a result of their rationalization and not of their automatic activation of unconscious processing. If their thinking patterns are hierarchical and/or dichotomous, these experiential learning activities can be challenging. It is important for practitioner-trainees to remember that the purpose of the exercises is not to blame but to examine privilege and oppression as a member of a particular group. The following experiential learning activities are designed to assist practitioner-trainees with understanding systematic racial privilege and oppression. This type of learning activity allows for integration of emotion with intellectual understanding of oneself and "others" (*transformative learning*).

CONCRETE STRATEGIES

Experiential Learning Activities: Role Play

1. If you are a person of color, adopt the perspective of a White person and state the fears and concerns that you believe such a person would bring to a discussion of race and privilege. Write your essay in the first-person singular. Then, take a moment to reflect.

2. Record your reflection.

3. If you are a White person, adopt the perspective of a person of color and state the fears and concerns that you believe such a person would bring to a discussion of race and privilege. Write your essay in the first-person singular. Then, take a moment to reflect.

4. Record your reflection.

McIntosh's (1989) list of White privilege indicates that White people have easy access to housing (both to rent and to own) in desirable neighborhoods, medical assistance, and their cultural music, food, TV programs, newspapers, magazines, and books. They have no fear of racial profiling and no emotional reactions due to their skin color. The following experiential learning activities are designed for transformative learning. It is important that the questions be answered without censoring and screening to obtain an individual's understanding of White privilege at the moment.

CONCRETE STRATEGIES

Assessing Your Oppression/Privilege in Relation to White Privilege

1. Reflect on the activities you have completed and answer the following questions:
   a. Describe the activities and interpersonal relationships you felt were the result of your White privilege.
   b. Describe the activities and interpersonal relationships you felt were the result of oppression because of your skin color.

2. How hard is it for you to find your cultural food at the local grocery store?
   a. How far do you have to travel to buy your cultural food?

3. How hard is it for you find your music locally?
   a. How far do you have to travel to buy your music?

4. Are you afraid of racial profiling?

5. How hard is it for you to find your cultural TV programs on standard channels?

6. How hard is it for you to find your cultural magazines locally?

7. How hard is it for you to find your cultural newspapers locally?

8. How hard is it for you to find your cultural books locally?

9. How hard is it for you to find bandages that match your skin locally?

10. How hard is it for you to find people from your race locally?

11. How often are you upset or frustrated due to your skin color?

12. How often do people stare at you due to your skin color?

(Continued)

(Continued)

13. How often do you see people of your race at a grocery store?

14. How many restaurants serve your cultural food locally?

15. How often are you labeled negatively due to your skin color?

16. How often are you the recipient of systematic privilege due to your skin color?

17. How often are you the recipient of systematic oppression due to your skin color?

 a. What have you learned about systematic oppression/privilege from participating in these activities?

 b. Which of your answers to the previous questions provide a clear example of systematic privilege?

 c. Which of your answers to the previous questions provide a clear example of systematic oppression?

 d. How would you use what you have learned from these activities in counseling/social work/human services?

 e. Talk about understanding the impact of White privilege with others who have completed these activities.

CONCRETE STRATEGIES

Consciousness Practice

Did you learn internalized oppression and privilege and systematic oppression and privilege consciously?

⚡ NOTE

1. www.stirfryseminars.com

5

Sexism

This chapter builds a foundation to support the social construction theory of gender by defining the differences between sex and gender, sex roles and gender roles, and sexual discrimination and sexism. The role of gender socialization in systematic oppression/privilege and internalized oppression/privilege is discussed. This chapter addresses gender not as an independent identity but as related to a person's other identities and purports that the whole person functions and interacts within sociocultural contexts. The whole person does not have only one identity at a time (e.g., gender). The whole person expresses behavior, feelings, and thinking, which are derived from combinations of multiple identities. This chapter begins to examine the whole person by exploring the intersection of race and gender within social contexts. It also explains that understanding the whole person requires understanding variations among men and among women as well as between men and women. The difficulties of transcending sexism and sexual discrimination due to embedded gender myths, systematic gender oppression/privilege, and internalized gender oppression/privilege are explored. Strategies for dismantling sexism and the benefits for both genders are discussed. This chapter also provides concrete strategies for transformative learning.

DIFFERENCES AMONG SEX, GENDER, AND SEXISM

Sex is the biological and physiological differences between males and females whereas gender is socially constructed by a particular society and ascribes gendered norms to individuals within that society. Individuals are expected to carry out these norms throughout the socialization process.

Sex is the product of biology, and gender is a process that may vary and reflects sociocultural expectations. Many individuals confuse not only sex and gender but also many concepts related to them such as sexual orientation, sexual identity, and gender identity. These concepts are briefly defined in the following paragraph for clarity.

Some individuals confuse gender with sexual orientation. Sexual orientation is determined by those to whom individuals are sexually (or erotically) attracted. There are four types of sexual orientation: (a) heterosexuality (heterosexuals are sexually attracted to members of the opposite sex), (b) homosexuality (homosexuals are sexually attracted to members of the same sex), (c) bisexuality (bisexuals are sexually attracted to members of both the same and the opposite sex), and (d) asexuality (asexuals are sexually attracted to no one). Sexual identity is who individuals are (e.g., lesbian, gay, bisexual, queer, heterosexual, asexual), which is different from gender identity. Gender identity is the concept of self as "male" or "female," and for most individuals it is related to anatomical sex (body parts). However, for some (e.g., transsexuals), their gender identity is different from their anatomical sex. Some transsexuals hormonally and/or surgically change their anatomical sex to match their gender identity. Gender identity is different from gender role. Gender role is what a society defines as appropriate behavior for males and females and can vary from culture to culture. The United States, like many cultures, recognizes only two gender roles: masculinity and femininity. The recent development of a third gender role, androgyny, combines socially defined appropriate male and female qualities.

The concept of more than two genders dates back to Mesopotamia (Murray & Roscoe, 1997). Some societies such as those of the indigenous cultures of American Indian tribes (e.g., Illinois, Sioux, Sac, Fox), the Indian subcontinent, the ancient Greeks, the Middle East, and Pacific Islanders have three genders: men, women, and a third gender (Blackwood, 1984; Goulet, 2006; Phillimore, 1991; Roscoe, 2000; Roughgarden, 2004; Wikan, 1991; Williams, 1986). The Native American *berdaches*, the *hijras* of India, and the *xanith* of the Middle East are biological males who behave, dress, and work and are treated socially as women. They are therefore not men; nor are they female women. Direct translation in English is "male-women" (Amadlume, 1987). Hearted women are biological females who work, marry, and parent as men; their social status is as "femalemen." They do not have to behave or dress as men to have the social responsibilities and prerogatives of husbands and fathers; what makes them men is enough wealth to buy a wife (e.g., in some African and American Indian societies). Historical examination of gender theories reflects that gender is a process that can be interrupted, reversed, or changed and that has been socially constructed.

Sexism is also socially constructed with systematic advantages on the basis of gender (male), and it includes but is much bigger and deeper than gender bias and gender discrimination. Gender discrimination is defined as "harmful actions towards others because of their membership in a particular group" (Fishbein, 1996, p. 7). Prejudice is prejudgment without any just ground, and discrimination occurs when prejudice is translated into behavior that denies individuals or groups of individuals equal treatment. Sexism is much bigger than individual prejudice and discrimination. It is governmental and institutional policies, laws, and rules that favor men. It is about the system giving social power and control to men over women and undermining the power and safety of women (Connell, 1987). Sexism ranges from the objectification of women, denigrating jokes about women, and job discrimination against women to violence against women. History indicates similarities between sexism and racism. Both are socially constructed in order to guarantee the privileged group's power by treating members of the "other" group as if they are not human beings. Both are deeply ingrained in the human psyche to an extent that both privileged and oppressed groups participate in perpetuating racism and sexism without conscious awareness. Both are based on inappropriate hierarchical and dichotomous thinking. The following reflection-based learning activities are designed to raise awareness of the impact of gender beliefs and their relation to a practitioner-trainee's own identity.

CONCRETE STRATEGIES

Reflection-Based Learning Activities

Close your eyes for 5 min, breathing in relaxation and breathing out tension. Then open your eyes.

1. How was gender portrayed by the media (TV, movies, computer games, popular music, etc.) when you were growing up? Write down your responses.

2. What gendered qualities do you regularly display or perform?

   a. Are there any gendered qualities you possess that you find yourself unwilling to perform? Write these down.

   b. Write down the conditions under which you're unwilling to perform these qualities. How do you feel when you do not perform them?

☒ SOCIAL CONSTRUCTION OF GENDER

Numerous research findings support that young children learn what is appropriate behavior for girls and boys at an early age through various social agents such as parents, the media, the toy and clothing industries, other adults, and peers (Coie & Dodge, 1998; Crick, 1996; Giles & Heyman, 2005; Maccoby, 1998, 2002; Ruble & Martin, 1998; Zhang, Lingin, Zhang, Wang, & Chen, 2003). Giles and Heyman conducted three studies on the relationship between beliefs about gender and aggressive behavior with preschool-age children (the age range was 3.6–5.0 years for the first study, 3.1–5.3 years for the second study, and 3.1–4.11 years for the third study). All three studies support the idea that young children perceive the world from their gendered belief system, which is fostered through socialization. The second study revealed that gendered beliefs are held universally. The researchers sampled children from various cultural backgrounds (African American, Asian American, European American, and Hispanic American), and gendered beliefs were persistent regardless of children's racial backgrounds. Other cross-cultural studies also support the idea that gendered beliefs are learned at an early age (Knobloch, Callison, Chen, Fritzsche, & Zillmann, 2005; Liben & Signorella, 1993; Susskind, 2003). Chinese, German, and American children ranging in age from 4.0 to 6.0 years chose movies with same-sex protagonists, and this tendency increased with age. Furthermore, regardless of country and age, children selected movies in line with their cultural gender expectations (Knobloch et al.). Children distorted situations if they were not congruent with their belief about gender (Liben & Signorella; Susskind). These studies indicate that transcending sexism, gender biases, and discrimination is challenging due to early childhood learning of gendered behaviors. The children's age range in the studies discussed above was from 3 to 6. By the time these children become adults, they will have lived in a gendered culture for a long time and will have been practicing gendered values, beliefs, and biases consciously and unconsciously.

The media reinforces the dominant values, gender stereotypes, and ideal images. Major themes in the media, as well as public polls, still favor men as superior by portraying them as if they have more power and more opportunities available to them. Most prime-time TV sitcoms objectify women and emphasize men and women's relationships on the basis of superficial qualities. Research on the role of women and adolescence magazines have suggested such sitcoms perpetuate gender and racial stereotypes, dominant cultural values, and unrealistic expectations (Currie, 1997; Frisby, 2004; Frith, Cheung, & Shaw, 2004; Hovland, McMahan, Lee, Hwang, & Kim, 2005; Poran, 2002; Sengupta, 2006). During the 1998 grand jury investigation of U.S. President Bill Clinton, Hillary Clinton's approval rating went up because of the way she handled her husband's sex scandal. Appearing in public with him while holding his hand and not expressing her opinion about her husband's affair was perceived as a wife who supported her husband. It was interpreted as a positive behavior. It was not perceived as a woman who could not assert her right as a wife. This was detrimental as a role model for American women, especially those in an abusive relationship. Would Mr. Clinton's rating have gone up if Mrs. Clinton were the one to have an extramarital affair in the Oval Office? Would the same Americans who rated Mrs. Clinton favorably rate Mr. Clinton favorably if he stood by her as a husband?

The following story illustrates the complexities of gender identity construction and behavior, which are results of the dynamic interaction among sociocultural context, gender socialization, gender-biased dominant cultural values, and the intersection of gender with other identities. The story illustrates the power of ingrained culturally appropriate gender behaviors, which often transcend intellectual understanding of gender equity.

PERSONAL STORY

Gendered Behavior

I didn't quite understand the decisions I was making as a wife. I often allowed my husband to have the first choice and tried to figure out how to satisfy my needs and wants afterward. For example, I wanted to continue my graduate studies after earning my master's degree. My husband said that he also wanted to continue his studies. As we discussed our dreams, I felt the only way we would receive financial support was for one of us to work while the other was going to school. I decided to work while he pursued his doctorate, even though I wanted to continue my studies, too. Yes, I let my husband fulfill his dream first, since he did not volunteer to work while I pursued my schooling. I did not insist because of the way I was culturally conditioned. I was socialized in a collectivism-oriented culture, which emphasized meeting others' needs first and not

(Continued)

(Continued)

doing to others what I did not want done to me. I, once again, had to experience life's challenges. Since I did not have U.S. citizenship, I was not able to get a job as a master's level social service professional, even though I was one of the top students (with one of the highest GPAs) in my master's program. The state of Minnesota required U.S. citizenship as a prerequisite to state jobs at my educational level at that time. Changing citizenship takes a lot of soul searching. I did not want to do it just because I needed a job, even though I knew I needed to work immediately. I took the first job I was offered, which did not require U.S. citizenship, because my husband's research assistantship barely covered the monthly rent (we had not anticipated failing to secure a student housing arrangement at the time of our arrival in St. Paul). I worked as a recreational worker for emotionally, neurologically, and mentally handicapped children at a residential facility. The minimum requirement for the position was a high school diploma. The director wanted my expertise; however, he was not willing to give me financial compensation for it. I eventually got a job at the master's level in Minnesota and enjoyed developing programs for neurologically and emotionally disturbed children. However, my husband got "homesick" and wanted to move back to Washington state without finishing his degree. He quit school without discussing it with me. He wanted to go back home and become a farmer since his parents told him farming was wonderful. I wanted to support him, yet I did not feel I could just walk away from my job. I wished I had known of his intentions at least 3 months in advance. Once again, I made accommodations to meet his needs. Even though it was difficult, I did not think about exploring other options, such as staying in Minnesota longer to have enough time to train my successor or staying there with the children while he explored his path as a farmer. I think it was my myth that the family needs to be together and at least one of the partners must make sure that it happens for the sake of the children.

Regardless of individuals' intellectual understanding of gender equality and how much they advocate for it, applying the concept of gender equality to their personal life is challenging at times for some women. The author is the product of a collectivistic culture (South Korea) that fosters the belief that women should put others' needs before theirs. Korea, like many Asian cultures, follows the Chinese scholar Confucius's (551–479 BC) philosophy. Women are underclass citizens under this patriarchal family system, which gives power and authority to men (Hu, 1988). The author was encouraged to follow her heart and explore her intellectual curiosity without cultural confinement within her family, but the fundamental cultural teaching of gender typing was deeply ingrained within her psyche (e.g., by school, media, her mother, other women). Her story demonstrates how the impact of her broader culture was stronger in shaping her gendered behavior than her family values, which did not emphasize gendered behaviors. Yet she combined her cultural values with her family value of "not doing to others what you do not want done to you." In addition, her behavior was influenced by the sociocultural context of the United States then. The sociocultural context of the United States now is much more into gender equality than in the past. Her intellectual understanding of gender equality did not have her strong emotional support at the time, and this led her to be influenced by the dominant cultural values, which were familiar to her from her own cultural gender socialization. It is also important to notice her gendered behaviors and gender equality ideas did not operate in a linear and sequential fashion. The following reflection-based learning activities on gender are designed for transformative learning, for which it is important not to censor or screen (Ferrer, Romero, & Albareda, 2005).

CONCRETE STRATEGIES

Reflection-Based Learning Activities on Gender

Close your eyes and breathe in and out slowly, evenly, and deeply for 5 min. As you breathe, go back in your timeline as far as you can to see whether you can recall experiencing gender issues during your childhood. Slowly open your eyes and do the following:

Memory on Gender

1. Describe your experience with gender issues. How did you feel about it then, and how do you feel about it now?
   a. Did you share your experience with someone? If you did, with whom did you share it, and what was his/her/zir response?
   b. If you did not share it with anyone, what did you do with it?

(Continued)

(Continued)

c. What was your feeling about your gender and the other genders?

d. What did you learn from your mother (or mother figure) about your gender?

e. What did you learn from your father (or father figure) about your gender?

f. What did you learn from your siblings (or sibling figures) about your gender?

g. What did you learn from your teachers about your gender?

h. If your parents applied gendered socialization practice, what was the main message? How does this message affect you now?

SOCIAL COMPARISON THEORY

Self-categorization theory was born out of social comparison theory by Festinger (1954). According to Festinger, individuals' evaluation of themselves is context dependent. In other words, individuals compare themselves to others, and they usually prefer to compare themselves with ingroup members who are perceived to share their beliefs, values, and attitudes. Self-categorization theory postulates that there are two main levels of self-definitions: (a) personal identity (individual self) and (b) social identity (collective self). Self-concept can change from personal to social identity according to the context. The self-categorization theory indicates that gender differences in self-concept are variable and context dependent.

Ingroup Versus Outgroup

Individuals show different parts of themselves depending on which group (ingroup vs. outgroup) they are dealing with at that time. When individuals compare themselves to other ingroup members, they use the personal identity category, but when they compare themselves to outgroup members, they use the social identity category. Individuals tend to be much more open and honest with the ingroup (Onorato &

Turner, 2001, 2004; Turner & Onorato, 1999). Guimond, Chatard, Martinot, Crisp, and Redersdoff (2006) conducted four studies to examine gender differences in self-construal and confirmed previous studies' findings that (a) women define themselves as higher than men in relational interdependence, and men define themselves as higher than women in independence/agency; (b) gender differences are reduced in ingroup comparisons of self-construal; and (c) gender differences are increased in outgroup comparisons of both relational interdependence and independence/agency. As shown in the previous section's discussion of the belief systems of preschool children, studies of gender discrimination show ingroup preference among children (Leaper, 1994; Maccoby, 1998; Powlishta, 1995) and outgroup gender bias among kindergartners (Kowalski & Kanitkar, 2003).

The impact of gendered socialization on an individual's identity construction, values, beliefs, and biases continues throughout one's life. Sexism, which is based on gendered socialization, has been perpetuated within various cultural and organizational structures (Jay, 1981). For example, inequality in women's career advancement in organizations and institutions is an area where men's ingroup loyalty perpetuates sexism and patriarchy. Lower ratings of female supervisors by male subordinates, unequal representation of women in high-level management, less social power for women, and slow promotion of women are some examples (Agars, 2004; Carli, 1990, 1999; Elias, 2004; Elias & Cropanzano, 2006). The United States claims to be a leading democratic country in Western societies and often intervenes in other countries to enhance or facilitate their democracy; however, its gender inequality is far from democratic practice (Almquist, 1987). In the United States, women occupy only 12.4% of board seats across all Fortune 500 companies, and only 5% of senior managers in Fortune 2000 industrial and service companies are women (Agars; Jackson, 2001). Valian (2004) sums up the causes of women's slow advancement by stating, "The small but systematic undervaluation of women culminates in women's smaller salaries compared to men's, and slower rates of promotion" (p. 211).

Automatic Activation

As indicated in Chapter 4 (racism), one of the most important discoveries of social psychology research and cognitive and neuroscience studies of memory in the past 2 decades is the recognition that unconscious learning processes are involved in stereotyping and prejudice. Banaji and Bhaskar (2001) depict gender as one of the most "fundamentally learned social categories" (p. 155) at an early age. As a result, transcending sexism is a challenge beyond intellectual understanding. Exhibiting gendered behaviors is quick and often unconscious. It only takes "300 milliseconds" (p. 155). Watching and reading gendered media images, being rewarded and/or approved for gendered behaviors, and repeating gendered intra- and interpersonal communication lead to strengthening gendered beliefs and values and become the automatic process of repeating these learning behaviors. As indicated by several studies, children start their gendered behaviors long before their conscious gender construction (Bandura & Bussey, 2004; Coie & Dodge, 1998; Crick, 1996; Giles & Heyman, 2005; Maccoby, 1998, 2002; Ruble & Martin, 1998; Zhang et al., 2003).

◊ SYSTEMATIC OPPRESSION/PRIVILEGE AND INTERNALIZED OPPRESSION/PRIVILEGE

Sexism as previously defined is systematic advantages for men on the basis of their gender. This means governmental, institutional, and organizational policies, laws, and rules are written to favor men and unfairly discriminate against women. In other words, women are oppressed by the system based on their gender. The concept of gender privilege is difficult for some men to understand because they do not feel privileged due to systematic oppression in relation to other-than-gender identities. For instance, a White man who has been struggling with poverty all his life would not understand that he has privilege because he is a White man. A further complication is that privilege often is invisible to privilege holders regardless of the type of privilege (e.g., race, sexual orientation, ability, age).

Both gender privilege and gender oppression are based on dichotomous and hierarchical thinking. They are based on a categorization by biological sex, with the male as superior or better (*hierarchical thinking*) than the female. Just like racial privilege and oppression, the groups are categorized in a hierarchy on the basis of their phenotypic characteristics of biology. Thus, gender privilege belongs to men regardless of their race, class, sexual orientation, disability, age, religion, education, and so on. "In other words, men cannot be oppressed as men . . . because a group can be oppressed only if there exists another group with the power to oppress them" (Johnson, 2006, pp. 38–39).

Some men do not feel privileged, but this does not mean they are not privileged in relation to their gender. White men in the United States are systematically gender privileged, which allows them to have easier access to education, housing, health care, and jobs compared with women and men in other racial groups. In addition, local and national laws and processes such as going through security systems at airports are friendlier for White men than for other racial groups. Some White men may not have access to housing and health care because access is determined not solely by race and gender but by income as well. However, they still have privilege because they are White and because they are men. Men of color are systematically gender privileged, not as much as White men but more than women of color. The relationship between men of color and White women is complicated by intersections of race, gender, education, sexual orientation, and class.

Learning about systematic gender privilege and oppression starts early and perpetuates unintentionally throughout life. Studies with elementary-school-age children have shown girls are more aware of their lower status than boys (Levy, Sadovsky, & Troseth, 2000; Liben, Bigler, & Krogh, 2001). Brown and Bigler (2004) showed that girls rated other girls as more negative than boys when they excluded peers. These findings suggest that it might have been due to the girls' internalized oppression. These tendencies were also shown in studies with adults. Both women and men responded negatively to women who showed a friendly but assertive leadership role (Valian, 2004). Valian's study suggests that women's responses might have been due to internalized oppression and men's responses might have been due to internalized privilege. Internalized privilege and oppression perpetuate and are perpetuated by systematic gender privilege and oppression, and these often take place without individuals' conscious awareness. Valian's examination of gender schemas and self-perception of entitlement also showed similar findings to those of the leadership study; women tended to be low in claiming entitlement compared with men, who tended to be high in claiming entitlement. The following reflection-based learning activities are about gender oppression/privilege and identity. Centering prior to doing these activities may lead to clarity and ability to focus.

CONCRETE STRATEGIES

Reflection-Based Learning Activities on Gender Oppression/Privilege

1. Indicate whether you belong to a privileged group or an oppressed group in relation to gender. The question is whether or not you belong to a privileged group according to your society regardless of your feeling of oppression or privilege.

2. How important is gender to your identity?

3. Close your eyes and breathe in and out slowly and evenly for 5 min. Pay attention to your feelings and the images that come to mind as you breathe. Slowly open your eyes and record or draw your feelings and/or images.

4. What have you learned from this exercise?

5. What was your understanding of systematic gender privilege and oppression before doing this exercise, and what is your understanding of it now?

6. Discuss your understanding of systematic gender privilege and oppression with others who have participated in the same experiential learning activities of this section.

7. What did you learn about yourself and others in your group from Question 6?

Individuals' internalized gender oppression/privilege affects their interpersonal and intrapersonal relationships on a daily basis. For instance, it affects how individuals relate to their family, friends, coworkers, institutions, governments, teachers, policymakers, managers, service workers, and therapists. Female clients often complain about their male partner being controlling and doing what he wants to do without discussing it with them. Some male clients cannot understand why they have to discuss decisions with their female partner because they "know for sure" what is good for her. Sometimes male clients ask for their female partner's opinion, but they get upset if their female partner does not agree with their plan. These examples are a part of men's socialization conditioning, which emphasizes their privilege over that of women. Internalized privilege and oppression at times interfere with interpersonal relationships between men and women without their conscious awareness.

The following reflection-, imagery-, and small-group-based learning activities are designed for transformative learning on gender issues (Ferrer et al., 2005; Power & Dalgleish, 1997).

CONCRETE STRATEGIES

Reflection-Based Learning Activities on Gender Issues

Practice identifying internalized gender oppression/privilege.

1. Reread the Personal Story box "Gendered Behavior" above and identify examples of internalized oppression. For instance, "I often allowed my husband to have the first choice and tried to figure out how to satisfy my needs and wants afterward" is an example of internalized oppression.

   a. Compare and discuss your examples with those of others.
   b. Rate your understanding of systematic gender privilege and oppression on a scale of 1 (very low) to 10 (100%).
   c. Write down your own examples of internalized gender privilege or oppression.

2. Close your eyes and breathe in and out slowly, evenly, and deeply for 5 min. As you breathe, go back in your timeline as far as you can to see whether you recall an experience with gender privilege or oppression at school during your childhood. Slowly open your eyes and do the following:

   a. Describe your experience with gender privilege or oppression at school.
   b. How did you feel about it then, and how do you feel about it now?
   c. Did you share your experience with someone? If so, with whom did you share it, and what was his/her/zir response? If you did not share it with anyone, what did you do with it?

(Continued)

(Continued)

    d. What was your feeling about your gender and the other genders in class?

    e. What did you learn from your teachers about gender?

    f. What did you learn about systematic gender privilege and oppression from your family when you were little? Be specific.

    g. Discuss concrete strategies to minimize internalized oppression for schoolchildren with others who have completed the experiential learning activities of this section.

THE INTERSECTION OF GENDER AND RACE

Most existing multicultural counseling theories compartmentalize the multiple identities of an individual as if each identity represents the whole person and is independent of the other identities. Thus, examining gender alone as if it operates in isolation and represents the total individual is artificial and does not lead to understanding an individual as a whole person. Gender is one important aspect of an individual's identity; however, it does not by itself represent the total person. The gender of an individual not only intersects with the individual's other identities but also is influenced by a particular sociocultural context. Race and gender cannot be treated as separate entities in determining a person's identity (Lee, 2006). Each individual has multiple identities, which are dynamic, fluid, and interacting constantly with the individual's sociocultural political context. Some individuals have a dominant identity that shows its characteristics across situations while others reveal different dimensions of multiple identities according to the particular sociocultural and political contexts within which they interact. Or some may identify with their dominant (salient or special) identity for about 50% of the time regardless of sociocultural context but show other identities according to sociocultural political contexts for the other 50%. Each identity is composed of multifaceted dimensions. Taking into account the complexities of these multifaceted dimensions, as well as those of an individual's multiple identities themselves, it is easy to miss who a person is in a particular sociocultural context if the complexities are simplified into static, dichotomous, and hierarchical categories. Chapters 4 through 9 in Part II of this book explore each identity in order to understand an individual as a whole person.

Oyserman and Markus (1993) illustrate the complexities involved in one's identity development; a categorical definition of self on the basis of gender reveals only a small part of who the person is, and if others assume they know this person only on the basis of gender, their assessment of this person may be vastly different from this person's own self-assessment. Oyserman and Markus, who pioneered the term *sociocultural self*, postulate that self-concept is defined in relation to sociocultural contexts. According to Markus (1977), self-schemas are "cognitive generalizations about the self, derived from past experiences, that organize and guide the processing of self-related information contained in the individual's social experience" (p. 64). Self-schema is the most consistent concept of self. Other self-concepts are temporary and depend on sociocultural contexts. There is no way to know about a person from appearance. For instance, when individuals see a woman of color, they know nothing about her attitudes toward and beliefs about her gender and race and the combination or intersection of her gender and race. One way to begin to understand the woman's worldview is through critically examining the intersections of her multiple identities in various sociocultural contexts. Oyserman and Markus eloquently describe the complexities involved in one's relationship to a particular sociocultural context:

> The independent contribution of each sociocultural context to one's self or identity cannot be evaluated. Each attribute or identifying feature both provides meaning to, and recruits meaning from, all the others. The resulting self is some melding, collaging, or weaving together of one's various sociocultural influences. (p. 195)

Research indicates that women of color are in *double jeopardy* or *double bind* status because on one hand they are pressured to put their race as the number-one priority to promote racial justice and on the other they are simultaneously pressured to put their gender as the number-one priority to dismantle gender inequality (Greene, 1994; Reid, 1984). Likewise, not all White women feel racial privilege even though they belong to a privileged racial group. If White women have been targets of persistent sexism on a personal, an institutional, or a cultural level, they may feel powerless against sexism and be incapable of feeling their White privilege. The same is true for men. There is no way to know about White men's experience with intersections of multiple identities and how their identities manifest in various sociocultural contexts. Kimmel (2000) reports that some men feel powerless due to the sociocultural context of how men's power is defined in the United States:

> Men's feelings are not the feelings of the powerful, but of those who see themselves as powerless. These are the feelings that come inevitably from the discontinuity between the social and the psychological, between the aggregate analysis that reveals how men are in power as a group and the psychological fact that they do not feel powerful as individuals. (p. 218)

Focusing on race or gender alone is creating something that does not represent the whole person (Collins, 1991). Race, gender, class, sexual orientation, age, disability, language, and region are mixed together like ingredients of a tossed salad to formulate a person's identity. How one identity interweaves with other identities is determined by a particular sociocultural context, a dominant identity (a salient or special identity) if there is one, intersections of multiple identities, and sociopolitical context. Practitioner-trainees need to think in terms of a holistic thinking style, which encompasses an examination of these complexities from a multilayered and multidimensional perspective. Dichotomous, linear, and hierarchical thinking styles do not facilitate critical examination of fluidity and the dynamic intersection of race and gender. Most beliefs and values are learned at an early age through socialization. As indicated in previous chapters, children learn these values prior to being able to critically and objectively examine them. Thus, they have a strong attachment to their learned beliefs and values, and it is hard to transcend them even if they understand the necessity of change intellectually in later life. A part of the difficulty is due to emotional attachment such as ingroup loyalty and the good feeling that comes with being rewarded by family, institutions, and culture. Thus, transcending sexism needs to include processing the emotional attachment to these values and beliefs. The following concrete strategies are designed to facilitate emotional processing of gender- and race-related experiences and their intersection.

CONCRETE STRATEGIES

Experiential Learning Activities on Emotional Processing

Prepare drawing materials (at least two sheets of drawing paper and a box of crayons, coloring pencils, or paints). Close your eyes and breathe in and out slowly and deeply for 5 min. As you are breathing in and out slowly, think and feel about your intersection of race and gender. Slowly open your eyes.

1. Draw your intersection of race and gender.

2. Write about what you drew.

3. What is your relationship to the following?
   a. Gender
   b. Race
   c. The intersection of gender and race

4. Have you been pressured to be loyal to race or gender by your community?
   a. How do you feel when you are pressured?
   b. How do you balance your need to be loyal to your inner beliefs and those of your community?
   c. How is your narrative similar to and different from that of your community (with regard to both race and gender)?

VARIATIONS AMONG MEN, AMONG WOMEN, AND BETWEEN MEN AND WOMEN

It is crucial to understand that there are variations among men, among women, and between men and women if practitioner-trainees are going to assess, diagnose, and treat a client from the client's worldview. A client's race, class, sexual orientation, impairment/disability, level of education, age, religion, language, region, and so on intersect with his/her/zir gender and determine variations among genders and within gender. As addressed at the beginning of this chapter, for a White man who has been poor all his life and does not understand he has White privilege, the perception of being a man in the United States may be very different from that for a

White man who grew up in the upper middle class and has benefited from White privilege. An Afro American woman who thinks the feminist movement is for White middle-class women may experience being a woman in a very different way from Afro American women who do not think this way about the feminist movement. Even some White women who struggle financially may think the feminist movement is only for White middle-class women.

There are variations among and within different cultures in gender conditioning. Assuming that Asian cultural gender conditioning is somewhat more biased toward boys and men does not allow for variations among and within Asian cultures. There are many cultures in Asia, just like there are many Latino and Black cultures. The more cultures that are included in a racial category, the more difficult it is to generalize them. Some Asian girls may be gender conditioned to play a subservient role, but so may many girls from other cultures. Some Asian girls may be encouraged to excel academically as much as boys, and so may girls from other cultures. Some boys from Mexican American cultures may be socialized to be gender biased toward boys at the preschool age and socialized to be gender balanced after preschool, and so may some boys from other cultural backgrounds. Each boy or girl accumulates information on gender identity and constructs his or her own gender identity.

Learning how to be aware of variations among men, among women, and between men and women relies heavily on a practitioner's ability to listen attentively, to ask appropriate questions, to not generalize (i.e., to detach from attribution error and social projection), to be aware of her biases (e.g., aversive racism, values, beliefs, attitudes), and to transcend inappropriate linear, dichotomous, and hierarchical thinking styles. The following experiential learning activities are designed to facilitate transformative learning on ingroups through narrative writing, drawing, and centering (Ferrer et al., 2005; Power & Dalgleish, 1997).

CONCRETE STRATEGIES

Experiential Learning Activities on Ingroups

Prepare drawing materials (at least two sheets of drawing paper and a box of crayons, coloring pencils, or paints). Close your eyes and breathe in and out slowly and deeply for 5 min. As you are breathing in and out slowly, think and feel how similar or different you are from other members of your race and gender ingroups. Slowly open your eyes.

1. Draw yourself in relation to your ingroups.

   a. Gender

   b. Race

2. Describe your differences and similarities in relation to your ingroups.

   a. Gender

   b. Race

3. How do you feel about your differences from your ingroups?

4. On the basis of your experience, what type of questions would you like to ask in order to find information on among- and within-group variations in relation to race and gender?

SEXISM AND INAPPROPRIATE THINKING STYLES/PATTERNS

Without dichotomous and hierarchical thinking, there is no sexism, gender discrimination, or gender biases. Gender biases, discrimination, and sexism are based on inappropriate dichotomous and hierarchical thinking styles, which consider men as more powerful and capable than women. This implies that one group is better than the other (*hierarchical thinking*). This thought pattern has been generalized to all women and all men as a group. Children learn gendered behaviors that are based on the same hierarchical thinking in early childhood, and these affect children throughout life. If children are socialized to value boys and girls equally, boys may not grow up believing they are better than girls. They may learn the difference between appropriate and inappropriate hierarchical and dichotomous thinking. Girls and boys may enjoy learning different ways of doing, thinking, and feeling from each other without insisting that their way is better than the others' way. Both boys and girls may learn to be compassionate, patient, and tolerant of each other. If children are taught that boys are strong in certain areas and girls are strong in other areas, they may learn to cooperate to make each other stronger rather than compete against or marginalize each other. If children are not forced into gender-typed behaviors, they may be able to express their true potential without being constricted by culturally defined gender-appropriate behaviors. By practicing differentiating between appropriate dichotomous thinking ("either/or") and inappropriate dichotomous thinking ("either/or") and including nondichotomous thinking ("both/and") on a daily basis, children may be able to learn to value others on the basis of their individual characteristics and qualities and not on the basis of gender alone.

⚜ STRATEGIES FOR AND BENEFITS OF DISMANTLING SEXISM

Creating a society that treats men and women with respect, justice, and equality requires (a) understanding the historical context of systematic gender oppression/privilege, (b) critically examining why systematic gender oppression/privilege is still so pervasive in everyday life, (c) being mindful of dismantling systematic gender oppression/privilege through shifting to holistic thinking, and (d) distinguishing an individual's group membership (privileged or oppressed) from that of his/her/zir personal experience. Knowing that individuals' personal experience may not be the same as their group membership is an important step toward understanding systematic gender oppression/privilege. When men do not differentiate between their group membership as men and their own individual behaviors, it is impossible for them to understand systematic gender oppression or internalized gender oppression. This is due to their belief that there is no sexism because they do not intentionally or unintentionally oppress women. They may not be perpetuating gender oppression, but this does not mean that systems (governments, institutions, organizations, etc.) have created policies, rules, or laws that treat women as equal to men.

The implementation of socialization practice that fosters gender equality from birth is essential to dismantling sexism. Gibran wrote in his 1923/1978 publication, *The Prophet:* "Your children are not your children. They are the sons and daughters of Life's longing for itself. . . . You may strive to be like them, but seek not to make them like you" (p. 17). Both men and women must stop teaching sexism and ethnocentrism to their children. They need to let their children discover life by themselves through interacting with each other. Parents need to facilitate empowerment without limiting or encouraging based on their children's gender or their own gender. It is necessary for parents not to generalize their experiences as if they are their children's. Other socialization agents like grandparents, aunts and uncles, teachers, camp counselors, and career counselors need to encourage children to empower themselves and pursue their interests on the basis of their abilities and desires and not on the basis of their gender. Children need to be socialized by watching and learning nondichotomous, nonlinear, and nonhierarchical ways of communicating with each other in order to transcend sexism.

At the personal level, individuals need to deconstruct dichotomous, linear, and hierarchical thought patterns when they are not appropriate. Transcending old ways of thinking, behaving, and feeling leads to dismantling sexism. In the process of deconstructing inappropriate dichotomous, linear, and hierarchical thinking, individuals will realize that there is no need for superiority and inferiority in interpersonal relationships. Individuals need to learn to communicate so that they will be able to work together toward workable solutions. Communicating with an "I" message instead of a "you" message is likely to facilitate workable solutions since "I" messages focus on an individual's own feelings, behaviors, and thoughts rather than blame the other (as occurs in a "you" message). The other party is likely to hear what the individual is expressing without being defensive when an "I" message is used. Women need to learn to assert themselves and not tolerate maltreatment from men. Some women learn to silence themselves while others express anger and frustration as a result of persistent sexism, sexual biases, and sexual discrimination. Being silent or expressing anger often does not convey how not to perpetuate oppression. Men need to learn to articulate their thoughts and feelings. Men, women, and transgenders need to practice accepting, respecting, and being patient with themselves and each other while learning to communicate in a nonhierarchical and nondichotomous way.

In order to reduce sexism at the institutional level, institutions need to change policies to reflect gender equality and practice gender-equality behaviors from the top down. Privilege holders at every level of an institution need to demonstrate equality-oriented behaviors. Institutions need to provide gender-equality educational programs that include deconstructing inappropriate thinking styles for employees on a regular basis, as well as recognize those who show gender-equality-oriented behaviors.

At the cultural level, individuals and institutions need to organize a group or groups to collectively demand the media show more gender-equality-based programs. Implementing gender equality collectively is still an unconventional concept at this point, and dismantling sexism at the cultural level requires the courage to be isolated from the majority. Transcending sexism and sexual discrimination at the individual, institutional, and cultural levels requires taking the path of least resistance, which requires mindfulness and courage.

Dismantling sexism at the personal, institutional, and cultural levels benefits everyone. Individuals will accept and respect each other regardless of gender. As a result, individuals will nurture each other emotionally and will be connected at the emotional level. Violence and hostility will not be plausible when there is an environment that fosters respect among individuals. Children will grow up with equal respect for men, women, and the transgendered. Individuals will learn to expand their way of being through thinking from a multidimensional, multilayered, and holistic perspective.

⚶ A PRACTITIONER'S ASSESSMENT OF SELF IN RELATION TO SEXISM, SYSTEMATIC OPPRESSION/PRIVILEGE, AND INTERNALIZED OPPRESSION/PRIVILEGE

The more practitioners are aware of their history with sexism and their relationship to systematic gender oppression/privilege and internalized gender oppression/privilege, the better prepared they are to assist clients. Practitioners' self-assessment starts with reflecting on their own gender socialization process, sociocultural contexts, and reinforcement histories in relation to sexism, sexual biases, and gender privilege and oppression. When practitioners examine their history without judgment or censoring but with critical reasoning skills, they will be able to obtain accurate self-assessment. This will assist practitioners in their attempts at accurate assessment of clients. The following is an example of a practitioner's self-assessment.

PERSONAL STORY

A Concrete Example of a Practitioner's Self-Assessment

I have a complex relationship to sexism and systematic oppression/privilege and internalized oppression/privilege. This is partly due to my multilayered socialization processes. There was a clear duality in Korean sex-role socialization when I was growing up. Girls were encouraged to achieve and excel as much as boys while they were in school. I do not remember feeling that boys and men had more power than girls and women. Sexism sets in by the time girls become a member of society by marrying or working prior to marriage. Even though I left Korea before I was aware of sexism pressure, I found myself in the same type of struggle as my friends in Korea. The role of a wife and a mother through gender socialization and newly gained knowledge on gender equality led me to want to care for both my children and my spouse while maintaining my professional career. I wanted to do the best I could in each of my roles, and I did not know how to do it well. There was not enough time in a day to do all I wanted to do for them and me. Each day, I had to figure out how to balance my roles for that day. I had to prioritize what was important on that day, and it was hard since I wanted to do everything and each item seemed equally important. I just could not put my needs and desires first. Socialization, the role of a wife as defined by my culture, wanting to express love in action, and my own personality played a significant role in perpetuating sexism through internalized oppression.

I grew up in a family where my mother's main role was being my father's wife, and she was content with her role. She used to tell me it was very important that I put my husband first when I got married. She would say this while she was preparing food for my father. I thought it was foolish of her to prepare food for my father since she had a person whose job was doing housework and cooking. She told me she had to prepare the food for my father since he liked her cooking more than that of the person who was hired to do the housework. It was amazing to watch her taking such pride in being a good wife and deriving such happiness from it. I thought it sounded boring, and my mother seemed more like my father's personal maid than a wife. However, I was surprised to find out how similar I was to my mother in terms of putting my husband's needs and wishes before mine—although I was very different from her in seeking a career while simultaneously maintaining my role as a wife and a mother. Without conscious awareness, I bought into strong Korean cultural myths, which state that marriage is a life commitment and women should stay married regardless of whether it is working out emotionally, psychologically, or spiritually. It took me a long time to figure out that staying in a sexism-based relationship perpetuates multigenerational sexism.

The author fluctuated in and out of internalized sexism due to childhood conditioning and persistent cultural myths on gender inequality in the United States. The power of learning through observation is apparent in her criticism of her mother's behavior, but she was following her mother and cultural gendered behavior. She was not able to sort out how much of putting members of her family first was due to her love for them and how much was due to ingrained sex-role conditioning in the broader social context. Her story shows a nonlinear and dynamic interaction between her family values and a broader cultural value; she put the cultural value ahead of her family values as a result of being surrounded by models who practiced gendered behaviors and the values put on these behaviors by them. The following reflection-based learning activities are designed to assess practitioner-trainees' gender construction history.

CONCRETE STRATEGIES

Experiential Learning Activities on Gender

1. Describe your relationship to your immediate family members from a gender perspective.

2. Identify sexism, gender bias, systematic oppression/privilege, and internalized oppression/privilege from your description.

3. Describe your experience in elementary, middle, and high school in relation to gender emphasis.

   a. Describe the impact of your experiences on you now.

4. How do the experiences described in Questions 1–3 affect you now in relation to your gender and in relation to other genders?

5. What is the most important thing you have learned by completing these experiential learning activities?

CONCRETE STRATEGIES

Consciousness Practice

What is it like being you in relation to your gender now?

6

Heterosexism

In this chapter, the differences among sexual orientation, homophobia, and heterosexism are described briefly. The impact of heterosexism on an individual's identity construction, internalized oppression/privilege, and internalized homophobia is explored in relation to the person's intersection of multiple identities. Particular attention is paid to early ingroup (family) rejection and its impact on the internalized oppression of nonheterosexuals. Variations within and among nonheterosexual individuals are discussed not only with regard to different salient characteristics of multiple identities and their intersection but also according to different theories of sexual orientation. Dismantling heterosexism at the personal, interpersonal, and institutional level is discussed. The chapter ends with experiential learning activities for practitioner-trainees to assess themselves in relation to their heterosexism, homophobia, and internalized oppression/privilege.

DIFFERENCES AMONG SEXUAL ORIENTATION, HOMOPHOBIA, AND HETEROSEXISM

As defined in the previous chapter, sexual orientation is to whom individuals are attracted sexually. Heterosexuals—those who are attracted to members of the opposite sex—are considered the norm in the United States. Homosexuals include men who are sexually attracted to members of the same sex and lesbian women who are sexually attracted to members of the same sex; bisexuals are sexually attracted to members of both the same and the opposite sex; and transgendered people are individuals who cross gender and may be attracted to members of both sexes but who may or may not want to change their anatomical structure. Transvestites, who do not intend to have sex-change surgery, include males who live as women and females who live as men (e.g., Billy Tipton, a woman, lived most of her life as a man and had a wife and three adopted sons). Bisexuals' and transgenders' concept of sexual identity challenges some heterosexuals whose dichotomous thinking style does not allow them to conceptualize sexual identity in flexible and fluid terms. Sexual orientation is only one aspect of a whole person, and it is a private aspect.

PERSONAL FEEDBACK

The following are some of my former students' responses to one of the multicultural counseling textbooks they were assigned:

> I am gay and the textbook perpetuates homosexual oppression. I feel this is done through the "common" labels that are used to define sexuality. This is extremely detrimental and limiting to anyone who does not fit in these boxes. Another example is the model of "Gay, Lesbian, and Bisexual Identity Formation." By making a list of how someone "becomes" gay, or at least aware of it, you are in a sense making homosexuality abnormal. I am enraged that there is not a model of "Heterosexual Identity Formation." I wonder who made the decisions about what is natural, normal, or standard? What I keep coming up with is that for the most part, white, upper/middle class, Christian men have sanctioned a code of conduct based on a system that benefits them and the position of power they hold. I see the power I have to change myself, but I feel more and more powerless against a system that feeds off of oppression.
>
> —Brad, 2005

> I can imagine it would be very tempting to not ask my clients pertinent questions for fear of making a fool of myself. But it is not ignorance that is the problem; it is what we do about our ignorance that will impact others and self, for better or for worse. Our textbook is a great example: Obviously it was created by people willing to make mistakes, and make mistakes they did: Their cursory treatment of transgender issues in the section on sexuality and the equally brief discussion of heterosexual identity development were problematic. The book's errors did give me ample opportunity to exercise my critical thinking skills. I just wish its authors had the courage and humility to preface the text with an overt admission of the book's flaws, instead of insisting the reader imagine that the book is a final authority on multicultural counseling.
>
> —Sarah, 2005

According to Blumenfeld (2000a), homophobia is "the fear and hatred of those who love and sexually desire those of the same sex. Homophobia includes prejudice, discrimination, harassment, and acts of violence brought on by that fear and hatred" (p. 263). Homophobia is one component of heterosexism (Thompson & Zoloth, 1989). Heterosexism is the institutionalized heteronormativity that perpetuates systematic oppression of those who have a nonheterosexual orientation (Kidd & Witten, 2008). "At times subtle, heterosexism is oppression by neglect, omission, erasure, and distortion" (Blumenfeld, 2000a, pp. 262–263). Heterosexism is socially constructed systematic advantages for heterosexuals on the basis of sexual orientation, and it includes heterosexual biases, discrimination, and prejudices. But it is more than minimization of, marginalization of, and belittling of nonheterosexuals. It is systematic privilege given to heterosexuals and systematic oppression of nonheterosexuals (Blumenfeld, 2000b). Heterosexism and homophobia lead some people to commit extreme violence against people who are only attempting to be themselves but who are doing so in a way that does not go along with socially constructed heteronormativity. Homophobia killed Matthew Shepard, a 21-year-old college student; Billy Jack Gaither, a 39-year-old gay man; and Brandon Teena, a transgendered individual (female to male). These people were killed because of who they were. David Warfield motivated students who were labeled "unmotivated" in high school and created an award-winning media communications academy but lost his job when he became Dana Rivers (Luschen & Bogad, 2003). Rivers was fired not because she was an incompetent teacher but because she became herself, which did not fit with the heterosexual standard. One gay student asked a question to the class:

> Why do I want to choose to be gay when the cost is so high? I am rejected by my parents, siblings, some friends, and relatives. There is a hole in my heart. I miss them. It's been very painful. Why do I want to choose pain?
>
> —Mike, 2001

The following reflection-based learning activities are designed to explore sexual orientation identity construction through transformative learning (Ferrer, Romero, & Albareda, 2005; Power & Dalgleish, 1997).

CONCRETE STRATEGIES

Reflection-Based Learning Activities

Close your eyes and breathe in and out slowly and deeply for 5 min. As you breathe, go back in your timeline as far as you can to see whether you recall an experience with sexual orientation during your childhood. Slowly open your eyes.

1. Describe your experience with sexual orientation.
   a. How did you feel about it then, and how do you feel about it now?
   b. Did you share your experience with someone? If so, with whom did you share it, and what was his/her/zir response?
   c. If you did not share it with anyone, what did you do with it?
   d. What was your feeling about your sexual orientation and other sexual orientations?
   e. What did you learn from your mother (or mother figure) about your sexual orientation?
   f. What did you learn from your father (or father figure) about your sexual orientation?
   g. What did you learn from your siblings (or sibling figures) about your sexual orientation?
   h. What did you learn from your teachers about your sexual orientation?
   i. If your parents applied heterosexuality-oriented socialization practice, what was the main message? How does this message affect you now?

SOCIAL CONSTRUCTION OF HETEROSEXISM

Heterosexism is systematic advantages for heterosexual individuals as a group on the basis of their sexual orientation over individuals with a non-heterosexual orientation. This means governmental, institutional, and organizational policies, laws, and rules are written to favor heterosexual men and women and unfairly discriminate against and oppress homosexuals, bisexuals, and the transgendered.

Institutional and Governmental Heterosexism

Institutional heterosexism and organizational heterosexism have been supported by governmental heterosexism. For example, two employees may receive different treatment on the basis of their sexual orientation due to unequal and unfair institutional and governmental policies. Institutions and organizations that provide health insurance to their employees often discriminate against nonheterosexual employees by not providing health insurance benefits for their partners while full health insurance benefits are given to the spouses of married employees. Sexual orientation is to whom an individual is attracted sexually, and expression of sexual attraction usually takes place in the private life of an individual and has nothing to do with an employee's ability to perform his/her/zir job. However, most nonheterosexual employees have been discriminated against at work not because of their quality of work performance but because of their sexual orientation.

One of the main governmental practices of heterosexism is banning nonheterosexual marriage in most U.S. states. Institutional heterosexism and governmental heterosexism are taking away the rights of nonheterosexual individuals not because of their actions but because of possible negative actions on the basis of who they are even though who they are does not interfere with what they do as employees or as citizens. Nonheterosexuals are not dangerous to others or themselves because of their nonheterosexuality, but institutional heterosexism and governmental heterosexism assume that they are dangerous to others and may become dangerous to themselves as a consequence of their nonheterosexuality. For the past 35 years, institutional heterosexism has been pervasive even in professional organizations such as the American Psychiatric Association. The APA considered a heterosexual orientation as the norm and considered homosexuality abnormal until 1973. Despite the disappearance of abnormality from the *DSM* in 1973, individuals with nonheterosexual orientation have been continuously devalued and pathologized within the counseling professions (Douce, 1998; Lucksted, 2004).

Internalized Oppression

Belief systems in relation to social identities are not based on factual information. They are constructed on the basis of cultural, societal, institutional, and family myths. Such belief systems perpetuate racism, sexism, classism, heterosexism, ageism, and other "isms." Most of them are based on dichotomous and hierarchical thinking that one belief is "right," "correct," and "better" than the others. Individuals with a nonheterosexual orientation as well as individuals with heterosexual orientation are conditioned to believe that something is wrong with or abnormal about nonheterosexual individuals (Garofalo, Wolf, Wissow, Woods, & Goodman, 1999; Remafedi, Farrow, & Deisher, 1991). One distinctively different characteristic of nonheterosexual individuals is common rejection by their primary ingroup, their immediate family.

Individuals who are targets of racism, sexism, classism, ableism, and other "isms" generally are not rejected by their own family due to who they are (i.e., a person of color, female, poor, or disabled). However, numerous individuals who are nonheterosexual often report rejection by their own family (Monette, 2004; Rich, 1990). Internalized oppression for nonheterosexual individuals may be more intense due to family rejection compared to that for other oppressed groups who have family support in dealing with the dominant culture. Harrison's foreword to Monette's book, *Becoming a Man*, depicts the psychological process of sense of self and internal and external isolation and secrecy of non-heterosexual orientation:

> When Paul Monette was nine and a half, and "primed for the sort of guilt that seals off all exits," his mother caught him and another boy with their pants unzipped and asked him what they were doing. "Nothing," he lied, and in that moment his life changed. His mother's suspicions, in no way alleviated by the lie, and his instinctive need to hide what he'd only just begun to understand as a pivotal—and disgraceful—difference between him and other boys predicted an alienation that would grow beyond his mother, ultimately separating Monette not only from most of the people with whom he came into contact but also, and much more destructively, from himself. (Monette, 2004, p. xiv)

Monette was socialized to believe he is "disgraceful" just like many individuals who are nonheterosexuals. Prossor's (1998) study indicated that parents tend to insist their children and adolescents have a heterosexual orientation even if their children and adolescents express a nonheterosexual orientation. "The implicit message my family gave me was not so much a condemnation as an embarrassed tolerance inextricably tied to a plea for secrecy" (Adams et al., 2000, p. 297). Rich (1990) also described family rejection as the worst prejudice. She struggled with the belief that others could not accept her if her family could not accept her, even though she understood the possibility of others accepting her intellectually. Her emotional pain from family rejection was overpowering her intellectual understanding. Struggling to be "normal," one of the author's former students, who was in his early 20s, fasted for 12 days to see whether he could be a heterosexual because his parents rejected him when he came out to them as a homosexual. They told him God could make him "normal" if he prayed hard enough. He thought his faith was as strong as his parents' and did not understand why God was not making him normal. Both his church and his parents disowned him, and his sense of self was shattered again because he was told—and he believed—that his church and his parents would always be there for him.

Most nonheterosexual individuals struggle internally due to heteronormativity around them from an early age. Being rejected by family because of who they are increases their feelings of alienation, isolation, and self-doubt. It is likely that such children learn to internalize their family's rejection and have difficulty transcending self-acceptance or others' acceptance in their adult life. As Rich (1990) stated, it is hard to transcend what is ingrained in early life, even after intellectual comprehension of family rejection. Nonheterosexuals deal with persistent systematic institutional and governmental oppression, family rejection, and peer rejection on a daily basis. It is understandable why the suicide rate is high among transgendered, gay, bisexual, and lesbian individuals compared to heterosexuals. The suicide rate for LGBT (lesbian, gay, bisexual, and transgender) youth is two to three times higher than for heterosexual youth. The suicide rate is also high among Afro American gay men compared to Afro American heterosexuals (Gibbs, 1997). The following reflection-based exercise is designed to raise awareness of heterosexism.

CONCRETE STRATEGIES

Experiential Learning Exercise

As you reflect on all the jobs you have had since you were old enough to have a job, how many of your jobs required you to be of a certain sexual orientation?

Internalized Homophobia

Homophobia is irrational fear of homosexuals and/or homosexuality and fear ranging from uncomfortable and uneasy feelings to feelings of intense hatred. Some of these feelings are from concern that others might think one is gay, and some of these feelings are from unconscious self-doubt about one's own sexual orientation (Adams, Wright, & Lohr, 1996; Herek, 2004; Riddle, 1985). Internalized homophobia is conscious or unconscious attempts to carry out heterosexism due to religious beliefs or heterosexual socialization and/or to repress one's homosexual desires (Adams et al., 1996). Discussing racism, sexism, classism, and other "isms" brings more intense feelings to those who have been personally and/or institutionally oppressed and marginalized than to individuals who were, who are, or who represent the oppressor. However, discussing homosexuality brings intense emotional reactions to individuals representing both the oppressed and the oppressor. This may be due to internalized homophobia.

When the author taught human sexuality, she observed how difficult it was for some students to differentiate between academic knowledge about homosexuality and their religious conditioning on homosexuality. Students who believed from their religious perspective that homosexuality was a sin were critical of homosexuals. Their emotional attachment to their religion hindered their academic learning. They insisted that homosexuality is a "sin" in "God's" eyes, yet they were not able to support their beliefs with evidence. Some students wanted to believe that homosexuals are the same as pedophiles despite the textbook's description that typical pedophiles are heterosexuals. Some heterosexual students insisted that they were against homosexuals being teachers because they were concerned about homosexual teachers' impact on children's sexual orientation. These students did not want to admit that it was their assumption that such teachers would influence children to become homosexuals because they believed it was a fact. These students' belief system would not allow them to hear that most jobs do not require an individual to be a certain sexual orientation and there is a wide range of teachers (good, bad, and in between; highly qualified, not qualified, and in between) with variations in sexual orientation. The issue of homosexuality seemed to stir a different set of deep emotions within these students, and these emotions created barriers against their learning. As a result, these students were not open to discussions like the following:

1. Limit to generalizability: If one homosexual teacher crosses the professional boundary in order to try to influence a student's sexual orientation, could people generalize such an action to all homosexual

teachers? Does that particular teacher represent the whole homosexual population? Remember a sample size of one $(N = 1)$ is not the
same as a sample size that represents a whole population $(N = all)$.

2. Have you known heterosexual teachers who cross the student-
   teacher boundary, which is as unethical as a homosexual teacher
   crossing the student-teacher boundary? Why do people not get as
   upset with heterosexual teachers as with homosexual teachers? Are
   heterosexual teachers not influencing children's sexuality as much
   as homosexual teachers?

3. If heterosexual teachers influence their students' sexuality, why do
   some students become homosexuals?

The following experiential learning activities are intended to introduce
compassion for others by taking an affective perspective position.

CONCRETE STRATEGIES

Experiential Learning Activities

1. In your mind, think about a TV commercial and change it for homosexual viewers.

2. Look around and observe events in your environments for a week,
   report back to class, and discuss your findings with other students.

3. Imagine yourself living in a homosexual world and that you are the
   only heterosexual. Write down your feelings.

4. For heterosexuals:
   a. Think and feel about how homosexuals feel in this heterosexual world.

5. For nonheterosexuals:
   a. How did you feel in your imaginary homosexual world?
   b. What can heterosexuals do to make you feel equal to them?

For most heterosexuals, it is difficult to examine the impact of sociocultural contexts of heterosexism and homophobia on nonheterosexuals. As indicated in previous chapters, privileges are invisible
to privilege holders. Experiential learning activities like those above
increase the possibility of transformative learning. These activities

force heterosexuals to pay attention to sexual orientation issues. Often they become aware that almost all events around them are comfortable for them because they are heterosexuals. Nonheterosexuals report that they are discriminated against on a daily basis because the world is heterosexual. Some homosexuals report that it is nice to be treated "normal" in their imagined homosexual world. They may say it is nice because they do not in their imagination have to deal with systematic oppression, marginalization, heterosexism, and homophobia. Some heterosexuals may be emotional because they are not able to put themselves in nonheterosexuals' place due to either their ingrained heteronormativity or their internalized homophobia. Some heterosexuals may be emotionally upset due to awareness of their insensitivity toward nonheterosexuals.

Ingroups Versus Outgroups
Within the Nonheterosexual Community

Although most individuals with a nonheterosexual orientation agree there is systematic oppression by heterosexuals as a group, at times they are not able to be supportive of other nonheterosexual groups. There is tension between some homosexuals and some bisexuals because some gay and lesbian individuals often do not accept bisexuals and transgenders. Deihl and Ochs (2000) discuss the inconsistencies among gay and lesbian liberation movements. The movement postulates their right to love whomever they please and their desire to be validated as who they are, but it excludes bisexual individuals. "When women and men come out as bisexuals, their gay and lesbian friends often tell them that they cannot really be bisexuals—that they are confused, or they are waiting to reap the benefits of heterosexism" (Adams et al., 2000, p. 279).

Transgender people cross gender and/or anatomical sex barriers. There are biologically female transgenders whose gender identity is male. They dress like men, change their name to a male name, and are interested in dating females. However, they have no desire to anatomically change to match their gender identity. Then, there are biologically female transgenders whose gender identity is male and who change their sex through surgical and hormonal treatment. There are biological males whose gender identity is female. They dress like females and are interested in dating males. Some of them change their biological sex and become women while other male transgenders dress like females and prefer to have relationships with biological females without changing their anatomical sex. Both bisexuals and transgenders transcend gender dichotomy and operate within a wider range of the gender spectrum than heterosexuals, gay men, and lesbians.

The inconsistencies among gay and lesbian liberation movements and the marginalization of bisexuals ("confused," "reap the benefits of heterosexism," etc.) might have been due to their dichotomous and hierarchical thinking styles/patterns, their tendency toward ingroup loyalty, or social projection. Inconsistencies and the lack of support for other nonheterosexual groups indicate that nonheterosexuals are affected by the dominant cultural values and beliefs that foster ethnocentric bias just like some heterosexuals. Even though they want others to transcend their hierarchical and dichotomous thinking styles/patterns to understand them (nonheterosexuals), they are not able to transcend their own embedded inappropriate hierarchical and dichotomous thinking styles to understand other nonheterosexual groups. Ethnocentrism and inappropriate thinking patterns are embedded in the American psyche (Singer & Kimbles, 2004; Takaki, 1993). Transcending these thought patterns and beliefs requires much more than intellectual understanding.

INTERSECTIONS OF RACE, GENDER, AND SEXUAL ORIENTATION

It is not possible to discretely figure out the impact of a single aspect of identity because of the intersections of multiple identities and their interlocking tendencies (Fukuyama & Ferguson, 2000; Gallor, 2005; Greene, 2000; Mobley, 1998). Holistic thinking, which examines both the details, such as the multilayered and multidimensional aspects of a person, and the whole picture needs to be implemented to understand the multiple identities of an individual within a sociocultural context. Croteau and Constantine (2005) eloquently summarize the importance of conceptualizing the intersection of multiple identities in understanding a person's worldview. There is no way to understand an individual fully without applying a holistic approach. An individual belongs to multiple "sociodemographic groups," which can be salient, "can be the basis for identity,

[and] can interact with one another in shaping experiences" (Croteau, Lark, Lidderdale, & Chung, 2005, p. 162). It is impossible to separate multiple identities because they are interwoven and intersect with each other. Gallor (2005) writes:

> I am a woman. I am a lesbian. I am Hispanic, with Spanish, Cuban, and Middle Eastern heritage. . . . I have never, however, articulated how these separate identities blend together to form and influence one whole "me," nor have I ever discussed how these identities have interacted with one another to influence my reality and worldview. . . . It is extremely difficult, maybe even impossible, to adequately illustrate how the heterosexist dominant discourse has had implications for me personally and professionally. The main reason for this difficulty is that it is impossible to separate my lesbian self from my Hispanic self or my gendered self from my lesbian self. (pp. 71–72)

Other scholars also propose treating issues of gay, lesbian, and bisexual identities as dependent on other identities (e.g., race, gender, class, age, disability) and related to sociocultural contexts (Bowman, 2003; Fukuyama & Ferguson, 2000; Greene, 2000; Morrow, 2003; Phillips, Ingram, Grant Smith, & Mindes, 2003). The concepts of interrelation and interdependence are key to understanding the intersections among race, gender, sexual orientation, class, disability, age, religion, region, and language. Understanding these concepts requires an individual to transcend inappropriate dichotomous and hierarchical thinking in order to conceptualize from a holistic perspective. The ability to understand the dynamics and complexities of the intersection of multiple identities within various sociocultural contexts requires fluid thinking (Lim-Hing, 2000). Fluid thinking operates within a wide spectrum from appropriate dichotomous, hierarchical thinking to diunital (both/and) and holistic thinking while maintaining the ability to critically examine the multidimensional and multilayered dimensions of multiple identities. Understanding these concepts from a multidimensional and multilayered perspective is necessary for transcendence but not sufficient for transcendence to occur. Mindful and persistent practice of applying these concepts in daily life needs to be followed for transformative learning. The following are experiential learning activities on the intersections of race, gender, and sexual orientation.

CONCRETE STRATEGIES

Experiential Learning Activities

Prepare drawing materials (at least two sheets of drawing paper and a box of crayons, coloring pencils, or paints). Close your eyes and breathe in and out slowly, evenly, and deeply for 5 min. As you are breathing in and out slowly, think and feel about your intersection of race, gender, and sexual orientation. Slowly open your eyes.

1. Draw your intersection of race, gender, and sexual orientation.

2. Write about what you drew.

3. Do you ever feel pressured to be loyal to your race, gender, or sexual orientation by members of one community?

   a. How do you feel when you are pressured?

   b. How do you balance your need to be loyal to your inner beliefs and your communities' requests?

   c. How is your narrative similar to and different from that of each of your communities (race, gender, and sexual orientation)?

There are numerous distinct variations in how an individual's multiple identities are experienced within him/her/zir. For some, all three identities (race, gender, and sexual orientation) function as salient identities, and for others, they vary according to sociocultural contexts or interact with each other to create a particular experience. Complexities in interrelationship and interdependence increase depending on whether the individual is a member of privileged group or an oppressed group or on the individual's own experience with being a member of a privileged group or an oppressed group with a particular identity—for example, a nonheterosexual, White woman who has been accepted for who she is by her family in relation to her sexual orientation but who has experienced institutional sexism throughout the socialization process. She may feel oppressed as a woman and not feel privilege as a White woman, but she may not feel she was oppressed due to her sexual orientation. Her identity construction and sense of self may be very different from that of a White woman who has been rejected by her family due to her sexual orientation in addition to experiencing institutional sexism throughout the socialization process. To discover how the intersections of multiple identities (race, gender, and sexual orientation) affect the identity construction of an individual, practitioners need to examine the individual's story from a holistic perspective.

CONCRETE STRATEGIES

Experiential Learning Activities

1. Indicate whether you belong to a privileged group or an oppressed group in relation to the following identities: (a) race, (b) gender, and (c) sexual orientation. Think about your answer to the question not in terms of whether or not you feel privileged but in terms of whether or not you belong to a privileged group according to your society.

2. Which of the above identities are important to you? Rank the above identities in order of importance, with 1 being the most important to you and 3 being the least important to you in relation to your identity construction. You can assign one number to more than one identity if they hold equal importance for you.

3. Close your eyes and breathe in and out slowly and evenly for 5 min. Pay attention to your feelings and the images that come to mind as you breathe. Slowly open your eyes and record or draw your feelings and/or images.

4. What have you learned from these activities?

〽️ SYSTEMATIC OPPRESSION/PRIVILEGE AND INTERNALIZED OPPRESSION/PRIVILEGE

Examining multiple identities simultaneously with their relationships to systematic oppression/privilege and internalized oppression/privilege becomes more complex because individuals' multiple identities not only interact with each other but also have different degrees of importance. In addition, they are affected by sociocultural contexts. Most internalized oppression and privilege operates unconsciously, and it is difficult to separate how much is from which identity. It is especially difficult to assess internalized sexual orientation oppression since children learn at an early age from their own family and other social agents such as schools, churches, the media, and storybooks that having a nonheterosexual orientation is not acceptable (Coie & Dodge, 1998; Crick, 1996; Giles & Heyman, 2005; Herek, 2000; hooks, 2000; Maccoby, 1998, 2002; Monette, 2004; Ruble & Martin, 1998; Zhang, Lingin, Zhang, Wang, & Chen, 2003). Monette's *Becoming a Man*, which depicts his own journey as a gay man in a heterosexual context, portrays how internalized oppression is shaped at an early age. His story reflects the powerful influence of heterosexual gender socialization on the development of self, describing unintentional cruelty toward non-gender-typed behaviors and its impact on nonheterosexual orientation development. Three studies conducted by Giles and Heyman showed early childhood learning of gendered behaviors. According to these studies, preschool children (ranging in age for the first study from 3.6 to 5.0 years, for the second study from 3.1 to 5.3 years, and for the third study from 3.1 to 4.1 years) perceive their world according to gendered beliefs regardless of their racial backgrounds. Other studies showed children's strong desire to support their beliefs. Children distorted situations in order to make them congruent with their beliefs on gender (Liben & Signorella, 1993; Susskind, 2003). These studies imply that the impact of systematic gender oppression/privilege and internalized gender oppression/privilege on children's development of self starts before they have developed clear critical reasoning skills. Research also showed that marginalized children exhibit similar characteristics to those of adults who are oppressed. These children were more aware of discrimination than the children from the dominant groups. They also noticed discrimination affecting them negatively (Altschul, Oyserman, & Bybee, 2006; Brody et al., 2006; Brown & Bigler, 2004, 2005; McKown & Weinstein, 2004; Pahl & Way, 2006). Research also showed that children of color are influenced much more by sociocultural contexts than White children, and these have implications in their classroom learning (Garcia Coll, Crnic, Lamberty, & Wasik, 1996).

It is apparent from these studies that internalized oppression/privilege starts before children are able to differentiate between facts and beliefs, and children's beliefs, values, and biases are shaped by the power of their social agents such as parents, teachers, churches, and the media. Due to ingroup loyalty, social projection, or asymmetric perception, children may leap to generalizations and/or accept social agents' beliefs and values as if they are facts.

In order to develop holistic thinking styles, individuals need to understand the role of internalized oppression/privilege and systematic oppression/privilege. It is not enough to shift from one personal thinking style to another without dismantling institutional and governmental heterosexism. The following experiential learning activities are designed for transformative learning about internalized oppression/privilege and systematic oppression/privilege.

CONCRETE STRATEGIES

Experiential Learning Activities on Internalized Oppression/Privilege and Systematic Oppression/Privilege

Keep an emotional diary for at least 10 days without analyzing the content. Your emotional diary should focus on how you felt about your interpersonal and intrapersonal relationships throughout the day. It should not describe what you did that day but how you felt about doing whatever you did. (See Chapter 2's experiential learning activities for an example.) Pay particular attention to your intrapersonal communication and keep your diary without censoring.

1. Go back to each journal entry 10 days later to critically examine the impact of internalized oppression/privilege and systematic oppression/privilege on each day. Tally whether your emotions were due to systematic oppression/privilege or due to internalized oppression/privilege.

2. Indicate whether you belong to a privileged group or an oppressed group in relation to the following identities: (a) race, (b) gender, and (c) sexual orientation. Remember to think about your answer not in terms of whether or not you feel privileged but in terms of whether or not you belong to a privileged group according to your society.

3. Which of the above identities are important to you? Rank the above identities in order of importance, with 1 being the most important and 4 being the least important in relation to your identity construction. What did you learn about yourself by comparing your tallies in Question 1 and your identity ranks in Question 3?

4. Close your eyes and breathe in and out slowly, evenly, and deeply for 5 min. Pay attention to your feelings and the images that come to mind as you breathe. Slowly open your eyes and write or draw your feelings and/or images.

5. What was your understanding about systematic privilege and oppression before you read this book, and what is your understanding about them now?

6. Discuss your understanding of systematic oppression/privilege and internalized oppression/privilege with others who have participated in the same experiential learning activities of this section.

Automatic Activation

As indicated in previous chapters, stereotypes, biases, prejudices, and beliefs are activated automatically. Internalized oppression/privilege, heterosexism, and homophobia are all part of beliefs, biases, and stereotypes, which are learned through early socialization. Cognitive and social psychology research in unconscious processing of stereotypes, prejudice, and implicit learning sheds light on the difficulty in transcending racism, sexism, heterosexism, and other "isms" due to automatic activation (Banaji & Greenwald, 1994; Chen & Bargh, 1997; Greenwald & Banaji, 1995; Henderson-King & Nisbett, 1996). Any strategies to dismantle heterosexism, homophobia, and internalized oppression/privilege need to consider the fact that automatic activation is from unconscious processing and develop methods to deal with stopping the automatic activation process. Transformative learning needs to take place to dismantle the automatic activation process prior to activation.

⟫ VARIATIONS WITHIN AND AMONG NONHETEROSEXUALS

Sexual orientation is a part of a person's whole identity. Other identities such as race, gender, class, disability, age, region, language, and religion interact with individuals' sexual orientation. Nonheterosexual individuals cannot be categorized as the same since there are various types of nonheterosexual orientation. In addition, each type of nonheterosexual orientation encompasses a wide range of differences according to sociocultural contexts and relationships with and dependence on other identities. In other words, there are variations among gay men, among lesbians, among bisexuals, and among transgenders as well as variations among all four types of nonheterosexuals as a group. Nonheterosexual orientation theories vary in their conceptualization of sexual identity. Both constructionists and essentialists believe individuals have stable sexual identity over their life span whereas queer theorists question the existence of a stable sexual identity (Gross, 2005). Queer theory's foundation is based on Foucault's (1990) idea of poststructuralism. Queer theorists propose deconstruction of conventional gender and sexual identity categories by postulating that sexual identity is not static and is changeable over the life span of an individual. Queer theories also include a wide range of sexual practices and sexual identities while challenging the biology of sex dichotomy as male or female. They argue that the discrete biological category of sex chromosomes to differentiate male (XY) and female (XX) excludes individuals who are missing one X chromosome (XO, Turner syndrome), individuals who have more than one X chromosome (XXY, Klinefelter syndrome), pseudohermaphrodites (who have either ovaries or testes with the opposite genitalia), true hermaphrodites (who have an ovary and a testis or a combined gonad), and "a six-day-old XX child with masculinized external genitalia" (Fausto-Sterling, 2000, p. 47). Labeling these individuals as men or women is determined by beliefs about gender and not by scientific information (Fausto-Sterling). Queer theory is not limited to sexual and gender identity or orientation. It extends to art, poetry, and politics. There are variations among different nonheterosexual groups in their perceptions of dominant models of homosexuality (Bolin, 1987; Marotta, 1981). Media representations of nonheterosexual models are mostly Euro White Americans and some Afro Americans. For example, some people of color with nonheterosexual orientation believe that they are not represented within the homosexual community since the dominant homosexual models represent White and middle-class values (Seidman, 1993). There are variations in region and its intersection with other identities such as race, gender, class, impairment/disability, age, language, and religion. Variations within a particular group of individuals with nonheterosexual orientation (i.e., transgender, bisexual, gay, lesbian) along with the multidimensional and multilayered intersections with other identities lead to a wide spectrum of multiple identities. The urban and rural experiences of gay men vary depending on intersections of race, social class, and other multiple identities. For example, Black gay men were racially discriminated against according to the Eurocentric standards of urban gay communities while these communities provided a sanctuary for White gay men (Green, 2007).

A practitioner's ability to assess an individual client without perceiving him/her/zir through the practitioner's own assumptions about nonheterosexual orientation is crucial in being aware of variations among nonheterosexuals as well as within a single nonheterosexual individual. The practitioner needs to be familiar with up-to-date research in the area of LGBT while having the ability to listen attentively to the client's narrative and observe the client's body language. A practitioner not only needs to attentively listen to the client's story but also needs to ask appropriate questions in relation to the intersections of race, gender, class, age, religion, and other identities in order to understand the client's experience as a nonheterosexual individual in complex sociocultural contexts.

The following personal story illustrates the intersection of race and sexual orientation. The story depicts prejudice against a nondominant sexual orientation by a nondominant racial group.

PERSONAL STORY

Asian and Gay

I have known a Vietnamese friend for 15 years. By the time we became good friends, he was a well-established professional who was looking for his future wife. He often shared the qualities he was looking for in a woman. He said he was interested in a woman's inner beauty. Some time ago, he invited a few friends over for dinner and fixed a delicious meal with the help of his male "friend." He never introduced his male friend as his partner, and it took me a long time to figure out they were indeed partners.

I invited him and his partner over for dinner, and he showed up alone about an hour late. He was always punctual, and I wondered whether he was OK. When he arrived, he was nervous, and I had never seen him that nervous before. When I asked him when he realized his sexual orientation, he told me he knew a long time ago but could not admit it to himself or to anyone else. He said it was taboo in his culture, and he tried to be "heterosexual" for a long time. That was why he was dating women, but he just could not go through with it. He said he knew intellectually I would accept him as a friend no matter what, but he could not bring himself to

(Continued)

(Continued)

tell me the truth. It was his partner who initiated the relationship because his partner could tell that he was gay. He said it is difficult to be gay and Vietnamese, explaining that his parents and siblings accept him but he can tell they wish he were straight. His parents, just like many Asian parents, want their children to have Vietnamese partners, and all of his siblings fulfilled his parents' desire except him. His partner is White.

My friend is much more comfortable around White people as a gay man, but he is loyal to his parents and siblings. He is also close to his Vietnamese community, whose members are not open to nonheterosexual relationships. He struggles with his multiple identities. Both being Vietnamese and being gay are equally salient to him.

HETEROSEXISM OR HOMOPHOBIA AND INAPPROPRIATE THINKING STYLES/PATTERNS

Both homophobia and heterosexism are examples of inappropriate dichotomous and hierarchical thinking. Both homophobes and heterosexists base their claim on an assumption that their standards are the norm, that they are right (*dichotomy*), and that everybody should be heterosexual. Directing hatred toward other people who have different concepts about sexual identity and committing violent acts against them (*dichotomy*) is to assume that one way is not only the right way to live but also the better way to live (*hierarchical thinking*). Homophobes oppress people with a nonheterosexual orientation on the personal, interpersonal, institutional, and cultural levels (Blumenfeld, 2000b; Thompson & Zoloth, 1989). If children are socialized to think from a diunital ("either/or" and "both/and") perspective and from a holistic perspective, they will critically examine the relationship between an individual's sexual orientation and systematic oppression. Holistic thinking provides the potential to value the differences as well as the similarities in human diversity. However, if children are socialized to think from a holistic perspective, they need to be in a sociocultural context that encourages and fosters a holistic thinking style. As long as the social context is heteronormativity oriented, dismantling heterosexism will not be possible.

STRATEGIES FOR AND BENEFITS OF DISMANTLING HETEROSEXISM

The first step toward dismantling heterosexism is learning to deconstruct inappropriate dichotomous and hierarchical thinking styles/patterns. The second step is understanding that a person's sexual orientation can only be understood in relation to other identities such as race, gender, class, age, disability, religion, region, and language. The third step is examining the impact of dominant oppressive discourse at the individual, interpersonal, and institutional levels on individuals with a nonheterosexual orientation. The fourth step is being ready to abandon taking the path of least resistance. Taking the path of least resistance perpetuates heterosexism. If each individual takes personal responsibility to raise consciousness on dismantling heterosexism at the personal and interpersonal levels, it will soon be spread to the institutional and cultural levels. Systematic oppression has been perpetuated by people within government (states, counties, cities, etc.), institutions (schools, colleges, universities, etc.), organizations, and society. It is each individual's responsibility to change the system by taking personal responsibility. For example, if someone says, "Homosexuals want their way all the time," you may want to ask the person to elaborate or define "all the time." You may ask a question like "Don't we, heterosexuals, want our way all the time, too?" Or you may want to say, "I do not understand your comment since we, heterosexuals, get systematic benefits that others don't get, such as health insurance benefits for our children and partner. We can marry anyone we want. The government does not tell us it doesn't recognize our marriage." It is at times difficult to take an initiative with sensitive issues.

The other way to dismantle heterosexism at the interpersonal level is to be a good listener for nonheterosexual individuals. Listening does not mean one has to feel guilty for being heterosexual. Listening means paying attention to other people with compassion.

At the institutional level, individuals can be allies for nonheterosexual individuals as a group and assist them in their attempt to change institutional or organizational policies. Individuals may organize a review of existing TV programs from children's programs including cartoons to educational programs, sitcoms, talk shows, news programs, and prime-time programs for heterosexism. They may do the same for children's books, teens' magazines, women's magazines, and men's magazines and demand that the media promote sexual orientation equality-based programs and advertisements and discourage programs with heterosexism. Mindful repetitions that integrate emotion and cognition are necessary to dismantle heterosexism.

There are numerous benefits for all people to dismantling heterosexism and homophobia. People will develop close relationships with each other on the basis of who they are and not on the basis of sexual orientation. All individuals will express their creativity and potential as who they are without socially constructed sexual orientation restrictions. This will lead them to being the authentic selves that they are meant to be.

☒ A PRACTITIONER'S ASSESSMENT OF SELF IN RELATION TO HETEROSEXISM, SYSTEMATIC OPPRESSION/PRIVILEGE, AND INTERNALIZED OPPRESSION/PRIVILEGE

Practitioner-trainees should reflect on the socialization process, various sociocultural contexts, and reinforcement history in relation to heterosexism-, homophobia-, and sexual-orientation-based oppression/privilege. There are many ways for the practitioner-trainee to assess self, and transformative learning by not judging or censoring is one way. Examining when and how practitioners' multiple identities function independently and interdependently is an important component of assessing their relationship to systematic oppression/privilege and internalized oppression/privilege. Practitioners need to raise multicultural consciousness by inclusion of multiple identities, their intersections with each other, and their degree of saliency within sociocultural contexts. The following experiential and reflection-based learning activities are designed for transformative learning about sexual orientation through narrative writing.

CONCRETE STRATEGIES

Experiential and Reflection-Based Learning Activities on Sexual Orientation

Close your eyes and breathe in and out slowly and deeply for 5 min. As you breathe, go back in your timeline as far as you can to see whether you recall an experience with heterosexism and homophobia during your childhood. Slowly open your eyes.

1. Describe your memory of sexual orientation privilege or oppression.
    a. How did you feel about it when you were a child and a teenager, and how do you feel about it now?

b. Did you share your experience with someone?

 (1) If you did, with whom did you share it, and what was his/her/zir response?

 (2) If you did not share it with anyone, what did you do with it?

c. What was your feeling about your sexual orientation compared to your parents' and friends' feelings about it?

d. What did you learn from your teachers about sexual orientation? Be specific.

e. What did you learn about systematic heterosexual privilege and nonheterosexual oppression from your family when you were a child? Be specific.

f. Do you belong to a privileged or an oppressed group, and how has this shaped your worldview?

g. Write down your intrapersonal communication, which is a reflection of your internalized oppression/privilege.

h. When was the first time you were aware of systematic oppression/privilege in relation to sexual orientation? Describe the incident in detail.

i. Is your sexual orientation different from that of your family members? If so, what overt and covert messages did you receive from your family, and how did these messages affect your relationship to your family?

2. Write down any heterosexist remarks you heard while growing up from (a) family, (b) friends, and (c) the media. How did you feel about them? Write down any heterosexist remarks you have made; how did you feel when you made them?

3. What is your experience with homophobia?

4. Write down your intrapersonal communication in relation to sexual orientation.

CONCRETE STRATEGIES

Consciousness Practice

Are you conscious of your heterosexism oppression/privilege now? Where is this experience?

7

Classism

I n this chapter, the complexities involved in class issues due to multiple determinants, the difference between class and status, and misunderstandings about classism are discussed. The intersections of class with race, gender, and sexual orientation are explored from a multilayered and multidimensional perspective. The interrelationship of systematic oppression and privilege and the effects of internalized oppression and privilege on class prejudice, class discrimination, and classism are discussed. The importance of sociocultural contexts in shaping class identity and classism is explored. Strategies for dismantling classism at the personal and institutional level are explored. The chapter concludes with self-assessment for a practitioner-trainee.

⧘ A DEFINITION OF CLASS AND CLASSISM

The major difference between traditional counseling and multicultural counseling is that a basic principle of multicultural counseling emphasizes understanding clients from their sociocultural contexts (e.g., race, gender, class, sexual orientation, disability, age, religion, language, region). Without considering sociocultural contexts, it is difficult to examine the effects of class on the whole person. Class includes economic security or insecurity, means of survival or taste, type of language, type of values and beliefs, dress code, location of residence, and much more. Class contextual factors are complex and complicated due to multiple determinants, unspoken subcategories having different nuances within a particular class, multiple meanings, and the tendency to deny the existence of class in the United States (Argyle, 1994; Langston, 2000; Liu, 2001). Langston writes:

> We experience class at every level of our lives; class is who our friends are, where we live and work, even what kind of car we drive. (p. 398)

The following section discusses the multiple determinants of class, the difference between class and status, and classism to illustrate the complexities involved in shaping a person's perception, worldview, communication style, and identity.

Multiple Determinants

There are multiple sociocultural contextual factors that determine class; income, education, occupation, prestige, power, lifestyle, wealth, property, leisure and consumption behavior, and acculturation are some of these determinants (Argyle, 1994; Brouwer, 2000; Geoghehan, 1997; Hacker, 1997; Heintz & Folbre, 2000; Hendry, Kloep, & Olsson, 1998; Sodowsky, Lai, & Plake, 1991). In addition to these multiple determinants, the cultural myth of the "American Dream" and intersections of race, gender, and class lead to the invisibility of class contextual factors (Boston, 1991). The "American Dream" is formulated on the assumption that everyone has an equal opportunity to succeed if he/she/ze works hard and perseveres (Mantsios, 2004). North American history supports this idea to an extent since individuals who were dissatisfied with England immigrated to the United States to build better lives for themselves. "The denial of class divisions functions to reinforce ruling-class control and domination. America is, after all, the supposed land of equal opportunity where, if you just work hard enough, you can get ahead, pull yourself up by your bootstraps" (Adams et al., 2000, p. 75). What is apparent is that social class has multiple meanings, and it may be conceptualized differently according to contextual factors and beliefs from one's own experience with it. For example, some people make the distinction between class and status within class, and this type of distinction leads to multiple meanings of social class.

Class Versus Status

Class and status are interdependent with a slight difference between them. Class is usually defined by income while status is defined by lifestyle within a class. For example, a farmer's income may be the same as a professor's (*class*), but the farmer may have a different lifestyle, practice a different type of parenting skills, and be perceived as having a different status than a professor in the United States. The distinction between class and status is determined by how an individual perceives the impact of class or status on his/her/zir identity development, whether or not systematic class oppression/privilege shaped his/her/zir identity, whether or not an individual's worldview is shaped by his/her/zir internalized class oppression/privilege, and how interactions of these are manifested in an individual's behavior and lifestyle.

Classism

Classism "constitutes a form of oppression that is structural, maintained by practices that constitute 'business as usual,' and played out at the individual, institutional, and cultural levels" (Adams, 2000, p. 380). Just like racism, sexism, and heterosexism, classism is a system of advantages for the middle and upper class as a group. It is much bigger than individual prejudice, bias, and discrimination. It means governmental, institutional, and organizational policies, laws, and rules are written to favor the middle class, the upper middle class, and the upper class and unfairly discriminate against people in a lower socioeconomic class. It is about the system (institutional and governmental policies and laws) giving social power and control to those who have economic and status security. Classism is the pattern of privilege and oppression that perpetuates so that privileged groups (e.g., the middle class and upper middle class) maintain their power over oppressed groups (Liu, Soleck, Hopps, Dunston, & Pickett, 2004). Both oppression and privilege are results of the socially constructed hierarchy, a categorical interrelationship of classes based on inequality. In order to have class privilege, a person needs to belong to a privileged group. Belonging to a privileged group or an oppressed group is not determined by the group members' perceived feelings but is determined by the hierarchical social structure. For example, individuals who are making what is considered a middle-class income may not feel class privilege because they are comparing themselves to people who make substantially more money. Or some individuals who are making a relatively lower-class income may not feel oppressed because their happiness and contentment are not dependent on their income. Johnson (2006) explains the difference between being a member of a privileged or an oppressed group and feeling privileged or oppressed:

> Living in a particular society can make people feel miserable, but we can't call that misery "oppression" unless it arises from being on the losing end in a system of privilege. . . . Being in a privileged category that has an oppressive relationship with another isn't the same as being an oppressive *person* who behaves in oppressive ways. (p. 39)

Researchers who do not make a clear distinction among classism, class prejudice, and class discrimination further complicate the understanding of class issues (Kilborn, 2001; Liu et al., 2004; Liu & Pope-Davis, 2003; O'Connor, 2001; Pope-Davis & Coleman, 2001). For example, Liu et al. divide "modern classism" into four types of classism: (a) upward, (b) downward, (c) lateral, and (d) internalized:

> Upward classism is defined as prejudice and discrimination directed toward individuals who are perceived to be of a higher social class. . . . Downward classism involves the prejudicial attitudes and discriminatory behavior against people and groups that are perceived to be "below" the perceiver. . . . Lateral classism reminds individuals that they also must be similar to each other to remain congruent with an economic culture. . . . Internalized classism results from a violation of the values, norms, and expectations of an individual's economic, culture, and social class worldview. (pp. 108–109)

The above definition of classism misses the basic foundation of classism. Classism is a form of oppression that is embedded in the social structure to systematically discriminate against the lower class that is on the losing end in a system of privilege. Liu et al. (2004) are not making a clear distinction among classism, class prejudice, and class discrimination. Classism includes class prejudice and discrimination, but it is much more. Not all individuals in the middle and upper classes discriminate against individuals in the lower class, but because the system (governmental, institutional, and organizational policies and rules) favors their group status, members of the middle and upper classes receive systematic benefits as a result of their membership in either class. Lower-class individuals may be prejudiced against middle- and upper-class individuals, but this prejudice is not classism since the lower class does not have systematic privilege and power over the middle and upper classes. The social structure is set up in a way that systematic privilege is only given to the middle class, the upper middle class, and the upper class and not to the lower class, regardless of prejudice. More research needs to be done to examine the effects of classism.

SOCIAL CONSTRUCTION OF CLASSISM

A primary socializing agent for the socialization of class is society (Bush & Simmons, 1992). Individuals learn their social class role early on through their interactions with family members, peers, teachers, and others, as well as through their sociocultural contexts such as school, church, and other institutions like governmental agencies, police, and hospitals (Gecas, 1992; Hill, 1992; Roediger, 1999; Zweig, 2000). Social class affects an individual's values, beliefs, and biases. Children experience classism in the early elementary grades when they are assigned to slow- or fast-track programs. Children in slow-track programs are not given privilege in the name of assisting their learning while such privilege is given to children in fast-track programs. More children from the lower class than from the middle class are in slow-track programs (Langston, 2000). These tracks determine whether or not access to better education is provided for children. Working-class and poor people are not given the same opportunity as middle- and upper-class people to maximize their potential by virtue of what class they are born into. They are considered less able on the basis of their class and not on the basis of their intellectual capabilities. Because systematic oppression takes place early in life, children have already been marginalized, minimized, and excluded before they are able to notice the impact of their parents' class on their thoughts, feelings, and actions. Early childhood experience shapes their perception, and children grow up to perceive outer reality through their childhood reality. The author once had a client whose inter- and intrapersonal communication was based on perceived self-inadequacy, which the author's client projected onto others as if they considered him inadequate. He vividly remembered going to elementary school with worn-out tennis shoes, and when his school gave him a new pair as a Christmas gift, he felt humiliated and perceived that everybody at his school knew he was poor. By the time he was the author's client, he was making a middle-class income; however, his inner experience of the world was the same as when he was in the primary grades. His basic belief was that others were laughing at him and thought they were better than him.

Privilege holders who think they care for humanity often practice unintentional class discrimination and prejudice. For example, after winter break, some elementary school teachers ask about children's holiday activities. If a teacher asks children what they got for Christmas, the teacher is assuming that everybody in class celebrates Christmas and every child in class received a Christmas present. This is unintentional discrimination against children who are from non-Christian families and who did not receive presents either due to their non-Christian faith or because their families could not afford them. These children may perceive the teacher's comments, which reflect the teacher's socioeconomic class and religion or religious preference, as excluding or marginalizing them. It is not that the teacher wants to intentionally discriminate against children, but the teacher's privilege does not allow for thinking about the possibility of some students not getting anything for Christmas nor celebrating it. Some children who did not receive presents may be forced to lie to be a part of the group. Well-meaning individuals who cannot fathom a world different from their own (*social projection*) unintentionally discriminate against others who face discrimination or classism on a daily basis.

⸙ SYSTEMATIC OPPRESSION/PRIVILEGE AND INTERNALIZED OPPRESSION/PRIVILEGE

Individuals often react to their environment due to internalized privilege and/or oppression rather than as a result of an event in the current reality. Internalization is one of the private thought processes of an individual's mind, and the process starts in early infancy. Developmental theorists such as Piaget (1969, 1972), Erikson (1964), Kohlberg (1987), and many others theorize learning begins at birth while scholars who focus on the importance of prenatal care to development theorize learning takes place during prenatal development. According to Piaget, infants learn about the world through sensorimotor interaction with their environment. Cognitive processing takes place through touching, seeing, tasting, and hearing in the sensorimotor stage. Infants are able to think before they can verbalize their thoughts, and this cognitive process takes place internally (Solso, 2001). This cognitive process is active and dynamic and interacts with psychosocial development in balancing assimilation and accommodation throughout childhood, adolescence, young adulthood, and adulthood. Learning to internalize privilege and oppression is achieved by a similar cognitive and psychosocial process. Systematic oppression challenges children's cognitive processes of balancing assimilation and accommodation. Systematic oppression communicates devaluing and marginalizing messages to children of a lower status or from a lower class. Children who are targets of systematic oppression are likely to develop internalized oppression while children who are targets of privilege are likely to develop internalized privilege. By repetition of these messages throughout children's lives, this process becomes automatic and gradually operates without their awareness. Unconscious learning and inconsistencies between knowledge and behavior such as those in the case of aversive racism make it difficult to assess the impact of internalized oppression/privilege on an individual's beliefs, values, and attitudes (Banaji & Bhaskar, 2001; Dovidio, Gaertner, Kawakami, & Hodson, 2002). The following reflection-based activities are designed to facilitate transformative learning on internalized oppression/privilege and systematic oppression/privilege.

CONCRETE STRATEGIES

Reflection-Based Learning Activities

1. Indicate whether you belong to a privileged group or an oppressed group in relation to the following identities: (a) race, (b) gender, (c) sexual orientation, and (d) class. Think about your answers not in terms of whether or not you feel privileged but in terms of whether or not you belong to a privileged group according to your society.

2. Which of the above identities are important to you? Rank them in order of importance, with 1 being the most important and 9 being the least important in relation to your identity construction.

3. Close your eyes and breathe in and out slowly and evenly for 5 min. Pay attention to your feelings and the images that come to mind as you breathe. Slowly open your eyes and record or draw your feelings and/or images.

4. What have you learned from these activities?

5. What was your understanding of systematic privilege and oppression in relation to class before completing these activities, and what is your understanding of them now?

6. Discuss your understanding of systematic privilege and oppression in relation to class with others who have participated in the same experiential learning activities of this section.

7. What did you learn about yourself and others in your group from Question 6?

Internalized oppression in one identity immobilizes individuals' ability to perceive their privilege in other identities. For instance, some White men from the working class have a difficult time understanding White privilege because their lived experience has been powerless. It is hard for them to understand that they still benefit from being White males even though their personal experience with poverty is so intense that they are not able to recognize their systematic privilege as White men. It is partly due to the heavy emphasis on economic success, which is often measured by income, occupation, and wealth, the single most important factor in defining success in the United States. Other types of success such as having internal peace, health, and harmony in the family have not been valued in the United States or many other capitalistic countries. As a result, being born into and socialized in a working or poor family in the United States has much more complex dynamics in identity construction than being born into a working family in a country that defines success in nonmaterial ways.

The following examples illustrate the impact of class identity construction on one's way of interpreting others, especially those outside of one's own social class. Students in one of the author's multicultural counseling classes were asked to describe challenging students in class and to identify the types of challenges. The following personal stories demonstrate interactions among systematic oppression/privilege, internalized oppression/privilege, the degree of intensity of class identity, and the intersection of multiple identities, which are major factors in determining the class and status of an individual.

PERSONAL STORIES

Class

There is a student in class who challenged me. He is male and from an upper-class family. He always brought his "pet" issues without regard to the class conversation. I thought he was full of himself and always saying he is better than everyone else. When I was trying to examine my feelings and thoughts about him by applying research methods, I couldn't really substantiate my thoughts and feelings from what he said and did.... This has been really difficult for me because for so long I have felt a great deal of jealousy and envy towards the upper classes. By admitting my true feelings rather than projecting onto him I have been able to accept myself and others for who we really are despite our economic (external) differences. I think I can build a relationship with him now. I realized that it wasn't his fault that he was born into the upper class and it wasn't my fault that I was born into the lower class.

—Pat, 2004

Specific behavior from a particular student that is bothersome is talking about food, wine, and culture in a "snobby" way, having a distasteful tone. He offers opinions from a place of privilege that don't reflect true under- standing. This student is male and from an upper middle class family. I am a female from a working class family. Learning that worldview is formulated from our family backgrounds helped me to understand this student and myself. It's possible I didn't really listen to him, the person. I might have framed him into my own perception of "snobby" people that I knew when I was growing up. It is hard to admit this. But it is possible.

—Mary Anne, 2004

There are so many students who challenge me! I'll just pick one, so it will be clearer for me. This student does not speak standard English. I am still trying to figure out if this is a result of socioeconomic status or a learning disability. My mind says it reflects this person's rural "hick," white-trash roots. I have a very hard time not assuming my superiority—of education, of upbringing, of intellect, of language skills, and ultimately, the superiority of me as a person over the other. I am learning about my bias. I can accept my bias more when I understand its roots. It is extremely difficult to be successful in therapeutic work with patients outside the white middle class if one maintains tradi- tional notions about the norm. One of the things I am doing is working inti- mately with this person to achieve greater empathy and understanding of his difference.

—Eli, 2004

The above stories provide multidimensional ways to understand the complex dynamics involved in perception. Pat's story reveals his jealousy and envy toward the upper class. How much of his jealousy and envy (inner experience) played a role in his perception of his classmate? Was his classmate "full of himself and always saying he is better than every- one else," or did Pat perceive him that way due to his internalized class oppression? Was Pat's internalized oppression blurring his ability to see his classmate objectively? How about Mary Anne's description? Is her comment, "He offers opinions from a place of privilege that don't reflect true understanding" a reflection of her internalized class oppression or her intersection of class and gender? Eli admits to her struggle with internalized privilege and its role in her ability to assess her classmate accurately. But how much is due to her class privilege, and how much is due to her intersection of gender and class?

All three of these students continued to work on transcending and transforming internalized privilege and oppression. They stated that they learned how much internalized oppression/privilege was linked to systematic privilege and oppression through working on their own internalized oppression/privilege. They also indicated that they realized their responses from internalized oppression/privilege were automatic and that they had an emotional attachment to their own beliefs and values, which were results of their social class. Understanding internalized privilege and oppression and their relationship to systematic oppression and privilege allows individuals to evaluate others' behavior from a multilayered and multidimensional perspective.

Automatic Activation

Reactions to internalized oppression/privilege in relation to class are as automatic as responses to racial and gender oppression/privilege. Research by Banaji and colleagues contributed to understanding automation of the unconscious processes involved in beliefs and attitudes (Banaji & Greenwald, 1994; Banaji & Hardin, 1996; Greenwald & Banaji, 1995). "The best intentions do not and cannot override the unfolding of unconscious processes for the triggers of automatic thought, feeling, and behavior live and breathe outside conscious awareness and control" (Banaji & Bhaskar, 2001, p. 142). Understanding the automatic activation process assists with the realization that transcending any unconscious learning process or habit is a challenging task that requires mindful practice of being aware of the process without being critical of oneself. It is possible that the initial reactions of Pat, Mary Anne, and Eli to their challenging classmates are from automatic activation. By accepting their feelings and thoughts as they were, all three of these students learned to understand the impact of their class, their internalized oppression/privilege, and their thinking style on their meaning making from a deeper level. The following reflection-based learning activities provide the opportunity to reflect on implicit learning from class conditioning.

CONCRETE STRATEGIES

Reflection-Based Learning Activities

1. Indicate whether you belong to a privileged group or an oppressed group in relation to class.

2. Describe your group's characteristics.

3. What assumptions were you led to believe about other groups when you were a child?

4. What assumptions do you have about other groups now?

5. Review the experiential learning activities on your values and beliefs (Chapter 3). How many of your values and beliefs were the result of class conditioning?

6. Review your intra- and interpersonal communication (Chapter 2).

7. How much of your intra- and interpersonal communication is related to class conditioning?

The following experiential learning activities provide the opportunity to develop compassion through taking someone else's role.

CONCRETE STRATEGIES

Experiential Learning Activities Through Role Play

Close your eyes as you breathe in relaxation and breathe out tension for 5 min. Imagine you were born into a poor family and have never received a birthday gift. You are 6 years old and sitting in a classroom where there is a birthday party being held for one of your classmates. Your classmate's mother has brought cake for everyone in class.

1. What thoughts are going through your mind as a child who has never had a party? Write them down.

(Continued)

(Continued)

2. Your classmate has invited some children to her birthday party on the coming Saturday. What are your thoughts and feelings? Write them down.

3. What thoughts and feelings come to you as you compare the above two situations to your own childhood experiences in relation to birthday parties?

4. How was your class portrayed by the media (e.g., TV, movies, books, popular music) when you were growing up? Write down your memories and feelings.

INTERSECTIONS OF RACE, GENDER, SEXUAL ORIENTATION, AND CLASS

As discussed in the previous chapters, defining self or self-identity by only one sociocultural context among multiple sociocultural contexts is as superficial as defining a person's identity by one identity (e.g., gender, class, race) among multiple identities and their intersections. Unidimensional approaches serve no purpose in understanding the whole person. It is only an illusion that they somehow assist with understanding the person. For example, Clement and Myles (1994) state that examining only the impact of class without considering the impact of gender "leads to the systematic neglect of gender relations as structured relations of domination and inequality between the sexes" (Katz-Gerro, 2006, p. 65). Ignoring class and only paying attention to gender also gives an inaccurate assessment of gender identity. A good example is some lower-class women do not feel that the feminist movement represents them because it represents only the White middle-class perspective (Crompton, 2001; Wright, 2001). "It has been shown that gender has different meanings when combined with different class locations or family statuses and so one would expect important cultural variations between different combinations of gender and class and of gender and family status" (Katz-Gerro, p. 77). Katz-Gerro's study examined the effects of gender and class and family status on consumption in Italy, Sweden, Israel, West Germany, and the United States. The results showed that gender had an independent effect on highbrow consumption regardless of class and family status in Israel, Italy, and Sweden while gender effect was interdependent with class and family status in the United States and West Germany. If the study had examined only U.S. and West German samples, the intersection of gender and class variations according to sociocultural contexts would not have been found. Individuals who are socialized in gender and class independent of sociocultural context may have conflict with those who are socialized in gender and class interdependent with sociocultural context because their values and beliefs are shaped through different gender and class relationships. Ignoring the intersections among a person's different identities creates barriers to transcending classism, racism, sexism, heterosexism, and other "isms." Including intersections among multiple identities requires a holistic thinking style, which allows for a multidimensional and multilayered perspective (Ogbu, 1988; Ridley, Hill, Thompson, & Ormerod, 2001; Robinson, 1999; Wilson, 1987; Yamada, Marsella, & Yamada, 1998). The purpose of the following reflection-based learning activities is to facilitate transformative learning in understanding the intersection of race, gender, sexual orientation, and class.

CONCRETE STRATEGIES

Reflection-Based Learning Activities

Prepare drawing materials (at least two sheets of drawing paper and a box of crayons, coloring pencils, or paints). Close your eyes and breathe in and out slowly and deeply for 5 min. As you are breathing in and out slowly, think and feel about your intersection of race, gender, sexual orientation, and class. Slowly open your eyes.

1. Draw your intersection of race, gender, sexual orientation, and class.

2. Write about what you drew.

3. Draw your relationship to (a) class, (b) gender, (c) race, (d) sexual orientation, and (e) the intersection of class, gender, race, and sexual orientation.

4. Have you been pressured to be loyal to only one group (e.g., race, gender, class) by your community?

(Continued)

(Continued)

    a. How do you feel when you are pressured?

    b. How do you balance your need to be loyal to your inner beliefs with your community's request?

    c. How is your narrative similar to and different from that of your community (e.g., race, gender, class)?

5. If you had difficulty participating in the above activities, explain.

6. When you evaluate another person or group of people, do you evaluate that person or group on the basis of multiple identities operating in various sociocultural contexts, or do you evaluate on the basis of a single identity?

Examining self and self-identity from a single-identity dimension or a single sociocultural context as if it is the only way to understand a person may be due to a habit of applying conventional thinking styles such as linear, dichotomous, and hierarchical thinking styles. As indicated earlier, hierarchical and dichotomous thinking styles are embedded in Americans' consciousness (Singer & Kimbles, 2004; Takaki, 1993; Thompson, 1977), and individuals need to work diligently in order to deconstruct their inappropriate application. Simplifying through inappropriate dichotomous and hierarchical thinking diminishes the possibility to consider human diversity as it unfolds in real life and to know the real person within the sociocultural context. In order to see the effects of intersections among multiple identities, individuals must be able to think holistically ("either/or" and "both/and").

VARIATIONS WITHIN AND AMONG CLASSES

There are variations among classes as well as within class. Some people are clear about who they are and feel content with their life even though their annual income is considered to be in a lower socioeconomic category while others are unhappy because they do not think they have enough money even though their income is in the upper-middle-class category. The example of farmer versus professor in the beginning of this chapter was provided to differentiate between class and status, and it was also an example of variation within class. The author once had a client who was a multimillionaire but who could not continue therapy on a regular basis until he became a Medicare client because he thought he could not afford to pay 20% of the therapy fee out of pocket. He was upset that his health insurance was paying only 80% and not 100%.

Class variations interact with other identities (e.g., race, gender, sexual orientation, impairment/disability, age, religion, language, region). For example, there are Koreans who immigrated to the United States because of the political condition of Korea. These people's main purpose of immigration was to provide a politically safer environment for their children, and they are willing to sacrifice themselves for their children's future. A significant portion of these immigrants are well educated and held professional jobs in South Korea. They also had enough money to immigrate and open businesses in the United States. However, there was a sudden change of status when they came to the United States primarily due to their inability to speak English fluently. The language barrier affects their ability to get a professional job, participate in community affairs, and develop close friendships with English speakers. Most of these immigrants opened minimarts, gas stations, motels, dry cleaning businesses, or restaurants since these jobs do not require extensive fluency in English. They work hard and long hours while trying to deal with cultural adjustment issues. Being demoted in status was very difficult for them to deal with since they came from a status-oriented culture. Most of them not only had to deal with their sudden status change but also grieved over the emotional connection they had with friends or coworkers in South Korea. Some men used to go out with their friends or colleagues after work to release work stress, to renew friendships, or to continue business in a more relaxed environment in South Korea. However, due to their language barrier, these men have not found this type of social relationship in the United States. They miss discussing politics, economics, and cultural events. They live in the United States, and their homes and businesses are in the United States, but some of them feel that they are living outside of the United States. Most of them associate with people from Korea—although it might be on a superficial level—because of commonality in race and language. They work hard and long hours, and most of them are economically successful. But their economic success is not necessarily driven by a capitalistic orientation. Their economic success fulfills some of their emotional needs and heals some of their pain from systematic oppression on the basis of race and language. They channel their energy into work when they are lonely, homesick, or frustrated due to the language barrier and cultural unfamiliarity.

Then, there are Korean immigrants who came to the United States because one of their immediate family members obtained naturalized U.S. citizenship through an interracial marriage. These immigrants vary substantially in terms of their prior socioeconomic status and education level in South Korea. If they are from a lower socioeconomic class with a lower educational level (high school or less), many of them consider America a paradise since it is much easier for them to get a job in the United States than in South Korea. These people feel they are rewarded for their hard work and enjoy both economic security and social rewards. Language and cultural barriers do not seem to frustrate them as much as the people whose class is demoted by coming to the United States since their U.S. living conditions are much better than their living conditions in South Korea. Their status is promoted since American classism is less oppressive compared to that of Korea, and their language barrier allows them not to notice the classism if they are discriminated against. If they are from a middle socioeconomic class and received a college education in Korea, they go through similar feelings to those of the immigrants who came to the United States for their children.

There are multiple variations among Blacks, Hispanics, Vietnamese, Chinese, Japanese, Russians, and other racial groups including Whites. Each group stated here has diverse subgroups. There are Blacks who were born in the United States to parents who were also born and raised in the United States, and there are Blacks who were born in the United States to immigrant parents from various African countries. There are different socioeconomic classes in each group. The intersections of race, gender, sexual orientation, and class are diverse among these groups since their relationships with each identity vary as well as the intersections among different identities vary. Each racial group has diverse variations within it as well as intersections with multiple identities operating in different sociocultural contexts. Thus, class alone does not describe the person. The person needs to be viewed from these multiple identities, intersections of multiple identities, and sociocultural contexts.

One of the author's client's intra- and interpersonal communication was discussed under "Social Construction of Classism" at the beginning of this chapter. His income level was in the middle-class category, but his perception and worldview were from what he learned when he was growing up as a boy from a poor family. The salient character of his identity was based on internalized oppression from his childhood social class experience. He had risen above poverty and achieved economic security in terms of his income and material possessions, but his inner experience was unchanged from that of his childhood. He was not able to appreciate his strengths and success due to automatic activation of the inadequate feelings and anxiety of his childhood. His chronological age is in his 50s. He lives in a nice house, but he does not experience privilege as a White male. His inner experience is still that of a boy who was laughed at by others due to holes in his shoes, no Christmas presents, and no electricity due to unpaid bills. Class identity may not affect individuals too much if they have a different salient identity such as sexual orientation, but it is crucial for understanding the intersections of multiple identities in order to understand a client's worldview.

〰 CLASSISM AND INAPPROPRIATE THINKING STYLES/PATTERNS

As previously defined, classism includes the patterns of privilege and oppression that perpetuate so that privileged groups (e.g., the middle and upper classes) maintain their power over oppressed groups (Johnson, 2006). Having power over another group is only possible when a society's framework is based on a dichotomous and hierarchical structure. Would poor and working-class children internalize minimization and marginalization if all children were socialized to have an appropriate dichotomous and hierarchical thinking framework along with the ability to critically examine an issue from a multilayered and multidimensional perspective? The middle- and upper-class children from this sociocultural context would not be likely to minimize or marginalize children from the poor and working class because they would not be conditioned to value middle-class attitudes and beliefs as better than working-class attitudes and beliefs. Poor and working-class children may know that they have fewer material things or less expensive things, but they would not be likely to equate it to being less of a person or less intelligent. Children from the middle and upper classes may know that they have more material things and expensive things, but they would not generalize it to other aspects of their identities and personal characteristics. All children may be able to accept their social class as it is, as well as other attributes of themselves that are distinctive.

Classism, class discrimination, biases, and prejudices are structured around inappropriate dichotomous and hierarchical thinking styles where higher income, a bigger house, and more wealth are valued as if people who have these things are better than those who have less. Having more material things than less may be better in some cases, but laws and governmental and institutional policies should not give one group of people systematic advantage because of their class. People who have more, as well as groups that have more, are systematically given more privilege and rights than those who have less. It is a fact that middle-class people have more income than lower-class people. To compare more income with less income, more material with less material, or more education with less education is to apply appropriate hierarchical thinking. However, a system that gives the advantage to high-income individuals and discriminates against people with low income is applying inappropriate hierarchical thinking. Leaping to the conclusion that having more material things or a higher income gives people the right to oppress others who have less is also based on inappropriate hierarchical thinking. There is a difference between having more and having less, but this does not lead to classism and class discrimination without inappropriate hierarchical and dichotomous thinking. Due to the automatic activation of hierarchical and dichotomous thinking styles, classism, class discrimination and class prejudice, and strongly held belief systems around class issues are perpetuated. It is almost impossible to deconstruct inappropriate thinking styles/patterns without practicing deconstructing strategies on a daily basis.

STRATEGIES FOR AND BENEFITS OF DISMANTLING CLASSISM

One of the most important strategies for dismantling classism and class prejudice, discrimination, and biases is processing class issues through transformative learning. Classism is based on multiple layers of complex emotions starting from the foundation of America, and these emotional complexities need to be addressed by being open and honest and acknowledging one's intrapersonal communication and feelings. Pat, Mary Anne, and Eli were able to begin their work in dismantling classism by being honest with themselves. Because of their willingness to be open and honest and acknowledge their thoughts and feelings, transformative learning occurred, and they were able to understand the impact of their classism on their perception and worldviews. Pat said, "By admitting my true feelings rather than projecting onto him [a challenging student in the class] I have been able to accept myself and others." The key here is that he was able to accept himself. In order to accept himself, he first admitted his true thoughts and feelings about his classmate. It took enormous courage to express how he really thought and felt. Mary Anne said, "It's possible I didn't really listen to him, the person. I might have framed him into my own perception of 'snobby' people that I knew when I was growing up. It is hard to admit this." Mary Anne bravely admitted the possible consequence of generalization on the basis of her previous experience. Eli had courage to admit that she had a hard time not assuming her superiority as a whole person. Her extraordinary effort was to intimately work with a very challenging student in order to transcend her bias from internalized privilege. Transformative learning occurred because all three took the risk of examining their real emotions and thoughts without judgment. Pat, Mary Anne, and Eli showed how to dismantle classism and social class discrimination at the personal and interpersonal levels. At the personal and interpersonal levels, dismantling strategies need to tap individuals' unconscious. The unconventional strategies discussed in Chapter 3 may assist individuals with examining their unconscious learning process. Narrative writing exercises, drawing, narrative movement, dream work, engaging in mindfulness, and consciousness-raising activities may also lead to exploring individuals' deeper level of beliefs and values in relation to class and the intersections of class with other multiple identities. Introspection needs to be applied for individuals to examine their current relationship to class and status, and the impact of the current sociocultural context on their relationship to class and status may help individuals understand dynamic and multilayered identity construction. Admitting class issues exist in the United States may also assist with raising consciousness.

Reflecting on one's own inter- and intrapersonal communication as well as others' interpersonal communication to examine beliefs is another way to dismantle classism, discrimination, and prejudice related to class issues. Another way to dismantle classism is to stop the automation of ongoing intrapersonal communication relating to class prejudices and beliefs. According to Banaji and Bhaskar (2001), "The best intentions do not and cannot override the unfolding of unconscious processes, for the triggers of automatic thought, feeling, and behavior live and breathe outside conscious awareness and control" (p. 142). Mindfulness and consciousness-raising activities will assist individuals with being aware of their automation. This needs to be practiced on a regular basis. "Thinking about what you would write is not the same as actually writing it" (Progoff, 1992, p. 11). Thinking about dismantling classism is not the same as actually dismantling classism.

At the institutional and governmental level, organize a small group and review policies in order to work toward equal access to benefits and privileges. Many institutions—for example, schools, temples, churches, homeless shelters, media production companies, county offices, and state offices—usually have a mission statement that advocates for equality for all people but often practice unintentional discrimination or perpetuate existing classism. Work collaboratively with others to dismantle classism at the institutional and governmental level in order to be more visible. The author taught a "Self and Community" program with a sociologist last year, and all students were required to intern during winter quarter. Their spring project was to return to class to evaluate their internship organizations on the basis of community psychology principles and provide them with concrete proposals for improvement. Many students interned at nonprofit organizations and learned the importance of understanding state and federal policies in order to help lower-income individuals and families. They were instrumental in changing organizations' policies, which facilitated serving lower-income individuals effectively. Some students provided concrete strategies for how to integrate state and federal policies to help lower-income individuals. Most students were gratified that they were able to contribute to their internship organizations. Some students chose to continue to volunteer on a part-time basis during the summer because they believed in making changes at institutional levels.

Dismantling classism benefits everyone because it will bring class equality for all people. Individuals will not have to create distance from each other on the basis of class difference. Individuals will not waste energy in marginalizing, minimizing, oppressing, and discriminating others. Individuals will not think, feel, and act superior or inferior on the basis of class. People will be able to interact with each other as they are without playing their class role, and their relationships will be based on their inner qualities and not on the superficiality of outer-class distinctions.

Progoff (1992) describes four dimensions of inner experience as discussed in Chapter 3, and the following experiential learning activities are about dialoguing with society in relation to class and the intersection of race, gender, sexual orientation, and class. The dialogue dimension is "inner dialogue" with self (Progoff, p. 125).

CONCRETE STRATEGIES

Experiential Learning Activities

You need to center prior to recording your inner experience.

1. Centering exercise: Close your eyes and imagine you are sitting in your cozy place. Practice three-dimensional breathing by moving your chest, rib cage, and stomach. Breathe slowly and evenly. Breathe in relaxation and see what is in your mind. If your mind is not with your body, ask your mind to be with your body. Breathe out tension and resistance. Breathe in relaxation and see what is in your mind. If your mind is with yesterday or tomorrow, inform your mind that the only reality you have is in this moment. Ask your mind to embrace your body and be still. Breathe out resistance and tension. Breathe in relaxation and appreciate your mind for trying; breathe out tension and resistance and slowly open your eyes.

2. The dialogue dimension: Close your eyes and breathe deeply and slowly while being aware of your emotions. Think about the society you grew up in while breathing deeply, evenly, and slowly. Sit still as you breathe deeply, evenly, and slowly. Open your eyes slowly and consider the following:

   a. How did your society treat you in relation to your class?

   b. Close your eyes, breathe deeply and evenly, and sit in silence thinking and feeling about yourself and the society in which you grew up. Begin a conversation with this society in your mind's eye and record your dialogue.

(Continued)

(Continued)

    c. When you finish writing, close your eyes again, breathe evenly and slowly, and feel your emotions without judgment or censoring. Then read the dialogue to yourself and take notes of any emotions that you feel. Observe whether these emotions are the same as what you felt before reading the dialogue. Record your emotional status.

    d. How did your society treat you in relation to the intersection of your race, gender, sexual orientation, and class?

3. The depth dimension is the process of integrating inner and outer life. If your inner experience is different from your outer life in relation to your class and your intersection of race, gender, sexual orientation, and class, how do you go about integrating them?

    a. Close your eyes again, breathe evenly and slowly, and feel your emotions without judgment or censoring. Just observe and attend to your inner voice. Describe your inner voice.

☗ A PRACTITIONER'S ASSESSMENT OF SELF IN RELATION TO CLASSISM, SYSTEMATIC OPPRESSION/PRIVILEGE, AND INTERNALIZED OPPRESSION/PRIVILEGE

Accurate assessment of a practitioner-trainee's class identity construction; multiple identities and their degree of importance; intersection of class, race, gender, and sexual orientation; and experience with systematic class oppression/privilege and internalized class oppression/privilege will assist her with understanding herself as a whole person and with understanding her clients' worldviews. Knowing and accepting herself as who she is will lead to less countertransference and accurate assessment of clients.

Completing all of the experiential learning activities in this chapter will assist the practitioner-trainee with achieving accurate self-assessment in relation to classism and systematic class oppression/privilege and internalized class oppression/privilege. The following reflection-based learning activities are designed for transformative learning on issues related to class and classism.

CONCRETE STRATEGIES

Reflection-Based Learning Activities

Close your eyes and breathe in and out slowly and deeply for 5 min. As you breathe, go back in your timeline as far as you can to see whether you recall an experience with classism or class issues during your childhood.

1. Describe your experience with classism or class issues.

2. How did you feel about it when you were a child and a teenager, and how do you feel about it now?

3. Did you share your experience with someone?

   a. If you did, with whom did you share it, and what was his/her/zir response?
   b. If you did not share it with anyone, what did you do with it?

4. What was your feeling about your class compared to that of your friends?

   a. What did you learn from your teachers about class?
   b. What did you learn about systematic class privilege and/or oppression from your family when you were a child? Be specific.
   c. Do you belong to a privileged or an oppressed group, and how has this shaped your worldview?
   d. Write down your intrapersonal communication, which is a reflection of your internalized class oppression/privilege.
   e. When was the first time you became aware of systematic oppression/privilege in relation to class? Describe the incident in detail.

5. Record any remarks about class you heard while you were growing up from (a) family members, (b) friends, and (c) the media. How did you feel about these remarks? Record any remarks related to class that you have made. What was your motivation for making such remarks? Write down your intrapersonal communication on class.

CONCRETE STRATEGIES

Consciousness Practice

Did you read this chapter consciously?

8

Ableism

There is confusion among different terms and the usage of the same terms in literature of impairment/disability. This chapter begins with clarification of terms like *disability, ableism, impairment*, and *disableism*, and the medical and social models are explained. The chapter addresses the fact that ableism is socially constructed, and consequences of ableism for both individuals with impairment/disability and individuals without impairment/disability are discussed. Consequences like internalized oppression/privilege and systematic oppression/privilege are discussed with personal stories for transformative learning. Strategies to dismantle ableism at personal, interpersonal, institutional, and cultural levels are discussed along with variations within a group as well as among groups. The importance of shifting thinking styles from dichotomous and hierarchical to holistic is described for examining intersections of race, gender, class, sexual orientation, and impairment/disability. A holistic thinking style is also emphasized for dismantling ableism at personal, interpersonal, institutional, and cultural levels. The chapter ends with reflection activities for a practitioner-trainee's self-assessment in relation to ableism, disableism, prejudice, and discrimination.

DIFFERENCE BETWEEN DISABILITY AND ABLEISM

A lack of attention has been paid to ableism despite attempts to include impairment and disability as a part of an important identity among multiple identities (Smith, Foley, & Chaney, 2008; Storey, 2007). This may be partly due to a research emphasis on ableism as the norm and partly due to confusion derived from using disableism and ableism interchangeably (Bolderson, 1991; Campbell, 2008; Goggin & Newell, 2000; Johnson & Moxon, 1998; Stainton, 1994). Disableism and ableism cannot be used interchangeably. There is a profound difference between the two in relation to their focus. Disableism focuses on the production of disability whereas ableism focuses on the production of ability. Disableism is "a set of assumptions and practices promoting the differential or unequal treatment of people because of actual or presumed disabilities" (Campbell, p. 152) whereas ableism is "a belief that impairment (irrespective of 'type') is inherently negative which should, if the opportunity presents itself, be ameliorated, cured or indeed eliminated" (Campbell, p. 154). The disability in ableism is defined by its deviance from ability, which suggests that people with disabilities as a group are inferior to people without disabilities (Gill, 1995; Henderson & Bryan, 1984; Longmore, 1995). Another factor contributing to the lack of attention paid to ableism might have been difficulty in categorizing impairment within a binary framework. Campbell explains the complexities of impairment:

> Within this illusionary binary world of fixed or chosen corporeal attributions the status of impairment is not so clear. Impairment is inherent within the body (or mind, cognition and so forth), however, impairment, despite often being characterized (etiologically) as "permanent" is in a broader sense "provisional." Impairments exist in a state of constant deferral, being open to the interventions of psycho-medical regimes posting corrections, cures or indeed elimination. (p. 159)

Terms like *differently abled* or *challenged* represent individuals' attempt to illustrate a wide spectrum of impairment.

Difference Between Impairment and Disability

The Americans With Disabilities Act of 1990 (ADA) defines disability in relation to an individual's ability to function in his environment. Disability is (a) a physical or mental impairment that substantially limits one or more of the major life activities of an individual, (b) a record of such an impairment, or (c) being regarded as having such an impairment (U.S. Department of Justice, U.S. Equal Employment Opportunity Commission, 2002/2005).

According to this definition, disability is not determined by a specific condition but by how the specific condition (impairment) affects an individual. Sandoz (2005) illustrated the distinction between impairment and disability by using a concrete example of a student with moderately impaired hearing who wore hearing aids in each ear and was able to hear lectures and discussions if the classroom was quiet and only one person was talking at a time. In this case, the student was not disabled if the other students did not create background noise during lectures and workshops. However, this student was disabled if there was background noise. This student was living with a hearing impairment, but whether he was going to be disabled or not was determined by his environment (i.e., classmates). If his hearing impairment was viewed from the medical model, he would have been forced to fix the problem, and he would not have had access to education because he could not have fixed the problem. The medical model, which assumes the impairment needs to be fixed and it is the individual's responsibility to fix it in order to make him/her/zir more like individuals without impairment, is not applicable in his case (Gill, 1995; Longmore, 1995). Other students being quiet is an example of the social model, which examines impairment from a holistic perspective. Its assumption is not based on pathologizing but based on improving the environment in order for the impaired person to function. There is a distinction between impairment and disability in this model. Impairment does not necessarily equate with disability in the social model. The social model critically examines structural and institutional ableism in order to improve physical structures and/or policies so that impaired individuals can find ways to not be disabled (Smith et al., 2008). Terms like *differently abled* or *challenged* are attempts to examine impairment from a spectrum perspective (nondichotomous and hierarchical), which includes multilayered and multidimensional characteristics of the impairment.

The medical model does not distinguish between impairment and disability. If an individual is impaired and the impairment cannot be fixed, the individual is disabled. The medical model is rooted in inappropriate hierarchical and dichotomous thinking that considers an individual without impairment better and more normal than an individual with impairment. The medical model focuses on pathologizing an individual with impairment in defining disability.

Ableism

Ableism is systematic oppression of individuals with impairments/disabilities on the basis of their disabilities. Ableism is much more than discrimination and prejudice against such individuals. It is systematic advantages for individuals without disabilities over individuals who are disabled/impaired. It is the fact that governmental and institutional policies, laws, rules, and structural designs of environment favor individuals without impairments/disabilities (Campbell, 2005). It is systematically blaming individuals with impairments/disabilities for their impairments and/or disabilities and assuming that they need to be "fixed" or "cured" (Longmore, 1995). According to Rauscher and McClintock (1997), "Deeply rooted beliefs about health, productivity, beauty, and the value of human life, perpetuated by the public and private media, combine to create an environment that is often hostile to" individuals with impairment/disability (p. 198). "Ableism is deeply and subliminally embedded within the culture" (Campbell, 2008, p. 153). Campbell (2001) defines ableism as

> a network of beliefs, processes and practices that produces a particular kind of self and body (the corporeal standard) that is projected as the perfect, species-typical and therefore essential and fully human. Disability is cast as a diminished state of being human. (p. 44)

The process of valuing nonimpairment and nondisability standards starts in early childhood through socialization by parents, teachers, peers, other adults, the media, and siblings. The impact of ableism on individuals with impairments/disabilities is similar to the impact of racism on people of color. Both lead to internalization of dominant values without conscious awareness (Burstow, 2003; Campbell, 2008). This affects individuals' relationship to self and others, whether it is on the interpersonal, institutional, or cultural level.

﹄ SOCIAL CONSTRUCTION OF ABLEISM

Discrimination against and oppression of individuals with impairment are practices constructed by society to give power and control to individuals without impairment and disability. Individuals without impairment and disability set the standard for the norm that assumes their way of doing things is "better" and "superior" than the way individuals with impairment/disability do things (Storey, 2007). From this perspective, the solution to problems of individuals with impairment/disability lies within them (Arms, Bickett, & Graf, 2008; Berry & Jones, 1991; Deegan, 2000; Fine & Asch, 2000; Sandoz, 2005; Shapiro, 2000). As described above, the solution for Sandoz's hearing-impaired student was dependent on other students, and he had no power to make other students assist him. "The accompanying *disability*—the hearing impaired student's inability to function and participate given the (constructed) circumstances—rests entirely in other program members' failures to acknowledge and take seriously the student's situation. He has been socially-disabled, by others' choices and actions" (Sandoz, p. 4). Other students probably did not know that their decision not to take the student's situation seriously was derived from ableism. Ableism is constructed on the basis of the medical model, which reinforces the belief that individuals with disability/impairment need to be fixed or cured to be normal (Smith et al., 2008). Otherwise, they are often viewed as abnormal on the basis of one aspect of multiple identities due to ableism (Olkin & Pledger, 2003; Reid & Knight, 2006). Ableism ignores the social model, which suggests that disability is a socially constructed phenomenon and individuals with impairment do not have to be disabled, because it wants to give power to groups or individuals without impairment. The medical model intentionally or unintentionally marginalizes, minimizes, and humiliates individuals with impairment.

It has been more than 16 years since the ADA was implemented. It was implemented on July 25, 1992, for employers with 25 or more employees and on July 26, 1994, for employers with 15 or more employees. This means that employers cannot discriminate against qualified individuals with disabilities. However, discrimination and prejudice against individuals with impairment and disability, as well as ableism, have continued despite the ADA. Impairment is only one dimension of a person's identity among multiple identities, and it may or may not disable the person's function, but impairment has been viewed as disability, and disability is considered a deficit in the United States. Persistent discrimination, prejudice, and ableism stem from multiple factors. One of the main reasons for their persistence is people's tendency to perpetuate cultural myths by generalizing and stereotyping on the basis of limited knowledge about disability. There are various types of impairment/disability—for example, physical impairment, sensory impairment, cognitive or intellectual impairment, learning disability, mental disorder (psychiatric disability), and chronic disease. Different types of impairment have different degrees of functionality. The following section examines a few existing categories of impairment/disability to explore how individuals with impairment/disability are treated at interpersonal, institutional, and cultural levels and how they are affected by such treatment.

Physical Impairment

According to a study by Freedman, Martin, and Schoeni (2004), about 20% of Americans have some type of impairment, and the number is steadily increasing.

Age-related impairment/disability increases with an aging population. There are visible and invisible physical impairments. Individuals whose physical impairment is visible are frequently treated as if they are lacking something intellectually. These individuals already struggle without others' mistreatment since they know they look different from others. They are socialized to believe that it is their fault that they have to struggle with their physical impairment/disability (Schultz & Decker, 1985). These individuals are also conditioned to believe that they are inadequate because a particular part of their body is different and to feel helpless when others minimize and marginalize them as people who lack intellectual capacity (French, 2000). They did not choose to be physically impaired/disabled (Frieden & Cole, 1985). Their impairment/disability is only one aspect of these individuals and does not represent them as whole people, although individuals who are able-bodied often treat them as if it does.

Learning Disability

The origin of learning disability is not low intelligence but the neurological circuit and is not well understood. Learning disability in the United States covers a wide range of academic challenges such as reading, writing, spelling, listening, speaking, reasoning, and organizing information. There are two types of learning disability, information processing difficulties (input, integration, storage, and output) and specific learning disabilities (reading, math, dyspraxia, speaking and listening, auditory processing, and nonverbal learning). For a long time, most teachers, parents, and members of the public have not understood learning impairments/disabilities. Due to others' lack of knowledge, individuals with learning impairments/disabilities have been treated as if they are intellectually inadequate (McDonald, Keys, & Balcazar, 2007).

Treating individuals with a learning disability as if they are inferior or stupid is an example of gross *generalization* on the basis of one aspect of one dimension of their identity among multiple identities. This type of generalization also ignores the impact of sociocultural contexts on these individuals. Adults with a learning disability often improve their reading and writing skills when they are not judged and criticized. Many dyslexic parents improve their reading skills by reading to their infants or pre-school children. They seem to read better since they are not afraid of their children judging them. Most children love to be read to by their parents, and they give unconditional positive regard to their parents. The following are two personal stories; one is from a 62-year-old man who lived all his life with a learning disability, and the other is from a 32-year-old woman who also lived all her life with a learning disability.

PERSONAL STORIES

INDIVIDUALS WITH A LEARNING DISABILITY

I had a client who came to therapy, though unwillingly, because of his wife's frustration with him. As I was trying to assess his problem, I discovered that he was learning disabled. He was a highly intelligent White male who had retired from his job. He said he refused to be a manager even though he was asked to apply for the position because he was afraid he would be forced to do lots of paperwork. His learning disability centered on dyslexia, or difficulty encoding and decoding information. Like many individuals with a learning disability, he tried to compensate for his problems without discussing it with anyone, even with his wife. Many of his strategies to cope with his learning disability were perceived as inattentive and inconsiderate by his wife, who did not know the characteristics of individuals with learning disabilities. He and his wife were very relieved to find out that there were actual explanations for his "inattentive" behaviors.

I had another client who knew she had some problems and quit college with only two more quarters to complete. She said she could not stand it

(Continued)

(Continued)

any longer. She was too exhausted to go through her elaborate strategies each day to cope with her academic life, and she did not want extra help for her condition. She was bright and creative but did not ask for assistance because she was too afraid of being "discovered as stupid." I wonder if she would have the same difficulty if she were finishing up school now, when people seem to have more knowledge about learning disabilities.

Mental Disorder (Psychiatric Disability)

Mental disorder or psychiatric disability is a complex concept and difficult to understand due partly to inappropriate systematic *hierarchical thinking.* There are various causes for psychological disorders. The cause could be hereditary, environmental, or developmental—or a combination of two or three of these. Various psychological disorders described in the *Diagnostic and Statistical Manual of Mental Disorders* are mostly based on observable characteristics of symptoms (American Psychiatric Association, 2000). Psychological disorders have multi-layered and multidimensional components, and observable symptoms represent only one aspect of these complexities. More attention is paid to physical illnesses, which are considered more legitimate than psychological illnesses, and medical treatment is used as a primary remedy for physical illnesses, while psychological disorders do not receive proper treatment and care compared to physical illnesses. The lack of understanding in relation to psychiatric disability, its impact on physical illnesses, and the "quick fix" approach among policymakers, managed care organizations, and the general public complicates developing effective treatment. Psychological disorders involve the whole person—the mind, body, and spirit—but individuals are often diagnosed only on the basis of observable symptoms. Psychological disorders are complicated by sociocultural contexts and require time to process both the conscious and the unconscious elements of the problem. The set number of sessions (e.g., 6, 12, or 20 visits a year) prescribed by most managed care organizations without considering the multiple factors involved in psychological disorders is an indication of the lack of understanding of the complexities of psychiatric disorders at institutional and cultural levels.

This lack of understanding of psychological disorders is illustrated by Deegan's (2000) personal experience with being labeled mentally ill. She describes how difficult it is to live with her condition when the cultural norm is based on being without impairment or disability:

> I was told I had a disease that was like diabetes, and if I continued to take neuroleptic medications for the rest of my life and avoided stress, I might be able to cope. . . . And that deep sense of loneliness came from the fact that although many people were talking to me about my symptoms, no one was talking to me about how I was doing. . . . Thus, to be with a person who is anguished is to risk experiencing the cry that is way down deep inside each of us. That is why the professionals have been so busy doing things to you, rather than being with you. . . . You may have been diagnosed with a mental illness but you are not an illness. You are a human being whose life is precious and is of infinite value. . . . Great danger is that you might undergo that radically devaluing and dehumanizing transformation from being a person to being an illness, from being Patricia to being "a schizophrenic" (or "a bipolar" or "a multiple"). (pp. 359–361)

Deegan's story reflects on ableism at individual, institutional, and cultural levels. The hiring by some institutions of untrained staff to save money, the tendency of some institutions to medicate for a quick fix without comprehensive assessment (prescribing appropriate medication for appropriate psychological disorders), the desire of some practitioners to label but not to help, the tendency of some practitioners to judge instead of listen to a client, and some practitioners' inability to understand psychiatric disability from a multilayered and multidimensional perspective constitute individual, institutional, and cultural discrimination, prejudice, and ableism (Stier & Hinshaw, 2007). Beliefs about, stereotypes about, and prejudice against individuals with psychiatric disorders are socially constructed to benefit individuals who are not impaired or disabled. The following reflection-based learning activities are designed to provide the opportunity for transformative learning about ableism by recalling an experience of marginalization by and of others.

CONCRETE STRATEGIES

Reflection-Based Learning Activities on Ableism

Close your eyes and breathe in and out slowly, evenly, and deeply for 5 min. As you breathe, go back to your timeline as far as you can to see whether you recall an experience with impairment/disability or being able- or not able-bodied during your childhood. Slowly open your eyes.

1. Have you ever minimized, marginalized, or laughed at someone because of his/her/zir disability and/or impairment?

   a. If you have, describe an incident. How did you feel about it then, and how do you feel about it now?

   b. Did you share your experience with someone?

      (1) If you did, with whom did you share it, and what was his/her/zir response?

      (2) If you did not share it with anyone, what did you do with it?

   c. What was your feeling about your impairment/disability and others' impairment/disability?

   d. What did you learn from your mother (or mother figure) about disability/impairment?

   e. What did you learn from your father (or father figure) about disability/impairment?

   f. What did you learn from your siblings (or sibling figures) about disability/impairment?

   g. What did you learn from your teachers about disability/impairment?

2. Have you ever been minimized, marginalized, or laughed at by someone because of your disability and/or impairment?

   a. If you have, describe an incident.

   b. How did you feel about it then, and how do you feel about it now?

   c. Did you share your experience with someone? If you did, with whom did you share it, and what was his/her/zir response?

   d. If you did not share it with anyone, what did you do with it?

   e. What was your feeling about your disability/impairment and others' disability/impairment?

   f. What did you learn from your mother (or mother figure) about disability/impairment?

g. What did you learn from your father (or father figure) about disability/impairment?

h. What did you learn from your siblings (or sibling figures) about disability/impairment?

i. What did you learn from your teachers about disability/impairment?

3. If your parents applied socialization practice with emphasis on lack of impairment/disability, what was the main message? How does it affect you now?

SYSTEMATIC OPPRESSION/PRIVILEGE AND INTERNALIZED OPPRESSION/PRIVILEGE

Systematic privilege has been maintained by the exclusion of individuals with disability/impairment, resulting in unequal access to power and justice. It is denying the fact that a person's impairment/disability is only one dimension of one identity among a person's multiple identities, and it may or may not disable the person's function. It is magnifying one dimension of one identity to represent the whole person, and impairment equates with disability, a deficit inherent in the person. Examples of systematic oppression, which denies equal access to people with disabilities and/or impairment at individual, institutional, and societal levels, are numerous (DeJong, 1982; Gee, Spencer, Chen, & Takeuchi, 2007; Linton, 1998). Individuals with a physical impairment/disability could not exercise their voting rights for a long time because the environment was not conducive to such activity; individuals with a physical impairment/disability could not vote because voting booths (environment) were made for able-bodied people. Governmental policy discriminated against individuals who were not able-bodied on the basis of their impairment or disability. Prison and jail populations have increased since institutionalized individuals with mental disorders were released to their communities without proper support and care. These individuals were not capable of requesting or demanding their treatment due to their disorders. The governmental policies and laws criminalized them to save money, which was an illusion since the government's expenses remained the same or increased to keep them in another kind of institution (jail or prison). Access to health care is denied by institutional policies that limit treatment for mental health to 6, 12, or 20 visits. This reflects the policymakers' lack of understanding about mental health and how the system oppresses people with mental health conditions. Systematic and institutional ableism denies individuals with impairment/disability access to achieving economic success while overvaluing economic success as if it is a total measure of a person's success. Systematic oppression and privilege lead to denying access to individuals with impairment/disability, and the above are only a few examples. There are extensive examples of systematic oppression, including denying individuals with impairment/disability access to housing, education, and health care (Barry, 1995; Caress & Steinemann, 2004; Rauscher & McClintock, 1997). Individuals with impairment/disability have been exposed to these types of ongoing systematic oppression by individuals without impairment/disability since early childhood. They have been conditioned to believe the privileged group's beliefs and assumptions are the norm, which is likely to lead to internalized oppression for individuals who cannot measure up to the norm. Many individuals with impairment/disability internalize societal norms and feel ashamed and embarrassed about being disabled (Brown, Connors, & Stern, 2000). According to Rosenwasser (2000), internalized oppression is

> an involuntary reaction to oppression which originates outside one's group and which results in group members loathing themselves, disliking others in their group, and blaming themselves for the oppression— rather than realizing that these beliefs are constructed in them by oppressive socioeconomic political systems. (p. 1)

Internalization is an inner experience, and meaning making from outerworld injustice reoccurs and accumulates on a daily basis (Burstow, 2003).

Ableism, discrimination, and prejudice are invisible to individuals with privilege but visible to individuals with disability/impairment (Asch, 1984). Deegan (2000) describes the experience of being objectified by professionals: "The professionals have been so busy doing things to you, rather than being with you." This description illustrates unintentional ableism due to internalized privilege. Some professionals who operate from a privileged perspective may "do things" to clients because they think they know better (*hierarchical thinking*). Some professionals may objectify individuals with impairment/disability due to their internalized privilege and beliefs about them. As a result of their unconscious processing, professionals may not be aware that they "do things" to clients rather than simply be with them.

It is important to understand that many people without disability/ impairment do not intend to exercise ableism. They behave without thinking about the impact of their behavior on individuals with impairment/ disability because privilege is often invisible to privilege holders. They probably have been allowed to practice their internalized privilege because it has been systematically given to them throughout their socialization process. The following personal stories reflect the impact of intentional or unintentional privilege and oppression on individuals with impairment/disability.

PERSONAL STORIES

Cancer From a Privileged Professional's Perspective

A nurse sent a young cancer patient home and asked him to start chemotherapy on Monday even though an oncologist had told him to start that Friday. The nurse knew that the oncologist went on vacation that afternoon, and she made a unilateral decision to start this patient's chemotherapy on Monday instead of Friday so her clinic did not have to pay the hospital for the weekend (the clinic was only open on weekdays). This particular nurse had a screensaver saying, "Oh! Lord! Please help my patients." Yet she had no understanding of how the young cancer patient felt about her decision.

Not Because She Was Not Able to Learn

I once had a community college transfer student who had a learning disability and needed to learn how to write a basic college research paper. When I called several offices that advertised they assisted students with special needs, each one informed me that it did not deal with students who needed to learn basic writing skills. I was confused about these offices' roles and how much they were operating from a privileged perspective. The student was highly motivated to learn and told me that she was put into a special education class until high school where she was not asked to do much. According to her, no one at her community college tried to teach her how to write. She transferred as a junior and wanted to work in human services. She had attended programs for students with learning disabilities but did not learn the necessary skills because she was not taught, not because she was not able to learn. What is the function of these programs: just to house students or to teach them to learn?

(Continued)

(Continued)

You Are So Lucky to Be Alive

A 25-year-old young man, a cancer survivor, is grieving through his cancer experience. People tell him how lucky he is to have survived and that he should be happy. His medical checkup indicates that he is cancer free, but he is struggling with understanding the meaning of cancer and his changed identity as a result of his experience with the disease. His physician looks at him and says, "You are so lucky to be alive. What are you complaining about? A lot of cancer patients would trade places with you."

No one is ready to listen to how he is feeling and what he has been struggling with. Everyone tells him he should not be complaining and he should be happy. No one seems to understand his posttraumatic stress because his physical cancer is gone, but it is still very alive in his inner experience.

Automatic Activation

Automatic activation is the result of unconscious processing of stereotypes, prejudice, and discrimination (Banaji & Greenwald, 1994; Chen & Bargh, 1997; Greenwald & Banaji, 1995: Henderson-King & Nisbett, 1996). Stereotypes, prejudice, beliefs, and values are activated automatically. Individuals learn to value the dominant cultural beliefs and myths at an early age. Physical beauty and health norms, internalized oppression/privilege and systematic oppression/privilege in relation to impairment and disability, and ableism are learned throughout the socialization process and are rooted deep in the American psyche. This is often a result of implicit learning, which is activated automatically without a person's awareness. The nurse described above who sent the young cancer patient away to save her clinic money, mental health professionals who are too busy to be with a client, and those teachers and staff members described above who ignored the student's learning disability even though their job was to assist students in need show inconsistencies between their behavior and what they claim to be. They behave as if there is no correlation between their implicit expressions and their explicit expressions (Dovidio & Gaertner, 2000, 2004, 2005; Schacter & Scarry, 2001). They seem to express their internalized privilege without conscious awareness. Implicit beliefs are activated automatically and affect perception and judgment without conscious awareness (Banaji & Hardin, 1996; Perdue & Gurtman, 1990).

INTERSECTIONS OF IMPAIRMENT/DISABILITY, RACE, GENDER, SEXUAL ORIENTATION, AND CLASS

Because multiple identities are interwoven, examining only disability/ impairment status as if it functions independently of other aspects of an individual's identities is artificial and provides no information about the whole person (Croteau & Constantine, 2005; Fine & Asch, 1981; Fukuyama & Ferguson, 2000; Gallor, 2005; Greene, 2000; McDonald et al., 2007; Mobley, 1998). In their illustration of the importance of examining intersections of gender and disability to prevent gender imbalance in special education and to understand multiple factors affecting learning, Arms et al. (2008) propose developing a theoretical framework "to address the multiple intersectionalities that students with disabilities may embody" (p. 356). Understanding interrelations and interdependence among multiple identities and various sociocultural contexts requires nondichotomous and nonhierarchical thinking. It requires holistic processing. For example, Reid and Knight's (2006) study found causes of learning disabilities and various psychological disorders in African Americans by examining intersections of race, class, and disability. Environmental racism and classism were the primary reasons for participants' learning disabilities and psychological disorders, which could not have been found without examining intersections of race, class, and disability. This study demonstrates the danger of symptom-only-based treatments without examining symptoms from a holistic perspective. Another example of the consequence of systematic oppression is illustrated by examining intersections of gender, sexual orientation, and impairment/disability. Laws prevent the partners of nonheterosexual persons with impairment from being included in health care decisions when the persons with impairment are too sick to make coherent decisions. Laws also prevent them from marrying legally in most states, and thus their right to include their partners in health care decisions is taken away by law (Smith et al., 2008) and not because they do not want to exercise that right. Insurance companies often do not provide the authorization for non-English-speaking clients to seek mental health help at out-of-network facilities even when the in-network facilities cannot provide an interpreter or a practitioner who speaks the clients' language. Their inability to understand cultural issues oppresses non-English-speaking clients who pay a premium equal to that of English speakers seeking the same mental health treatment.

Examining an individual through one identity as if it operates independently of all other identities is an illusion. Individuals can be understood only by examining the intersections of multiple identities and various sociocultural contexts, as well as by examining how these intersections interrelate and are interdependent. The following reflection-based learning activities are designed to assist with transformative learning about the complex relationships among these intersections.

CONCRETE STRATEGIES

Reflection-Based Learning Activities on Intersections

Prepare drawing materials (at least two sheets of drawing paper and a box of crayons, coloring pencils, or paints). Close your eyes and breathe in and out slowly, evenly, and deeply for 5 min. As you are breathing in and out slowly, think and feel about your intersections of disability/impairment, race, gender, class, and sexual orientation. Slowly open your eyes.

1. Draw your intersections of disability/impairment, race, gender, class, and sexual orientation.

2. Write about what you drew.

3. Have you been pressured to be loyal to disability/impairment, race, gender, class, or sexual orientation by any of these communities?

   a. How do you feel when you are pressured?
   b. How do you balance your need to be loyal to your inner values and your communities' requests?
   c. How is your narrative similar to and different from that of each of your communities?

\\\ VARIATIONS WITHIN AND AMONG INDIVIDUALS WITH IMPAIRMENT/DISABILITY

There are variations within individuals with the same type of impairment/disability since people have different degrees of impairment/disability and different meanings associated with their impairment/disability. Variations within the same type of impairment and the same degree of impairment may be caused by different experiences with intersections of multiple identities.

Furthermore, some individuals may be disabled by the impairment regardless of environmental settings while others may not be disabled by the impairment as a result of environmental accommodation and/or restructuring. The student in Sandoz's (2005) example, as described above, was disabled only if other students did not reduce the noise level. He was not disabled if his classmates decided to reduce the noise. Thus, in some situations, whether an individual is disabled or not is determined by the feasibility of environmental accommodations and how they are carried out in practice. There are also variations between different types of impairment/disability. Some types of impairment result in daily functional difficulty, and other types of impairment are context bound. Some types of impairment are invisible while other types are visible. Impairment/disability and an individual's experiences with other identities such as race, gender, class, or sexual orientation may be interdependent.

A practitioner needs to listen to a particular client's story attentively and ask specific questions in order to assess his/her/zir impairment/disability experiences with intersections of other identities. The practitioner also needs to be able to assess the impact of inappropriate dichotomous and hierarchical thinking styles on accurate assessment and treatment. The following personal stories illustrate variations in impairment/disability.

PERSONAL STORIES

VARIATIONS IN IMPAIRMENT/DISABILITY

Life Is All About Love

I met a man who was diagnosed with multiple melanoma about 5 years ago, and his prognosis was poor. However, he felt that his soul was awakened by cancer, and he realized what is important in life. He said he learned that life is all about love. He said he defined success by material achievement prior to having cancer. Now he is working hard to help children in poverty. He said he wants to help those in need as payment for all the blessings he has received. He has been seeking alternative treatment and is in remission. His spirits are high, and he has been working hard internationally to accomplish his goal. He practices the concept that life is all about love on a daily basis with his family, his community, and his project.

(Continued)

(Continued)

His Body Is Alive, but His Spirit Is Gone

Brian had cancer when he was 21, and now he is 31 and cancer free. However, he has been grieving since he was 13—for his parents' breakup, his father's abandonment, his girlfriend's betrayal with his friend while he was away at college, and then cancer. He was a happy child who excelled in school sports, music, and other activities prior to his parents' divorce. He became angry when he was a teen, and he has been depressed ever since breaking up with his girlfriend. He has lost the will to live, and surviving cancer did not seem to bring his spirit back. His body is alive, but his spirit is gone. He has no dreams. He is still numb. He has been numb for 18 years. Is he alive?

Cancer or Bipolar?

Pat is 25 years old and was diagnosed with bipolar disorder at 21. She had been moody and agitated ever since her sister's sudden death when she was 15. Her mother never thought she was bipolar but that she was reacting the way she did because of her sister's death and because she was a teenager. Her condition grew worse as she got older, yet Pat refused to go to a psychiatrist or a psychologist. She was emotionally intense when she was up and when she was down. Her thoughts raced constantly, and she became increasingly pessimistic when she was down and filled with grandiosity when she was up. She completed college despite her ups and downs. When she was up, she was overconfident and engaged in many projects. She was manic and unable to sleep. She often stayed up for a while making poor choices like drinking and driving and being generous with her money with friends who used her. When she was down, she would sleep most of the time and was filled with regrets and shame about her poor choices. She lost many friends due to making poor choices when she was manic but refused to recognize her problem. A series of reckless behaviors led her to involuntary psychiatric hospitalization at age 21 when she was diagnosed as bipolar. She was put on lithium and stayed in the hospital for about 10 days. She had at least six bipolar episodes after the initial hospitalization and went through 10 different medications, none of which seemed to work. Her mother brought her home whenever she was in one of her highs or lows to help her out.

> When her mother's friends told her that Pat needs to make it on her own rather than with her mother's help, her mother asked them if they would not help their son or daughter if he or she had cancer, and they said cancer is different. Pat's mother does not think cancer is any different from bipolar. She believes that her daughter will return to her previous state if her mood can be stabilized. Can we compare cancer to bipolar disorder?

☒ ABLEISM AND INAPPROPRIATE THINKING STYLES/PATTERNS

Ableism is a systematic problem. It is the result of systems and social structures giving advantage to individuals who are not disabled or impaired over individuals with impairment/disability. Governmental policies, laws, and rules and even the physical structures and designs of buildings give advantage to the privileged group, which consists of individuals who are not impaired or disabled. Ableism is constructed on the basis of hierarchical thinking that favors the values, beliefs, and attitudes of individuals without impairment/disability. It is not possible to have ableism without inappropriate dichotomous and hierarchical thinking. *Dichotomous thinking* has only two boxes, such as good and bad. As a result, people who are not impaired or disabled put "different" into a "bad" box in order to put themselves into a "good" box (self-appraisal theory). In *hierarchical thinking,* anything "different" is considered inferior to anything "not different." From a holistic perspective, on the other hand, "different" is interpreted as more than just "bad" or "good." The holistic perspective includes more than appropriate dichotomous and hierarchical thinking. For example, from a holistic perspective, any physical difference in one part of a person's body is considered only one dimension of one identity among multiple identities of the person. A person comprises a wide range of different dimensions, such as personality, intelligence, ability to provide empathy, ability to draw, ability to feel, ability to think and reason, and so on. In addition, the difference is only one layer of one dimension of the person, and there are many layers to this one dimension. If people think in a holistic way, it will be difficult to conceptualize a person as inferior or inadequate on the basis of only one difference in one aspect of a person's multiple dimensions and the multiple layers of one dimension. It is not possible to perpetuate ableism without inappropriate thinking styles/patterns.

Individuals with impairment/disability would not be labeled as inadequate or inferior if they lived in a society where people think and conceptualize from a holistic perspective. The author's clients would not have felt that their disability was inferior if people's dominant thinking patterns were not based on hierarchy. These clients were treated as if they were stupid when their difficulty was due to a neurological impairment.

ℕ STRATEGIES FOR AND BENEFITS OF DISMANTLING ABLEISM

Ableism needs to be dismantled at the personal, interpersonal, institutional, and cultural levels (Castaneda & Peters, 2000; Hehir, 2002). Deconstructing inappropriate dichotomous, hierarchical, and linear thinking styles/patterns is the main strategy for dismantling ableism at all levels. Thinking about such deconstruction is not enough to dismantle ableism. At the personal and interpersonal levels, individuals need to practice deconstructing ableism on a daily basis in order to minimize automatic activation. As individuals deconstruct inappropriate dichotomous and hierarchical thinking styles in relation to ableism, they will start to develop a diunital and holistic thinking style. Another strategy at the personal level is for individuals to examine their own stereotypes, biases, and assumptions in relation to disability/impairment and to critically examine their validity and purpose (Smith et al., 2008). Revisiting their internalized privilege and oppression in relation to ableism and restructuring cultural assumptions and standards are included in this process (Olkin & Pledger, 2003; Smith et al.). This process will gradually allow them to recognize individuals with impairment/disability as whole people who have multiple identities, talents, and unique characteristics and that their impairment/disability is only one dimension of one identity among multiple identities. This process will be likely to assist individuals with thinking of those who are impaired as people who have impairment/disability and not as impaired/disabled people. "Once people with disabilities are admitted inside the human and moral community, the task becomes one of creating an environment where all humans—including those with impairments—can flourish" (Adams et al., 2000, p. 338).

Another strategy at the personal and institutional levels is learning to conceptualize disability and impairment from the social model perspective by stopping the automatic tendency to perceive them from the medical model perspective. Individuals without impairment will gradually become aware of human-made barriers in architectural designs that lead to disablement. As these individuals without impairment gain the new perspective that individuals with impairment do not choose to be disabled, they will understand that institutions at times impose disability on individuals with impairment by enforcing cultural norms (Bryan, 2000; Donaldson, 2002; Gutierrez-Jones, 1998). Cognitive restructuring from the medical model to the social model allows individuals to think about what can be improved so that individuals both with and without disability/ impairment will have equal access to an institution. By shifting their focus from the medical model to the social model, individuals not only advocate for individuals with impairment/disability but also work together to promote equal access at institutional and governmental levels.

There are several concrete strategies for dismantling institutional ableism. First is educating members of institutions about disability and impairment. Disability/impairment awareness can begin for all members of an institution through reading, listening to speakers both with and without impairment, role-playing activities to increase compassion, and watching videos on a regular basis throughout the year (Olkin & Pledger, 2003; Smith et al., 2008). Institutions need to critically examine the physical structures of buildings and the degree of accessibility by individuals with impairment/disability in addition to reviewing policies and regulations to make sure that equal access is provided for individuals with impairment. The Rehabilitation Act of 1973 and the ADA have provided specific guidelines to eliminate discrimination against individuals with disability in terms of employment and physical accessibility (U.S. Department of Justice, U.S. Equal Employment Opportunity Commission, 2002/2005; U.S. Equal Employment Opportunity Commission, 2008). Disability advocates emphasize legal and political rights. What needs to be improved is social inclusion and cultural interdependency between people with impairment/disability and people without impairment/disability.

Dismantling ableism benefits all. Individuals with disability/ impairment will flourish, and other individuals will build genuine relationships with individuals with impairment/disability on the basis of human qualities (Overboe, 1999). Both parties will be able to learn from and support each other in discovering their potentiality and learning about each other's culture. Individuals may be able to connect who they are as people with all their unique characteristics. The concept of being differently abled will be understood and celebrated.

🕷 A PRACTITIONER'S ASSESSMENT OF SELF IN RELATION TO ABLEISM, SYSTEMATIC OPPRESSION/PRIVILEGE, AND INTERNALIZED OPPRESSION/PRIVILEGE

Psychologists and counselors specializing in various psychological disorders have been invited to be guest speakers by the author's multicultural counseling program since 1996. Every one of them has stated the importance of practitioners knowing themselves as a prerequisite to being competent practitioners. Smith et al. (2008) support this notion by stating that counselors' self-assessment in relation to ableism is one of the important components of practitioner training and education. The more practitioners are willing to examine their inner experiences with ableism, discrimination, and prejudice related to disability/impairment, the more they will be clear about who they are, and in turn this knowledge will assist them with accurate assessment of clients. The following reflection-based learning activities are designed to facilitate transformative learning about ableism for practitioner-trainees (Ferrer, Romero, & Albareda, 2005; Power & Dalgleish, 1997).

CONCRETE STRATEGIES

Reflection-Based Learning Activities on Ableism

Close your eyes and breathe in and out slowly, evenly, and deeply for 5 min. As you breathe, go back in your timeline as far as you can to see whether you recall experiencing any events related to impairment/disability in your childhood. Slowly open your eyes and do the following:

1. Describe your experience with impairment/disability.
    a. Which group did you identify with, the privileged or the oppressed?
    b. How did you feel about your experience with impairment/disability when you were a child and a teenager, and how do you feel about it now?

c. Did you share your experience with someone? If you did, with whom did you share it, and what was his/her/zir response?

   d. If you did not share it with anyone, what did you do with it?

   e. What was your feeling about your impairment/disability or lack thereof compared to that of your parents and friends?

   f. What did you learn from your teachers about ableism?

   g. What did you learn about systematic ableism privilege and impairment/disability oppression from your family when you were a child? Be specific.

   h. How did your group membership shape your worldview?

   i. Write down your intrapersonal communication, which is a reflection of your internalized oppression/privilege in relation to ableism.

   j. When was the first time you became aware of systematic oppression/privilege in relation to ableism/disability? Describe an incident in detail.

   k. Is your ableism/disability status different from that of your family members? If so, what overt and covert messages did you receive from your family, and how did these messages affect your relationship to your family and your worldview?

2. Write down any remarks about individuals with impairment/disability you heard while you were growing up from (a) family, (b) friends, and (c) the media. Write down any remarks you have made about individuals with impairment/disability. How did you feel when you made these remarks, and how do you feel about having made them now?

CONCRETE STRATEGIES

Consciousness Practice

What is it like being a person with or without impairment?

9

Other "Isms" Due to Age, Language, Religion, and Region

The purpose of this chapter is to examine "isms" related to age, language, religion, and region from a multilayered and multidimensional perspective. The chapter discusses the social construction of "isms," which are rooted in inappropriate hierarchical and dichotomous ethnocentric bias, and the necessity of transformative learning in examining systematic oppression/privilege and internalized oppression/privilege. The chapter also explores the complexities involved in the intersections among race, gender, class, sexual orientation, impairment/disability, age, language, religion, and region. It discusses the importance of understanding within-group and between-group variations, as well as of dismantling "isms." The chapter concludes with an emphasis on the accurate self-assessment of a practitioner and the impact of the self-assessment on her ability to understand clients' worldviews.

OTHER "ISMS"

There are identities besides race, gender, sexual orientation, class, and impairment/disability that construct a person's whole identity. Age, language, religion, region, size, and other identities are also significant aspects of constructing a person's overall identity. These may be more dominant (salient or special) identities for some individuals than those identities previously discussed. In this chapter, age, language, religion, and region are explored.

Ageism

The social structure of the United States segregates people according to age. This segregation leads to indifference toward other age groups, especially children and the elderly. Often, children and the elderly are discriminated against, marginalized, and silenced. They are oppressed by the system on the basis of their age. Ageism is more than discrimination against children or the elderly, however. It is more than prejudice, marginalization, and minimization. It is systematic advantages for dominant groups on the basis of chronological age. This means governmental, institutional, and organizational policies, laws, and rules are written to favor dominant age groups. Ageism is systematic oppression by which governmental and institutional policies and regulations give power to the dominant age groups (Calasanti, Slevin, & King, 2006).

The Elderly

Ageism is systematically marginalizing, institutionalizing, discriminating against, and taking away power, responsibility, and dignity from older adults (Nelson, 2002a; Nelson, 2005).

Due to the culture's emphasis on youth, older adults are often silenced in the United States, where older people not only have to deal with the developmental challenges related to aging but also are victims of ageism. They are often silenced before they can fully describe their problems as if those problems are due to the "natural aging process." The author's older clients frequently tell stories about how their health care providers do not listen to them. At times, their problems are not due to the aging process and could be remedied if they were heard. Many of the author's older clients feel they are treated as if their external changes equate to an internal deterioration of their intelligence and emotion. They feel objectified and treated as if they are no longer individual human beings (Burbank, 2006). Research supports the author's clients' narratives (Ivey, Wieling, & Harris, 2000; James & Haley, 1995; Reyes-Ortiz, 1997). Health care providers are not the only ones who marginalize and minimize the elderly. Ageism takes place at interpersonal, institutional, and cultural levels (Cuddy, Norton, &

Fiske, 2005; Greene, Adelman, Charon, & Friedmann, 1989; Hirsch & Vollhardt, 2002; Jones, Veenstra, Seamon, & Krohmer, 1997; Pasupathi & Lockenhoff, 2002). The youth orientation of U.S. culture tends to frame aging as a negative life event that needs to be avoided and denied. Excluding or silencing the elderly as if they don't exist is one way of focusing on youth. However, such exclusion—treating the elderly as "other"—often leads to elder abuse (Cook-Daniels, 1995; Hirsch & Vollhardt; Jones et al.; Kidd & Witten, 2008; Quinn & Tomita, 1986). The following is a personal story of an 80-year-old client who was treated as if her external changes equated to an internal deterioration of her intelligence.

PERSONAL STORY

One older client told me that she went to a self-service gas station and the attendant charged her about $10 more than the actual bill. She could not go back to the meter to check the price since another person had already started using the pump. She felt she had no choice but to pay the requested amount, which hurt because she was devalued due to her external appearance. Some older adults feel that they are pushed away from their culture as worthless people.

Old age is a part of the life cycle and needs to be accepted and appreciated as a part of the natural process of life. The unique characteristics of old age, such as not being able to see or hear very well, are a necessary part of the developmental process of aging. Both physical and biological aging change an individual's body shape and structure. However, the cultural myth in the United States that youth is better than old age, coupled with a belief in technological reconstruction, leads to some Americans' obsession with staying youthful "forever." This type of sociocultural context encourages many people to buy into commercialism, which emphasizes maintaining youth by consuming such products as antiaging creams, diet pills, and plastic surgery while considering the elderly as "other." Technological advancement may temporarily allow for a "youthful appearance," but it cannot prevent the neurological and physiological process of aging. Technological advancement cannot prepare individuals to deal with the emotional and psychological processes of human development that are taking place inside them. Inappropriate application of technology may cause further internal conflict for aging individuals since it enables their discontent with the natural developmental process. Being fixated on outer appearance is a form of denial and grandiosity, and it does not allow for dealing with the reality of the present moment. It blinds individuals to learning from the positive experience of getting old. Such discontentment with the natural aging process and desperate attempts to conquer nature's mysterious unfolding of life often leads to avoiding the elderly through unintentional discrimination, prejudice, and ageism. The concept of being "over the hill" at age 40 is incomprehensible to cultures that accept the natural process of aging by accepting inner and outer changes as processes of life. There is rich experience that can only come from fully living each stage of development. Individuals gain wisdom from integrating all of the experiences of each developmental stage to foster an intellectual and emotional understanding of life's unfolding mysteries.

Generalizations about old age on the basis of external appearances, cultural myths about old age, and denial of external appearances are invalid because physical aging is only one aspect (dimension) of aging among multiple dimensions and aging is only one identity among multiple identities of an elderly person. Chronological age and physical appearance do not give much information about an individual or a group of individuals. Physical appearance and chronologically old age do not provide information about the elderly person's health-related factors, psychosocial factors, spiritual factors, cognitive functions, or emotional functions. Studies indicate substantial individual differences in cognitive as well as emotional functions of the elderly due to differences in their psychosocial factors, health conditions, lifestyles, support systems, educational level, and gender (Bosma, van Boxtel, Ponds, Houx, & Jolles, 2003; Elwood, Pickering, & Gallacher, 2001; von Hooren et al., 2007). If the sociocultural context fosters living each moment to the fullest by embracing the mysterious unfolding of life, the elderly may enter another level of consciousness and transformation. If the sociocultural context encourages individuals to accept the reality of who they are, they will realize that birth and death are not results of human technology but of the natural process of life as its mysteries unfold. The elderly would enjoy living life without discrimination, prejudice, and ageism. They may also enjoy reflecting on, synthesizing, and integrating their life experiences. The following is a personal story of a 67-year-old colleague who was marginalized solely on the basis of her chronological age, which is only one aspect of her aging.

A colleague of mine who is 67 years old sprained and cracked her ankle while she was hiking up a steep mountain. She has been physically active all her life; she hikes, walks, and bikes regularly.

When she went to see the doctor, the nurse told her that it was going to take her a long time to heal since she is not a "young chick" anymore. Then the nurse proceeded to tell her she should act her own age by restraining her "rigorous" physical activities. When she began to recover much "faster than normal," however, both the doctor and the nurse were surprised. They did not know what to say to her. She was not fitting into their expectations of what is normal on the basis of her chronological age. They did not consider her personal health. In addition to getting regular exercise, she eats balanced and nutritious meals, is intellectually and emotionally satisfied with her work, and is surrounded by supportive friends and family.

Children

Children also suffer due to ageism. Children are often treated as if they do not have a voice. Many children are victims of domestic violence, neglect, or physical, emotional, or sexual abuse (Attar, Guerra, & Tolan, 1994; Cooley-Quile, Turner, & Beidel, 1995a, 1995b; Dempsey, 2002; Egeland, Carlson, & Sroufe, 1993; Frederick & Goddard, 2007; Groves & Zuckerman, 1997; Hudley & Novac, 2007; Jenkins & Bell, 1997; Marans & Adelman, 1997; Phillips, Voran, Kisker, & Howes, 1994). Children who report abuse to their parents often are minimized and become a target for suspicion instead of being protected from their abuser. Therefore, they become powerless at an early age and as a result have a higher tendency throughout their life to perceive the world from a victim's perspective. The author remembers a Japanese international student who, during a book seminar, could not stop crying about how many school-aged children are maltreated in the United States. This student said that in Japan she was raised in a poor family but had an abundance of love from family and neighbors. She asked, "How come the United States, which is supposedly the richest country in the world, ignores its own children?" The answer to her question is complex due to cultural differences, which are based on different values and belief systems.

From a collectivism-oriented cultural perspective like that of Japan, it is difficult to comprehend that the community does not take care of its children but a governmental agency such as the Department of Social and Health Services intervenes to take care of them. An individualistic society like that of the United States that takes pride in individual choice, rights, and freedom may lead the neighborhood people to be hesitant to help children in need because they do not want to impinge upon another's rights or invade another's privacy. The U.S. social system is set up so that others do not adopt a nurturer's role like they would in a collective culture. The extent of others' responsibility is reporting to an appropriate agency like Child Protective Services. Sociocultural contexts affect how each society provides intervention for children who are in need.

Research findings indicate the impact of emotional traumas on children's intellectual, social, emotional, and physical development (Hart, Binggeli, & Brassard, 1998; Harvey et al., 2003; Sanchez-Hucles, 1998; Shaley, 2002; van der Kolk, 2002). Many children are exposed to a spectrum of psychological and emotional traumas, but adults often do not intervene due to the lack of visible evidence. In an individualistic society like that of the United States, it is difficult for social agents like schools and Child Protective Services to intervene on the behalf of children who are exposed to emotional traumas because their policies require visible evidence. There is indication of delayed impact that is not evident at the time of trauma. Deater-Deckard, Dodge, and Sorbring (2005) found that lack of parental emotional support increases stress hormone release, and these children develop social reasoning bias. Social reasoning bias is selectively attending to only faulty judgment, which originated from psychological and emotional traumas such as being threatened, witnessing family and/or community violence, living in a hostile environment, and receiving little to no emotional support (Cooley-Quile et al., 1995a, 1995b; Hudley & Novac, 2007). Faulty judgment leads to selectively attending to social cues that are threatening and violent or to perceiving social cues as threatening and violent even if they are not (Huesmann, 1998; Novac, 2003; Waldman, 1996). By the time children and adolescents who are exposed to psychological and emotional stress manifest aggressive behavior due to social reasoning bias, it is almost too late to help them. The link between the neurobiology of the brain and the development of social reasoning bias derived from maltreatment of children indicates that once children learn to make meaning out of their environment, they view the world from that perspective (Cecchi, Khoshbouei, Javors, & Morilak, 2002; Deater-Deckard et al.; Downey, Khouri, & Feldman, 1998; Hudley et al., 1998;

Huesmann). The impact of emotional and psychological traumas on the development of the brain and social reasoning bias due to neurochemical changes needs to be considered for others to intervene at an earlier stage of children's development (Hudley & Novac, 2007).

Even well-meaning parents often unintentionally minimize their children due to *hierarchical thinking* patterns, which lead them to think they know what is best for their children. Some parents are so caught up in satisfying their own needs that they unintentionally ignore their children while rationalizing that they are good parents. Some parents who want to spend a great deal of quality time with their children cannot do so because they have to work to provide food and shelter. Some states provide health insurance and develop educational programs to aid these children, but they hardly provide children with emotional nurturing. The following reflection-based learning activities are designed to provide practitioner-trainees with a transformative learning experience.

CONCRETE STRATEGIES

Reflection-Based Learning Activities on Ageism

Close your eyes and breathe in and out slowly, evenly, and deeply for 5 min. As you breathe, go back in your timeline as far as you can to see whether you recall an experience with ageism. Slowly open your eyes.

1. Have you ever minimized, marginalized, or laughed at someone because of his/her/zir age (e.g., an elderly person or a child)?

   a. If you have, describe an incident.
   b. How did you feel about the incident then, and how do you feel about it now?
   c. Did you share your experience with someone? If you did, with whom did you share it, and what was his/her/zir response? If you did not share it with anyone, what did you do with it?
   d. What was your feeling about your age and that of others (e.g., elderly people and children)?
   e. What did you learn from your mother (or mother figure) about age?
   f. What did you learn from your father (or father figure) about age?
   g. What did you learn from your siblings (or sibling figures) about age?
   h. What did you learn from your teachers about age?

(Continued)

(Continued)

2. Have you ever been minimized, marginalized, or laughed at by someone because of your age?

   a. If you have, describe an incident.

   b. How did you feel about the incident then, and how do you feel about it now?

   c. Did you share your experience with someone? If you did, with whom did you share it, and what was his/her/zir response? If you did not share it with anyone, what did you do with it?

   d. What was your feeling about your age and that of others (e.g., elderly people and children)?

   e. What did you learn from your mother (or mother figure) about elderly people and children?

   f. What did you learn from your father (or father figure) about elderly people and children?

   g. What did you learn from your siblings (or sibling figures) about elderly people and children?

   h. What did you learn from your teachers about elderly people and chilren?

Language

People who speak English as their second language are able to articulate as well as others in their primary language. They often understand a lot more English than they are able to speak. Each language has a different grammatical structure, and it is especially difficult for ESL (English as a second language) speakers to thoroughly express themselves in English exactly like native English speakers. For example, Koreans answer the opposite way from North Americans when asked a question with negatives such as "Don't you want to go with me?" If Koreans want to go, they say, "No, I want to go with you" instead of "Yes, I want to go with you." When Koreans hear "Yes, I want to go with you," they do not understand what the reply means. On one occasion when the author shared this example in class, her Japanese students were delighted to hear that Koreans interpret English the same way as they do. Immigrants, international students, and refugees face more barriers in speaking English if their language structure and linguistic emphasis are different from those of English, because the style of verbal expression in an individualism-oriented culture is different from (not better than) that of a collectivism-oriented culture. For example, most North American students inform their professors that they will not be in class the next day by saying, "I won't be in class tomorrow because of a doctor's appointment." They usually state their intent before giving a short explanation for it. Most students from collectivism-oriented cultures, in contrast, would first describe their situation in detail and then describe their intent. They would say, "I have not been feeling well lately. First, I thought it was due to lack of sleep, but the feeling is persistent even if I sleep. I am not really sick but don't have energy . . . ," and at the end of their explanation they would say, "I really don't want to miss the class, but I think I need to see the doctor, and tomorrow is the only day available for the doctor to see me. Otherwise I will have to wait another 3 weeks." North Americans usually get impatient listening to this (circular) style of description because they are used to stating their intent first and then giving a brief description. When ESL speakers read nonverbal expressions of impatience, they become distracted and unable to articulate clearly.

As the author became more acculturated to the North American way of communication, her way of communicating according to the Korean language changed without her conscious awareness. The author's mother used to tell her that she had to read her letters at least two or three times in order to comprehend what she was really saying. The author's mother was confused because at the beginning of her letters, the author did not write like other Koreans, who traditionally describe the weather and nature (e.g., the color of the sky, trees) at the beginning of their letters. For example:

Dear Mom,

The sky is clear blue like a deep ocean waving at me to come and swim. The leaves are falling like they have been evacuated from their own home or country. They don't know where to go, and they wander around aimlessly, which reminds me of my life in the United States . . . .

Korean writers would continue in this manner for a while, and then they would make their main points in the middle of the letter, usually to close with ending remarks like the following:

My heart is filled with many more things I would like to share with you, and they are as big as the Gold Mountain; however, I need to put down my pen for now since time is running out . . . .

The way the author wrote to her mother was like a Korean translation of an American letter. The author would start out with "Hi Mom," then include her main points, and then write "Bye." The author's mother was expecting to connect with her daughter through the author's written expression of her personal experiences with the weather, the leaves, the skies, and so on. The Korean language uses a wide range of adjectives and adverbs to express different degrees of emotion and the process of understanding. As the author became more fluent in English, her way of verbal expression also changed from one of process orientation to one of product orientation. The author was focusing on her goals and objectives and not on processing her various emotions. As a result, the author's letters focused on her goals and objectives rather than on processing her feelings. The author's style of written expression changed partly due to the acculturation process and partly due to adopting the English language. To the author's mother, who was still in a collective culture that emphasized relationships more than goals and objectives, the author's letters did not make sense. In fact, the letters reminded the author's mother of an unfinished product without an introduction or an end; she had a difficult time comprehending them because she was hoping they would connect her with her daughter. Without knowing it, the author had abandoned the Korean way of letter writing. The author thought American letter writing was much more functional at that stage of her life. This was the result of acculturation. The author was in a hurry, and her mind was busy with planning her next task, with meeting her goals. The author did not have any time where she could just sit down and simply think of her mother. She did not have the psychological space to enjoy life as she was used to it in Korea. The author's busy life led her to be aware of the importance of time, and she became focused on how to save time to do all she had to do as a mother, wife, teacher, and therapist. The author found herself getting impatient with letters from Korea, which had lots of "unimportant" things at the beginning, so she skipped the first part of the letters to read the main part and then went back to read the letters from the beginning. The author had changed from a girl who watched leaves falling in autumn and cried because she had empathy for the poor dying leaves to a woman who was too busy to enjoy letters from her mother that were filled with a poetic expression of her love.

Sociocultural contexts affect learning English. For example, some concepts that the author has learned in the United States are very difficult to translate into Korean because Koreans do not deal with these concepts or because the author does not know a Korean way of expressing them. For example, most Korean college psychology textbooks do not describe Anna Freud's defense mechanisms correctly. When the author first read the Korean translation of defense mechanisms, she knew that it was incorrect. However, she did not know how to articulate defense mechanisms using a Korean vocabulary because she did not study psychology in Korea.

ESL speakers are immigrants, international students, diplomats and their families, and refugees. They represent various races (e.g., African Americans, American Indians, American Jews, Asian Americans, South Americans, Middle Eastern Americans, Central Americans, Caribbean Americans, Biracial Americans, Multiracial Americans), classes, ethnicities, sexual orientations, ages, impairments/disabilities, education levels, regions, religions, and languages. Their struggle does not end with language. They also struggle with adapting to new cultural values, rules, and customs (Bemak & Greenberg, 1994; Boothby, 1994; Chiu, 1995; Chung, 2001; Cross, 1995; Oropeza, Fitzgibbon, & Baron, 1991). Their intersection with multiple identities and sociocultural contexts determined them as whole individuals, and multiple factors affect their English proficiency levels. For example, most international students do not dare ask questions in class in front of the other students because they are afraid of being laughed at or not being able to express themselves adequately in English. They have anxiety about speaking English. Their English speaking becomes worse when listeners seem impatient (nonverbal language) because of their sentence structures and pronunciations. Some listeners may behave as if international students have a hearing or an intellectual disability. Native English speakers may talk to them loudly instead of pronouncing their words clearly and speaking slowly. Another example is understanding sociocultural context of refugees prior to their arrival to the United States may bring them to a different level of understanding, including with regard to their English proficiency. Refugees were forced out of their own countries before they came to the United States. They were forced to relocate whereas immigrants wanted to come to the United States. Being forced to leave one's country is a painful experience and affects refugees' adjustment in the United States. Being forced to relocate creates various kinds of helplessness, which manifests as "ungratefulness" toward America. If helping professionals (e.g., social workers, counselors, physicians, nurses) expect refugees to be "grateful" for shelters and food stamps, they are only looking at one dimension of one aspect of the sociocultural context and ignoring the other aspects of the sociocultural context in addition to ignoring the psychological and emotional dimensions of refugees. If they look upon refugees as "ungrateful" individuals who are taking resources away from North Americans, they may communicate this unintentionally to refugees through verbal and nonverbal language, which can lead to individual or institutional racism and classism. Due to wars, natural disasters, or political upheavals, refugees went through physical, mental, and emotional traumas prior to being forced out of their countries (El-Sarraj, Tawahina, & Heine, 1994; Kozaric-Korvacic, Folnegovic-Smale, Skringjaric, Szajnberg, & Marusic, 1995; United Nations, 1995).

There are other difficulties among immigrants, diplomats' families, and refugees. The lack of proficiency in English changes parents' status. Parents may no longer be authority figures. Instead, they have to rely on their children as their English translator, which creates a role reversal dilemma. Children who used to rely on their parents for emotional, psychological, and financial support take the role of parents in terms of providing information about what is going on in the culture while still relying on their parents for financial support. Emotional and psychological relationships between parents and children go through several changes during different stages of acculturation, and the process becomes much more complicated due to different degrees of acculturation between children and parents. Parents try to exert their authority in other areas in an attempt to maintain their place in the family structure. Most parents emphasize values they brought with them from their country and often do not consider the fact that their children are becoming Americans by going to American schools and being exposed to American mainstream culture. These children are at times frustrated since their parents are not the same as when they were in their own country. There are various complicated problems between parents and children due to unrealistic expectations and forced role reversals due to language.

People who have insufficient proficiency in English are discriminated against as if their lack of English proficiency is a representation of who they are as a whole person (Poyrazli & Lopez, 2007; Yeh & Inose, 2003). There are many factors to consider before passing judgment. Age, reason for coming to the United States, age at the time of arriving in the United States, class, gender, level of education, social support, degree of difference between an individual's own language and English, opportunity to practice English, degree of acculturation, years of residence in the United States, and years of schooling completed in the United States affect an individual's oral, written, and listening proficiency of English (Acevedo,

Loewenstein, Agron, & Duara, 2007; Acevedo et al., 2000; Ardila, Ostrosky-Solis, Rosselli, & Gomez, 2000; Coffey, Marmol, Schock, & Adams, 2005). Often, ESL speakers are treated as if they are deaf. They do not have a problem hearing. ESL speakers just have a problem comprehending what is said. ESL speakers want to tell listeners that they are hearing fine and their problem is understanding what they hear. They want to tell listeners that they are not deaf or retarded even though they might appear to be, but they do not tell them, partly due to carrying out their culturally conditioned interpersonal etiquette and partly due to being fatigued from trying to pronounce English. They, at times, forget that they speak their own language as fluently as Americans speak English. In addition, ESL speakers have other issues such as cultural adjustment, coping with the lack of social support, and dealing with regulations imposed by Immigration and Customs Enforcement (Andersen, 1994; Constantine, Kindaichi, Okazaki, Gainor, & Baden, 2005; Fernandez, 1988; Lewthwaite, 1996; Oropeza et al., 1991; Poyrazli & Lopez, 2007).

The following experiential learning activities are designed to provide the opportunity for developing empathy and compassion for people who are different from practitioner-trainees.

CONCRETE STRATEGIES

Experiential Learning Activities on Limited English Speaker(s)

Close your eyes and breathe in and out slowly and deeply for 5 min. As you breathe, go back to your timeline as far as you can to see whether you recall an experience with language. Slowly open your eyes.

1. Have you ever minimized, marginalized, or laughed at someone because of the way he/she/ze spoke?

   a. If you have, describe the incident.
   b. How did you feel about the incident then, and how do you feel about it now?
   c. Did you share your experience with someone? If you did, with whom did you share it, and what was his/her/zir response?

(Continued)

(Continued)

  d. If you did not share it with anyone, what did you do with it?
  e. What was your feeling about your language and that of others?
  f. What did you learn from your mother (or mother figure) about English spoken by nonnative speakers?
  g. What did you learn from your father (or father figure) about English spoken by nonnative speakers?
  h. What did you learn from your siblings (or sibling figures) about English spoken by nonnative speakers?
  i. What did you learn from your teachers about English spoken by nonnative speakers?

2. Have you ever been minimized, marginalized, or laughed at by someone because of the way you speak English?

  a. If you have, describe the incident.
  b. How did you feel about the incident then, and how do you feel about it now?
  c. Did you share your experience with someone? If you did, with whom did you share it, and what was his/her/zir response?
  d. If you did not share it with anyone, what did you do with it?
  e. What was your feeling about the way you speak English and the way others speak English?
  f. What did you learn from your mother (or mother figure) about the way you speak English?
  g. What did you learn from your father (or father figure) about the way you speak English?
  h. What did you learn from your siblings (or sibling figures) about the way you speak English?
  i. What did you learn from your teachers about ESL speakers?

Religion

There are various religions. Religion for some people is a source of strength in reaching inner peace and harmony. There are religious people and groups who practice their religious teachings of love and tolerance (Coward, 1986; Hunsberger & Jackson, 2005). There are also religious people and groups who, due to their religious ethnocentrism and ingroup loyalty, minimize, marginalize, oppress, and discriminate against people with different beliefs and lifestyles (Altemeyer, 2003; Bizumic & Duckitt, 2007; Juergensmeyer, 2000; Laythe, Finkel, Bringler, & Kirkpatrick, 2002; Laythe, Finkel, & Kirkpartrick, 2001). Some of these religious individuals commit acts of violence out of hatred toward those who are different.

The focus of this section is limited to persons and groups who discriminate against, marginalize, and condemn others with different beliefs and/or no religion. People who are intolerant of others in the name of religion need to understand that people who have different religious affiliations and/or different beliefs feel equally strongly about their own religions and/or beliefs. Judging or discriminating against other people or groups of people on the basis of religion is doing exactly the opposite of what religion claims to accomplish. The central theme of most religions is loving others and being compassionate toward and tolerant of others (Coward, 1986; Leak, 2006). Thinking that one religion is better than other religions for oneself is different from generalizing that one religion is better than other religions for all people (*hierarchical thinking*). This is an example of generalization on the basis of personal experience (sample size = 1) and projecting that everyone should think and feel in the same way (*social projection*). The phenomena of social projection and asymmetric perception seem to blind individuals from their ability to put themselves into others' position (Pronin, Gilovich, & Ross, 2004; Robbins & Krueger, 2005). Religious ethnocentrism, social projection, and asymmetric perception interfere with their ability to differentiate between expressing their passion and love for their own religion and marginalizing or oppressing others on the basis of difference in or lack of religious beliefs. Religious ethnocentrism is based on inappropriate hierarchical and dichotomous thinking.

Children are often praised or punished according to "right" and "wrong" behaviors. "Right" and "wrong" behaviors imply a moralistic undertone, and morals are often tied to religious values and principles even when they are prejudicial and discriminatory against other individuals and/or groups (Fulton, Gorsuch, & Maynard, 1999). How well children follow these values and principles is partly determined by how the significant adults in their lives (e.g., parents and teachers) communicate these values/morals to them. Some adults communicate their own wishes and expectations for children as if they are God's expectations

(Altemeyer, 2003). These parents and other adults use religion as a tool to threaten children to behave. Often, instead of directly stating that they are not pleased with a certain type of behavior, some parents say, "God watches you and knows everything about you." The author has seen numerous students and clients struggle with unnecessary guilt as a result of religious socialization and religious ethnocentrism. They expressed they were frightened as children because not only did they think they needed to behave but they also thought their thoughts needed to be "pure" at all times. "Pure thoughts" imply that they think, feel, and do what is acceptable by their religious beliefs at all times. The author once had a client who was a White North American by birth and had lived in the United States all her life. She was over 60 and a virgin because at the onset of puberty she was extremely frightened by the sexual feelings she began to have. She thought she was the only one who felt that way, and she wanted to stay far away from boys to make sure she would not "sin." She was a highly intelligent, kind, and compassionate person who had been grieving for her lost dream of getting married and having her own children.

Using religion as a tool to threaten children to behave has emotional undertones; burdens children with fear, guilt, and shame; and leads to formulation of implicit biases and attitudes about sense of self and others (Greenwald & Banaji, 1995; Rudman, 2004). Some of the author's students and clients were scared to honor or believe in themselves because they felt that honoring self and having confidence in self were against their religion. From their religious perspective, doing something for themselves or honoring themselves was considered selfish. When I asked them how they interpreted the Bible verse, "Love your neighbor as yourself" (Luke, 10:27), they said "as" means "same," but they were taught to love and be considerate of other people more than themselves. When the author asked them why they were feeling guilty or selfish for doing something for themselves, they stated that their socialization processes in relation to religion discouraged self-care and encouraged self-sacrifice. As a result, this caused internal conflict since their gut feeling did not match their intellectual understanding.

Others are socialized with institutional religious superiority, which often leads to unintentional discrimination against outgroup members (Bizumic & Duckitt, 2007). For example, hospitals that are affiliated with religions often practice unintentional discrimination against people with other religious affiliations or no religious affiliation. These hospitals accept patients from different religious affiliations; however, they do not provide local resource information from other religious groups. If the purpose of such hospitals is only to promote their own religion, they should accept only people of that faith or inform their patients about their intention of only providing their own religious resources for patients and families. If the purpose is to provide services for all people, they need to make sure resources of other faiths and of nonbelievers are available to pursue if patients and families desire to do so.

There are *multilayered* and *multidimensional* aspects of religions that are deeply embedded in individuals' emotional, sociological, and political aspects of life. After 9/11, some individuals harassed several of the author's students because they are Muslim, especially those whose facial features and skin color match the Muslim stereotype. These students are Americans. They were born and raised in the United States. They speak English fluently. However, in a fear-driven sociocultural context, they were discriminated against due to their religion and phenotypic physical characteristics. Because religions accompany strong emotion, people defend their religion and try to persuade others about their religious superiority. If religious people truly cared for their spirituality, they would be much more focused on their own behavior and thinking styles in order to experience harmony, peace, and stillness rather than on telling others what is best for them out of their own religious ethnocentrism. Most religions emphasize becoming a whole person through Godlike behavior. For example, being Christian means behaving like Christ, who died for Christians' salvation. In Buddhism anybody can become a Buddha by living life like Shakyamuni, who became a Buddha through enlightenment. From these perspectives, transcendence and transformation or enlightenment come through one's own internal work and not through judging other people from a hierarchical thinking style (Blackmore, 2004). The minimization of other religions, ethnocentric bias toward one's own religion, and outgroup bias due to religious differences are religious prejudice. Hate-related behavior such as violence toward others in the name of religion is a severe type of oppression (Kidd & Witten, 2008). It is similar to racism, sexism, heterosexism, classism, ableism, ageism, and other "isms."

The following reflection-based learning activities are designed to provide the opportunity for practitioner-trainees to examine their values and beliefs about religion.

CONCRETE STRATEGIES

Reflection-Based Learning Activities on Religion

Close your eyes and breathe in and out slowly and deeply for 5 min. As you breathe, go back to your timeline as far as you can and see whether you can recall an experience with religion. Slowly open your eyes.

1. Have you ever minimized, marginalized, or laughed at someone because of his/her/zir religion?
   a. If you have, describe the incident.
   b. How did you feel about the incident then, and how do you feel about it now?
   c. Did you share your experience with someone? If you did, with whom did you share it, and what was his/her/zir response? If you did not share it with anyone, what did you do with it?
   d. What was your feeling about your religion/lack of religion and that of others?
   e. What did you learn from your mother (or mother figure) about religion?
   f. What did you learn from your father (or father figure) about religion?
   g. What did you learn from your siblings (or sibling figures) about religion?
   h. What did you learn from your teachers about religion?

2. Have you ever been minimized, marginalized, or laughed at by someone because of your religion/lack of religion?
   a. If you have, describe the incident.
   b. How did you feel about the incident then, and how do you feel about it now?
   c. Did you share your experience with someone? If you did, with whom did you share it, and what was his/her/zir response?
   d. If you did not share it with anyone, what did you do with it?
   e. What was your feeling about your religion/lack of religion and that of others?
   f. What did you learn from your mother (or mother figure) about your religion/lack of religion?
   g. What did you learn from your father (or father figure) about your religion/lack of religion?
   h. What did you learn from your siblings (or sibling figures) about your religion/lack of religion?
   i. What did you learn from your teachers about your religion/lack of religion?

Region

There is a great deal of variation within the United States in relation to region. Some people from rural areas are different from some people from cities. There are different spectrums of cities and towns in the United States. New York City offers a variety of cultural events like plays, musicals, concerts, and art exhibits on a daily basis. Many immigrants, refugees, and international students find it odd that there are not that many cities like New York in the United States. They might come from very geographically small nations with a capital where there are a lot of activities like there are in New York. They might assume that all big cities in the United States would offer at least as much as their capital city in their country of origin (*generalization*). They might be surprised to hear that some people from rural areas in the southern parts of the United States still have outhouses instead of indoor toilets because this does not fit into their schema of cities in the United States.

Due to ethnocentrism and social projection, individuals tend to favor their own regions. Individuals have a tendency to forget that their own experience with their particular region belongs to them. It is their own experience (sample size $N = 1$, which is not generalizable to others' experiences), and there are numerous different experiences by different people. Insisting their own experience is the only valid experience and considering all other people's experiences are not as valid as theirs is *egocentric* and *hierarchical* thinking. There is also regional disparity related to economic disparity. Individuals who live in privileged areas may discriminate against individuals who live in oppressed areas such as those that are targets of environmental racism and high-crime areas. The following reflection-based learning activities are designed to provide transformative learning in understanding regional discrimination, biases, and prejudice.

CONCRETE STRATEGIES

Reflection-Based Learning Activities on Regional Bias

Close your eyes and breathe in and out slowly and deeply for 5 min. As you breathe, go back to your timeline as far as you can to see whether you recall an experience with region. Slowly open your eyes.

1. Have you ever minimized, marginalized, or laughed at someone because of where he/she/ze was from (region)?
   a. If you have, describe the incident.

(Continued)

(Continued)

    b. How did you feel about the incident then, and how do you feel about it now?

    c. Did you share your experience with someone? If you did, with whom did you share it, and what was his/her/zir response? If you did not share it with anyone, what did you do with it?

    d. What was your feeling about your regions (where you came from and where you lived then) and those of others (where they came from and where they lived then)?

    e. What did you learn from your mother (or mother figure) about people from different regions?

    f. What did you learn from your father (or father figure) about people from different regions?

    g. What did you learn from your siblings (or sibling figures) about people from different regions?

    h. What did you learn from your teachers about people from different regions?

2. Have you ever been minimized, marginalized, or laughed at by someone because of where you came from and/or where you lived (regions)?

    a. If you have, describe the incident.

    b. How did you feel about the incident then, and how do you feel about it now?

    c. Did you share your experience with someone? If you did, with whom did you share it, and what was his/her/zir response?

    d. If you did not share it with anyone, what did you do with it?

    e. What was your feeling about where you came from and where you lived and where others came from and where they lived?

    f. What did you learn from your mother (or mother figure) about where you came from and lived?

    g. What did you learn from your father (or father figure) about where you came from and lived?

    h. What did you learn from your siblings (or sibling figures) about where you came from and lived?

3. What did you learn from your teachers about where you came from and lived?

SOCIAL CONSTRUCTION OF "ISMS"

This book has discussed racism, sexism, classism, heterosexism, ableism, and other "isms," and the recurring theme has been the dominant groups having systematic privilege and power over the nondominant groups. As a result, governmental and institutional policies, regulations, and laws are structured around the dominant groups' standards and norms as if they are the only ones that matter. Croteau, Lark, and Lance (2005) illustrate the hierarchical nature of "isms" by summarizing Robinson's (1999) concept of "discourse":

> According to Robinson (1999), the "isms" are socially constructed through an interlocking system of discourses that rank social identities (e.g., valuing White people over people of color, those who are able-bodied over those with disabilities, and men over women). These discourses are referred to as "dominant" discourses to emphasize that the key principle within these discourses is one of dominance, or the valuing of one group over another. (p. 4)

"Isms" are based on ethnocentrism, and ethnocentrism is based on inappropriate dichotomous and hierarchical thinking. Ethnocentrism considers the ingroup superior and better than the outgroup (Aboud, 2003). Children as young as 5 years show that they not only have learned to be loyal to their ingroup but also have learned to dislike other children who do not conform to the norms of the ingroup (Abrams, Rutland, & Cameron, 2004; Abrams, Rutland, Cameron, & Margues, 2003; Nesdale & Brown, 2004). By the time these children grow up to be teens and adults, they will be ingrained with ingroup favoritism, social projection, and ethnocentrism. They are likely to selectively perceive events in their environment as fitting into their beliefs. The personal stories and research findings in this chapter support Robinson's (1999) definition of "isms." Not only are "isms" based on a *hierarchical* system; they are also based on *dichotomous* thinking. For example, ageism is constructed by institutional and societal age segregation in the United States. Age segregation divides individuals into "us" versus "them" (*dichotomous thinking*). Age segregation in the United States is forced upon individuals because U.S. society constructed rules and regulations on the basis of chronological age but treats them as if they are based on facts. Age segregation leads to ageism. Age segregation sets rules as to when children should start school, when they become adults, and when adults should retire from work. In other words, developmental tasks in each stage in the United States are socially constructed on the basis of chronological age and White middle-class values. These developmental tasks are considered "normal" and forced upon individuals who are not White or of the middle class (Hagestad & Uhlenberg, 2005; Mayer & Schopflin, 1989). Individuals who do not perform these developmental tasks according to what is considered "normal" by the dominant culture are pressured to conform according to these standards, even though they are not represented in formulating this normalcy. The author once had a Japanese American client who was socialized at home to be considerate of others by putting others first and reinforced for being obedient and quiet. However, his teacher wrote in his report card that he was too shy and needed to be "sociable with other children," implying that he needed to talk more with other children. Talking more with others is considered being "sociable" and a positive quality in the mainstream American values. The teacher imposed these mainstream values on the author's client without considering his cultural background, and his parents wanted him to follow the teacher's recommendation at school since teachers are valued and respected in Japanese culture. He was marginalized on the basis of who he was, a Japanese American, despite his excellent academic performance. Being a good student was not good enough for the teacher, and being a good son was not good enough for his parents because he did not please his teacher at school. He was confused due to this chaotic reinforcement between school and home, and it affected his identity construction.

Unintentional or intentional marginalization of international students, immigrants, and refugees on the basis of their proficiency in English is an example of linguistic ethnocentrism (Fadiman, 1997; Pedersen, Lonner, Draguns, & Trimble, 2007; Poyrazli & Lopez, 2007; Simon & Lynch, 1999). The injustice of socially constructed ethnocentrism is evident when monolingual North Americans discriminate against, minimize, and are prejudiced against others who demonstrate insufficient English proficiency when it does not interfere with their ability to perform their job. Religiously based prejudice, discrimination, and bias are also socially constructed on the basis of inappropriate dichotomous and hierarchical thinking. Targets for religiously based "isms" have changed over the years in the United States. Race was a target for religious "isms" from the 1940s to the 1970s, and sexual orientation was a target for religious "isms" in the 1990s (Hunsberger & Jackson, 2005).

Division and hierarchy are the foundation of socially constructed racism, sexism, heterosexism, classism, ableism, ageism, and other "isms" related to language, religion, and region. The fundamental principle underlying "isms" is unequal power distribution and systematic privilege and oppression to maintain unequal power distribution through implicit and explicit conditioning throughout the socialization process. The "isms" are due to ethnocentrism.

≈ SYSTEMATIC OPPRESSION/PRIVILEGE AND INTERNALIZED OPPRESSION/PRIVILEGE

Both dominant and nondominant groups perpetuate the appropriate social norms and standards without conscious awareness since conditioning starts before individuals are able to apply their own critical reasoning skills. When dominant groups perpetuate their own standards and norms, it is because of their internalized and systematic privilege. When nondominant groups perpetuate the dominant groups' norms and standards, it is because of accumulated internalized oppression. Children learn about systematic privilege and oppression throughout the socialization process, and these become internalized privilege and oppression without the children's conscious awareness (Altschul, Oyserman, & Bybee, 2006; Brody et al., 2006; Caughy, Nettles, O'Campo, & Lohrfink, 2006; Jackson, Barth, Powell, & Lochman, 2006; McHale et al., 2006). Understanding individuals' own internalized privilege and oppression in relation to age, language, religion, and region requires examining systematic privilege and oppression with critical and analytical reasoning skills while allowing for self-exploration of the emotional consequences of critical analysis. In other words, transformative learning needs to occur in order for individuals to transcend and heal from wounds created by both systematic oppression/privilege and internalized oppression/privilege. Intellectual understanding alone does not transcend and transform "isms." The following personal story may be an example of internalized oppression.

PERSONAL STORY

One of my closest friends from middle school came to the United States to stay with her sister who was a naturalized citizen. She arrived 3 months later than I did, and she understood that she would be attending college. But she realized that her sister was interested in using her as a babysitter rather than letting her go to college. About a year later, she got a job at a bank and moved out of her sister's house. I had not heard from her in a while when one day I received a letter from her. The letter was written in English, and she had changed her name to an American name. When I wrote back to her, I wrote in Korean, explaining that I did not feel like I knew her when she used another name and that I preferred to write in Korean because I could not articulate in English about our relationship since our friendship from middle school was developed in Korea using Korean language. I did not hear from her for another 2 years.

She called to tell me she wanted to visit me. We were so glad to see each other after so many years. When we met, she said she preferred speaking in English because she had forgotten the Korean language. I could understand if we were with non-Korean speakers, but I didn't know why we needed to speak in English when only we were visiting. I assumed her Korean listening and speaking proficiency was as good as mine since she came to the United States 3 months later than I did. So I spoke in Korean and she spoke in English when only the two of us were visiting. It was very confusing. She said she liked being an American, avoided Koreans, and disliked Korean culture. She was interested in perfecting her English to an extent that she'd had numerous surgeries to alter her vocal cords. She said she wanted to be born with blue eyes and blond hair after this life and asked me what I wanted to be in my next life. I told her I was too busy living this life and had never thought about the next life or what I wanted to be.

We see each other whenever I pass her city on my way to or from Korea. I gave up speaking in Korean to her since it was confusing to use two languages to converse. When my 5-year-old son asked me why I spoke in English with her when I spoke Korean with all other Koreans, I found it was a hard question to answer to a 5-year-old child. Her attitude toward other Koreans stayed the same. She wanted nothing to do with Koreans or Korean culture. So, she would drop me off to see other Korean friends and would come and pick me up. I often wondered whether her behavior was a sign of internalized oppression. Even if she has not been personally oppressed because she is a person of color, she has been acculturated in a country where being White is favored institutionally and culturally over being a person of color.

The following reflection-based learning activities are to facilitate individuals' understanding of systematic oppression/privilege and internalized oppression/privilege through transformative learning. When individuals complete both reflection-based and experiential learning activities in relation to age, language, religion, and region, they are likely to gain new knowledge about complexities of identity construction from intersections among age, language, religion, and region. This new knowledge is a byproduct of experiencing emotional and intellectual understanding through transformative learning.

CONCRETE STRATEGIES

Reflection-Based Learning Activities on Oppression/Privilege

Close your eyes and breathe in and out slowly and deeply for 5 min. As you breathe, go back to your timeline as far as you can to see whether you recall an experience with a certain *age** or *age* issues during your childhood.

1. Describe your memory of *age* privilege or oppression.

2. How did you feel about it when you were a child and a teenager, and how do you feel about it now?

3. Did you share your experience with someone?

   a. If you did, with whom did you share it, and what was his/her/zir response?

   b. If you did not share it with anyone, what did you do with it?

4. What was your feeling about your *age* compared to that of your friends?

5. What did you learn from your teachers about *age*?

6. What did you learn about systematic *age* privilege and/or oppression from your family when you were a child? Be specific.

7. Did you belong to a privileged or an oppressed group, and how has this shaped your worldview?

8. Write down your intrapersonal communication, which is a reflection of your internalized *age* oppression/privilege.

(Continued)

(Continued)

9. When was the first time you became aware of systematic oppression/privilege in relation to *age*? Describe the incident in detail.

10. Write down any remarks about *age* you heard while you were growing up from (a) family, (b) friends, and (c) the media. How did you feel about them? Write down any remarks related to age that you have made. What was your motivation for making these remarks? Write down your intrapersonal communication on *age*.

*Repeat the same activities by replacing *age* with *language, religion,* and *region*.

Automatic Activation

Researchers define age, race, and gender categories as "primitive" or "automatic" categories because responses to them are easily activated (Butler, 1969; Fiske & Neuberg, 1990; Hamilton & Sherman, 1994; Nelson, 2002b, 2005; Schneider, 2004; Swann, Langlois, & Gilbert, 1999). The theory that stereotypes and prejudice in the areas of race, gender, and age are automatically activated is supported by various research findings (Banaji & Greenwald, 1994; Chen & Bargh, 1997; Greenwald & Banaji, 1995; Henderson-King & Nisbett, 1996; Schacter and Scarry, 2001; Susskind & Hodges, 2007). Because attitude is gradually formed throughout the socialization process, prejudicial attitudes can be automatically activated in individuals often without their conscious awareness. Children learn to discriminate or reject intergroup children on the basis of their ingroup social identity whether it is race, gender, class, religion, language, or region (Brewer, 2001; Killen, 2007; Killen, Richardson, Kelly, Crystal, & Ruck, 2006; Nesdale & Brown, 2004; Nesdale, Durkin, Maass, & Griffiths, 2005a, 2005b; Verkuyten, 2007).

Object relations theory postulates that caregivers' role is crucial in early emotional development, primary identification, and dependence. Aviram (2007) writes:

To various degrees, identification with caregivers become[s] the emotional experience of self (Fairbairn, 1952). Fairbairn's theory suggests that if primary identification persists into adulthood and dependence needs are directed beyond the family, primary identification with these parental substitutes would minimize differentiation between self and group. In such cases, primary identification with the group continues to function as a defensive operation promoting an over-identification with the group to compensate for the experienced inadequacy of the infantile character. (p. 6)

Object relations theories explain from an emotional developmental perspective the ingroup and outgroup relationship in the early stage of life. Unmet early childhood emotional needs may have an impact on overidentification with the ingroup because the ingroup is experienced as the self. The emotional component in ingroup identification may be a catalyst for automatic activation of prejudice against the outgroup. Identification with the ingroup is a dynamic relationship between an individual and the group within a particular sociocultural context. The group identity is often called collective identity, and when the individual is minimized, oppressed, or marginalized, collective identity is automatically activated, the self–group boundary becomes a blur, and the individual reacts (Aviram, 2007). This reaction may be expressed as strong dislike against outgroups that oppressed, marginalized, and minimized collective identity. "The stronger the identification with the ingroup the greater is the likelihood of outgroup hatred" (Aviram, p. 9). Due to this deep-rooted emotional component and automatic activation, it is difficult to transcend "isms" related to age, language, religion, and region.

⧹⧹ INTERSECTIONS OF RACE, GENDER, SEXUAL ORIENTATION, CLASS, IMPAIRMENT/ DISABILITY, AND OTHER IDENTITIES

An individual can only be understood when his multiple identities and their intersections are examined because multiple identities (e.g., race, gender, class, sexual orientation, impairment/disability, language, religion, region, age) are interrelated to different degrees and manifest their characteristics in various sociocultural contexts. When counterdiscourse includes only intersections of some identities and neglects other identities, one still does not know the whole person. For example, race may be the only important (dominant or salient) identity for some people but not for others. Individuals' whole identity construction needs to be explored by examining intersections of multiple identities.

Assessment of intersections of multiple identities needs to be based on the person's narrative and not other people's assumptions. This is a challenging task not only because of the tendency to simplify by dichotomous thinking but also because a comprehensive practical and theoretical model is not available.

Bieschke, Croteau, Lark, and Vandiver (2005) summarize the dilemma of inclusion of all social identities:

> While we strongly believe that the counterdiscourse needs to more fully integrate multiple social identities and cultural contexts, such a shift toward complexity and inclusiveness will be painful, giving rise to unexplored conflicts and necessitating difficult exploration and dialogues. (p. 203)

Without fully integrating multiple identities, intersections of multiple identities, and sociocultural contexts, clients will not be accurately assessed and treated, and knowing a client's worldview will be impossible. The following reflection-based experiential learning activities are designed to identify one's dominant identity, one's multiple identities, and their intersections.

CONCRETE STRATEGIES

Reflection-Based Experiential Learning Activities

A. Salient Identity

1. Indicate whether you belong to a privileged group or an oppressed group in relation to the following identities: (a) race, (b) gender, (c) class, (d) sexual orientation, (e) age, (f) disability/impairment, (g) religion, (h) language, and (i) region. The question is not whether you feel privileged but whether you belong to a privileged group according to your society.

2. Which of the above identities are important to you? Rank the above identities in order of importance, with 1 being the most important to you and 9 being the least important to you.

3. Close your eyes and breathe in and out slowly and evenly for 5 min. Pay attention to your feelings and the images that come to mind as

you breathe. Slowly open your eyes and write or draw about your feelings from Question 2.

4. What have you learned from these activities?

B. *Intersections*

Prepare drawing materials (at least two sheets of drawing paper and a box of crayons, coloring pencils, or paints). Close your eyes and breathe in and out slowly, evenly, and deeply for 5 min. As you are breathing in and out slowly, think and feel about your intersections of disability/impairment, race, gender, class, sexual orientation, age, language, religion, and region. Slowly open your eyes.

1. Draw your intersection of disability/impairment, race, gender, class, sexual orientation, age, language, religion, and region.

2. Write about what you drew.

3. Have you been pressured to be loyal to disability/impairment, race, gender, class, sexual orientation, age, language, religion, or region by each community?

   a. How do you feel when you are pressured?
   b. How do you balance your need to be loyal to your inner values and your communities' requests?
   c. How is your narrative similar to and different from that of each of your communities?

VARIATIONS WITHIN AND AMONG AGE, LANGUAGE, RELIGION, AND REGION

Variations within age, language, religion, and region are as diverse as variations among age, language, religion, and region. Not all elderly adults feel marginalized, discriminated against, and silenced. Not all people whose first language is not English feel that they are discriminated against or minimized because of their insufficient English proficiency. Not all people with religious affiliation show religious prejudice against those whose belief systems are different from theirs. Not all people living in a particular region demonstrate regional biases toward people who live in different regions. People from the same state are different from region to region. People from the same region in the same state are also different from each other. Making *generalizations* that people from the same regions have the same characteristics is judging people on the basis of one external aspect of one identity among multiple identities. *Generalizations* about one region being better than the other regions is geographic ethnocentrism on the basis of hierarchical thinking. Most people have the tendency to prefer what is familiar to them, but they do not have to put down other people's familiarity in order to justify their preference.

People are different even if they come from the same region regardless of the size of the region. Some people in small towns do not care for city life or city people, but not all people in small towns do not care for city life or city people. People from the same region have different family histories (birth order, socioeconomic class, religion, racial and ethnic backgrounds, etc.), and these have affected their worldviews. In addition, people show their preferences, biases, prejudices, and discrimination to different degrees and at different intensities. Thinking holistically by including individuals' multilayered and multidimensional aspects facilitates understanding and perceiving variations within as well as among groups in relation to age, language, religion, and region. The following personal story is an example of regional dialectic differences within the United States.

PERSONAL STORY

Region and Language in the United States

Virginians' dialect is different from that of Washingtonians. When we moved to Virginia to pursue our master's degrees, my partner and I went to a hardware store to buy a few things for the apartment. At the end of our purchase, the clerk said, "You all come back." My partner started to follow the clerk even though I said I did not think he wanted us to come back literally. Since I frequently trusted native speakers' linguistic interpretations as more sound than mine, I followed my partner, who followed the clerk to the back of the store. When the clerk realized we all followed him to the back, he looked puzzled. We had a good laugh about that. A Washingtonian did not know "You all come back" was the same as "Come again."

OTHER "ISMS" AND INAPPROPRIATE THINKING STYLES/PATTERNS

Dichotomous and hierarchical thinking patterns perpetuate the cycle of "isms" against age, language, religious, and regional equity. Within this frame of reference, it is impossible to transcend and discover or create a new vision of relating to people with different religious affiliations, people with no religious affiliation, people in different age groups, non-English speakers or ESL speakers, and people with different regional backgrounds.

Whether they speak with an accent, struggle to pronounce English words, or explain in a circular style, some people are able to speak another language as well as Americans speak English. If these people are not judged from a hierarchical thinking perspective, which puts English proficiency on the top, native English speakers may have compassion for their struggle to articulate rather than being impatient with them. It is not possible to give power and privilege to one group over the other groups if society does not value dichotomous and hierarchical thinking. "Isms" are not possible when all social identities are given equal power by society and by people. "A shift toward complexity and inclusiveness will be painful" partly due to long-held beliefs of ethnocentric bias in each demographic group and partly due to the long-held practice of simplifying the complex issues (Bieschke et al., 2005, p. 203). Changing one's thinking style from simple "either/or" thinking to "both/and" thinking is a difficult task both emotionally and intellectually. However, not changing it because it is painful and difficult will allow "isms" to perpetuate generation after generation, just like they have been doing since America's birth. Ethnocentrism of dominant groups will perpetuate at individual, institutional, and cultural levels. It will also become more difficult to change.

STRATEGIES FOR AND BENEFITS OF DISMANTLING "ISMS"

Dismantling "isms" requires deconstructing inappropriate dichotomous and hierarchical thinking and developing and practicing diunital and holistic thinking at the personal, interpersonal, institutional, and cultural levels. It is important to pay attention to an individual's responsibility in dismantling "isms" because "although oppression is often institutionalized at societal levels, it is necessarily enacted in the context of interpersonal relationships" (Birrell & Freyd, 2006, p. 52). Deconstructing inappropriate thinking styles leads to deconstructing negative *generalizations* about old age, children, ESL speakers, religion, and region at the personal, interpersonal, institutional, and cultural levels. For example, deconstructing inappropriate thinking styles will lead to awareness of the consequences of limits to generalization, awareness of the consequences of excluding some sociodemographic identities, awareness of evaluating an individual's worth on the basis of one single aspect (e.g., class) of an identity among multiple identities, and awareness of an inaccurate assessment of a person. Similarly, individuals will become aware that generalizing about their own identity, one language, one religion, or a certain age on the basis of hierarchical and dichotomous reasoning only perpetuates "isms," which are based on ethnocentrism.

At personal and interpersonal levels, individuals can assess their own implicit attitudinal biases and stereotyping by taking the Implicit Association Test (IAT). This can be done alone in front of a computer. An individual is instructed to press keys rapidly without thinking in response to a pair of tasks on a computer screen (http://implicit.harvard.edu/implicit/). The IAT results will indicate which area one should work on in order to deconstruct his/her/zir biases related to sexism, racism, heterosexism, ableism, and other "isms." This is a task at an individual level, but it affects institutional and cultural levels since individuals make up institutions and societies. At the institutional level, children at school and home can be taught to favor the ingroup without rejecting or putting down the outgroup (Verkuyten, 2007). Susskind and Hodges (2007) found that middle school children want to see their ingroup positively without desiring to see the outgroup negatively. Preschool children viewed both the ingroup and the outgroup positively when they were asked to rate them independently. However, when they were asked to rate both groups simultaneously, they rated the ingroup much more positively (Kowalski, 2003). Hopeful tendencies toward dismantling marginalization and minimization of the outgroup were shown by children in middle childhood who demonstrated fairness in their rating of the ingroup and the outgroup (Rutland, 2004). According to Rutland, this was a result of social pressure put on them to be fair. This study suggests that children can be taught to be mindful of social justice and equity for others. They need role models who work across differences collaboratively. Counterdiscourse within the multicultural movement needs to happen if the movement is really serious about implementing multicultural counseling competencies and becoming a role model for processing pain and difficult emotional issues through affective transformation in order to engage in counterdiscourse.

In terms of dismantling the violence cycle for children, Ortega, Beauchemin, and Kaniskan's (2008) study revealed a family-based intervention approach as the most effective strategy. The study found that giving immediate attention and support to families with a higher stress level was crucial, and reducing family stress by identifying specific types of factors was suggested. Using a narrative approach has been effective in dismantling "isms" associated with psychological traumas because it provides material for narrative analysis of trauma experiences, which can provide insight for victims and professionals (Harvey, Mishler, Koenen, & Harney, 2000; Sorsoli, 2007). Incorporating students' religious identity into treatment strategies is another way to dismantle "isms" related to religion.

Person-to-person contact is another way to dismantle "isms" (Floyd & Shinew, 1999). Peterson (2007) described how to transcend "isms" by observing men gathering at someone's home and sharing a meal for more than 20 years. Each gathering was informal with a low level of tension, and the focus was hospitality. There were only four "informal expectations":

> no telling of jokes that demean another person or group, no discussion of professional sports, no self-aggrandizement through "hero" stories, and no networking for personal gain. (p. 74)

The gathering started with six men getting together once a month to provide mutual support and share their inner stories in the early 1980s. This longitudinal gathering showed the power of person-to-person contact in dismantling "isms." Peterson (2007) concludes:

> What *Another Level* demonstrates is that men of various backgrounds and living in different locations are able to build strong, positive relationships that transcend social boundaries of race and geography and do this outside of institutionalized settings. Intentional "hanging out" together and holding each other accountable to clear "expectations" has allowed these men to build a strong sense of mutual trust and has encouraged trust-worthiness to be a primary characteristic of their friendships with each other. (p. 80)

There are numerous benefits for dismantling inappropriate hierarchical, dichotomous, and linear thinking and learning holistic thinking. Holistic thinking will allow individuals to accept each other's identities as just each other's identities. There are no better or worse identities. For example, if individuals apply a holistic thinking style to interactions with the elderly, they will accept old age as part of life's natural developmental process. Instead of alienating old people, they will include them in the community and society and learn from their experiences. Children, teenagers, and young adults will accept the elderly as they are. They may learn things from old people's experiences that they could not learn from technology and material goods. They may learn how to cope with the unavoidable aging process from the elderly and reassess their priorities in order to live life to the fullest. Adults may learn from children's creative thought process, innocence, and spontaneity, all of which lead adults to revitalization, and children may learn to value and accept themselves. Individuals may also be willing to learn from collectivism-oriented cultures about how to protect their children as a community. In a collectivistic society, neighborhood adults and relatives take care of children whenever there is a need. This means almost everything from providing love to disciplining the children. Loving and disciplining neighbors' and relatives' children is included as a part of the responsibility of adults in the community whether their parents provided these needs or not.

If individuals use a diunital thinking style from a multilayered and multidimensional perspective, they will be able to see the beauty of each region. Individuals may enjoy and learn from each other's experiences in regions to which they have not been. Each region offers its distinctively beautiful gifts, which are not comparable to those of another region. Individuals who were socialized in cities may love New York City's cultural events because New York City offers familiar activities that they learned to value. The big, old mansions along the Gulf of Mexico in Louisiana, Mississippi, and Alabama are beautiful with rich history and Southern traditions, and they may remind some individuals of scenes from *Gone With the Wind*. Individuals may learn that people in different regions dress up more than in other regions. Individuals who live in Minnesota may love the colorful leaves of "10,000 lakes" without thinking that their region is better than other regions. Santa Fe's stars and adobe houses, Washington's Puget Sound and mountains, the Creator's masterpiece that is the Grand Canyon, and the endless farmland in Montana, Idaho, Washington, Oregon, Vermont, Massachusetts, Florida, and California all have their distinctive beauty. There are too many beautiful places in the United States to list them all. These places are not comparable because each is unique in its beauty and people who live there. Some value a particular region that may not be understood by people in other regions. There also are differences in dialect and accent in each region. People from the East Coast pronounce English words differently from those on the West Coast or in the South. All of these differences are celebrated and enjoyed without ethnocentrism in a holistic thinking perspective. The following personal story illustrates illogical assumptions based on inappropriate hierarchical thinking.

PERSONAL STORY

Dismantling inappropriate hierarchical and dichotomous thinking allows individuals to critically examine the purpose and function of ethnocentrism, prejudice, discrimination, and oppression. For example, if I say I am better than you because I am a college professor, I also need to examine the purpose and function of my statement. If my purpose and function are to put you down because I have more formal education, it is a result of my narrow perspective about education. I may have more formal education than you, but that does not necessarily mean that I have more education since education comes from various life experiences including formal education. You may have less formal education but many more life experiences than I do. My statement has no function. If my purpose is to make you do something for me, I need to just ask you. If I am trying to impress you on the basis of my education in order to make you do something for me, my assumption that you will do it because you are impressed by my formal education is illogical and is based on hierarchical thinking.

〰 A PRACTITIONER'S ASSESSMENT OF SELF IN RELATION TO OTHER "ISMS," SYSTEMATIC OPPRESSION/PRIVILEGE, AND INTERNALIZED OPPRESSION/PRIVILEGE

Accurate assessment, intervention, and treatment of a client are dependent on a practitioner's awareness of her values, beliefs, biases, and prejudices. In order to provide counseling services to those whose cultural backgrounds are different from her own, the practitioner needs to know pathways to understanding the client's worldview (Constantine et al., 2005). Understanding her worldview with desire to know the client's worldview will facilitate her ability to understand the client's worldview. When the practitioner has no awareness of the impact of race, gender, sexual orientation, impairment/disability, age, language, religion, and region on her own values, attitudes, beliefs, and biases, she may unintentionally pathologize clients not because she consciously assumes she is better but because of her lack of knowledge about the impact of multiple identities, intersections of multiple identities, systematic oppression/privilege, and internalized oppression/privilege on the client's worldview (Robb, 2006). Knowing oneself takes the courage to be open and honest with oneself, the ability to reflect, and the ability to assess oneself from unconventional and conventional modes of inquiry. The following activity is designed for a practitioner-trainee to assess identities and oppression/privilege related to age, language, religion, and region.

CONCRETE STRATEGIES

Self-Assessment on Multiple Identities and Systematic Oppression/Privilege and Internalized Oppression/Privilege

Close your eyes and breathe in and out slowly, evenly, and deeply for 5 min. As you breathe in and out, think and feel about your self-assessment of age, language, religion, and region and related systematic oppression/privilege and internalized oppression/privilege. Be mindful of your thoughts and feelings without censoring and without judgment. Slowly open your eyes.

1. Describe your self-assessment of age, language, religion, and region. Which identities will create countertransference, and what are you planning on doing to minimize it?

2. We have discussed nine identities. State which identities you belong to in a privileged group and which ones you belong to in an oppressed group.

   a. Describe your thoughts and feelings about being in the privileged groups as well as in the oppressed groups.
   b. How did the above (Question 1) shape your identities?

c. What do you need to do (how do you need to think, feel, and behave) in order to minimize your experience of being in the privileged and/or oppressed group as a practitioner? Describe your answer in detail.

d. Rank your identities from 1 to 9, with 1 being the most important and 9 being the least important: (a) race, (b) gender, (c) class, (d) sexual orientation, (e) disability, (f) age, (g) language, (h) religion, and (i) region.

e. Write down your barriers to becoming a multiculturally competent practitioner on the basis of your ranking.

f. What did you learn from Question 1, and how does your learning hinder or facilitate your becoming a practitioner?

CONCRETE STRATEGIES

Consciousness Practice

Are you conscious now? Where is your conscious experience?

10

Deconstructing Inappropriate Hierarchical, Dichotomous, and Linear Thinking Styles/Patterns

This chapter discusses challenges involved in deconstructing inappropriate hierarchical, dichotomous, and linear thinking styles/patterns. The chapter discusses the need to deconstruct inappropriate thinking styles through transformative learning due to a history of emotional attachment to these inappropriate thinking styles. Specific and concrete strategies for deconstructing these thinking styles are explained, and examples of how to deconstruct such thinking styles and experiential learning activities relating to multiple identities (race, gender, sexual orientation, class, age, language, religion, and region) are provided. Practitioner-trainees are encouraged to use their daily recording of inappropriate hierarchical, dichotomous, and linear thinking styles/patterns from Chapter 2 for their experiential learning material.

This chapter provides another way to deconstruct inappropriate thinking styles by examining internalized oppression and privilege. Practitioner-trainees are encouraged to use their recording of internalized oppression/privilege from the learning activities in Chapters 5–9. and, step by step, to work through deconstructing hierarchical, dichotomous, and linear thinking applied in internalized oppression and privilege. This chapter emphasizes diligent and mindful practice of deconstructing inappropriate thinking styles since implementation of conceptual understanding is only possible through walking the talk of equity and justice.

◊◊ REASONS FOR CHALLENGE

Identifying inappropriate hierarchical, dichotomous, and linear thinking styles/patterns is the first step to deconstructing these inappropriate thinking styles, which have been "vehicles of oppression" (Root, 1992, p. 4). However, it is difficult to identify them since cultural values and beliefs are structured around these thinking styles. The article "Race and Sexual Orientation in Multicultural Counseling: Navigating Rough Waters" articulates the difficulty eloquently:

> The dominant White Eurocentric worldview upon which social institutions and interpersonal norms are built in this country is my "home" cultural perspective; the worldview that comes quickest and most natural for me is the worldview that is privileged in this society. Furthermore, the sense of White privilege is the socially defined space that I began life with, my first "given" so to speak. In that sense, it is the base out of which I construct my life as a White gay man in a racist and heterosexist world. (Croteau & Constantine, 2005, p. 179)

As stated above, most individuals who are socialized with the "dominant White Eurocentric worldview" have been inundated with hierarchical, dichotomous, and linear thinking styles from birth. Thus, sorting out inappropriate hierarchical, dichotomous, and linear thinking styles from appropriate thinking styles is challenging since dichotomous and hierarchical thinking styles have been a part of individuals' thought process and have contributed to shaping their worldviews. The fact that dominant values are embedded in the American psyche has been evidenced by a variety of research in relation to race, gender, sexual orientation, class, impairment/disability, age, language, religion, and region. Controversies between a multicultural perspective that is race based and a multicultural perspective that is inclusion based illustrate embedded hierarchical thinking, creating division within the multicultural perspective. A multicultural perspective that is race based is theorizing that "race and racism is primary and superordinate to other issues of diversity and oppression" (Bieschke, Croteau, Lark, & Vandiver, 2005, p. 205). Race may be a primary identity for some people but creates exclusion for those whose primary identity is not race based. Statements like "I still find it hard to believe that heterosexism and homophobia could be as painful or difficult to bear as racism" (Croteau & Constantine, 2005, p. 171) are from a *hierarchical* perspective with ethnocentric bias. A multicultural perspective that considers only one social identity as the most important identity in comparison to other identities is hierarchical. As long as individuals with multicultural backgrounds only want to be inclusive of what they value and believe and exclude the other identities they do not value, achieving equity and justice for all people will not be feasible.

Hierarchical, dichotomous, and linear thinking styles have been a part of giving individuals a sense of accomplishment, reward, affirmation, and confidence (Nash, 1992; Nugent, 1994; Powlishta, Serbin, Doyle, & White, 1994; Root, 1992). These thinking styles have assisted individuals with learning culture-specific ingroup values, which help their identity construction (Farver, Kim, & Lee, 1995; Friedlmeier & Trommsdorff, 1999; Stetsenko, Little, Gordeeva, Grasshof, & Oettingen, 2000). Ingroup favoritism, which is one type of ethnocentric bias, is automatically processed and automatically activated partly because individuals have been conditioned to favor ingroups since early childhood. Individuals have not been conditioned to think of the impact of their ingroup favoritism on outgroups. Research on aversive racism and implicit learning provides excellent examples of how intellectual understanding of justice and equity is separate from long-held beliefs about ingroup favoritism that are embedded in White superiority (*hierarchical* thinking) and division (*dichotomous* thinking). In Chapter 4, it was discussed that individuals who showed aversive racism believed that they were allies of people of color (Dovidio & Gaertner, 2000, 2004, 2005; Dovidio, Kawakami, & Gaertner, 2002; Gaertner & McLaughlin, 1983). Ingroup favoritism includes more than intellectual and rational dichotomous and hierarchical reasoning. It encompasses a wide range of emotions from joy and euphoria to loneliness and fear. These emotions are intertwined with relational dynamics such as approval or rejection of significant people in individuals' lives. Knowles and Peng (2005); Ponterotto, Utsey, and Pedersen (2006); and Robbins and Krueger (2005) discuss the little progress that has been made to embrace people who are different, and this can be explained from a perspective of ingroup favoritism to enhance collective self-esteem without necessarily thinking of consequences of ingroup ethnocentric bias on outgroups (Aberson, Healy, & Romero, 2000; Rubin & Hewstone, 1998; Verkuyten, 2007).

DECONSTRUCTING THROUGH TRANSFORMATIVE LEARNING

Due to deep-rooted emotional attachment to ingroup favoritism, deconstructing inappropriate hierarchical, dichotomous, and linear thinking must focus on understanding the affective transformative process as well as the rational transformative process (Boucouvalas, 1997; Cranton & Roy, 2003; Daloz, 1999; Kovan & Dirkx, 2003; Mezirow, 2000a; O'Sullivan, Morrell, & O'Connor, 2002; Yorks & Kasl, 2002). In order for the affective transformative process to occur, individuals need to accept themselves as they are. It is necessary that they do not judge or censor themselves to be aware of inner experience. There are various methods to facilitate affective transformation such as narrative writing, imagery, and silence. The narrative writing can be in journal form or of an autobiographical nature. Both have been effective for self-knowledge, healing, and spiritual awareness (Baldwin, 1991; Cameron, 1992; Cappacchione, 1992). Imagery plays a vital role in integrating conscious and unconscious material. Unconscious material can be brought to a conscious level through writing and/or drawing imagery (Cameron; Kast, 1993; Progoff, 1992). Silence is a powerful tool for accessing inner experience, and silence is one way to communicate. There are some experiences that cannot be articulated by words but need to be experienced in order to gain insight. How to use silence as an accurate assessment and effective therapeutic tool will be discussed in Chapters 13 and 14. Individuals need to practice these strategies mindfully and diligently on a regular basis for affective transformation to occur. The following experiential learning activities use imagery, memory, and reflection to facilitate transformative learning about compassion.

CONCRETE STRATEGIES

Experiential Learning Activities on Compassion

Recall some of your emotional pain. Write down your responses to the following questions. Be honest with yourself. This activity is only for your awareness. You can destroy your written responses at the end of this activity. Regardless of your race, gender, class, education, sexual orientation, religion, and age, you must have experienced at least one incident where you felt powerless, hopeless, and helpless.

1. Recall the times you were minimized, misunderstood, discriminated against, shamed, embarrassed, and/or oppressed. Try to recall your feelings in detail.

   a. Who minimized you?
   b. How old were you?
   c. What did you do?
   d. What was most helpful to make you feel better?
   e. What was the lesson from this experience?
   f. How does this incident affect you now?

After you have completed your responses to the above questions, proceed with the following questions.

2. Think and feel about how other people are discriminated against because of their differences. Imagine their oppression, anger, frustration, shame, isolation, alienation, hurt, humiliation, self-doubt, confusion, loneliness, betrayal, and so on.

   a. Write and/or draw your feelings and thoughts.
   b. What do you think would help these people feel better or regain self-respect?
   c. What would you do differently today after attempting to understand their pain by remembering your own pain or wound?
   d. Are you still insensitive or judgmental? Do you still feel superior to these people? Explain.

Automatic activation of inappropriate thinking patterns/styles can be stopped by thinking about other people's "isms" as equal to one's own. This allows an individual to evaluate "isms" through "controlled processing" and resist or avoid the use of stereotypes (Devine & Monteith,

1999; Macrae, Bodenhausen, Milne, & Jetten, 1994; Wegener, Clark, & Petty, 2006). The above experiential learning activities are designed to stop automatic inappropriate thinking by encouraging individuals to remember their own pain and experiences with minimization, marginalization, or oppression. This allows individuals to consider other people's pain equal to their own pain. The affective transformative process begins when practitioner-trainees take the personal affective position in an attempt to feel the client's feelings through remembering their own painful experiences. When this experiential learning activity is used in class with multicultural counseling students and in diversity workshops for professionals, most students and professionals are able to be compassionate toward others whose pain has been caused by injustice and inequity. These are moments of affective transformation. Deconstructing long-held beliefs of hierarchical and dichotomous thinking styles/patterns requires more than just cognitively understanding the concept of deconstruction of inappropriate thinking styles/patterns. It requires the affective transformative process.

For rational or cognitive transformative learning, choose one specific example from your daily recording of intrapersonal communication of inappropriate thinking styles to begin deconstructing. In Chapter 2, there were concrete strategies designed to assess individuals' inappropriate hierarchical, dichotomous, and linear thinking on the basis of daily recording of inner dialogue (intrapersonal communication). Reread your responses to these learning activities and pick one example of hierarchical thinking to begin deconstructing. One effective way to deconstruct is to work with a specific and concrete personal example of a hierarchical, dichotomous, or linear thinking style. To describe thinking styles in an abstract or a conceptual way sounds intellectual and sophisticated but does not lead to a change. A change requires both intellectual and emotional understanding of conceptual strategies and concrete steps to implement them. Focusing on specifics and operationalizing inappropriate thinking styles are necessary for the rational transformative process. This process is similar to behavior modification. Selecting a reachable learning objective on the basis of a baseline is the first step. Developing instructional strategies to reach the learning objective requires not only finding an appropriate reward for a particular individual, as well as an appropriate time and frequency of administering the reward, but also defining success operationally. The following is a copy of the experiential learning activities from Chapter 2.

CONCRETE STRATEGIES

Inappropriate Hierarchical Thinking and Intrapersonal Communication

The purpose of these activities is to gain conscious awareness of how you think and how your thinking style affects your interpersonal communication. It is important that you do not judge, censor, or minimize your inner dialogue (intrapersonal communication).

Experiential Learning Activities

Reread your recorded inner dialogue (intrapersonal communication) and do the following.

1. Examine whether you used inappropriate hierarchical thinking and what happened as a result. Draw a picture to symbolize the results or describe the results in writing.

2. If you used an inappropriate hierarchical thinking style, describe the first time you were exposed to it.

3. Did your parents, siblings, and/or schoolteachers use inappropriate hierarchical thinking styles while you were growing up? What did they say? How did these statements shape your intrapersonal communication?

4. Close your eyes for about 5 min while breathing in and out slowly and evenly. Reflect on your answers to the previous questions. Open your eyes and write down your relationship to the inappropriate hierarchical thinking style.

5. Think of one incident where you were frustrated with a client, a co-worker, a family member, or a friend. What were your assumptions? What did you expect? Was your frustration related to inappropriate hierarchical thinking? If so, explain.

6. Estimate the percentage of inappropriate hierarchical thinking in your inner dialogue each day.

The following is the author's response to the above questions in relation to one example of hierarchical thinking.

CONCRETE STRATEGIES

1. I used to think Americans are dirtier than Koreans because they wear street shoes in the house. This was a gross generalization on the basis of whether one wears shoes in the house or not.

2. I cannot remember the first time I was exposed to this inappropriate hierarchical and dichotomous thinking. Thinking that Americans are dirtier than Koreans came from dichotomous thinking rather than hierarchical thinking.

3. My parents and teachers emphasized always doing my best, and if my assessment was that I did my best, I needed to be satisfied that I did my best regardless of how others evaluated my behavior. I don't remember what my sister said. She was 10 years older than me, and I don't remember her influence on me when I was little. My parents and teachers, however, affected me greatly. My intrapersonal communication includes asking myself whether I did my best at a particular time and then, if my assessment is I did, letting it go. My success level is determined by process (effort) and not the product (achievement).

4. I don't really have a relationship with appropriate or inappropriate hierarchical thinking styles since they are not my primary thinking styles. Sometimes I am misunderstood by those who think hierarchically. They interpret my nonhierarchical comments in a hierarchical way. For example, if I say, "I finished" because I am delighted that I have completed an activity and not because I want to put another person down, others might say something like "I know I am lazy. You don't have to remind me" or "I know you are thinking I am not motivated." I am often puzzled by these statements because I don't understand why they would come to that conclusion from my statement.

5. I have not been frustrated with clients. I have been frustrated with coworkers, however, because I expect them to deliver their promised commitments but they do not always do so. I am from a family that considered commitment a high priority, and I often forget that this is not a high priority for some people. It is not related to hierarchical thinking.

6. 1%

Process of Deconstructing the Hierarchical Thinking

My desire not to wear shoes in the house still persists. Visitors usually take off their shoes in my house even though they are not required to do so. I no longer look at the issue with critical Korean cultural eyes. I know the custom of wearing or not wearing shoes in the house differs from culture to culture. I just prefer not wearing shoes in the house, and I do think the house stays cleaner when shoes are not worn inside; I do not, however, think Americans dirty because they wear shoes in the house. My children have asked why they have to take their shoes off in the house while their friends wear shoes inside their houses. I told them that different cultural groups teach different cultural customs and values to their children and I prefer some Korean customs and values, including not wearing shoes inside the house. If someone wears shoes inside in Korea, he or she is considered "crazy" because taking off shoes inside is the norm. However, it is normal to wear shoes inside in the United States, so it does not bother me if my guests wear shoes inside my house. I know that I am in the United States and the United States has different customs from Korea.

It was discussed in Chapter 3 that writing and reflecting on inner experiences gives access to unconscious processes, and the writing process builds, integrates, and synthesizes separate aspects of an individual's inner life. It was also explained that consciousness studies indicate that objective and subjective experiences are not separated in the inner world and do not operate linearly and sequentially but interact simultaneously (Blackmore, 2004; Metzinger, 2003; Searle, 1997). Through writing down her answers to the questions above, the author learned that hierarchical thinking can be based on dichotomous thinking. The following is another experiential learning exercise to assist practitioner-trainees with deconstructing dichotomous thinking. It is a copy of the reflection-based learning activities from Chapter 2 about inappropriate dichotomous thinking styles.

CONCRETE STRATEGIES

Inappropriate Dichotomous Thinking and Intrapersonal Communication

The purpose of these activities is to gain conscious awareness of how you think and how your thinking style affects your interpersonal communication.

(Continued)

(Continued)

It is important that you do not judge, censor, or minimize your inner dialogue (intrapersonal communication). Read your response to the following questions and write the process of deconstructing inappropriate dichotomous thinking.

Reflection-Based Learning Activities

Record your inner dialogue (intrapersonal communication) on a daily basis for at least a week to 10 days and then do the following:

1. Examine whether you used an inappropriate dichotomous thinking style and what happened as a result. Draw a picture to symbolize the results or write them down.

2. If you used an inappropriate dichotomous thinking style, do you recall the first time you were exposed to it?

3. Did your parents, siblings, and/or schoolteachers use inappropriate dichotomous thinking while you were growing up? How did this shape your intrapersonal communication?

4. Close your eyes for about 5 min while breathing in and out slowly and evenly. Reflect on your answers to the previous questions. Open your eyes and write down your relationship to the inappropriate dichotomous thinking style.

5. Think of one incident where you were frustrated with a client, boss, or friend. What were your assumptions? What did you expect? Was your frustration related to inappropriate dichotomous thinking? If so, explain.

6. Estimate the percentage of inappropriate dichotomous thinking in your inner dialogue each day.

Individuals must complete these experiential learning activities with each self-identified inappropriate thinking style in order to deconstruct these thinking styles. Every time an inappropriate thinking style is deconstructed, an individual gains self-knowledge that is only available through experiencing both rational and affective transformation by completing these learning activities. As individuals complete these writing activities on deconstructing inappropriate thinking styles, they are learning not only how to integrate reasoning (intellect) with affect (emotion) but also how to think holistically. Individuals are transforming through participating in these experiential learning activities. Conceptual learning alone will not be effective in deconstructing inappropriate hierarchical, dichotomous, and linear thinking because it will be based on only an intellectual assumption of how it is going to be done rather than on learning from actually experiencing. By practicing deconstructing inappropriate thinking styles, individuals will discover that holistic thinking will lead them to understand that most human qualities and relationships are multifaceted, multilayered, and interrelated. They are too complex to fit into simple generalizations.

░ INTERNALIZED OPPRESSION/PRIVILEGE AND THINKING STYLES/PATTERNS

Another way to deconstruct inappropriate hierarchical, dichotomous, and linear thinking is to examine the extent of one's internalized privilege and oppression in relation to multiple identities (e.g., race, gender, sexual orientation, class, impairment/disability, age, language, religion, region) as discussed throughout Part II of this book. Studies have implied that internalized privilege and oppression are due to constant and consistent exposure to systematic privilege and oppression in relation to race, gender, class, sexual orientation, disability, age, language, religion, and region, and this is also based on inappropriate *dichotomous* and *hierarchical* thinking (Barry, 1995; Brody et al., 2006; Brown & Bigler, 2004: Bryan, 2000; Caughy, Nettles, O'Campo, & Lohrfink, 2006; Cuddy, Norton, & Fiske, 2005; Donaldson, 2002; Garofalo, Wolf, Wissow, Woods, & Goodman, 1999; Greene, Adelman, Charon, & Friedmann, 1989; Gutierrez-Jones, 1998; Hirsch & Vollhardt, 2002; Jackson, Barth, Powell, & Lochman, 2006; Jones, Veenstra, Seamon, & Krohmer, 1997; Levy, Sadovsky, & Troseth, 2000; Liben, Bigler, & Krogh, 2001; McHale et al., 2006; McKown & Weinstein, 2004; Nelson, 2002a; Nelson, 2005; Pasupathi & Lockenhoff, 2002; Perdue & Gurtman, 1990; Remafedi, Farrow, & Deisher, 1991; Thompson & Zoloth, 1989; Valian, 2004). For example, pathologizing non-White students could be viewed as ingroup favoritism, which may be due to the practitioner's internalized racial privilege as a result of having learned to value the dominant cultural values, or it could be due to her internalized oppression. She may have no conscious awareness of her racial prejudice. In order to minimize the pathologization of non-dominant group members, practitioners need to be aware of their values, beliefs, and biases and the impact of these values, beliefs, and biases on their ability to be multiculturally competent. The following questions are designed to examine the relationship between inappropriate thinking styles and an individual's affective and cognitive information on internalized privilege and oppression. Thus, portions of previous experiential learning questions on racism, sexism, heterosexism, classism, ableism, and ageism from Chapters 4 through 9 are brought up due to their feasible relevancy in understanding an individual's foundation of inappropriate hierarchical, dichotomous, and linear thinking styles. It is important to participate fully in the following learning activities in order for both a rational and an affective transformative process to take place. Conceptual understanding alone does not transcend ingrained inappropriate thinking patterns that are the basis for ethnocentrism.

CONCRETE STRATEGIES

Experiential Learning Activities for Race Experience and Inappropriate Thinking Styles

Please reread your responses to Questions 1 and 2.

1. Describe your memory of White privilege or racial discrimination, prejudice, or racism at school.

   a. How did you feel about it then, and how do you feel about it now?

   b. What did you learn from your teachers about race? Be specific.

2. What did you learn about race from your family when you were little? Be specific. If your parents applied racialized socialization practice, what was the main message? How does that message affect you now?

3. How much of your inappropriate hierarchical, dichotomous, and linear thinking is related to one or more of the above questions?

4. Read one of your race-related examples of inappropriate hierarchical, dichotomous, or linear thinking. Deconstruct the thinking style and rewrite your example in a nonhierarchical, nondichotomous, and nonlinear way.

CONCRETE STRATEGIES

Experiential Learning Activities for Gender Experience and Inappropriate Thinking Styles

1. Indicate whether you belong to a privileged group or an oppressed group in relation to gender. The question is whether or not you belong to a privileged group according to your society regardless of your feeling of oppression or privilege.

2. Describe your experience with gender privilege or oppression at school.

   a. How did you feel about it then, and how do you feel about it now?
   b. What did you learn from your teachers about gender? Be specific.

3. What did you learn about gender from your family when you were little? Be specific.

   a. If your parents applied gendered socialization practice, what was the main message? How does that message affect you now?

4. How much of your inappropriate hierarchical, dichotomous, and linear thinking is related to one or more of the above questions?

5. Read one of your gender-related examples of inappropriate hierarchical, dichotomous, or linear thinking. Deconstruct the thinking style and rewrite your example in a nonhierarchical, nondichotomous, and nonlinear way.

CONCRETE STRATEGIES

Experiential Learning Activities for Sexual Orientation Experience and Inappropriate Thinking Styles

1. Indicate whether you belong to a privileged group or an oppressed group in relation to sexual orientation. The question is whether or not you belong to a privileged group according to your society regardless of your feeling of oppression or privilege.

(Continued)

(Continued)

2. Describe your experience with sexual orientation privilege or oppression at school.

   a. How did you feel about it then, and how do you feel about it now?
   b. What did you learn from your teachers about sexual orientation? Be specific.

3. What did you learn about sexual orientation from your family when you were little? Be specific. If your parents applied gendered socialization practice, what was the main message? How does that message affect you now?

4. How much of your inappropriate hierarchical, dichotomous, and linear thinking is related to one or more of the above questions?

5. Read one of your sexual orientation–related examples of inappropriate hierarchical, dichotomous, or linear thinking. Deconstruct the thinking style and rewrite your example in a nonhierarchical, nondichotomous, and nonlinear way.

CONCRETE STRATEGIES

Experiential Learning Activities for Class Experience and Inappropriate Thinking Styles

1. Indicate whether you belong to a privileged group or an oppressed group in relation to class. The question is whether or not you belong to a privileged group according to your society regardless of your feeling of oppression or privilege.

2. Describe your experience with class privilege or oppression at school.

   a. How did you feel about it then, and how do you feel about it now?
   b. What did you learn from your teachers about class? Be specific.

3. What did you learn about class from your family when you were little? Be specific. If your parents applied class socialization practice, what was the main message? How does that message affect you now?

4. How much of your inappropriate hierarchical, dichotomous, and linear thinking is related to one or more of the above questions?

5. Read one of your class-related examples of inappropriate hierarchical, dichotomous, or linear thinking. Deconstruct the thinking style and rewrite your example in a nonhierarchical, nondichotomous, and nonlinear way.

CONCRETE STRATEGIES

Experiential Learning Activities for Disability/Impairment Experience and Inappropriate Thinking Styles

1. Indicate whether you belong to a privileged group or an oppressed group in relation to impairment/disability. The question is whether or not you belong to a privileged group according to your society regardless of your feeling of oppression or privilege.

2. Describe your experience with impairment/disability privilege or oppression at school.
   a. How did you feel about it then, and how do you feel about it now?
   b. What did you learn from your teachers about impairment/disability? Be specific.

3. What did you learn about impairment/disability from your family when you were little? Be specific. If your parents applied nondisability or nonimpairment socialization practice, what was the main message? How does that message affect you now?

4. How much of your inappropriate hierarchical, dichotomous, and linear thinking is related to one or more of the above questions?

5. Read one of your impairment/disability-related examples of inappropriate hierarchical, dichotomous, or linear thinking. Deconstruct the thinking style and rewrite your example in a nonhierarchical, nondichotomous, and nonlinear way.

CONCRETE STRATEGIES

Experiential Learning Activities for Age Experience and Inappropriate Thinking Styles

1. Indicate whether you belong to a privileged group or an oppressed group in relation to age. The question is whether or not you belong to a privileged group according to your society regardless of your feeling of oppression or privilege.

2. Describe your experience with age privilege or oppression at school.

   a. How did you feel about it then, and how do you feel about it now?
   b. What did you learn from your teachers about age? Be specific.

3. What did you learn about age from your family when you were little? Be specific. If your parents applied age segregation socialization practice, what was the main message? How does that message affect you now?

4. How much of your inappropriate hierarchical, dichotomous, and linear thinking is related to one or more of the above questions?

5. Read one of your examples of inappropriate hierarchical, dichotomous, or linear thinking. Deconstruct the thinking style and rewrite your example in a nonhierarchical, nondichotomous, and nonlinear way.

CONCRETE STRATEGIES

Experiential Learning Activities for Language Experience and Inappropriate Thinking Styles

1. Indicate whether you belong to a privileged group or an oppressed group in relation to language. The question is whether or not you belong to a privileged group according to your society regardless of your feeling of oppression or privilege.

2. Describe your experience with language privilege or oppression at school.

   a. How did you feel about it then, and how do you feel about it now?
   b. What did you learn from your teachers about language? Be specific.

3. What did you learn about language from your family when you were little? Be specific. If your parents applied language proficiency socialization practice, what was the main message? How does that message affect you now?

4. How much of your inappropriate hierarchical, dichotomous, and linear thinking is related to one or more of the above questions?

5. Read one of your examples of language-related inappropriate hierarchical, dichotomous, or linear thinking. Deconstruct the thinking style and rewrite your example in a nonhierarchical, nondichotomous, and nonlinear way.

CONCRETE STRATEGIES

Experiential Learning Activities for Religion Experience and Inappropriate Thinking Styles

1. Indicate whether you belong to a privileged group or an oppressed group in relation to religion. The question is whether or not you belong to a privileged group according to your society regardless of your feeling of oppression or privilege.

2. Describe your experience with religious privilege or oppression at school.
   a. How did you feel about it then, and how do you feel about it now?
   b. What did you learn from your teachers about religion? Be specific.

3. What did you learn about religion from your family when you were little? Be specific. If your parents applied religion-oriented socialization practice, what was the main message? How does that message affect you now?

4. How much of your inappropriate hierarchical, dichotomous, and linear thinking is related to one or more of the above questions?

5. Read one of your religion-related examples of inappropriate hierarchical, dichotomous, or linear thinking. Deconstruct the thinking style and rewrite your example in a nonhierarchical, nondichotomous, and nonlinear way.

CONCRETE STRATEGIES

Experiential Learning Activities for Region Experience and Inappropriate Thinking Styles

1. Indicate whether you belong to a privileged group or an oppressed group in relation to geographic region. The question is whether or not you belong to a privileged group according to your society regardless of your feeling of oppression or privilege.

2. Describe your memory of regional privilege or oppression at school.
   a. How did you feel about it then, and how do you feel about it now?
   b. What did you learn from your teachers about region? Be specific.

3. What did you learn about region from your family when you were little? Be specific. If your parents applied region-oriented socialization practice, what was the main message? How does that message affect you now?

4. How much of your inappropriate hierarchical, dichotomous, and linear thinking is related to one or more of the above questions?

5. Read one of your examples of region-related inappropriate hierarchical, dichotomous, or linear thinking. Deconstruct the thinking style and rewrite your example in a nonhierarchical, nondichotomous, and nonlinear way.

☷ DILIGENT AND MINDFUL PRACTICE

An individual's salient (dominant or special) identity, the importance of belonging to the ingroup, and sociocultural contexts of developmental milestones also influence the individual's thinking styles. The following is feedback from one of the author's former students on deconstructing inappropriate dichotomous and hierarchical thinking:

Starting to know my special identity and realizing my own personal bias were what helped to deconstruct dichotomous and linear thinking . . . (a) $N = 1$ which stressed not only the importance of this concept to research, but also in the realization that my experience is equal to myself and can only be generalized to me, (b) how situations, people's identities, and experiences are multi-layered and multi-dimensional which led to acceptance of multiple existence of reality. (Kim, 2005)

The next step after identifying sources of inappropriate hierarchical, dichotomous, and linear thinking styles/patterns and writing down how to deconstruct inappropriate thinking styles is mindful practice of appropriate thinking styles and statements. Understanding the impact of inappropriate thinking styles/patterns on equity and justice for all people is not the same as applying this understanding in practical situations. Deconstructing inappropriate thinking styles/patterns requires diligent and mindful practice on a daily basis. At the beginning, this is a tedious procedure because it seems the individual is repeating the same concept (deconstructing inappropriate hierarchical, dichotomous, and linear thinking). The individual is repeating the same concept over and over again in order to break the illusion that it will be automatically transferred to application since he/she/ze understands the concept intellectually. There is no automatic transfer. A transfer is only possible through repeating the tedious procedure until it becomes second nature. When the application becomes automatic, the automatic activation of inappropriate hierarchical, dichotomous, and linear thinking stops. Transferring from an inappropriate thinking style to an appropriate thinking style is like learning a foreign language. The only way to master verbal and written expression of a foreign language is to practice. No amount of understanding grammatical structures will assist with speaking and listening proficiencies. Deconstructing inappropriate thinking styles starts as higher-level information processing, which takes more time, whereas activation of inappropriate thinking styles is automatic and processed at a lower level. Lower levels of information processing and inconsideration of the target (an individual, individuals, or a group) lead to automatic activation whereas higher levels of processing and consideration of the target take time and allow for "controlled processing" (Gilbert & Hixon, 1991; Macrae, Hewstone, & Griffiths, 1993; Wegener et al., 2006). Strategies to achieve "controlled processing" are applying critical reasoning skills, participating in self-assessment through Internet Web sites, and being aware of emotional attachment to dominant and nondominant values, beliefs, stereotypes, and prejudices. The more individuals apply "controlled processing" (Wegener et al.), the more they will be able to avoid or stop the automatic activation process.

It is important to learn to apply "controlled processing" in order to slow down or stop the automatic processing of inappropriate thinking styles. Inappropriate hierarchical, dichotomous, and linear thinking affects individuals' perception, and perception affects individuals' inter- and intrapersonal communication. For example, did they hear another person marginalizing or laughing at them, or did they interpret (perceive) the information according to a hierarchical thinking style? Did they examine their intrapersonal and interpersonal communication by applying scientific inquiry skills learned from conducting an experiment or critiquing research articles, or did they interpret the information from a perspective of internalized oppression or privilege? Critical inquiry like these questions will facilitate controlled processing, and this process will also assist practitioner-trainees with decreasing automatic usage of inappropriate hierarchical, dichotomous, and linear thinking styles/patterns.

〰 TRANSFORMATION AT THE INSTITUTIONAL LEVEL

Deconstructing inappropriate hierarchical, dichotomous, and linear thinking styles/patterns at an individual level creates a foundation for institutional and cultural transformation for equity and justice for all people. Teachers who diligently and mindfully practice deconstructing inappropriate hierarchical, dichotomous, and linear thinking styles can be models for students. They can use holistic and inclusive languages to instruct students. Research indicates that both preschool children and preadolescents assigned positive attributes to both ingroups and outgroups when instruction did not force them to pick one group over the other. When instruction was given to assign attributes to both genders instead of picking one gender or the other (dichotomous instruction), there was less ingroup favoritism in gender attribute studies (Kowalski, 2003; Powlishta, 1995; Susskind & Hodges, 2007). Preschoolers in Kowalski's study viewed both ingroups and outgroups positively when they were instructed to respond nondichotomously. Teachers can also help students interpret events in multiple ways. Teachers, managers, supervisors, and coaches may model ingroup favoritism, but this does not always indicate outgroup exclusion. Ingroup favoritism may occur without intergroup comparison or outgroup negativity (Bennett et al., 2004; Brewer, 2001; Susskind & Hodges).

At the institutional level, social and human services institutions, academic institutions, and health-providing organizations such as hospitals and clinics need to promote a holistic thinking style that fosters cooperation and interdependence. Practitioners should not be afraid of consulting each other with their cases to assist individuals from multicultural backgrounds. In this setting, practitioners will openly and honestly discuss their cases with each other and seek constructive feedback about their methods of assessing, diagnosing, and treating clients with diverse backgrounds.

It takes time, effort, and energy to deconstruct inappropriate hierarchical, dichotomous, and linear thinking patterns. The progress may be slow because it is so unfamiliar to what people have been doing. An old Korean proverb says, "A big mountain is a collection of dust" meaning big issues grow slowly over time and must be deconstructed in the same way. Whatever individuals do to transcend discrimination and "isms," no matter how insignificant it is, leads to a path to a change. Each small and insignificant act, thought, statement, feeling, and attitude against "isms" adds up to create a big change. Social change starts with one individual. One individual becomes a group of individuals, and when the group of individuals practices appropriate thinking styles diligently and mindfully, change slowly takes place and affects more people. Groups of individuals become a society by taking a small step each day to deconstruct inappropriate hierarchical and dichotomous thinking.

CONCRETE STRATEGIES

Consciousness Practice

Is your inner experience right now the same as it was before you read this chapter?

Part III

A Practitioner's Awareness of the Client's Worldview

C ompleting the experiential and reflection-based learning activities in Parts I and II is a prerequisite for transition into Part III, which integrates knowledge from previous chapters. Chapter 11 explores existing identity development models for both dominant and nondominant groups. Knowledge gained from previous chapters about the impact of internalized oppression on nondominant groups will assist with understanding complexities of identity development from a multilayered and multidimensional perspective. Practitioner-trainees will be able to contrast and compare identity development of dominant and nondominant groups and will gain a deeper understanding about the impact of systematic privilege and oppression on the process of identity construction. Chapter 12 demonstrates how to integrate intellectual understanding of identity models and theories with emotional understanding by applying them to self. This process allows practitioner-trainees to examine their own multiple identity development, dominant identity (salient or special identity), dynamics in identity and sociocultural contexts, and thinking patterns/styles. The experience of applying theoretical conceptualization to practical situations will assist practitioner-trainees with attempting to understand their clients' worldviews.

Experience gained through exploration of multiple identity construction enables practitioner-trainees to understand the importance of their clients' multiple identities and intersections among them. This understanding is the foundation for accurate assessment, diagnosis, and treatment. Chapter 13 provides concrete strategies for accurate assessment, which incorporates a practitioner's knowledge and skills with her ability to integrate emotion. It discusses the importance of a practitioner's role in examining the *Diagnostic and Statistical Manual of Mental Disorders (DSM)* and professional ethics codes (American Counseling Association, 2005; American Psychological Association, 2002; National Association of Social Workers, 1999) for their relevance for multicultural populations. It also emphasizes the importance of a practitioner's role in developing strategies to utilize the current *DSM* in an ethical manner in order to serve clients with multicultural backgrounds. Chapter 14 is the final product of what it means to be a multiculturally competent practitioner. It provides case studies for practicing multicultural competencies in addition to experiential learning activities.

11

Identity Development

Through his chapter explores Erikson's (1950, 1964, 1968) conception of personal and social identity development and how social identity was expanded to include cultural identity as sociocultural contexts changed by growing interests in visibility of nondominant groups (e.g., race, gender, sexual orientation). Various models of identity development are discussed to illustrate similarities and differences among groups such as monoracial groups, nondominant racial groups, biracial and multiracial groups, the dominant (White) group, and gay and lesbian groups. The role of internalized privilege and oppression in shaping an identity of a victim or an agent is explored. Each model of identity development is examined to evaluate the impact of inappropriate hierarchical, dichotomous, and linear thinking styles/patterns on identity construction.

※ IDENTITY

Conception of Identity Development

Erikson (1950, 1964, 1968) conceptualized ego/identity development as a dynamic interplay between an individual and the sociocultural context. It is "the organization of self-understanding that defines one's place in the world" (Schwartz, Montgomery, & Briones, 2006, p. 5). Ego identity and ego diffusion (age 12 to 18 or older) are one of Erikson's (1964) eight psychosocial stages of development. According to Erikson, for some individuals, reassessing their given or expected identity by family and other social agents (identity formulated by external influences) starts in the adolescent stage. Erikson postulated that identity confusion is a part of identity development since identity changes over a lifetime as an individual interacts with his/her/zir environment. According to Erikson, revision of identity is one of the most important developmental tasks for adolescents and adults. Erikson's theory of identity development has two categories, personal identity and social identity. Personal identity is composed of beliefs and values that are internally consistent and coherent with one another, and these manifest similarly across situations. Social identity is the group(s) with which a person identifies and toward which he/she/ze shows ingroup favoritism (Schwartz et al., 2006). A person's social identity is constructed through ingroup identification.

Erikson was a pioneer in the concept of identity development, and Marcia (1966, 1980) and Loevinger (1976, 1983; Blasi & Loevinger, 1976) developed more detailed concepts of identity development. Marcia expanded Erikson's theory and postulated four stages of identity development: (a) identity diffusion, a process by which an adolescent reassesses and explores possible identities in various areas; (b) foreclosed identity, the continuation of an adolescent's expected or given identity during childhood; (c) moratorium, the active stage of an adolescent's identity search in which he/she/ze has reached a deeper level of exploration yet has not made a commitment; and (d) achieved identity, when an adolescent has made a commitment.

However, these theories are based on cultural values and beliefs that were dominant due to the sociocultural context at the time of the theories' development. As nondominant groups gained visibility, scholars expanded Erikson's concept of social identity to include cultural identity and started to examine the impact of acculturation, assimilation, and enculturation on identity development (Arce, 1981; Dufrene & Herring, 1994; Padulla & Perez, 2003; Phinney, Horenczyk, Liebkind, & Vedder, 2001). According to these scholars, *cultural identity* is a special type of social identity that is defined as belonging to a cultural group because of an individual's identification of beliefs, values, and ideals. Cultural identity may change through *adaptation*, which occurs when individuals from different cultures come into contact with a new culture. *Acculturation* represents changes in one's cultural identity as one adapts to a new culture. An acculturated person is flexible enough to support changes that occur as a result of adapting to a dominant culture without losing his/her/zir *internal consistency* and coherence that generate positive feelings about the group(s) with which the person identifies. The acculturation process for immigrants, international students, diplomats and their families, and refugees is different from that for members of nondominant racial groups whose dominant language is English and who are born in the United States. The acculturation process within each group (i.e., people of color born in the United States, immigrants, international students, refugees) is unique as a result of class, sexual orientation, disability, age, religion, region, and gender (Bhatia & Ram, 2001; Gibson, 2001; Markus, Steele, & Steele, 2000; Phinney et al., 2001; Sandhu, 1997a).

Identity Development and Changes

Changes in identity occur when individuals change and/or their socio-cultural context changes and their previous identity no longer represents them internally and/or externally (Bosma & Kunnen, 2001). In these situations, individuals tend to respond to these identity crises in one of three ways: (a) confronting the challenge and purposefully revising their identities to cope with it, (b) relying on external demands and responding to fit external expectations, or (c) avoiding or ignoring the situation. Existing models of identity development for monoracial groups, biracial and multiracial groups, and gay and lesbian groups are briefly reviewed to examine the complex process of identity changes among different groups. All identity models reviewed in this chapter indicate there arc individual variations within as well as among groups in terms of their identity development and changes. The three phases described by Bosma and Kunnen show up in different stages of different models. All individuals start out with the *assimilation* stage in all identity models reviewed in this chapter except Root's (1998, 1999). Root's focus was on resolution of each stage and not developmental stage progression.

☓ MODELS OF IDENTITY DEVELOPMENT FOR NONDOMINANT MONORACIAL GROUPS

The major models of identity development in the literature are briefly discussed in this section in order to understand the complexities involved in identity development. Nondominant monoracial or ethnic identity development models, biracial and multiracial identity development models, White racial identity development models, and nonheterosexual orientation identity development models are discussed.

Cross's Psychology of Nigrescence

This model, first introduced in 1971, is the most well known and has been revised for the past 35 years. The latest model (Cross & Vandiver,

2001; Vandiver, Cross, Worrell, & Fhagen-Smith, 2002) divides the pre-encounter stage into three levels (assimilation, miseducation, and self-hatred), the immersion-emersion stage into two levels (anti-White and intense Black), and the internalization stage into three levels (nationalist, biculturalist, and multiculturalist). The latest model is thus composed of eight stages: pre-encounter assimilation, pre-encounter miseducation, pre-encounter (racial) self-hatred, immersion-emersion anti-White, immersion-emersion intense Black involvement, internalization nationalist, internalization biculturalist, and internalization multiculturalist. Individuals in the *pre-encounter assimilation* stage identify themselves from an individualistic perspective as an American. Individuals identify with the dominant cultural group and have no desire to be aware of their Blackness. Individuals in the *pre-encounter miseducation* stage accept their group stereotypes and distance themselves from their Black community. Individuals in the *pre-encounter (racial) self-hatred* stage have a negative image of being Black due to internalized oppression of racism and racial stereotypes. Individuals in the *immersion-emersion anti-White* stage often demonstrate emotional intensity about their Black culture as well as White culture by rejecting White people, society, and culture and accepting only Black people and culture. Individuals in the *immersion-emersion intense Black involvement* stage are actively engaged in Black involvement and operate from a dichotomous thinking style where they idealize and romanticize being Black. Individuals in the *internalization nationalist* stage have an Afrocentric worldview and are actively engaged in Black culture but not to the degree shown by individuals in the previous stage (immersion-emersion intense Black involvement). Individuals in the *internalization biculturalist* stage show balance between their Black culture and the dominant White culture. They are grounded in both Black culture and the dominant culture. Individuals in the *internalization multiculturalist* stage identify with multiple identities equally and are comfortable having multiple identities.

Helms's People of Color Racial Identity Model

A distinctive characteristic of Helms's (1995) theory is that a healthy racial identity depends on overcoming internalized racism and racial biases and stereotypes. Helms prefers the term *people of color* instead of *minority* since people of color are not always the numerical minority and Whites are not always the numerical majority even though Whites still exercise power regardless of their numerical status (Helms, 1995; Helms

& Cook, 1999). Helms's model is an integration of the models of Atkinson, Morten, and Sue (1989); Cross (1971); Erikson (1968); and Kohut (1971). Helms's model is composed of six stages: conformity, dissonance, immersion, emersion, internalization, and integrated awareness. Individuals in the *conformity* stage manifest their internalized racism by assimilating to the dominant cultural values or by conforming to the dominant culture's stereotypes of their group. Individuals in the *dissonance* stage experience anxiety and ambivalence over their belongingness since they are aware they do not fit in with the dominant culture yet lack knowledge about their own racial group. Individuals in the *immersion* stage operate from a dichotomous and hierarchical perspective. They idealize their group and reject the dominant cultural values. Individuals in the *emersion* stage show strong commitment to the ingroup, and their identity is centered on ingroup values and beliefs. Individuals in the *internalization* stage have internalized their racial identity and function as bicultural individuals. Individuals in the *integrated awareness* stage display multicultural competency by showing commitment to their own ingroup while understanding and respecting other racial and ethnic groups' needs to maintain their own identities. They are the ones who apply diunital and holistic perspectives.

Phinney's Model of Ethnic Development

Phinney and colleagues (Phinney, 1989, 1990, 1992; Phinney & Alipuria, 1990; Phinney & Rotheram, 1987a, 1987b; Phinney & Tarver, 1988) conducted research in developmental psychology to investigate the applicability of Erikson's (1950, 1964, 1968) and Marcia's (1966, 1980) identity development theories with nondominant racial group adolescents. Phinney's model was born out of this research and consists of three stages. Phinney puts Marcia's identity diffusion and foreclosure together as the *first stage* where acceptance of dominant cultural values leads to internalized negative ethnic stereotypes about adolescents' own group. However, adolescents do not express the dominant group preference. The *second stage* is moratorium where adolescents are beginning to be aware of their ethnicity. They show emotional intensity ranging from anger toward the dominant culture to guilt, shame, and anger toward themselves. The *third stage* is identity achievement where adolescents have achieved a healthy bicultural identity by accepting their racial and ethnic identity while integrating some parts of dominant cultural values.

Atkinson et al.'s Model of Minority Identity Development

This model was developed by Atkinson, Morten, and Sue (1989, 1998) and is based on the assumption that all minority groups develop personal and group identities as a result of an internal struggle due to oppression. The model is composed of five stages: (a) conformity, (b) dissonance, (c) resistance and immersion, (d) introspection, and (e) synergetic articulation and awareness. Individuals in the *conformity* stage assimilate to the dominant cultural values and devalue their race, which results in negative attitudes about themselves and their racial group. They follow the dominant group's evaluation of other racial groups. Individuals in the *dissonance* stage experience internal conflict over their pro-White attitude and emerging awareness of their own race. Individuals in the *resistance and immersion* stage accept and value their own racial or ethnic cultural values and identify with the ingroup while rejecting the dominant cultural values. They show a wide range of emotion from anger to guilt. Their anger toward the dominant group increases as they understand racism and their guilt for having a pro-White attitude in the *conformity* stage. This leads them to resist dominant cultural values. Their attitude toward other racial groups fluctuates between being empathetic and being intolerant due to ingroup favoritism. Individuals in the *introspection* stage question their resistant attitude toward the dominant group in the previous stage as a result of their secure racial or ethnic identity. They understand systematic oppression by the dominant group but are able to also understand variations within dominant group members. They also question their blind loyalty to their ingroup and explore balancing their personal self with ingroup identification, which leads them to see both positive and negative sides of their ingroup members. Individuals in the *synergetic articulation and awareness* stage have a positive racial or ethnic identity for themselves and their ingroup. They understand that racial identity is one aspect of multiple identities and have a positive attitude toward other minority groups and appreciate constructive aspects of the dominant culture. Their desire to deconstruct oppression extends beyond their own racial or ethnic group. They are interested in deconstructing all forms of oppression.

Ethnic Identity for Chicanos and Latinos

Ruiz's (1990) model was constructed through case study analysis of Mexican Americans and other Latinos. This model is composed of five stages: causal, cognitive, consequences, working through, and successful resolution. Individuals in the *causal* stage show little awareness of their racial and ethnic culture. Individuals in the *cognitive* stage are eager to assimilate with the dominant culture because they associate success in assimilation with economic success in life. Individuals in the *consequences* stage reject their own culture in the process of assimilation. Individuals in the *working through* stage start to develop ethnicity-specific consciousness as they become intolerant of assimilation to the dominant culture. They struggle with their inner conflict between assimilation and desire to reclaim their racial and ethnic identity. Individuals in the *successful resolution* stage have increased self-esteem as a result of identifying with their racial and ethnic heritage.

⚟ MODELS OF IDENTITY DEVELOPMENT FOR BIRACIAL AND MULTIRACIAL GROUPS

Poston's Model of Biracial Identity Development

Poston's (1990) biracial identity model is composed of five stages of development. In Stage 1, biracial children develop *personal identity* through early socialization experiences as people, and such identity is not associated with race. In Stage 2, young biracial children are *compelled to choose an identity* and usually select just *one racial identity.* Sociocultural contexts, facial and physical features, peer groups, family, and so on influence the children's selection of race. In Stage 3, biracial individuals *experience emotional intensity* from guilt to self-hate for their choice. Individuals in Stage 4 begin to *explore their other race* while maintaining identification of the previous chosen race. Individuals in Stage 5 *integrate* their biracial heritage and become biracial, valuing and identifying with both cultures.

Jacobs's Model of Biracial Identity Development

Jacobs's (1977, 1992) model is based on interviews and play therapy with children from Black and White biracial families. His theory consists of three stages. Children under 4.5 years of age are usually in the *precolor constancy* stage, which means they understand that skin color is permanent. They have no racial identity incorporated into their personal identity unless they have had negative experiences. Children at around 4.5 years of age in the *postcolor constancy* stage start to prefer Black and reject White and then prefer White and reject Black. This is a natural prerequisite state for developing biracial identity (Jacobs, 1992). How successfully children reach their biracial identity is related to how parents communicate the biracial issues to them. Children usually reach the *biracial identity* stage between 8 and 12 years of age, as they understand complex aspects of their lineage of parents representing two different racial groups. They reach biracial identity by understanding their parental lineage, rather than their skin color, is a determining factor of biracial identity achievement. What is unique about this theory is that Jacobs allows for a nonlinear perspective of identity development by indicating that individuals may return to previous stages as they mature to adolescence and adulthood. This model is fluid and includes an understanding of the impact of cognitive development in adolescence and developmental challenges in adulthood.

Root's Meta Model of Biracial Identity Development

Root's model (1990, 1998, 1999) is unique in that it is based on a resolution process rather than a developmental stage process. Her model consists of four different ways of deriving resolution, and there is no one best or true resolution. Each resolution has a different outcome. One resolution is *accepting a culturally assigned identity.* This resolution works out for those individuals who are satisfied with an assigned identity and are supported by both an immediate and an extended family. The negative aspect of accepting assigned identity is when an individual relocates to a new community and is assigned another identity. This leads to internal conflict because the person not only has to deal with loss of self but simultaneously has to figure out who he/she/ze is supposed to be now. A second resolution is *identifying as biracial* and drawing from strengths of both cultures. The difficulty arises when an individual is no longer able to hold onto a biracial identity. The third resolution is that an individual *chooses one racial identity.* The individual does not feel minimized or marginalized if he/she/ze is accepted by his/her/zir chosen ingroup and does not deny aspects of his/her/zir other racial group. The difficulty arises when he/she/ze is misperceived by others in the community due to his/her/zir chosen identity. The fourth resolution is *incorporating a new identity* with previous racial heritages. This new multiracial identity minimizes conflict. The difficulty occurs when the new identity is not able to incorporate the individual's previous racial heritages.

⅀ MODELS OF IDENTITY DEVELOPMENT FOR WHITES

Studying White identity development assists both White individuals and individuals from nondominant cultures with understanding internalized privilege/oppression, racism, sexism, classism, heterosexism, ableism, ageism, and other "isms." As emphasized by helping professional organizations (American Counseling Association, 2005; American Psychological Association, 2002; National Association of Social Workers, 1999), practitioners' awareness of themselves increases their ability to see clients from the clients' worldviews. White identity development may assist White practitioners' understanding of their own identity development, and as a result, they may be able to better understand their clients' identity development. Practitioners of color may understand why some White practitioners are color blind and what needs to be done for them to be at the stage where they show multicultural competency by studying White racial identity development.

Helms's Model of White Racial Identity (WRI) Development

Since 1984, Helms has been dedicated to refining her model of White Racial Identity (WRI) development (Helms, 1990, 1995; Helms & Cook, 1999; Helms, Jernigan, & Mascher, 2005). Her most recent model consists of seven stages of identity development: contact, disintegration, reintegration, pseudoindependence, immersion, emersion, and autonomy (Helms & Cook). Individuals in the *contact* stage deny White privilege and racism in society and show no desire to learn about their own privilege or racism. Individuals in the *disintegration* stage experience anxiety, guilt, and conflict due to their beginning of awareness of White privilege and racism. They feel guilty for Whites' oppression and desire justice for Blacks but are anxious due to an inner conflict of wanting to be accepted by their ingroup (White) and desire for outgroup justice (Black). Individuals in the *reintegration* stage show racist characteristics and feel anger and fear instead of guilt and anxiety toward individuals from nondominant cultures. They blame victims of systematic oppression as if personal, institutional, and cultural marginalization, minimization, and oppression are the victims' own problems and not the oppressors'. Individuals in the *pseudoindependence* stage begin to intellectually understand ongoing racism and Whites' responsibility without integrating their emotion (lack of transformative learning). As a result, they blame other Whites for racism and White privilege without reflecting on their own internalized privilege and racism. Individuals in the *immersion* stage genuinely want to have accurate information about racism and White privilege and their own internalized privilege. Some individuals become allies for racial justice. Individuals in the *emersion* stage embrace other Whites who share a similar understanding of racism and understand the responsibilities of Whites and the roles of oppressed and oppressor. Individuals in Helms's last stage, *autonomy*, are able to function from the perspective of a diunital, multilayered, and multidimensional thinking style, which allows them to avoid activities that benefit them due to their White privilege, and are actively engaged in reducing all forms of oppression.

Ponterotto's Model of White Racial Consciousness Development

Ponterotto's (1988) model is designed for racial consciousness development of practitioner-trainees. This model is conceptualized from Ponterotto's experience as a White professor teaching mostly White graduate students about multicultural counseling. His model consists of four stages: preexposure, exposure, zealot-defensive, and integration.

Individuals in the *preexposure* stage have no awareness of their own racial identity or the racial identity of people of color. They assume racism is a thing of the past. Individuals in the *exposure* stage begin to understand individual, institutional, and cultural racism and oppression. They experience anger because they have been misinformed about the history of multicultural America and feel guilty for accepting stereotypes of other racial groups without questioning them. These individuals' emotional intensity increases as they discover they are also racist in relation to subtle racism like aversive racism. They are torn between sharing their knowledge with friends and family and taking a path that is least resistant in order not to alienate or be alienated by them. Individuals in the *zealot-defensive* stage show two different types of behavior. Individuals in the *zealot* stage are prominority and explore personal and collective guilt for being benefactors of White privilege. Individuals in the *defensive* stage react to their anger and guilt by personalizing critical analysis of systematic oppression by Whites. Individuals in the *integration* stage not only accept their own subtle and unintentional racism and realities of racism as they are; they also report empowerment through deconstructing their own racism and desire to learn about other cultural groups. They not only want to reclaim their White identity but also want to know more about their other identities (gender, sexual orientation, class, disability, religion, region, age, etc.). They are able to apply a diunital thinking style to deal with racial issues.

Sabnani et al.'s Model of White Racial Identity

Sabnani, Ponterotto, and Borodovsky (1991) integrated the models of Hardiman (1982), Helms (1984, 1990), and Ponterotto (1988) and came up with a five-stage model (preexposure or precontact, conflict, prominority and antiracism, retreat into White culture, and redefinition and integration). Individuals in the *preexposure or precontact* stage have no racial identity or White privilege awareness, although they unconsciously identify with Whiteness and accept stereotypes about nondominant groups. Individuals in the *conflict* stage begin to acquire knowledge about nondominant groups and question how they can be a part of a group that has oppressed people of color. These individuals are in a state of confusion with various emotions (anxiety, guilt, and depression) due to conflict between their desire to conform to their ingroup norms and their desire to have nonracist values. Individuals in the *conflict* stage experience anger and guilt for conforming to the dominant cultural value–oriented socialization and toward White culture in general. Individuals in the *prominority and antiracism* stage identify with nondominant groups by resisting racism in order to transcend guilt and confusion from the previous stage. Individuals in the *retreat into White culture* stage overidentify with Whiteness with defensiveness about White culture. They retreat from the conflicting situation of the *prominority and antiracism* stage because they are questioned or misunderstood by both the ingroup (White) and the outgroup (nondominant group). They are not understood by other Whites because they are prominority, and they are questioned by the minority groups. Individuals in the *redefinition and integration* stage achieve their redefinition of White identity and have a realistic perception of their racial group as well as other racial groups. Their focus shifts from racial issues to dismantling all forms of oppression. They are open to learning all sorts of cultural activities from their own ingroup as well as outgroups.

Rowe et al.'s Model of White Racial Consciousness (WRC)

A significant contribution of this model is the theory that Whites' racial identity development and people of color's identity development do not follow a linear process (Rowe, Behrens, & Leach, 1995; Rowe,

Bennett, & Atkinson, 1994). The White Racial Consciousness (WRC) model consists of seven types of individuals. *Dominative* individuals may act out racist attitudes directly or indirectly since they believe Whites are superior. *Conflictive* individuals value a Eurocentric worldview without supporting racism or inequality. *Integrative* individuals have positive racial attitudes and are rational and pragmatic. *Reactive* individuals hold prominority attitudes without awareness of their role in perpetuating racism. *Avoidant* individuals minimize racial issues due to a lack of exploration. *Dependent* individuals have racial understanding based on other people's opinions. *Dissonant* individuals are conflicted due to incongruence between their racial beliefs and experience.

Sue et al.'s Model of White Racial Identity

Sue et al. (1998) integrated the previous identity models. The unique characteristic of their theory is that it emphasizes the strengths of both developmental and typology models. There are five stages in the model: conformity, dissonance, resistance and immersion, introspection, and integrative awareness. Individuals in the *conformity* stage are individualistic and ethnocentric with minimal awareness of their racial and cultural identity. They deny White privilege and the existence of racism. Individuals in the *dissonance* stage experience internal conflict between their old beliefs and their new knowledge about the existence of racism. Some individuals retreat to the conformity stage, and others work through their conflict and move to the next stage. Individuals in the *resistance and immersion* stage begin to understand White privilege and systematic oppression and are aware of their own role in perpetuating racism and how they are benefactors of unearned White privilege. They feel guilty about having been misinformed about the multicultural history of America and for participating in the systematic oppression of nondominant groups. Some individuals in this stage overidentify with the nondominant groups to a point of rejecting their own White identity. Individuals in the *introspection* stage redefine Whiteness with accurate information about systematic oppression, White privilege, and racism. Guilt, anger, and defensiveness are not their primary feelings as they were in the previous stage; instead, these individuals begin a personal search for deeper meaning about being White. They may experience feelings of isolation due to disconnection from their prior identity as well as feelings of loss, confusion, and frustration due to not understanding the nondominant cultural individuals' experiences. Individuals in the *integrative awareness* stage value racial and human diversity and understand themselves as racial and cultural beings. They have inner strengths that make them who they are, and they work toward deconstructing all forms of oppression.

MODELS OF IDENTITY DEVELOPMENT FOR GAYS AND LESBIANS

Cass's Model of Homosexual Identity Formation

Cass's (1979) model was born out of her clinical experience with gay and lesbian clients. She divides public and private aspects of identity and proposed six stages of identity development: identity confusion, identity comparison, identity tolerance, identity acceptance, identity pride, and identity synthesis. Individuals in the first stage (*identity confusion*) feel inner turmoil due to incongruity between their personal feelings and thoughts toward same-sex persons and societal values on homosexuality. Individuals in the second stage (*identity comparison*) are beginning to be aware of their homosexual self while experiencing social alienation. These individuals' public identity may be heterosexual while their private identity may be homosexual. Individuals in the third stage (*identity tolerance*) tolerate their homosexuality rather than accepting it. Individuals in the fourth stage (*identity acceptance*) identify themselves as homosexual and increase contacts with other gay and lesbian individuals. For some, their public and private identity becomes congruent while others still keep two different identities. Individuals in the fifth stage (*identity pride*) immerse themselves in gay and lesbian culture and reject heterosexual values. Individuals are proud to claim their own identity and are angry for past alienation and frustration due to systematic oppression. Individuals in the sixth stage (*identity synthesis*) integrate their gay or lesbian identity into their personal identity. They increase their contacts with heterosexuals because they accept them as they are.

Fassinger's Inclusive Model of Lesbian and Gay Identity Formation

This model integrates previous gay and lesbian identity models, racial identity models, and feminist theories in addition to framing a continuous and circular process (Fassinger, 1998). The model consists of four phases:

awareness, exploration, deepening or commitment, and internalization and synthesis. Individuals in the first phase (*awareness*) realize that heterosexuality is not a universal norm and admit that they have thoughts and feelings of sexuality that differ from social norms, expectations, and socialization of family. Individuals in the second phase (*exploration*) explore their sexual feelings in depth. On one hand, they feel anger toward the systematic sexual oppression that led them to be socialized in a heterosexist and homophobic sociocultural context. On the other hand, they are excited about belonging to a gay or lesbian community. Individuals in the third phase (*deepening or commitment*) gain in-depth self-knowledge about their sexual identity. Individuals in the fourth phase (*internalization and synthesis*) accept their sexual identity and integrate it with their personal identity. They have inner peace and fulfillment and are able to maintain their integrated self-identity across different contexts. They interact with other individuals on the basis of their inner qualities regardless of their sexual orientation (Fassinger & Miller, 1997).

⫸ VARIATIONS AMONG AND WITHIN RACIAL GROUPS

In terms of identity development, it is important to be mindful of variations among racial groups and nonheterosexual orientation groups as well as variations within a monoracial group, a multiracial group, and a particular nonheterosexual orientation group. Furthermore, not all people will go through linear identity development as described by some models. Some individuals go through nonlinear and circular paths (Jacobs, 1977, 1992; Rowe et al., 1994). Racial identity development and nonheterosexual orientation development intersect with other identity developments (gender, class, disability, age, religion, language, region, etc.). Therefore, racial identity and nonheterosexual orientation development need to be examined in relation to gender, class, disability, age, language, religion, region, and so on in order to understand a person and his/her/zir worldview (Root, 1998).

Victim Versus Agent

As indicated, racial and other identity development does not always progress linearly and sequentially. Developmental stages, types, or phases can be blurred because there are variations among individuals within each stage, phase, or type. For example, some individuals of a nondominant culture may not be able to move to the next stage of their identity development because they have not resolved inner conflicts rooted in systematic oppression and internalized oppression. This may be due to their sociocultural contexts not providing the structure for transformative learning where the affective transformative process can take place. Or it may be due to an inability to admit their internalized oppression. Many studies described in Part II indicate children learn ingroup favoritism at an early age as they interact within sociocultural contexts, as well as how ingroup favoritism leads to intergroup discrimination, which often results in intergroup oppression. Models of identity development for nondominant mono- and biracial groups reviewed in this chapter indicate that the first stage of identity development is assimilation (Atkinson et al., 1989, 1998; Cross, 1971; Cross & Vandiver, 2001; Helms, 1995; Jacobs, 1992; Poston, 1990; Ruiz, 1990). Nondominant group members try to be like dominant group members by rejecting their own cultural values in the assimilation stage. These individuals learn internalized racism through the process of assimilation. Jackson, Barth, Powell, and Lochman's (2006) study demonstrates the power differential shown at an early age as a result of learning internalized oppression and internalized privilege. White children asserted their power even though there were only a few of them while Black children did not assert their power even though substantially more of them were present unless the teacher was also Black. This study suggests the role of internalized oppression in identity construction of individuals of nondominant groups. Many studies reviewed in this book indicate that prior to claiming their own racial and sexual orientation identity development as their own, children, adolescents, and adults assume socially constructed dominant White and heterosexual values as the norm for all people including themselves. Research on race, gender, class, and sexual orientation indicates that children of nondominant groups judge themselves on the basis of the dominant cultural values, which results in negative self-image and internalized oppression (Coie & Dodge, 1998; Crick, 1996; Gecas, 1992; Giles & Heyman, 2005; Hill, 1992; Maccoby, 1998, 2002; Prossor, 1998; Rich, 1990; Roediger, 1999; Ruble & Martin, 1998; Zhang, Lingin, Zhang, Wang, & Chen, 2003; Zweig, 2000). Research also shows that children distort situations in order to fit their beliefs (Liben & Signorella, 1993; Susskind, 2003).

Internalized oppression and negative self-image become a part of these individuals' worldviews. The worldview that they are powerless over their position in their lives is the worldview of the victim and not the agent. Herman (2004) depicts how people of color become victims of internalized oppression: "The more ethnic discrimination one experiences, the more one internalizes the racial categorization of others" (p. 744). Systematic oppression at institutional and governmental levels leads nondominant group members to powerless and helpless positions. In other words, they are victims of injustice and inequity whether it is due to their race, gender, sexual orientation, class, disability, age, language, religion, or region. The victim's worldview developed by internalized oppression needs to be processed through transformative learning in order to be transcended. Processing the affective component of the victim's worldview takes time. Jacobs (2006) writes:

> I think the developmental perspectives on one's internal and external worlds are important. Here one's reflection on those frames of reference developed through cultural contexts, early relationships and life stages that provide opportunities for future reflection, re-authoring, and transformation. Crisis, loss, grieving, and discomfort invite transforming old frames to new frames and the recognition of the personal power of giving voice to the process and change. Stillness, paying attention, exploring relationships from both personal and professional contexts affords opportunities to examine the many meanings of transformative moments. (pp. 121–122)

The personal story of Pat in Chapter 7 (classism) reveals the complexities involved in internalized oppression and its impact on his perception and worldview. Complexities of internalized oppression include but are not limited to the interwoven relationship between systematic privilege and oppression and internalized oppression and privilege within a person. For example, a person may be a target of internalized racial and class oppression but an internalized privilege holder in relation to gender, language, and sexual orientation. It is difficult to sort out how much of the victim identification is from race and how much is from class. For instance, intense emotional reactions from some of former Senator Hillary Clinton's supporters in the 2008 U.S. presidential election can be examined through the lens of internalized gender oppression. Their intense emotional reactions may be partly due to pervasive systematic injustice done to women in general and partly due to being victims of gender oppression throughout their personal lives. If these women chose to vote for the Republican candidate, Senator John McCain, because his running mate was a woman, Sarah Palin, even though they are Democrat, it suggests an intensity and degree of their internalized gender oppression. They may have thought they were supportive of Senator

Clinton, but their strong emotion around internalized gender oppression may have led them to choose a woman over their political party philosophy or what Senator Clinton represented as a candidate.

The structure provided in academic settings and in practitioner training programs is necessary to process the affective component of internalized oppression whether the oppression is related to race, gender, sexual orientation, class, disability, age, language, religion, or region. Individuals need to develop strategies to transform from a victim to an agent identity.

Students in the author's multicultural counseling program are encouraged to evaluate their intrapersonal communication to assess whether their worldview is based on a victim perspective or an agent perspective. They are asked to assess factors contributing to their perspective. Often students share the roots of their perspective (either victim or agent) with each other and are surprised to find the link between their perspective and their internalized oppression. Students are encouraged to process their perspective from a multidimensional and multilayered perspective to assess the purpose and benefits or losses of being a victim or an agent. Students with a victim perspective are encouraged to think and feel about their strengths despite injustice and inequity. They are encouraged to imagine their strength as they think about how they have made it this far academically and/or professionally. They are asked to hold on to the image and do a centering exercise. This is repeated randomly throughout the quarter. The following are three of the author's former students' experiences with acknowledging their victim identity both emotionally and intellectually.

PERSONAL STORIES

Victim Identity

When I am being judgmental and seeing their behavior as victimizing me it keeps me stuck in these feelings. Then I feel angry and defeated and cut people off. Then I feel isolated and depressed. This intensifies my special identity as a victim and perpetuates this cycle . . . Regardless of the special identity of the target group that we are working with, we need to avoid empowering one group at the expense of another . . . Empowering one group to feel valuable by devaluing another is oppressive and patriarchal.

—Bob, 2001

(Continued)

(Continued)

I specifically had problems talking to the Whites in my class about racial issues. I remember referring to all of them as "You White People" which exemplifies my bias (prejudice) and assumption that all White people are the same and whose behavior mirrored those who acted ignorantly towards my family or me. I still struggle with this unrealistic deeply embedded emotional pain because of my experiences with some White people throughout my lifetime.

—Jim, 2001

My personal internalized oppression had deluded me into believing that I was a helpless victim. A victim can only be reactionary and my dichotomous and linear meaning making in the beginning of this course was that limiting.

—Emily, 2005

The following experiential learning activities are designed for practitioners/practitioner-trainees to assess their racial and sexual orientation identity development.

CONCRETE STRATEGIES

Experiential Learning Activities on Racial and Sexual Orientation Identity Development

1. Describe your racial identity development. Review the racial identity models in this chapter and read your description of your racial identity development. Which model or models explain your racial identity development? If you cannot find the model that describes your development, describe it on the basis of what you have learned from the models.

2. On the basis of your experience on Question 1, how would you go about assessing the racial identity development of a client?

3. Describe your sexual orientation identity development. Compare your description to Fassinger's (1998) inclusive model. How was your development similar to and/or different from the model?

4. On the basis of your experience on Question 3, how would you go about assessing the sexual orientation identity development of a client?

5. Reread your journal writing from Chapter 2. Evaluate whether you have a victim or an agent identity.
   a. What experiences led you to have this identity?
   b. What are you gaining if your worldview is from a victim perspective?
   c. What needs to be done for you to transform your victim identity to an agent identity?

SIMILARITIES AND DIFFERENCES BETWEEN DOMINANT GROUP AND NONDOMINANT GROUP IDENTITY DEVELOPMENT

A review of the racial identity development of non-White and White individuals and nondominant sexual identity development indicates that there are predominant similarities between them. All three groups (Whites, non-Whites, and those with a nondominant sexual orientation) start with believing the dominant White cultural beliefs and values are the norm. The nondominant groups' racial identity development and nondominant sexual orientation groups' identity development begin by questioning blind acceptance of White cultural values including the stereotypes of nondominant groups. Racial or sexual orientation identity develops as individuals learn to value their racial heritage or accept their sexual orientation. White individuals also start out believing White values are the norm for all White and other racial groups. White individuals' identity development begins by becoming aware of their oppressor role as a group through examining White privilege, racism, and systematic oppression. White individuals formulate racial identity as they reject what they believed to be the norm and acknowledge they have been a participant in perpetuating racism, a benefactor of White privilege and insensitivity to other racial groups' rights. As a result, they redefine their White racial identity to value other racial groups and human diversities and work toward deconstructing all forms of oppression. All three groups need to work through the impact of systematic oppression/privilege and internalized oppression/privilege on their awareness of sense of self. All three groups are at times rejected by their ingroups, if ingroup members are still perpetuating White privilege, heterosexism, and systematic oppression/privilege.

The dominant and nondominant racial groups are different in that people of color start from an oppressed position and empower their identity through transcending oppression while White individuals start from an oppressor's position and empower themselves by transcending their role as oppressors. Both racial groups obtain a sense of fulfillment through reclaimed racial identity, and both are open to building a genuine relationship with each other as individuals who are proud of their identities. Both racial groups want to work toward deconstructing all forms of oppression by being aware of their racial identities.

Finding similarities and differences between heterosexual and non-heterosexual identity development was not feasible due to the unavailability of a heterosexual identity development theory.

A commonality among all stage or developmental models is that it is possible to be firmly grounded in one's own identity while accepting others' identities as their own. Individuals in Cross and Vandiver's (2001) *internalization biculturalist* and *internalization multiculturalist* stages, Helms's (1995) *integrated awareness* stage, Phinney and Alipuria's (1990) *third stage* (identity development), Atkinson et al.'s (1989, 1998) *synergetic articulation and awareness* stage, Poston's (1990) fifth stage, Helms et al.'s (2005) *autonomy* stage, Ponterotto's (1988) *integration* stage, Sabnani et al.'s (1991) *redefinition and integration* stage, Rowe et al.'s (1994) *integrative* type, and Sue et al.'s (1998) *integrative awareness* stage indicate all individuals in these stages are able to think diunitarily (both). Individuals in these stages or types demonstrate that it is possible to think diunitarily and holistically. If holistic thinking is the cultural norm instead of existing inappropriate dichotomous and hierarchical thinking, people would not need to go through an inner struggle in developing their multiple identities, would be able to reach diunitarily based stages early, and would begin to celebrate their differences and work together toward a better life for all people.

CONCRETE STRATEGIES

Consciousness Practice

Did you read this chapter consciously?

12

Multiple Identities

T he purpose of this chapter is to illustrate the multiplicities and complexities of multiple identity development through providing concrete examples in order to facilitate practitioners' ability to assess and treat clients accurately by including their multiple identities. The chapter explores the difficulties involved in changing implicit attitudes and beliefs by examining cognitive information processing models and presents thorough and concrete strategies to deal with these difficulties. An example of assessing multiple identity development according to the White Racial Consciousness model is provided, and concrete strategies for how to apply this model to assess multiple identities are explored with experiential learning activities for practitioner-trainees. A concrete example describing the author's multiple identity development is provided to help practitioner-trainees assess their own multiple identity development. The chapter ends with demonstrating how practitioner-trainees can incorporate their experience with multiple identity development into assessment of clients.

※ CHALLENGES OF ASSESSING MULTIPLE IDENTITIES

Chapter 11 discussed racial and sexual orientation identity development. For some individuals these are salient (dominant or special) identities, but these individuals also have other social identities that affect them. Some individuals may have two or three equally salient identities while others may have only one salient identity. Some change their salient identity according to all sociocultural contexts while others change their salient identity only in some sociocultural contexts. Some individuals' salient identity remains constant regardless of the sociocultural context. Not all individuals' salient identities are the same. Various scholars and researchers have called for including all of an individual's identities in order to fully understand the individual and his/her/zir worldview (Berry & Sam, 1997; Croteau & Constantine, 2005; Cross, 1995; Paniagua, 2005; Ponterotto, Casas, Suzuki, & Alexander, 2001).

> An individual can be fully understood only in a holistic manner that includes understanding the influences and interactions of the individual's multiple sociodemographic groups, some or all of which may be salient "identities" for the individual. (Croteau & Constantine, 2005, p. 162)

Some researchers have studied only some of an individual's multiple identities and found that an individual's identity is an integration of these identities, which manifest according to sociocultural contexts (Falicov, 1995; Fukuyama & Sevig, 1999; Hays, 2001; Hickson & Phelps, 1997; Passalacqua & Cervantes, 2008; Reid & Knight, 2006; Robinson & Howard-Hamilton, 2000; Swartz-Kulstad & Martin, 1999; Thompson, 2007; Warwick, 2002). Passalacqua and Cervantes presented three case studies to illustrate the importance of examining a client's identity through intersections of gender, culture, and religious or spiritual orientation in order to provide effective assessment and treatment. They emphasized Robinson and Howard-Hamilton's position:

> Robinson and Howard-Hamilton (2000) affirmed that attention to the intersection of gender, culture, class and race is salient to understanding that psychosocial identities embody each of those constructs and determines one's psychological framework. These authors warned against allowing one identity construct to define an individual's character. (p. 231)

Passalacqua and Cervantes (2008) discussed the impact of practitioners' lack of understanding of multiple identities on effective assessment and treatment:

> Many cultural groups, both within mainstream America and immigrants, may hold mainstream religious beliefs as well as various combinations of indigenous spiritual beliefs that compose their human experience. Failure to assess these various belief systems in

a systematic way could lead counselors into an unexamined psychological arena that is loaded with various ethical dilemmas and value discrepancies that may influence both assessment and treatment of clients or their respective families. (p. 230)

As indicated above, not examining a client from a holistic perspective leads to inaccurate assessment and ineffective treatment because the information the practitioner gathered is incomplete on the basis of partial identities. Thompson (2007) examined the intersection of sexual orientation and intellectual disability and found within-group prejudice and discrimination among queer individuals against those with intellectual disabilities. "If a queer or queerly informed pedagogy is only for those learned enough to know queerness and to aptly perform it—whether as teacher or student—then queerness is limited to an elite" (Thompson, 2007, p. 52). The impact of ingroup discrimination on identity development is much more painful than that of outgroup discrimination due to one's expectation of ingroup support and acceptance. Psychological complexities of ingroup rejection cannot be understood accurately without examining the intersection of multiple identities. Reid and Knight (2006) examined the intersections of disability, race, class, and sexual orientation and found the major contributing factors to learning disabilities and psychological disorders were environmental racism and classism. These contributing factors were found as a result of examining the intersections of multiple identities. Examining only one identity would have made this conclusion impossible. The economic disparity between Whites and people of color was revealed by examining the intersection of race and class (Marable, 2000; Regents of the University of Michigan, 2006; Smith, 2005).

The above researchers demonstrated the importance of examining the intersections of an individual's multiple identities by examining two to four identities. Needed is a model that integrates an individual's multiple identities since understanding a person holistically means including all of the identities that affect the whole person. Nine identities are examined in this book, and some individuals may have many more than nine affecting who they are. To understand an individual holistically, one has to process all of a person's multiple identities, their intersections, and the saliency of each identity simultaneously. This requires integration of complex cognitive processing and affective processing. Cognitive information processing, especially the formation of attitudes involving stereotyping and prejudice, will be examined in the following section in order to facilitate an understanding of what is necessary to treat members of nondominant groups and members of dominant groups as equals in the diverse human community.

Cognitive Information Processing

Implicit attitude, implicit memory, and implicit learning have been known to be barriers to transcending unequal treatment and injustice toward others who are or who are considered outgroup members. Implicit attitudes are automatically activated and often expressed in an individual's nonverbal behaviors and prejudicial judgments. Banaji and associates (Banaji & Bhaskar, 2001; Banaji & Greenwald, 1994; Banaji & Hardin, 1996; Blair & Banaji, 1996; Greenwald & Banaji, 1995) demonstrated repeatedly the relationships between implicit learning and stereotypes. Their research indicated that once implicit attitudes are formed, individuals are resistant to new information (Banaji & Bhaskar, 2001; Rydell, McConnell, Strain, Claypool, & Hugenberg, 2007). Different researchers have proposed different cognitive processing models for attitudes: (a) the single attitude model (Fazio, 1995), (b) the dual attitude model (DeCoster, Banner, Smith, & Semin, 2006), and (c) the meta-cognitive model (Petty, Brinol, & DeMarree, 2007). The single attitude model postulates an automatic linking between incoming stimuli and stored knowledge or beliefs in memory. Stored memories are automatically activated by incoming stimuli often without an individual's conscious awareness. The dual attitude model postulates separate storage in the brain for implicit (automatic) and explicit (deliberate) learning. According to Petty et al., implicit attitudes are a result of associative cognitive information processing such as "evaluative conditioning" (p. 660). Explicit attitudes are a result of propositional cognitive information processing such as "thinking about message arguments" (p. 660), and associative processing and prepositional processing operate independent of each other. Rydell et al.'s study found resistance to implicit attitude change as counterattitudinal information increased. They concluded "this knowledge may be important for understanding why attitudes, especially long-established attitudes built upon many associations in memory, are so difficult to change over long periods of time" (p. 876). Teasdale and Barnard's (1993) interactive cognitive subsystem (ICS) postulates that the prepositional system processes cognitive units and the implicational system processes implicit information such as emotion, body language, and other implied cognitive meaning within the ICS. Stott (2007) writes:

> Within ICS, it is evident that an emotion such as fear will often be closely accompanied by familiar propositional appraisals such as "I am in danger." However, such appraisals reflect the *output* of implicational code representing a schematic danger scenario, rather than being a prerequisite for the emotion of fear. (p. 43)

The meta-cognitive model (MCM) integrates parts of the single and dual attitude models (Petty et al., 2007). This model does not postulate two different storage areas or different processing like the dual attitude model. It postulates that both positive and negative evaluations can be made from either associative or prepositional processing. According to the MCM, "an individual may not hold a belief intellectually but, due to an idiosyncratic metacognitive stance toward internal feeling states, a conflicting view of reality emerges, presented as an emotional belief" (Stott, 2007, p. 44). Furthermore, the MCM supports previous research findings about the difficulty of successful negation (Deutsch, Gawronski, & Strack, 2006) and proposes adding motivation to aid successful negation. These theories differ in terms of their conceptualization of mechanisms in information processing, but they agree on conceptualizing implicit attitudes. They agree that implicit attitudes are spontaneous, automatic, emotional, and hard to change. Understanding that negating stereotypes is difficult from a cognitive information processing perspective assists in recognizing that stereotypes and prejudice are embedded in Americans' psyche (Deutsch et al.; Rydell et al. 2007; Stott). It is important to realize that admitting negative consequences of stereotyping is a difficult task for many North Americans, primarily due to their tendency toward high self-appraisal and cultural conditioning involving ethnocentric bias (Dudek, 2008; Pronin, Gilovich, & Ross, 2004; Takaki, 1993; Taylor & Brown, 1988).

The examination of cognitive processing of attitude information illustrates the challenges involved in changing implicit attitudes that are based on long-held beliefs of normalized White middle-class values. Adding motivation for successful negation suggests difficulty in changing the affective process. Emotion and cognition are two sides of the same coin. They are inseparable (Lazarus, 1982; Power & Dalgleish, 1997). Individuals with posttraumatic stress disorder (PTSD), for example, intellectually understand that the trauma they experienced sometime ago is not likely to happen again, but they are not able to shut off internally their emotional experience with the trauma. Ehlers and Clark (2000) and Foa and Rothbaum (1998) explained PTSD patients' persistent and strong emotional reactions to trauma as their inability to contextualize and integrate their traumatic memories into their autobiographical memory.

Reviewed studies indicate that it is difficult to change stereotypes and implicit attitudes without considering emotion and cognition as inseparable. Hinnant and O'Brien (2007) found integration of emotion and cognition includes taking both a cognitive and an affective perspective, which are positively associated with each other. They defined cognitive perspective taking as individuals' ability to imagine "how things are experienced from another's point of view" (p. 304) and affective perspective taking as "the ability to understand the feelings of another by taking that person's point of view" (p. 305). Affective perspective taking leads to more accurate empathy toward another than taking a cognitive perspective. In order to facilitate transformative learning, each chapter of this book provides concrete strategies for experiential learning or reflection-based learning activities, which at times require participants to take a cognitive perspective, an affective perspective, or both. The conventional academic setting has minimized the emotional aspect of learning, and research evidence has shown that integrating both emotional and cognitive aspects of learning is an effective way to increase multicultural competencies. It is no longer effective to teach multicultural competencies according to conventional teaching and learning models because they are not likely to provide a transformative learning experience, which has a higher probability of reducing prejudice, discrimination, and bias. Multicultural counseling training and education programs need to provide an opportunity for practitioner-trainees to transform both thinking styles/patterns and emotions. Delphin and Rowe (2008) demonstrated how to increase cultural competence through an interactive workshop for community mental health professionals. Participants were actively involved in identifying their own social and salient identities, and they learned through the interactive process about the automatic nature of personal and social biases including their impact on the treatment process. The identity model proposed is based on a holistic perspective, which includes both appropriate dichotomous thinking ("either/or") and diunital thinking ("both/and"). Inclusive of a person's multiple identities, it is constructed to represent the whole person by examining intersections of multiple identities, the salient identity, and sociocultural contexts. It is conceptualized on integration of cognition and emotion, and it is based on a transformative model, involving transformation of both affective and cognitive processes.

⟨⟨ FLUIDITY OF IDENTITY DEVELOPMENT

An individual's identity formation goes through a dynamic and fluid process while intersecting with multidimensional and multilayered aspects of multiple identities and contexts. For instance, one dimension of identity development runs along the continuum while simultaneously interacting with other identity dimensions to different degrees. These complex relationships can only be understood by using multidimensional and multilayered thinking styles that simultaneously explore multiple dimensions, multiple intersections, and variations within as well as among identities. This holistic thinking perspective, which excludes inappropriate dichotomous, hierarchical, and linear thinking while integrating emotional and intellectual understanding of multiple identity development, will capture the fluidity and dynamics of multiple identity development.

Multiple Identity Assessment by the WRC Model

Awareness of their own identity development assists practitioners with understanding its impact on how they think, behave, and feel toward clients' worldviews (Pack-Brown, 1999). Practitioners who are unable to understand their own racial identity development are viewed as having difficulty with clients' worldviews (Helms, 1990, 1995). According to Helms (1990), a precursor to being a nonracist White person is understanding and accepting White culture as part of White racial identity development. Several studies indicate there are positive correlations between more advanced levels of racial identity development and higher levels of multicultural counseling competencies (Castillo et al., 2006; Middleton et al., 2005; Ottavi, Pope-Davis, & Dings, 1994; Vinson & Neimeyer, 2000). This chapter is devoted to showing practitioners and practitioner-trainees how to assess their own multiple identities in an attempt to raise their multicultural competence. Both the White Racial Identity (WRI) model (Helms, 1984, 1990, 1995) and the White Racial Consciousness (WRC) model (Rowe, Bennett, & Atkinson, 1994), which were discussed in Chapter 11, have been used efficiently to assess White practitioners' racial identity development. In addition, the WRI model has predicted racial prejudice for both male and female White undergraduate students (Carter, 1990; Castillo et al., 2006; Pope-Davis & Ottavi, 1994).

The model proposed by this book is the first comprehensive multiple identity development model that simultaneously examines the multiple identities discussed in Part II. Most if not all models in Chapter 11 indicated the internal struggles an individual faces as he/she/ze moves from one stage to another in developmental stage models or from each resolution situation to the next in the resolution model. Practitioners and practitioner-trainees who belong to a privileged group may not have too much to write at this time, and that is all right. Accept the process as it is. Not censoring or judging will assist them with gaining insight through narrative reflection writing and imagery. Centering may help bring clarity and stillness. As indicated in Chapter 3, practitioner-trainees may learn something about themselves as they mindfully complete the assessment. Completing these activities will allow them not only to know about themselves from a holistic perspective but also to gain insight on how to inquire about a client's multiple identities.

All the identity models discussed in Chapter 11 have been modified to assess practitioner-trainees' multiple identities, and the WRC model has been modified to assess practitioners' and practitioner-trainees' multiple identity development as an example. The following experiential learning activities are designed for assessing multiple identities. Identities relating to race, gender, class, sexual orientation, impairment/disability, religion, age, region, and language are assessed. Practitioners and practitioner-trainees need to add other areas of identity that are important for them.

CONCRETE STRATEGIES

Experiential Learning Activities

Close your eyes. Breathe in and out slowly for 3 min or as long as it takes to create calmness and stillness within you. Then open your eyes.

1. Racial identity development

   The WRC model can be used to assess racial identity with a slight modification. *Dominative* type individuals promote their own race (e.g., Japanese) and do not have personal relationships with members of other racial groups but tolerate them when they have to. *Integrative* type individuals are comfortable with their own racial identity as well as with others' racial identities and ethnicities. They have personal relationships with members of their own racial group, Whites, and members of other non-White racial groups. *Conflictive* type individuals act as if they support racial equity; however, they are racially prejudiced with subtle issues that are not apparent at face value. *Reactive* type individuals ignore their own personal responsibility, although they claim they understand systematic and institutional oppression and internalized oppression around race.

   a. Choose a type that describes your racial identity development at this point in your life. Rate yourself on a scale of 1 to 10, with 1 being the beginner state and 10 being 100% of that type.

   b. Draw whatever images come to your mind as you participate in this activity.

2. Gender identity development

   The WRC model can be used to assess gender identity with a slight modification. *Dominative* type individuals promote their own gender and have minimal personal relationships with people of other genders but tolerate them when they have to. *Integrative* type individuals are comfortable with their own gender identity as well as with the gender identities of others. They have personal relationships with people of the same and different genders. (3) *Conflictive* type individuals act as if they support gender equity; however, they are sexist with subtle issues that are not apparent at face value. *Reactive* type individuals ignore their own personal responsibility, although they claim they understand systematic and institutional oppression and internalized oppression around sexism.

   a. Choose a type that describes your gender identity development at this point in your life. Rate yourself on a scale of 1 to 10, with 1 being the beginner state and 10 being 100% of that type.
   b. Draw whatever images come to your mind as you participate in this activity.

3. Class identity development

   The WRC model can be used to assess class identity with a slight modification. *Dominative* type individuals promote their own class and have minimal personal relationships with members of other classes but tolerate them when they have to. *Integrative* type individuals are comfortable with their class as well as other classes. They have personal relationships with people from all types of class. *Conflictive* type individuals act as if they support class equity; however, they are classists with subtle issues that are not apparent at face value. *Reactive* type individuals ignore their own personal responsibility, although they claim they understand systematic and institutional oppression and internalized oppression around class.

   a. Choose a type that describes your class identity development at this point in your life. Rate yourself on a scale of 1 to 10, with 1 being the beginner state and 10 being 100% of that type.
   b. Draw whatever images come to your mind as you participate in this activity.

   (Continued)

(Continued)

4. Sexual orientation identity development

The WRC model can be used to assess sexual orientation identity with a slight modification. *Dominative* type individuals promote their own sexual orientation and have minimal personal relationships with those who have other sexual orientations but tolerate them when they have to. *Integrative* type individuals are comfortable with their own sexual orientation as well as with other sexual orientations. They have personal relationships with people of the same and different sexual orientation. *Conflictive* type individuals act as if they support sexual orientation equity; however, they are heterosexists with subtle issues that are not apparent at face value. *Reactive* type individuals ignore their own personal responsibility, although they claim they understand systematic and institutional oppression and internalized oppression around sexual orientation.

a. Choose a type that describes your sexual orientation identity development at this point in your life. Rate yourself on a scale of 1 to 10, with 1 being the beginner state and 10 being 100% of that type.

b. Draw whatever images come to your mind as you participate in this activity.

5. Impairment/disability identity development

The WRC model can be used to assess impairment/disability identity with a slight modification. *Dominative* type individuals promote their own status of ability/disability and have minimal personal relationships with people who have a different status of ability/disability but tolerate them when they have to. *Integrative* type individuals are comfortable with their own status of ability/disability as well as with that of others. They have personal relationships with able and disabled individuals. *Conflictive* type individuals act as if they support ability/disability status equity; however, they are biased with subtle issues that are not apparent at face value. *Reactive* type individuals ignore their own personal responsibility, although they claim they understand systematic and institutional oppression and internalized oppression around impairment/disability.

a. Choose a type that describes your impairment/disability identity understanding at this point in your life. Rate yourself on a scale of 1 to 10, with 1 being the beginner state and 10 being 100% of that type.

b. Draw whatever images come to your mind as you participate in this activity.

6. Religious affiliation identity development

   The WRC model can be used to assess religious affiliation identity with a slight modification. *Dominative* type individuals promote their own religion and have minimal personal relationships with people who are not religious or who believe in different religions but tolerate them when they have to. *Integrative* type individuals are comfortable with their religiosity or lack thereof as well as with those who subscribe to other religions. They have personal relationships with people who have the same religion, people who have a different religious affiliation, and people who have no religion. *Conflictive* type individuals act as if they support religious diversity; however, their prejudice shows with subtle issues that are not apparent at face value. *Reactive* type individuals ignore their own personal responsibility, although they claim they understand systematic and institutional oppression and internalized oppression around religion.

   a. Choose a type that describes your religious affiliation identity development at this point in your life. Rate yourself on a scale of 1 to 10, with 1 being the beginner state and 10 being 100% of that type.

   b. Draw whatever images come to your mind as you participate in this activity.

7. Age identity development

   The WRC model can be used to assess age identity with a slight modification. *Dominative* type individuals promote their own age group (e.g., children, youth, elderly) and have minimal personal relationships with members of other age groups but tolerate them when they have to. *Integrative* type individuals are comfortable with their own age as well as with other ages. They have personal relationships with members of all different age groups. *Conflictive* type individuals act as if they are against ageism; however, they display ageism with subtle issues that are not apparent at face value. *Reactive* type individuals ignore their own personal responsibility, although they claim they understand systematic and institutional oppression and internalized oppression around age.

   a. Choose a type that describes your age identity development at this point in your life. Rate yourself on a scale of 1 to 10, with 1 being the beginner state and 10 being 100% of that type.

   b. Draw whatever images come to your mind as you participate in this activity.

(Continued)

(Continued)

8. Regional identity development

   The WRC model can be used to assess regional identity with a slight modification. *Dominative* type individuals promote their own region and have minimal personal relationships with people of other regions but tolerate them when they have to. *Integrative* type individuals are comfortable with their own regional identity as well as with regional identities of others. They have personal relationships with people from various regions. *Conflictive* type individuals act as if they have relationships with people from various regions; however, they are biased with subtle issues that are not apparent at face value. *Reactive* type individuals ignore their own personal responsibility, although they claim they understand systematic and institutional oppression and internalized oppression around regions.

   a. Choose a type that describes your regional identity at this point in your life. Rate yourself on a scale of 1 to 10, with 1 being the beginner state and 10 being 100% of that type.

   b. Draw whatever images come to your mind as you participate in this activity.

9. Language identity development

   The WRC model can be used to assess language identity with a slight modification. *Dominative* type individuals promote their own language and have minimal personal relationships with people who speak other languages but tolerate them when they have to. *Integrative* type individuals are comfortable with their own language as well as with the languages of others. They have personal relationships with people who speak different languages with different degrees of proficiency. *Conflictive* type individuals act as if they support equality for ESL speakers; however, they are biased with subtle issues that are not apparent at face value. *Reactive* type individuals ignore their own personal responsibility, although they claim they understand systematic and institutional oppression and internalized oppression around ESL speakers.

   a. Choose a type that describes your language identity development at this point in your life. Rate yourself on a scale of 1 to 10, with 1 being the beginner state and 10 being 100% of that type.

   b. Draw whatever images come to your mind as you participate in this activity.

The Author's Multiple Identity Development

I am going to use myself as an example to illustrate the complexities involved in multiple identity development. As I examined my nine areas of identity (race, gender, class, sexual orientation, impairment/disability, religion, age, region, and language), I realized my thoughts, feelings, and behavior at times change depending on which identity I am dealing with. I had contradictory thoughts and feelings as I examined one of my identities in relation to the others from a *multidimensional* and *multilayered* perspective. I had different emotions with different identities, as I have experienced lots of pain from discrimination in relation to some identities and no pain in relation to others. For example, I have no perceived discrimination experiences with class, impairment/disability, age, sexual orientation, religion, or region. At least that is what I think and feel at this time. In those identities, I hold a privilege and have seen myself unintentionally being like my oppressors. For example, I thought small-town living fostered narrow perception mainly because I was raised in a big metropolitan area in South Korea. I longed for city-type activities since that was all I knew, and when I came to the United States I expected every city to have extensive cultural activities (*generalization*). It took some maturity for me to admit that I was ethnocentric in relation to assuming city activities are "better" than rural activities (*hierarchical thinking*). As I questioned the validity of my assumptions about small-town living, I realized that I had no evidence to support my assumptions. My learning about the positive aspects of small towns came after awareness of my *hierarchical* and *egocentric thinking*. I have since learned to enjoy small-town activities and appreciate quiet small-town living. If I had continued my biases against small towns, I probably would not have tried small-town activities.

I have, however, been discriminated against due to my race, gender, and language. I have been a victim of my own sexism as well as that of others. Multiple layers and multiple dimensions in relation to sexism interlocked with other oppressions. I was a sexist, for example, when I put myself last as a wife and a mother, and then there was another layer of sexism that family and society placed upon me. I operated in two different ways simultaneously: I was a sexist who was oppressing myself at home while maintaining professionalism at work by portraying myself as egalitarian. I did not know I was a sexist for a long time. I thought I was putting myself last because of my love for my family, but I was conditioned as a girl to do so, although I did not practice it when I was growing up. I internalized sexism and was not able to differentiate how much was due to love for my family and how much was due to my internalized sexism.

My experience with racism reflects my perception as a person who grew up as a member of a majority group and became a minority group member. Although it was painful to be the object of racism in the United States, its impact on my physical, emotional, psychological, and spiritual well-being was not as paramount as it has been for some people of color who were born and raised in the United States. These people of color were born a minority and will stay a minority in the United States. I was not conditioned to internalize racism in Korea, and this experience influenced the way I dealt with racism.

My parents belonged to the privileged class in South Korea, from which I benefited. When I moved out on my own to come to the United States, however, my class changed. I was marginalized as a blue-collar worker in the United States, but I did not pay that much attention to this maltreatment because I loved working and being financially independent from my parents. Because I perceived working as my choice and a path to newfound financial freedom, I cherished those moments of counting pennies and waiting long minutes for the bus. My class status changed, but it also boosted me to become my own person. The way I dealt with the classism affected me positively. I was glad to have lower-class status and learn the value and management of money. My penny-pinching lifestyle taught me self-confidence and not to fear my financial situation. I know I can work anywhere and anytime if I need to.

Discrimination due to language affected me severely when I first came to the United States, and the experience stayed with me for a long time. It only got better when my language skills improved and I was not laughed at as frequently. I felt sharp pain, anger, powerlessness, and sadness when experiencing discrimination in relation to my language. When I first came to the United States, I was discriminated against by my statistics professor and my research methods professor. I felt humiliation and powerlessness. I felt so alone and isolated. Regret for coming to the United States, missing the love and caring of my family, feeling obligated to carry out my own commitment, and anger toward ethnocentric people were intermingled and created all sorts of feelings to different degrees within me. It took some years for me to realize that it is all right to speak with an accent since I do speak Korean. Since then, I have been enjoying seeing the world from two cultural perspectives, which gives me a different perspective.

I do not recall an experience with marginalization in relation to my sexual orientation, impairment/disability, age, or religion. I know I am a privilege holder for being heterosexual and able-bodied with no known physical, mental, emotional, or learning impairment. I am positive my cultural sensitivity toward those who are targets of systematic oppression has increased over the years with my interests in social justice. There is no way I can really understand their pain caused by oppression, but I am compassionate toward them by remembering my pain from being an ESL speaker and a target of racism and sexism. I have no strong emotional attachment to my chronological age since I get a year older each year like everyone else. Age has not been an important part of who I am. However, I am aware of ageism against young children and the elderly. I am not sure what my relationship to religion is. Religion was not emphasized during my childhood. My mother was a Buddhist, and I assumed my father was also a Buddhist although I never saw him going to a temple. My parents sent me to a private Methodist middle and high school because it was considered one of the best schools, not because of the religion it promoted, and my parents put no restrictions on my participation in religious activities or lack thereof. I explored various religions by attending different churches and temples when I was in middle school. I believe spirituality plays an important role in healing, but spirituality is not synonymous with religion. I consider myself spiritual but without a conscious connection to a particular religion.

I have thus been oppressed and the oppressor simultaneously, and these experiences have shaped my identity construction. I was oppressed in relation to race, gender, and language and was simultaneously an unintentional oppressor in relation to sexual orientation, age, and region.

My identity changed with my negative and positive experiences with the nine identities discussed in this book, and the change progressed in divergent directions. Some of my thinking styles used to be *linear, dichotomous,* and *hierarchical,* and they are gradually transforming into a holistic perspective. Some parts of my thinking are totally changed. Other parts of my thinking style are changing somewhat, and other parts are staying the same. I do not know what my dominant identity is at the conscious level, but it is important for me to seek internal balance and wholeness.

I have learned that it is dangerous to evaluate another person solely on the basis of one identity as if that identity represents him/her/zir as a whole (*generalization*). In exploring my identity development, I have discovered that I hold different degrees of prejudices in various identities and these different degrees, different dimensions, and different layers manifest themselves in various ways as I interact with others. Sometimes I am conscious of them, and other times I am not conscious of them. I have learned that my thoughts, feelings, and attitudes have changed substantially in some areas and not at all in other areas. My thoughts, feelings, and attitudes are fluid, and I do not know which ones will stay the same and which ones will change. I have realized that I can have preferences without judging those of others as inferior (*nondichotomous thinking*). Some of my preferences have remained the same while over the years others have changed.

Practitioner-Trainees' Multiple Identity Development

CONCRETE STRATEGIES

Experiential Learning Activity

Describe your multiple identity development and try to answer the following questions:

1. Have you stayed the same, changed somewhat, or changed completely? As you read my examples, you may have found that, like me, you are much more affected by the development of some identities and less by the development of others. You may also have found that development of some identities is intertwined with that of others with different degrees of impact. If you reflect on your responses to the experiential learning activities, you will discover different layers of each identity dimension and their intersections with each other.

2. How would you describe your different degrees of emotional intensity in relation to different sociocultural contexts?

3. Which of your identities are constructed out of oppressed experience, and which identities have led you to be the oppressor?

4. Are your thinking patterns/styles consistent when you are the oppressed and the oppressor?

5. What are your feelings as an oppressor and as the oppressed?

6. What have you learned from being an oppressor? What have you learned from being oppressed?

7. Have you changed your dominant (salient) identity throughout your life, or have you stayed the same?

8. Do you have a dominant identity?

9. Do you use the same or different criteria to assess your identity construction?

Practitioner-trainees may discover that their identities have complex relationships with each other. These relationships have changed for some practitioner-trainees over the years, and they have stayed relatively stable for others depending upon their mobility, openness, motivation, ability to reflect, experience within particular sociocultural contexts, level of consciousness, and ability to listen to their inner self. For some, their identities have changed with their priorities to meet their developmental tasks in each stage, as well as when the focus was shifted from external to internal identity.

A practitioner's accurate assessment of a client's worldview is determined by the practitioner's ability to assess her own multiple identity development from a multilayered and multidimensional perspective and to integrate intellectual with emotional understanding of multiple identity construction. The following experiential learning activities are designed for practitioner-trainees to apply what they learned from assessing their own multiple identity development to assessing that of clients.

CONCRETE STRATEGIES

Experiential Learning Activities

Reread your description of your multiple identity development.

1. Which identities are likely to lead you to countertransference, and what do you need to do to minimize it?

2. What is your dominant (salient) identity? Describe how it may facilitate or hinder your ability to assess a client's worldview.

(Continued)

(Continued)

3. As a practitioner, what do you think are important questions you need to ask your clients on the basis of your experience with examining your own multiple identity development?

4. What have you learned about your ability to be flexible and fluid?

5. Use colored crayons, colored pencils, watercolors, or colored pens and drawing pads or paper to draw your inner- and outer-world experiences with your multiple identities.

6. Discuss the following with other individuals who have completed these experiential learning activities:

   a. What did you learn about yourself through drawing?
   b. What were your thoughts about multiple identities before and after describing your own multiple identities?

A substantial amount of experiential and reflection-based learning activities have been presented throughout this book in order to provide the opportunity for practitioner-trainees to integrate the intellectual aspect of learning with the emotional aspect of learning. These learning activities involved narrative writing, imagery, role-playing (both cognitive perspective taking and affective perspective taking), centering, consciousness-raising exercises, and drawing. If the practitioner-trainees have completed each learning activity in conjunction with the chapter content, they are ready to integrate and synthesize all that they have learned both cognitively and affectively. They are ready to assess and treat culturally diverse clients from a multilayered and multidimensional perspective. They are ready to assess clients from a holistic perspective.

CONCRETE STRATEGIES

Consciousness Practice

Are you the same "you" as you were 2 hours ago?

13

Culturally Appropriate Assessment

The purpose of this chapter is to develop a comprehensive assessment tool for clients who are culturally different from clients who are culturally different from practitioners. This means assessment will be based on a perspective of understanding the client's culture and his worldview. In order to assess a client whose worldview is different from the practitioner's, the practitioner needs to have accurate self-assessment of her own worldview. The fundamentals of accurate assessment for culturally different clients are discussed. Why the treating practitioner should complete the intake, the impact of the practitioner's communication style on the assessment, the practitioner's ability to think in a multilayered and multidimensional style while making the assessment, and the practitioner's ability to incorporate scientific inquiry into the assessment are also discussed.

Comprehensive assessment techniques to understand a whole person are discussed. These include the client's communication style, his multiple identities, the intersections of his multiple identities, the dominant identities of the client and his family members, and the acculturation levels of the client and his family members. In addition, how to incorporate the *Diagnostic and Statistical Manual of Mental Disorders (DSM-IV-TR)* and professional ethics codes for culturally different clients are discussed.

⟋⟍ FOUNDATION FOR ACCURATE ASSESSMENT

Assessment is the foundation for developing an effective treatment for the client. Accurate assessment is especially crucial for clients from diverse cultural backgrounds. D'Andrea and Heckman (2008) state that emphasis on social justice is one of the major forces in the multicultural counseling movement, and there are various articles on social justice and multicultural counseling in the *Journal of Counseling & Development*'s second special issue on multiculturalism (Comstock et al., 2008; Crethar, Rivera, & Nash, 2008). Social justice evolves around providing equality and justice for all people regardless of their race, gender, sexual orientation, class, disability, age, language, religion, and region. This book has focused on providing both cognitive and affective transformation of practitioner-trainees so they will be able to implement fair and accurate assessment and treatment. This is the first comprehensive assessment tool that includes assessing multiple identities of a client. The foundation for an accurate assessment is discussed in this section.

Intake and Effective Treatment

The practitioner-trainee needs to decide how she is going to demonstrate respect to a client. Some mental health clinics call clients who are incapable of managing their daily lives "consumers." The term *consumer* is applied to individuals who are not capable of exercising their consumer rights either due to systematic oppression/internalized oppression or due to their psychotic states. They are not allowed to choose or are not capable of choosing a more effective program for them; nor can they choose which facility is best suited for their situation. On a daily basis they rely on case managers for taking pills and keeping doctors' appointments and are challenged by a lack of life skill competencies. Who decided to call them consumers? What does this label mean in a materialistic sociocultural context, and how does it relate to clients who cannot exercise their consumer rights due to their mental, emotional, physical, and/or financial condition? How do these individuals feel being called consumers, especially when they know that they have no power to exercise their rights? What does calling clients consumers do to the relationship between a practitioner and clients who are able to afford treatment fees? Did anyone ask them how they want to be called?

The other issue the practitioner-trainee needs to think about is who is going to conduct the intake if she is working for an agency that separates treatment practitioners from intake practitioners. Changing from a practitioner completing intakes to one in a fragmented system where duties are assigned to "specialists" under the guise of efficiency also reflects the impact of sociocultural context on treatment of clients. The American Counseling Association's (ACA, 2005) *Code of Ethics and Standards of Practice*, the American Psychological Association's (APA, 2002) *Ethical Principles of Psychologists and Code of Conduct*, and the National Association of Social Workers' (NASW, 1999) *Code of Ethics* state a commitment to the welfare of the public they serve. If practitioners and organizations are committed to the welfare of clients, they need to seriously examine whether the intake conducted by a person who is not going to provide treatment for a client is a sign of commitment to the welfare of the client.

It has been the author's experience that most clients do not seek therapy until they are no longer able to tolerate a situation and are pressured by someone, forced by court or work to seek therapy. Initially they are vulnerable and nervous to talk about their problem to a stranger. Therefore, the first encounter with a helping professional will determine the client's attitude and ability to build rapport. If he exposes himself psychologically and emotionally at the intake and then is assigned to another stranger to start treatment, this poses a problem for the practitioner since key information is gathered at the time of intake. If the practitioner develops treatment strategies on the basis of another person's (the intaker's) written report, it must be assumed that the person gathering the intake information has the same worldview as the practitioner, the same amount of knowledge in multicultural counseling competencies, the same biases and prejudices, the same way of observing nonverbal language of the client, the same tone of voice, the same verbal communication skills, and so forth.

During intake, when the practitioner listens attentively to the client's presenting problem, therapeutic goals, psychosocial and physical developmental history, intrapersonal and interpersonal relationships, problem-solving strategies, and cultural experiences, the practitioner not only learns the client's history, strengths, and weaknesses and recurring themes in the client's life but also can learn from the client's nonverbal language. The client's nonverbal expressions of his story are a rich text of the client's worldview and meaning making. Verbal and nonverbal information from the intake can provide a structure for developing an effective treatment program.

Effective Verbal and Nonverbal Communication Styles

In general, the quality of a practitioner's attitudes determines how much information the practitioner gets from the client. The practitioner may unintentionally express her negative attitudes through verbal and nonverbal communication. Miller and Miller (1997) postulate four types of verbal communication styles—(a) small talk, (b) control talk, (c) search talk, and (d) straight talk—that accompany four types of listening skills. Small talk helps build rapport. This type of verbal communication does not have that much substance but is pleasant and light. Examples include "How are you today?" and "My dog is so cute, and she makes me relax. Do you have a pet?" This type of talking leads to conventional listening, which does not trigger intense emotional response, is pleasant to listen to, and shows one's interest in a topic but requires only as much energy as one chooses to expend.

Control talk (*fight talk* and *spite talk*) is used not to generate information but to use power and control to resist change, change others, or force a certain outcome. It focuses on keeping score or getting even. Fight talk is a one-up position of power (*hierarchical*), which discounts and devalues others. It often uses punitive (e.g., blaming, attacking, scolding) and aggressive (e.g., name-calling, belittling, arguing, labeling) language and focuses on the person (*judging/putting down*) rather than the issues. Examples are "You are lazy and stupid," "You are wrong," "Do it this way because I told you to," and "You are paranoid. Go find the real cause of your problem." Such fight talk often stirs up resentment and frustration and creates resistance, rigidity, and tension. It damages interpersonal relationships and claims the speaker's superiority and righteousness (*hierarchy* and *dichotomy*). Spite talk attempts to influence others through a passive-aggressive style. Spite talkers exercise power through powerlessness (helplessness and hopelessness) and often lie and distort situations to obtain power. Contrary to fight talk, spite talk exerts control from a one-down power position (inferior position of *hierarchy*). It leads to shame and guilt. Examples are "Nobody ever listens to me" and "It's OK to do this your way. I am sure it will come out better than if we do what I want." It reflects low self-esteem and pain in response to a particular situation. It drains and diffuses energy. Control talk leads to reactive listening. The reactive listener interrupts the speaker, ignores critical information, judges constantly instead of listening, forces agreement, and superimposes solutions. In other words, reactive listening minimizes the speaker, generates tension, leads to poor decisions, prolongs the resolution, and damages interpersonal relationships.

Search talk is intended to explore facts, clarify misunderstanding, brainstorm, evaluate alternatives, expand knowledge, and gain perspective. Examples are "I'm wondering if I understood the facts correctly" and "I am confused about the process versus the product." Search talk reduces tension, increases information, and leads to raising questions on the basis of observation. It may be frustrating if it continues without leading to resolution or action. Search talk leads to explorative listening, which leads to attentive listening, generating possibilities, and increasing the quality of information rather than getting stuck in a conventional and reactive listening style. Search talk and explorative listening are effective strategies to improve the practitioner's clarity and to get more information from a client. For example, the practitioner may say, "I am wondering whether you could explain a little bit more about your relationship to your work situation. I want to make sure that I understand it clearly."

Straight talk focuses on one's own experience, accepting reality as it is rather than denying, blaming, or avoiding it. Individuals who use this type of verbal communication own their contributions and respond to and deal with tension in inter- and intrapersonal conflicts peacefully by putting energy into positive change. They focus on a collaborative effort with interpersonal and work-related issues. This collaborative effort leads to a richer interchange with others and allows the straight talkers to recognize they are the authority on their own experience but not on the experience of others. Straight talk builds trust as individuals share their real feelings, desires, and thoughts about particular issues. Examples are "I think I didn't get your input. I am sorry I interrupted you. Please accept my apology," "I'm thinking about going to graduate school, but the thought of graduate school scares me and I don't know why," and "I am frustrated because our task is working on the project for 30 minutes and we have only 10 minutes left." Straight talk leads to attentive listening, which reduces interpersonal tension, establishes rapport, and builds trust.

The effective verbal communication style for practitioners is a combination of search talk and straight talk. The mood for search talk is calm, tentative, inquisitive, and supportive. A practitioner is interested in learning about the client's worldview. Search talk often consists of open questions. The mood of straight talk is caring, serious, centered, and focused. Combining straight talk and search talk will likely lead to rapport. When there is rapport, it is easier for the clients to openly express their inner experiences such as what they are thinking and feeling about themselves and others. Building rapport is based on the art component of therapy. It is based on emotion that connects people. It is about how the client feels toward the practitioner. When clients feel accepted and valued and that what they have to say is heard by the practitioner, they open up. The practitioner builds rapport on the basis of nonverbal communication as well as verbal communication. Having in-depth knowledge of counseling theories, including multicultural theories, does not lead to automatic rapport. It is the art component, which consists of emotion, intuition, and attitude from both conscious and unconscious learning, that leads to this rapport. This component is derived from transformative learning, which integrates the knowledge component with the emotional component of that knowledge. It is a practitioner's implicit expression of beliefs, values, and biases toward clients and their worldviews (Banaji & Greenwald, 1994; Chen & Bargh, 1997; Greenwald & Banaji, 1995; Schacter & Scarry, 2001). It is activated automatically and affects the practitioner's perception and judgment without her awareness (Banaji & Hardin, 1996; Perdue & Gurtman, 1990). In order to learn from a transformative learning perspective, the practitioner needs to be mindful of her biases, beliefs, stereotypes, and prejudices and the possibility of racism.

The following experiential learning activities are designed to identify the practitioner's communication styles and provide the opportunity to modify them if she wants to be an effective practitioner.

CONCRETE STRATEGIES

Experiential Learning Activities

Close your eyes and breathe in relaxation and breathe out tension. As you breathe slowly and deeply for about 5 min, recall the verbal and nonverbal communication styles of your social agents (e.g., parents, grandparents, uncles, teachers). Slowly open your eyes.

1. Personal activity:
    a. Describe your father's (or father figure's) verbal communication style.
    b. How did you feel when he talked to you?
    c. Describe your mother's (or mother figure's) verbal communication style.
    d. How did you feel when she talked to you?

    e. Describe your own verbal communication style.

    f. Describe similarities and differences between your verbal communication style and those of your parents.

    g. Describe your father's (or father figure's) nonverbal communication style.

    h. How did you feel about his nonverbal communication style?

    i. Describe your mother's (or mother figure's) nonverbal communication style.

    j. How did you feel about her nonverbal communication style?

    k. Describe your own nonverbal communication style.

    l. Describe similarities and differences between your nonverbal communication style and those of your parents.

    m. What have you learned from these experiential learning activities?

2. Role-playing:

    a. Divide the class into small groups of four. Pair up in your small group. One pair will role-play, and the other pair will observe to give feedback. The first pair will decide who is going to be a counselor and who will play the client.

        (1) Start regular counseling practice skills for 10 min in each session. The client may talk about whatever issue he/she/ze would like to discuss. The counselor should use control talk.

        (2) The client should observe his feelings throughout the session.

        (3) The other pair will give feedback about what they observed.

        (4) The person who played the client will give feedback about his/her/zir feelings and thoughts.

        (5) Repeat the procedure until everyone has had the chance to be counselor, client, and observer. Videotape the sessions and examine the nonverbal language of both the client and the counselor (e.g., body posture, tone, hand gestures).

        (6) Discuss what you learned from this activity and implications for effective counseling.

Accurate assessment of the client's worldview depends on the practitioner's ability to assess herself accurately. Concrete strategies for accurate self-assessment of the practitioner's worldview are discussed throughout this book. Each practitioner needs to assess her ability to hear the client's narrative from the client's point of view while being aware of her own worldview, thinking patterns, biases, and so on. If the practitioner is not able to do this, she is not qualified to assess the client from his worldview. Furthermore, the practitioner needs to assess her ability to build rapport with clients from multicultural backgrounds.

If a practitioner's communication style is *control talk* and *reactive listener*, she will have difficulty listening to clients' stories because she may be engaged in intrapersonal communication in order to formulate her own statement instead of listening to clients. This is automatic and often an unconscious process. The practitioner needs to get feedback from others about her talking style, assess her own listening style, and work on improving communication toward *search talk/explorative listening* and *straight talk/attentive listening.* The nonverbal language of *control talk* is anger, resentment, disengagement, indifference, defiance, and hopelessness. So, the practitioner may say the correct words to be empathetic and respectable by using *search* and *straight talk*, but her client may be more affected by her nonverbal language and assume that she is nonempathetic. Nonverbal language is much more powerful than verbal language, and people take cues from nonverbal language (*body language*) when there are discrepancies between the verbal and the nonverbal language (Miller & Miller, 1997). Miler and Miller summarize that "nonverbals precede verbals. . . . Nonverbals are more powerful than verbals. . . . Nonverbals are implicit: words are explicit. Nonverbals punctuate interaction" (p. 76). There are other verbal cues such as tone of voice and type of words used. Cue words for control are "you" statements and "I" statements. For example, the control talker may say, "You shouldn't be doing that," instead of saying, "I am having difficulty understanding what you did. I wonder whether you can help me by explaining it in detail." *Control talk* also uses cue words like *should, ought, have to, always, never,* and *everyone*.

If a practitioner's communication style is *search talk/explorative listener* and *straight talk/attentive listener,* she will be able to be compassionate and empathetic toward clients who are control talkers and reactive listeners. What and how a practitioner verbalizes reflect how the practitioner listens to clients. For instance, if the practitioner's communication style is *control talk*, she is likely to use *reactive listening* even though a client may be utilizing straight talk. Miller and Miller (1997) emphasize the importance of both communication skills (*knowledge*) and caring attitude (*art*). When the practitioner cares and has appropriate communication skills, she not only resolves issues effectively but also feels good about herself. This strengthens the positive relationship between practitioner and client. Clients can build rapport and trust when the practitioner's verbal communication (*search* and/or *straight talk*) is congruent with her nonverbal communication (*caring attitude*). When the practitioner cares about the client but is not able to express her care, she is often misunderstood. For instance, a practitioner may care about her clients deeply but use *control talk* (an inappropriate communication skill) without awareness. Clients may perceive her as controlling and not understanding their worldviews. When the practitioner has appropriate communication skills but does not care about her clients, she may be perceived as a manipulative person. Lastly, if the practitioner does not have effective communication skills and does not care about her clients, she may be engaged in unintentional psychological abuse.

One of the multicultural counseling competencies of the Association for Multicultural Counseling and Development (Roysircar, Arredondo, Fuertes, Ponterotto, & Toporek, 2003, p. 6) is "Counselor Awareness of Client's Worlview . . . [defined as] culturally skilled counselors understand how race, culture and ethnicity may affect personality formation. This implies "culture-specific knowledge building is necessary for responsible and ethical practice." A practitioner who is truly multiculturally competent shows empathy when clients are defensive because she understands clients' defensive behaviors are often a result of past painful experiences. Being genuine with defensive clients is not possible within dichotomous, hierarchical, and linear thinking styles, which frame one party as "good" or "superior" and the other as "bad" or "inferior." If the practitioner is reacting to the client's defensive behaviors, she needs to investigate whether her thinking style is based on inappropriate dichotomous, linear, and hierarchical thinking. When a practitioner can examine the client's defensiveness from a multidimensional and multilayered perspective, it allows for a wide range of explanations from a simplistic "either/or" interpretation to a complex "both/and" interpretation. This process is likely to lead the practitioner not to react but to use the information to assess the client in relation to stress, personality, problem-solving styles, thinking styles, and salient identities and to examine the client's history of internalized and systematic oppression and so on. Watching for any nonverbal cues such as facial expression, posture, movement, and tone of voice will assist the practitioner with understanding the meaning of the client's defensiveness. The practitioner may use active listening by saying, "It sounds like you were really frustrated" or "I am hearing you are really hurt by your friend not being there for you." The client may feel support from active listening and begin to decrease defensiveness and resistance. Effective verbal and nonverbal communication skills provide a foundation for gathering information for an accurate assessment.

Some practitioner-trainees may feel frustration due to continually having to revisit the concepts of inappropriate thinking styles. These concepts have been repeated intentionally throughout the book because it is difficult to change implicit attitudes (Deutsch, Gawronski, & Strack, 2006; Rydell, McConnell, Strain, Claypool, & Hugenberg, 2007; Stott, 2007). It is easy to remember the words, but it is hard to implement words into action. Shifting from inappropriate dichotomous, linear, and hierarchical thinking styles to a holistic thinking style needs to be practiced on a daily basis while being patient with gradual progress. It took most individuals a lifetime to automatically activate linear, dichotomous, and hierarchical thinking, and it is going to take a long time to transcend inappropriate thinking styles.

Incorporating Scientific Inquiry Into Clinical Inquiry

One of the ways to become an effective practitioner is to acquire the ability to apply psychological research methodology critique skills to the therapeutic setting. Research inquiry demands critical reasoning skills and paying attention to details in order to differentiate sound research from inadequate research. It requires objective scientific inquiry and not personal subjective inquiry. Objective scientific inquiry will aid practitioner-trainees in learning to ask specific questions by using the client's own words instead of interpreting the client's words through their worldview. Assessment of a client also requires objective scientific inquiry in order to accurately hear a client's story without personal bias. In order to obtain accurate information, the practitioner must use objective scientific inquiry with a warm and accepting attitude. If the practitioner uses objective inquiry with a nonjudgmental tone of voice and nonjudgmental body language, the client will feel the practitioner is interested in helping him. Practitioner-trainees who want to improve their research skills can practice by analyzing primary research articles on a particular issue related to multicultural populations and critique the articles in terms of research design, sample size, threat to internal and external validity, author accuracy in interpreting tables, and so on. Applying research skills to therapy includes (a) the practitioner paying close attention to generalizations made by both the client and the practitioner; (b) the practitioner asking for clarifications rather than interpreting the client's statements from the practitioner's worldview; and (c) the practitioner asking for specific information. Corey's (2005) *Case Approach to Counseling and Psychotherapy* gives the following example:

Ruth: I know that being so afraid has closed in on my life in so many ways. I feel ready to take this on, but it would be too overwhelming to become so honest with myself and everybody else in lots of areas of my life all at once.

Therapist: So you would like to challenge fear and express yourself more openly, but you want to do so in small steps. Is that right?

Ruth: Sure. (p. 269)

The practitioner interprets Ruth's comments as wanting to progress "in small steps." Ruth has no choice except to agree with the therapist due to the power differential in the relationship. If Ruth were a woman of color, the impact of the power differential in the relationship could be more intense due to systematic racism she has experienced throughout her life. Or, it could be more intense due to trusting an expert's opinion more than her own. Counseling and psychotherapy textbooks that include dialogues between a therapist and a client often show the therapist's dialogues as interpreting the client's dialogues. This type of communication frequently leads the client to follow the therapist's interpretation. The therapist in the example could gather information by using Ruth's statements to explore how she wants to proceed. The therapist could say, "Would you give me some examples of how being so afraid has closed in on your life?" "Do you need to be honest with everybody all at once?" "You said you need to be honest with yourself and everybody else. Is it practical to do that for both you and everybody else at the same time?" "You said you need to be honest with yourself and everybody else in lots of areas. In what area would you like to start?" or "Who is everybody? Would you name these people for me?" There are various ways to explore what and how Ruth wants to start. The therapist's role is to create an environment where the client makes changes, transcends, experiences, or transforms and not to lead the client toward the therapist's worldview.

In the author's multicultural counseling program, students are required to submit one abstract per week for 5 weeks. They need to use primary research articles and indicate a hypothesis, a research design (correlational or experimental), independent and dependent variables, the statistical significance of tables, and internal and external validity. This is an attempt to provide students with the opportunity to incorporate scientific objective inquiry skills into counseling skill practice in addition to writing research synthesis papers. At the end of the quarter, students are required to submit a research synthesis paper including a minimum of 10 primary research articles. By the 5th week, students' ability to shift their clinical inquiry from general to specific is dramatic. Prior to completing their weekly research abstract assignments, students usually assume that they understand what a peer is describing in their peer counseling sessions. For instance, when a student who is playing the client's role says, "I am really depressed," a student who is playing the counselor's role often says, "Yeah, I know what you mean." However, the same student who is playing the counselor's role learns to ask for more information by applying scientific inquiry to make sure he/she/ze understands what the student who is playing the client's role meant during the research synthesis project. So, it usually changes from "Yeah, I know what you mean" to "Tell me more about your depression. What do you think when you are depressed?" "What do you say to yourself when you are depressed?" "What are you thinking right at this moment?" and so on.

By applying details of research skills such as quantitative reasoning and limiting generalization, practitioner-trainees can assist clients who overgeneralize by inquiring about specific information through search talk. Having objective scientific inquiry skills assists practitioners not only with being able to develop accurate assessment skills and treatment programs but also with knowing how to differentiate excellent from mediocre multicultural counseling research. An effective practitioner needs to incorporate well-done research findings to understand the multicultural population. Making the division between clinical and counseling psychology and experimental and academic psychology does not prepare future practitioners to be competent practitioners. Practitioner-trainees need to be thoroughly trained in both clinical and research preparation. They need to know about counseling skills, quantitative and qualitative research analytical skills, and clinical skill building with an emphasis on intuition, inter- and intrapersonal awareness of emotion, compassion for culturally different individuals, and respect for human diversity.

A practitioner creatively interweaves the art and knowledge aspects of counseling and psychotherapy to facilitate a client's path to discovering self from a multilayered and multidimensional perspective. Effective assessment cannot be based on inappropriate dichotomous and hierarchical thinking. A client's story derived from applying an inappropriate dichotomous and hierarchical interpretation may represent only a small portion of the client's worldview, or it may distort the story to the extent it is no longer the client's story. In order to assess the client's worldview, the practitioner needs to assess the client from a holistic perspective. Most practitioner-trainees may remember from physiological psychology or general psychology that talking is a sequential activity processed by the left side of the brain. Verbal expression is highly praised in the U.S. school environment. In addition to sequential processing like language, the left side of the brain processes logical, temporal, and rational information. The right side of the brain processes emotional, intuitive, creative, and atemporal information. Intuition looks at a situation as a whole rather than in part. People need both sides of the brain to process their thoughts, feelings, and actions. For accurate assessment, practitioners need to inquire about information concerning both sides of the brain and be mindful of their interpretation of the client's stories from both sides of their brain.

Interpretation of Silence by Different Cultures

The practitioner should not interpret silence from the North American perspective when she is assessing clients from multicultural populations. Not all cultures interpret talking more as a positive quality. Some cultures value silence as a much more desirable quality than talking or value both talking and silence. In fact, valuing speaking as more important than silence is a Eurocentric concept based on hierarchical thinking (Covarrubias, 2007; Miike, 2007; Tu, 1996). Native American culture and numerous Asian cultures consider silence a part of communication since they define communication as a process and not a product (Braithwaite, 1990; Carbaugh, 2001; Clair, 1998; Covarrubias; Miike, 2003). The author once had a Japanese American client who was encouraged to show respect to his elders by being silent. He was praised for being quiet at home, but his teachers indicated that he was a good student but too quiet. His parents were concerned about his school behavior and told him he should be more outgoing at school. He was frustrated and confused since he was expected to be outgoing at school but silent at home. Covarrubias explains the ethnocentric bias held by Westerners on silence:

> Situated or perhaps caught in a Eurocentric sociocultural bipolar worldview—speaking is good, silence is bad—conceptualizations about what constitutes proactive communication inspire some scholars (among other people) to treat silence as an ontological and epistemological vacuum waiting for talk to happen. Silence is treated as a suspended animation, stand-by position until real communicative opportunities ensue. (p. 267)

Covarrubias (2007) makes a distinction between consumptive silence and generative silence. Silence is "interpersonal malfunction" (p. 268) in consumptive silence but "functions to enable the thriving of a particular way of being in, learning about, and experiencing her world" (p. 269) in generative silence. Cultures that place importance on generative silence value "peace," "respectfulness," and "perseverance" but devalue "impatience" (p. 269). When the practitioner asks questions of clients from the nondominant value orientation, she needs to wait without showing impatience. The client may be thinking or feeling about the practitioner's questions; interlinking them with memories, beliefs, and values; and actively processing them by engaging in intrapersonal communication. The importance of inner experience was discussed in Chapter 3, and awareness of inner experience can be expressed in various modes such as silence, drawing, movement, writing, and verbal description. Understanding a client from his worldview also implies that silence may be a part of his culture and his way of learning to change feelings, beliefs, and behavior. The practitioner who is not comfortable with silence needs to examine her assumptions about silence and her relationship to silence by reflecting on her developmental stages. Her discomfort can be expressed through her body language and interfere with the therapeutic process. The practitioner can also learn to be in silence as the client is actively engaged in being who he is in silence. The practitioner can pay attention to her intrapersonal communication and experience her feelings and thoughts in the moment in silence. When the client expresses he is through processing in silence either by verbal or nonverbal language, the practitioner may ask, "Would you like to share your process with me?" The practitioner must accept whatever decision the client makes. This is one way of showing that the practitioner accepts the client as he is by honoring his wishes. The following is an example of using silence as a powerful tool.

PERSONAL STORY

Silence, the Powerful Assessment Tool

I took a projective test course from a behaviorist in my master's program in Virginia. The professor spent a substantial amount of time critiquing the validity and reliability of projective tests. He also emphasized applying objective scientific inquiry when administering and scoring projective tests. He asked us to measure with a stopwatch how long the test taker looked at the picture, changes in intonation, eye contact with the picture and with the test administrator, frequency of rotating the picture, and so on. We had to administer each projective test to five people. I apply some of the techniques I learned in this course when I am in silence with clients.

I am as alert when I am engaged in conversation with verbal clients as when I am engaged in a session with a silent client. When I ask a question and the client stays in silence, I measure unobtrusively the duration of silence and body language, facial expression, and other expressions like sighing, coughing, crying, and smiling. The following is an example.

Client: I am sorry. I am not a talker.

Practitioner: Nothing to be sorry about. There are various ways to process, and silence is one of them. Take your time.

We sit in silence. Both the client and I are actively engaged in meaning making. I try to provide a comfortable space for the client by not distracting his process while observing unobtrusively until he talks or breaks the silence with nonverbal language, such as tears rolling down his cheek, a smile, or a facial color change. Such nonverbal language communicates to me. I record the client's specific nonverbal expression and add a symbol that signifies to me to return to the subject later to get more information. Then I ask one of, some of, or all of the following questions.

Practitioner: Are you indicating that you are done processing? Would you like to share what you are thinking and feeling? Would you like to draw what came to you now? Shall we do a centering exercise before I ask you another question?

(Continued)

(Continued)

Client: No, I am OK. I can't really describe what I am thinking and feeling, but your question made me think about lots of things.

If the client does not want to share his process, I honor his wish. I consider silence as one way of communicating. It is not important to me that the client verbalizes. What is important is that the client is actively engaged in the therapeutic process through verbal or nonverbal meaning making. What I need to learn is whether my assessment of the client is accurate.

Accurate Listening

Accurate listening requires the practitioner to empty her mind in order to follow what the client is expressing verbally and nonverbally. It requires putting herself into the client's position (empathy) in order to hear what he is saying, acknowledging the client's experience, inviting more information for clarity, and checking the accuracy of her interpretation by listening actively with specific inquiry. Accurate listening is similar to Miller and Miller's (1997) attentive listening. This listening skill reduces tension, builds trust, and leads to the most accurate information. Whether the practitioner is an attentive listener or not is determined by the client and not by her. The practitioner may think and feel she is an attentive listener, but her clients may not feel and think that way. Reviewing the findings of research on asymmetric perception of self and others, differential evaluations on subjectivity and objectivity, and introspections about self versus others in relation to the practitioner's therapeutic skills help ensure that her actions match her intent (Andersen, 1984; Andersen & Ross, 1984; Baumeister, 1998; Chen & Bargh, 1997; Dunning, Meyerowits, & Holzber, 1989; Epley & Dunning; 2000; Heath, 1999; Pronin, Gilovich, & Ross, 2004; Pronin, Kruger, Savitsky, & Ross, 2001; Pronin, Lin, & Ross, 2002; Steele, 1988; Taylor & Brown, 1988).

One way for practitioner-trainees to evaluate their listening style is to get feedback from videotaping their listening behaviors in various situations such as counseling practice sessions and small-group discussion sessions. In addition, video feedback is an excellent source for learning about practitioner-trainees' nonverbal communication skills. Whether a client feels valued, accepted, trusted, and/or understood by the practitioner can be assessed from the practitioner's nonverbal communication.

What are barriers to accurate listening? Practitioners need to examine their own barriers to accurate listening. One barrier could be a cultural context that fosters a fast lifestyle as ideal. Students often write about their mind racing in their process learning assignments. The purpose of these inner-experience narrative writing assignments is for students to learn about themselves without being graded or judged in order to promote self-awareness in an academic setting. Some students state that their racing mind distracts them from attentively listening to lectures, small-group discussions, and peers during counseling practice sessions. A practitioner's thinking styles may also be a barrier to accurate listening if she applies dichotomous, hierarchical, and linear thinking styles inappropriately. As indicated earlier, if the practitioner is a dichotomous thinker, she may interpret the client's nondichotomous verbal communication as dichotomous.

The author once had a student whose thinking style was dichotomous and hierarchical, and he applied this thinking style in counseling skill practice. Other students were frustrated because they felt he was not listening to their issues. The following is an example of their skill practice.

Student client:	I have ambivalent feelings about going home for Thanksgiving. I love to see my mom and enjoy a few days with her, but I am not sure whether I would like to be harassed by my relatives who come to dinner. They are always saying something about my lifestyle.
Student counselor:	Why don't you go see your mom?
Student client:	I want to see my mom but . . .
Student counselor:	(Interrupts the client.) There is no "but." Just go see her. (The student client tries to say something, but the student counselor continues to talk.) I don't see any problem in that. I think it's good that you want to see your mom. (The student counselor continues to talk about what the client should do.)

As the group and the author were reviewing the session by videotape, the author stopped after the student client's first dialogue and asked the student counselor for a key word to describe the presenting problem. He said the client wanted to see her mom. When the author asked him about the meaning of *ambivalent*, he knew the definition but was not able to help the client explore her "ambivalent feelings" because he focused on "I love to see my Mom" and interpreted "love to see my Mom" dichotomously, and it was creating an either/or (*seeing mom* or *not seeing mom*) situation rather than focusing on exploring the client's "ambivalent" feelings. If the student counselor was able to help the client explore her ambivalence in depth, she may have come up with several avenues for possible solutions. One possibility would have been to ask how many relatives have harassed her, how many of them would be present, and how long each one would stay. Another might have been to suggest she discuss her "ambivalent feelings" with her mother to see if she might be able to help. Exploring the possibility of having an early dinner with her mother and then visiting people who were not critical of her lifestyle would have been another good suggestion. The student counselor might also have explored the meaning of *harass* with the student client by exploring specific comments or behaviors that, in her mind, constitute harassment. The student client, however, felt that she was not heard because the student counselor missed her ambivalence and told her she should go to her mother's; he was telling his story rather than listening to her story. He wanted to be a "good counselor," but his thinking style kept him from listening accurately. Even though he said he understood intellectually, it was challenging for him to transcend inappropriate dichotomous thinking.

Another barrier to accurate listening is a practitioner's own anxiety. Sometimes the desire to become an effective practitioner makes one overly critical of herself. Being critical of oneself in the therapeutic process distracts the practitioner from paying attention to the client's story, much like students who are so preoccupied with the amount of pages they have been assigned to read that they cannot complete the reading. This distracts students from concentrating on reading and comprehending what they have read. When students spend too much time figuring out whether they will be able to reach a goal, it distracts them from reaching that goal. Distraction prevents them from reading, but reading is the only way to reach their goal. If the practitioner wants to be an effective therapist, she must clear her mind and focus on the client's story in the moment.

Anxiety is not from the outside. What individuals perceive as an anxiety-producing situation may have originated from external cultural or familial contexts such as high expectations from others, trauma, racism, sexism, heterosexism, ableism, and classism. However, one's internal interpretation from external cues is an internal process and often automatic. It is from one's own anticipation based on the past and projected into the future. Most people who have shared their anxiety with the author have expressed that anxiety is from their logical, rational mind. Their brain is working logically and rationally with irrelevant information such as a past traumatic experience as if it is from the present situation. The mind is complex with values, beliefs, biases, prejudices, and memories. Because thinking is a private process that has no feedback loop, it can be exaggerated without actual basis. This can lead to physiological symptoms such as dry mouth, rapid heartbeat, rapid pulse, shallow breathing, sweating, and "butterflies in the stomach." The brain often cannot separate reality from assumed reality. For this reason, many people think their anxiety is based on facts and forget that physical symptoms are created by exaggerated interpretations of internal processing. They can be anxious on the basis of their exaggerated interpretation and send the body an emergency-situation message to activate the sympathetic division of the autonomic nervous system. As a result, these individuals may secrete more stress hormones than needed and create a hormonal imbalance.

One way to reduce anxiety and stress is by breaking the automatic activation cycle. Activities like centering (breathing exercises), meditation, and yoga will decrease anxiety. One can also use the body movement activities that were introduced in Chapter 3 (Halprin, 2003; Schure, Christopher, & Christopher, 2008).

﹏ ASSESSMENT IN RELATION TO RACE, GENDER, SEXUAL ORIENTATION, CLASS, DISABILITY/IMPAIRMENT, AGE, LANGUAGE, RELIGION, REGION, AND THEIR MULTIPLE INTERSECTIONS

Assessment Related to Race

Some White practitioners who have learned and understood systematic privilege for Whites and systematic oppression for people of color feel guilt and shame for their race and compassion for people of color. They want to make sure they do not add more pain to the lives of people of color. These practitioners say they feel like they are walking on eggshells because they do not want to hurt their clients of color's feelings and do not know what is appropriate behavior. White practitioners need to know that practitioners of color may have an advantage if a client identifies with their skin color (Helms & Carter, 1991). However, skin color is only one aspect of multiple factors influencing the effectiveness of therapy. White practitioners also need to know that if practitioners of color have not resolved their own pain from systematic oppression and internalized oppression, there will be a problem of countertransference. Furthermore, the degree of acculturation, degree of racial identity development, type of thinking patterns, degree of awareness of their values and beliefs, relationship to privilege/oppression, and communication styles of practitioners of color influence their ability to translate intellectual understanding of multicultural competencies into practice. There are great variations among practitioners as a whole, and there are great variations among White practitioners as well as among practitioners of color. There are also great variations within practitioners of any particular racial group.

Regardless of their racial background, practitioners need to accept the fact that it is impossible to know how to initially assess a client of color since there are so many spoken and unspoken specific cultural beliefs, values, customs, attitudes, and individual variations. For instance, some Black clients want to be called Black while other Black clients want to be called Afro American. Clients who want to be called Black at one point in life might well have wanted to be called Afro American at another point in life. The only way to know how to address them is by asking how they want to be identified. "Walking on eggshells" only perpetuates racial stereotypes and creates barriers to building rapport. Instead of being fearful of hurting the feelings of clients of color, ask them what is the appropriate way to interact with them.

White practitioners do not need to walk on eggshells or suffer from White guilt because that does not transcend racism or racial prejudices. White practitioners need to think about the effective way to assist clients so that clients can transcend their suffering from systematic oppression. Assessing clients accurately assists practitioners with developing an effective treatment program, and this is one step closer to transcending their clients' suffering. Practitioners of color need to be mindful of not generalizing on the basis of their own experience. Their experience may be very different from that of clients even if their skin color is the same. Both practitioners of color and White practitioners need to actively share their resources with each other and ask for assistance from each other in order to develop accurate assessment of clients.

Other crucial aspects of assessment are the difference between the client's degree of racial identity and that of his family, the difference between the client's degree of acculturation and that of his family, and how these factors influence the presenting problem (Helms, 1994a, 1994b). There are several assessment scales relevant to measuring White racial identity and the racial identity of people of color and other acculturation scales for various racial groups (Anderson et al., 1993; Cortes, Rogler, & Malgady, 1994; Dawson, Crano, & Burgoon, 1996; Marin & Gamba, 1996; Nguyen, Messe, & Stollak, 1999; Paniagua, 2005; Sodowsky & Lai, 1997; Sodowsky, Lai, & Plake, 1991; Tropp, Erkut, Garcia Coll, Alarcon, & Garcia, 1999; Yamada, Marsella, & Yamada, 1998). Practitioners may want to research these scales to see whether they are effective instruments for their clients. Practitioners need to be able to assess clients concerning multiple identities and the clients' relationships to these multiple identities in terms of experience with privilege and oppression. Practitioners also need to be able to assess the intersection among these multiple identities and the power of the client's salient (dominant or special) identity in the client's worldview.

When a practitioner has to use the *Diagnostic and Statistical Manual of Mental Disorders (DSM-IV-TR)*, she needs to critically examine the validity of the *DSM-IV-TR* for a client whose cultural values are not represented by the *DSM-IV-TR*. A practitioner needs to pay close attention to whether each axis is assessed by the practitioner's worldview or the client's worldview while being mindful of the fact that the *DSM-IV-TR* is based on the mainstream cultural norm. A practitioner needs to critically analyze how she would experience and react to the world and life if she had to deal with racism on a daily basis since childhood. For example, if a client demonstrates dysthymic disorder characteristics according to the *DSM-IV-TR* description, the practitioner needs to ask whether it is ethical to label the client as dysthymic when the symptoms are primarily due to systematic oppression. In other words, the practitioner needs to be able to differentiate symptoms of dysthymic disorder due to an individual situation (without internalized oppression) from the same symptoms due to systematic societal oppression.

Assessment Related to Gender

A practitioner needs to be mindful of how her relation to gender interacts with the client's experience with gender. The practitioner needs to be clear about her assumptions, beliefs, values, biases, and attitudes about gender before completing an assessment of a client on gender. Knowing about her relationship to gender and being aware of her tendency to countertransfer will assist her with attentively listening to the client's story. Being clear about her relationship to gender and her role as a helping practitioner facilitates her desire to have a mindset that is flexible, fluid, and ready to hear the client's story without judgment.

The practitioner needs to conceptualize that gender and a client's multiple identities are interrelated and that, for some clients, gender is a dominant (salient or special) identity while it may not play a significant role for others. For still other clients, gender may play a significant role in particular sociocultural contexts. The practitioner needs to pay close attention to a client's narrative about his experience as a family member, a student in class, an employee at work, and so on. Clients have a wealth of information about themselves that they may not be able to share with the practitioner because they do not know what information is important for accurate assessment of their presenting problem, unless the practitioner asks specific questions in a way that the client perceives as the practitioner being genuinely concerned about the client.

Read the following statement from Ruth and formulate what kind of questions the practitioner should ask her in order to understand her experience as a woman within her sociocultural context.

Ruth: All my life I've had others tell me who and what I should be, and John has picked up where my parents and church left off. I don't know what my life is about apart from being a wife and a mother. What would our kids think if John and I split up? How would it affect them? Would they hate me for what I'd done to the family? I know I am tired of living the way I am, but I'm not sure what I want. And I'm scared to death of making any more changes for fear that it will lead to even more turmoil. John and the kids liked the "old me" just fine, and they seem upset by the things I've been saying lately. (Corey, 2001, p. 101)

What specific questions could the practitioner ask Ruth in order to assess her gender identity development; the sociocultural contexts in which her gender identity developed; whether or not she has been affected by sexism, systematic oppression, and internalized oppression; and the degree of their effect on her, if any? Accurate assessment relies on the practitioner's ability to ask questions from Ruth's story and not from the practitioner's interpretation of her story. This is the time to apply the practitioner's knowledge from critiquing psychological research articles and research methods. For example, what does the practitioner learn about Ruth when she says, "All my life I've had others tell me who and what I should be"? Write down a response to this question before proceeding.

When the author read Ruth's comment, she was not able to respond because she had no idea who Ruth meant by "others," how they have communicated and continue to communicate to her who and what she should be, and in what sociocultural contexts these communications have taken and continue to take place. The author needed more information from Ruth and would have liked to say to her, "Ruth, you said that all your life you've had others tell you who and what you should be. I was wondering whether you could give me some examples of who told you who you are and what you should be." The author might have found the type of relationship Ruth had with these people. After listening to her story, the author might have asked, "What was the earliest experience of this sort that you can remember, and how old were you?" The author might have learned from Ruth about her developmental stage, which would have suggested her cognitive and emotional development at the time of the first memory. If her first memory was from about 8 or 9 years old, the author may have evaluated her reaction from Piaget's (1969, 1972) concrete operational cognitive stage, Erikson's (1964, 1968) industry versus inferiority psychosocial stage, or Kohlberg's (1987) level II, conventional stage of moral reasoning, while assessing her gender-typed behavior reinforcement history if she was a member of the dominant group. The author might also have thought of developmental tasks at that age and evaluated the developmental appropriateness of external demands on Ruth. The author might have asked the follow-up questions from a developmental perspective, which would have revealed another aspect of Ruth. If she was from a non-dominant group, the author might have asked questions relevant to the acculturation levels of Ruth and her family, to the non-White gender identity development of Ruth and her family, and to developmental tasks relevant to her culture. The author might have asked questions that would have revealed Ruth's experiences with systematic oppression and internalized oppression.

The above is an example of why a practitioner needs to have knowledge about both conventional and multicultural developmental psychology (e.g., *cognitive, psychosocial, moral*), gender studies, acculturation processes, racial identity development, and so on in the left side of her brain in order to listen with accurate empathy.

By listening to clients attentively and asking specific questions from their general statements, practitioner-trainees will begin to learn about clients' beliefs, attitudes, and biases on gender. This is one of the reasons why the intake needs to be completed by a practitioner who is going to treat the client. Because so much information is available at the time of intake, the practitioner can build her specific questions on the intake information throughout treatment. The following experiential learning activities are designed to help practitioner-trainees implement both the cognitive and the affective knowledge they have gained throughout the book in assessing a client.

CONCRETE STRATEGIES

Experiential Learning Activities

Form a small group with three or four individuals who are reading this book and who have participated in the suggested activities.

1. Discuss Ruth's gender identity development; the sociocultural context of her gender identity development; whether or not she was affected by sexism, systematic oppression, and internalized oppression; and to what extent she was affected.

2. Role-play counselor and client with another classmate. The student who plays the client should talk about his/her/zir history with sexism and gender development. The student who plays the counselor should practice asking specific questions to understand the client's sociocultural context for gender identity development and experiences with systematic privilege/oppression and internalized privilege/oppression.

3. Give feedback to each other. The student who played the client role may express when he/she/ze felt comfortable about exploring gender-related issues and when he/she/ze felt uncomfortable.

4. Change roles and repeat Questions 2 and 3.

Assessment Related to Sexual Orientation

A practitioner needs to review the experiential learning activities in which she has participated in this chapter prior to assessing a client, as well as to assess her standing in relation to heterosexism, homophobia, systematic privilege/oppression, and internalized privilege/oppression. A practitioner also needs to reflect on her relationship, if any, to organized religion(s).

A practitioner also needs to assess her ability to think from a multi-layered and multidimensional perspective in addition to her ability to be flexible with her thinking since a client's sexual orientation intersects with other types of identities. Individuals' worldviews are constructed by various beliefs and values, which have accumulated through diverse inner and outer experiences. When the author gave a diversity training workshop at a state university for senior counselors, a practitioner who identified herself as a lesbian revealed her dominant identity is a result of oppression she felt from classism when she was growing up and not from her sexual orientation. She said she knew intellectually that she was not that little girl, but she could not help being stuck in that stage.

A practitioner needs to listen attentively to a client's story and ask specific questions by applying techniques she has learned from the scientific mode of inquiry. The following experiential learning activities are designed to help practitioner-trainees implement both the cognitive and the affective knowledge they have gained throughout the book in assessing a client.

CONCRETE STRATEGIES

Experiential Learning Activities

Read the following case study and think about specific questions you would ask to assess whether the client's presenting issue is due to sexual orientation.

Glenn is a 33-year-old gay Black student. He says:

> The year began with a feeling-out process that included the selection of our first small group. As is always my way, I waited to be picked and expected that a group of White people would not choose to include me. For many years the voice of my mother has echoed in my ear, "The White man is not trustworthy, so you must be twice as good and always expect to be attacked." These lessons were taught to me not out of any malice or desire to do me harm but rather for me to be forewarned and thus forearmed. All my life I have held this knowledge in the back of my mind, and my feeling was that it did not affect me. I felt I was above these "limitations" as I have always had White friends and felt a connection to the White world. In high school I refused to associate with other students of color at lunchtime, a common hour for students to have unscheduled time together. I recall feeling no desire to be anywhere around the Black students.

(Continued)

(Continued)

When I came out to my community, they rejected me. My family, my church, and my friends... They couldn't accept me. I can handle being rejected by Whites but not my own community.

I have discovered that for many years now I have given away my power. I have given to others the ability to make myself acceptable, and in doing so I lost myself. For many years I have acted as I thought I needed to be accepted in the White world, to not be a "nigger" as I was taught.

1. Write down your specific questions (scientific inquiry) in order to assess whether Glenn's presenting problem is due to acculturation, class, or the intersection of race, gender, class, and sexual orientation. Do you see any other issues creating the problem for him? Write down your responses.

2. Form a small group with three to five individuals who are reading this book and participate in the following activity.

   a. Discuss the questions a practitioner needs to ask in order to find out what identities are important to Glenn and whether or not his sexual orientation is one of them.

   b. Practice how to ask these questions by role-playing, with one student assuming the counselor's role and one assuming the client's role. The student who plays the client needs to give feedback to the student who plays the counselor. Reverse roles and continue to focus on how to ask these questions. The student who is playing the client needs to give constructive feedback in response to how questions are asked.

3. How was assessing sexual orientation issues different from and/or similar to assessing issues related to race and gender for you and for your group?

Assessment Related to Class

A practitioner needs to clear her mind by centering before seeing a client or a group of clients. It is extremely important that a practitioner's mind be clear and calm before she assesses a client. Assessment is a difficult task since a client brings multiple identities that interact with complex and diverse sociocultural contexts in addition to his worldview. Each client's worldview is constructed according to various beliefs, values, biases, interactions with the environment, and so on.

It is important for a practitioner to know her own history and experience with her own class and classism before assessing a client in relation to the impact of class on his worldview. In addition, the practitioner needs to remind herself that there are multiple determinants of class and multiple meanings to class and they interact with other identities (e.g., race, gender, sexual orientation, disability, age, language, religion, region). The practitioner also needs to check her thinking pattern/style to assess her ability to think from a multilayered and multidimensional perspective in addition to her capacity for transformative learning. The practitioner needs to remind herself that she is there to assess the client with no prejudgment or assumptions.

The practitioner needs to listen attentively to a client's story and ask specific questions by applying techniques she has learned from conducting research or critiquing primary research journal articles. The following experiential learning activities are designed to help practitioner-trainees implement both the cognitive and the affective knowledge they have gained throughout the book in assessing a client.

CONCRETE STRATEGIES

Experiential Learning Activities

Read the following case study and think about specific questions you would ask to assess whether the client's presenting issue is due to class identity.

Minja, a 41-year-old Korean woman, says:

> My life has been so difficult. I've been hoping it will get better, but it's getting worse. I guess I can stand others laughing at me because of my English, but I can't stand my children laughing at me. They treat me like I know nothing. (She sobs for a while.) I am sorry. I didn't mean to cry. We went to church earlier than usual, and no one was there but us. Kids were playing, and I sat by the piano watching them running out of the room. I started to play the piano, and my daughter was shocked to hear me. She asked me, "Mom! Where did you learn to play the piano so well?" I said, "I majored in piano when I was in college." My daughter looked at me as if I was much more than what she used to think of me. My children thought I was not well educated because of my broken English and the type of work I do. I used to stay home to take care of the

(Continued)

(Continued)

children in Korea, but now I have to work as a janitor. I didn't tell my family in Korea I have a low-class job. I feel so stupid because I can't help my children with their homework because I don't understand what they need to do. It hurts me so much to see my husband struggling with his demoted status. He used to be a manager in a big company. I am emotionally, intellectually, and physically exhausted.

1. Write down your specific questions in order to assess whether Minja's presenting problem is due to acculturation, class, or the intersection of race, gender, and class. Do you see any other issues creating the problem for her? Write down your responses.

2. Form a small group with three to five individuals who are reading this book and participate in the following activity.

   a. Discuss Minja's class identity development; the sociocultural context of her class identity development; whether or not she was affected by classism, sexism, racism, systematic oppression, and internalized oppression; and to what extent she was affected.

   b. Role-play counselor and client with another classmate. The student who plays the client should talk about his/her/zir history with classism, sexism, racism, and class identity development. The student who plays the counselor should practice asking specific questions to understand the client's sociocultural context for class identity development and experiences with systematic privilege/oppression and internalized privilege/oppression.

   c. Give feedback to each other. The student who played the client role may express when he/she/ze felt comfortable exploring class-related issues and when it was uncomfortable.

   d. Change roles and repeat Questions 2 and 3.

3. How was assessing class issues different from and/or similar to assessing issues related to race, gender, and sexual orientation for you and for your group?

Assessment Related to Impairment/Disability

A practitioner needs to examine her understanding of the difference between impairment and disability and the difference between the medical model and the social model of disability and/or impairment. The practitioner also needs to assess whether she believes in one model over the other and how that will affect the way she will assess a client in relation to impairment/disability. In addition, the practitioner needs to assess her thinking style/pattern and rate her thinking style in terms of degree of dichotomous and hierarchical thinking, diunital thinking, multilayered thinking, and multidimensional thinking. The practitioner needs to assess her ability to integrate the emotional aspect of learning. For example, the practitioner may understand the theoretical concept of the social model, but her emotion may not be present. What is important is not if the practitioner has a holistic thinking style but the practitioner's ability to accept her thinking styles and ability/inability to integrate emotional aspects of the theoretical concept at this point as they are. When the practitioner is able to accept her multiple identities, thinking styles, and level of emotional integration as they are, she is able to assess a client much more accurately. The following experiential learning activities are designed for practitioner-trainees to practice research skill-based scientific inquiry in assessment.

CONCRETE STRATEGIES

Experiential Learning Activities

Read the following case study and discuss how to accurately assess whether the client's presenting problem is related to his impairment and whether or not the impairment is disabling him.

Alex, a 27-year-old Native American college graduate, says:

> I was told I should come and see you even though I don't have any mental problems. Because I am different, people think I have a mental problem. No one understands me. I am free spirited and not bought out by the culture. I have always been this way. I am intense when I am creating my art, but people say I am bipolar. I used to be very depressed. I had lost a lot. My parents divorced when I was 13, my girlfriend betrayed me when I went to college, and then I had cancer . . . so many losses. So I was depressed for a long time, but I don't want to be. I work without sleep when I feel I don't have much time left and too much to do. I was near death. I tasted it. I know my time is limited so I bury myself in my artwork, and people say I am manic. I got cancer because I stuffed away my pain. Now I express how I feel—how I truly feel—and then I am labeled as having mania. I am expressing my true feelings in honoring spirit. That's my culture. I worship my ancestors because I believe in rituals and ceremonies. Is that crazy? I am true to my Native American culture and am called crazy by White people. I think they are the ones who are crazy. They want me to take drugs to calm me down. I don't want to take drugs because it kills my creativity. I am an artist. There is no life for me without being me. I am me when I create.

(Continued)

(Continued)

1. Write down your specific questions (scientific inquiry) in order to assess whether Alex's presenting problem is due to disability/impairment or the intersection of race, gender, class, sexual orientation, and disability/impairment. Do you see any other issues creating the problem for him? Write down your responses.

2. Form a small group with three to five individuals who are reading this book and participate in the following activity.

   a. Discuss the questions a practitioner needs to ask in order to find out what identities are important to Alex and whether or not his impairment/disability is one of them.

   b. Practice how to ask these questions by role-playing, with one student playing the counselor's role and the other student playing the client's role. The student who plays the client needs to give feedback to the student who plays the counselor. Reverse roles and continue to focus on how to ask these questions. The student who is playing the client needs to give constructive feedback in response to how questions are asked.

3. How was assessing impairment/disability issues different from and/or similar to assessing issues related to race, gender, class, and sexual orientation for you and for your group?

4. Is Alex impaired, or is his problem due to others' misunderstanding him as a person (an artist) and/or a Native American?

Assessment Related to Age, Language, Religion, and Region

Age

When a practitioner is assessing children, it is important to make sure that the environment is conducive to free expression. The author often asks children to draw or engage in play therapy since some children can express their thoughts and feelings much better through these activities than through words, especially when they are pressured to say certain things by adults. The practitioner needs to have appropriate training by taking courses in psychotherapy through expressive arts and/or play therapy or be trained by experts in the field. Sometimes taking pressure off of children by engaging in activities like walking or activities of a child's choice while asking questions for assessment also helps children respond spontaneously. It is also important to interview parents/guardians and siblings to access family dynamics and the child's position in the family since most nondominant cultures are collectivism oriented. Family and extended family play an important role in a child's life in collectivism-oriented cultures.

When assessing the elderly, a practitioner must treat them with dignity and respect. A practitioner needs to consider the sociocultural context of American culture, which is youth oriented. Nelson (2005) states, "Age prejudice in this country is one of the most socially-condoned and institutionalized forms of prejudice" (p. 208). It is imperative for a practitioner to understand cultural exclusion of the elderly and its impact on elderly people's sense of self. The practitioner needs to ask her elderly clients to determine an appropriate tone of voice by experimenting until she finds their comfort level, and she also needs to ask about the best way to communicate since research reports show conflicting results on "baby talk." Some elderly clients were marginalized by "baby talk" while others reported that they were helped by this type of communication (Nelson, 2005). The practitioner may also want to ask whether making eye contact shows respect in an elderly client's culture or whether it is a sign of disrespect. The following experiential learning activities are designed to help practitioner-trainees implement both the cognitive and the affective knowledge they have gained throughout the book in assessing a client.

CONCRETE STRATEGIES

Experiential Learning Activities

Read the following case study and discuss how to accurately assess whether the client's presenting problem is related to her age. Betty is an 82-year-old White woman.

> Betty was referred to therapy by her longtime best friend because of her suicidal ideation. She has lived her life by the teachings of her church. She was active in church all her life, but the responsibilities were taken away from her for no apparent reason. She feels they were taken away because the church officials consider her old. She says she is able to drive and is physically healthy. She would like to help others like she used to, but everybody treats her like she is not capable. She says, "I feel so useless. I believed all my life that my essence is devoting

(Continued)

(Continued)

my time for others, but I can't because no one will let me." She says her husband doesn't talk to her, and her kids only call her when they need something. She doesn't want to live like this. She would love to go for a drive with her husband, but he only does what he wants to do and spending time with her is not what he wants to do. He never was a talker, but she has spent 60 years hoping he would talk to her someday. She says she regrets not leaving her husband when she was younger, but she didn't leave him because of her religion, and now she is too old to leave.

1. Write down your specific questions (scientific inquiry) in order to assess whether Betty's presenting problem is due to age, religion, class, race, or the intersection of age, religion, class, and race. Do you see any other issues creating the problem for her? Write down your responses.

2. Form a small group with three to five individuals who are reading this book and participate in the following activity.

   a. Discuss the questions a practitioner needs to ask in order to find out what identities are important to Betty.

   b. Practice how to ask these questions by role-playing, with one student assuming the counselor's role and the other student assuming the client's role. The student who plays the client needs to give feedback to the student who plays the counselor. Reverse roles and continue to focus on how to ask these questions. The student who is playing the client needs to give constructive feedback in response to how questions are asked.

3. How was assessing age issues different from and/or similar to assessing issues related to race, gender, sexual orientation, class, and disability for you and for your group?

4. Is Betty's presenting problem due to others' misunderstanding her as a person?

Language

A practitioner needs to make sure she does not speak loudly to a client whose first language is not English because hearing is not the problem. The problem is how to make meaning out of what is heard. Instead of talking loudly, a practitioner needs to pronounce English words clearly and slowly. The author has observed that most North Americans, in interacting with non-English speakers or speakers of English as a second language (ESL), speak too fast for them. They usually slow down and pronounce clearly for a while (maybe 5 or 10 s), but then they go back to their own speed with less clear pronunciations. Because English is often not pronounced as it is spelled, it is hard for ESL speakers to understand what is said. Pronouncing *water* as "warer," for example, and changing vowels depending on where stress marks (accents) are put confuses ESL speakers. It is a challenging task to figure out what "warer" is for ESL speakers whose first language is monosyllabic. These ESL speakers pronounce each syllable, which makes it difficult for a native English speaker to understand what is said. It is important for a practitioner to repeat what was said slowly or ask the client to "spell it out" with a warm and nonthreatening attitude. A practitioner may want to say that she probably speaks too fast in pronouncing words, and that may not make much sense. She should encourage the client to ask for pronunciations to be repeated. The practitioner can encourage the client to ask questions or give some nonverbal signals so the practitioner can slow down and pronounce more clearly. The practitioner needs to ask the client whether her speed and pronunciations are all right for him. The following experiential learning activities are designed to help practitioner-trainees implement both the cognitive and the affective knowledge they have gained throughout the book in assessing a client.

CONCRETE STRATEGIES

Experiential Learning Activities

Read the following case study and discuss how to accurately assess whether the client's presenting problem is related to her English proficiency. Hanako is a 24-year-old Japanese international student who has been in the United States for about 6 months.

> Hanako was sent to the campus counseling center by her advisor. She came to the office, but she talked very little. She communicated with her head (by nodding or shaking it). She cried softly throughout the session. She said she came because her advisor wanted her to seek counseling. She said her roommate treats her like a child. Her roommate laughs at her a lot and talks to her loudly as if she is deaf. She feels she is stupid most of the time, and she misses her home. She said she doesn't like dormitory food and the dorm is too loud to sleep in. She feels like she made a mistake coming to the United States to study.

(Continued)

(Continued)

1. Write down your specific questions (scientific inquiry) in order to assess whether Hanako's presenting problem is due to English speaking or the intersection of race, gender, and other social identities. Do you see any other issues creating the problem for her? Write down your responses.

2. Form a small group with three to five individuals who are reading this book and participate in the following activity.

   a. Discuss the questions a practitioner needs to ask in order to find out what identities are important to Hanako.

   b. Practice how to ask these questions by role-playing, with one student assuming the counselor's role and the other student assuming the client's role. The student who plays the client needs to give feedback to the student who plays the counselor. Reverse roles and continue to focus on how to ask these questions. The student who is playing the client needs to give constructive feedback in response to how questions are asked.

3. How was assessing language issues different from and/or similar to assessing issues related to race, gender, sexual orientation, class, disability, and age for you and for your group?

4. Is Hanako's problem due to others' misunderstanding her as a person?

Religion

When dealing with people whose self-concept is oppressed rather than lifted by their religion, listen to their story and be compassionate about their situation. Ask them questions in a nonthreatening way so they may try to figure out their problem for themselves. Judging their religion would lead them to be distant from the practitioner, and they may not share their intrapersonal messages (self-talk). Both believers and nonbelievers should not ridicule or pressure one another. The following experiential learning activities are designed to help practitioner-trainees implement both the cognitive and the affective knowledge they have gained throughout the book in assessing a client.

CONCRETE STRATEGIES

Experiential Learning Activities

Read the following case study and discuss how to accurately assess whether the client's presenting problem is related to religion. Chuck is a 44-year-old White male.

> Chuck came to counseling due to a fight in church. He has been a pastor of the church for the last 3 years. When he got to the church, it was in debt, and the size of the congregation was very small. For the last 3 years, he has worked hard to build the church, and it went pretty well until the fight. The fight started when he chose not to side with a female church member who wanted him to testify against her husband in a divorce proceeding. The female church member wanted him to say that he saw her soon-to-be-ex emotionally abusing her. Chuck felt he couldn't say that because he had not witnessed emotional abuse. The female church member got upset and created an unfounded rumor about Chuck that he did not care for her. Some church members are upset with Chuck because they believe the female church member's story, and some are saying that Chuck made the right decision not to testify. There are several loud members in the church's female support group, and they are asking Chuck to quit. This fight has upset Chuck's wife to an extent that her health has been compromised. He doesn't know what to do.

1. Write down your specific questions (scientific inquiry) in order to assess whether Chuck's presenting problem is due to religion or the intersection of race, gender, class, and other identities. Do you see any other issues creating the problem for him? Write down your responses.

2. Form a small group with three to five individuals who are reading this book and participate in the following activity.

   a. Discuss the questions a practitioner needs to ask in order to find out what identities are important to Chuck and whether or not religion is one of them.

   b. Practice how to ask these questions by role-playing, with one student assuming the counselor's role and the other student assuming the client's role. The student who plays the client needs to give feedback to the student who plays the counselor. Reverse roles and continue to focus on how to ask these questions. The student who is playing the client needs to give constructive feedback in response to how questions are asked.

(Continued)

(Continued)

3. How was assessing religion issues different from and/or similar to assessing issues related to race, gender, sexual orientation, class, disability, age, and language for you and for your group?

4. Is Chuck's problem due to others' misunderstanding him as a person?

Region

Regions have significant meaning to sense of self for some people while regions have no meaning for others even though they are the product of a particular region. One's place of birth, the place where one is raised for most of his/her/zir childhood, and the nation one left behind by force or by choice have significant meaning and are part of a person's identity formation. Certain regions in the United States have distinctive foods, cultures, dialect, customs, beliefs, political convictions, and so on that shape a part of a person's identity. A practitioner needs to listen attentively to assess which part of the regional characteristics are embedded in the meaning making of a client. The following experiential learning activities are designed to help practitioner-trainees implement both the cognitive and the affective knowledge they have gained throughout the book in assessing a client.

CONCRETE STRATEGIES

Experiential Learning Activities

Read the following case study and discuss how to accurately assess whether the client's presenting problem is related to region. Barb is a 35-year-old Afro American woman.

> Barb came to the community mental health center because it accepts clients according to a sliding scale. Barb is frustrated because she thinks where she and her family are living is a dangerous place for them. She said her husband is a proud man who is the first person to own a house in his family. Barb wants to move because a chemical dumping site is only five blocks away from their house. She thought the house was very reasonably priced when they bought it and didn't know the price was low due to the toxic waste. She said she is concerned about her two young children being exposed to chemicals at an early age.

She said her husband says chemicals are not bad, but she can smell them from her house. She said she and her husband fight almost on a daily basis because she wants to move and he doesn't. She said she'd rather rent a place since they can't really afford a decent house in other areas.

1. Write down your specific questions (scientific inquiry) in order to assess whether Barb's presenting problem is due to region or the intersection of race, gender, class, sexual orientation, religion, language, age, or disability/impairment. Do you see any other issues creating the problem for her? Write down your responses.

2. Form a small group with 3 to 5 individuals who are reading this book and participate in the following activity.

    a. Discuss the questions a practitioner needs to ask in order to find out what identities are important to Barb and whether or not region is one of them.

    b. Practice how to ask these questions by role-playing, with one student assuming the counselor's role and the other student assuming the client's role. The student who plays the client needs to give feedback to the student who plays the counselor. Reverse roles and continue to focus on how to ask these questions. The student who is playing the client needs to give constructive feedback in response to how questions are asked.

3. How was assessing region issues different from and/or similar to assessing issues related to sexual orientation, class, disability, age, language, and religion for you and for your group?

4. Is Barb's problem due to others' misunderstanding her as a person?

⁂ ASSESSMENT OF THE INTERSECTIONS OF MULTIPLE IDENTITIES (RACE, GENDER, CLASS, SEXUAL ORIENTATION, IMPAIRMENT/DISABILITY, AGE, LANGUAGE, RELIGION, AND REGION)

An accurate assessment examines a client from a holistic perspective. The client's multiple identities, sociocultural and sociopolitical contexts, social stressors, limitations, strengths, resources, trauma, and salient (dominant or special) identities are components of the whole person, the client (Ridley, Hill, Thompson, & Ormerod, 2001). "Any psychological assessment that fails to consider the person's important identities is incomplete. In addition, any psychological assessment that fails to examine the interaction among these variables is inaccurate" (Pope-Davis & Coleman, 2001, p. 202). Accurate assessment requires a practitioner who can think from a multilayered and multidimensional perspective and who accepts her values, beliefs, and attitudes and is able to grant the same to others. Each client has different degrees of experience with various identities, and these different degrees, different dimensions, and different layers manifest themselves in both inter- and intrapersonal relationships. A practitioner needs to apply a multidimensional and multilayered perspective to examine a client from his multiple identities based on race, gender, class, ethnicity, sexual orientation, impairment/disability, age, language, religion, region, and so on. The practitioner assists the client in examining whether he is a member of the majority (dominant) or the minority (nondominant) and privileged or oppressed groups in each identity. The practitioner can assess whether the client is aware of the benefits from unearned privileges and the degree of internalized privilege as a result of being a member of a dominant group(s). The practitioner can also assess whether the client is aware of the impact of systematic oppression and the degree of internalized oppression as a result of being a member of a nondominant group(s). For example, the client may have no experiences with discrimination related to class, gender, disability, age, sexual orientation, language, region, and religion but intense discrimination and oppression experiences related to race. A practitioner can assess how this experience with oppression has influenced other aspects of the client's identity formation and how this has affected the client in his inter- and intrapersonal communication and overall sense of self.

In order to assist the client with examining multiple selves with different degrees of privilege and oppression history, the practitioner can ask the client to rank his multiple identities (e.g., race, gender, class, ethnicity, sexual orientation, impairment/disability, age, religion, region, language) in relation to their importance. This not only can facilitate the client's understanding of multilayered and multidimensional aspects of his multiple identities but also provides the practitioner with a way to develop an effective treatment for the client. The practitioner needs to ask specific questions using the client's words from the client's story to provide him with an opportunity to examine the complex intersections of his race, gender, class, ethnicity, sexual orientation, disability/impairment, age, language, religion, region, and other relevant social identities. The practitioner also needs to be flexible by understanding that the client's importance of identities may change with various sociocultural contextual experiences, and the change may be expanded to diverse directions or his identities may stay the same despite sociocultural contextual changes. The client's importance of identities may change with his thinking style (e.g., from a linear, dichotomous, and hierarchical to a holistic perspective). Some parts of a client's thinking may totally change, other parts may change somewhat, and still other parts may stay the same.

Part of accurate assessment derives from the practitioner's ability to view the client holistically, which implies the practitioner is able to view the client as a person with emotion, intellect, multiple identities, a complex sociocultural and familial history, a particular relationship to oppression and privilege, and particular thinking styles/patterns. Treatment success partly depends on accurate assessment; partly depends on the practitioner's ability to understand her own values, beliefs, biases, and worldview; and partly depends on the practitioner's ability to be free from inappropriate dichotomous, linear, and hierarchical thinking and to conceptualize from a multilayered, multidimensional, diunital, and holistic perspective.

〲〲 RATING SCALES FOR THINKING STYLES, MULTIPLE IDENTITIES, AND DOMINANT IDENTITIES

The presenting problem may have to do with differences in thinking styles and dominant identities of the client and other parties who are involved. A practitioner needs to integrate all the information from the intake and subsequent sessions: the client's thinking styles, multiple identities, intersections of multiple identities, and dominant identity or identities and the acculturation levels of the client and/or his family. For multiple identity and dominant identity assessment, the practitioner may ask the client directly to rate his identities on a Likert scale, which ranges from 1 to 10, with 1 being almost no exhibition of specified characteristics and 10 being 100% exhibition. The practitioner may want to collect assessment data for the client's family members when she has sessions with them. However, asking the client to rate his family members' thinking styles, multiple identities, and dominant identities may also give her another perspective. Quantifying thinking styles, multiple identities, and dominant identities of the client and the client's family members assists the practitioner with figuring out if the problem or conflict derives from differences in thinking styles or dominant identities. As discussed earlier, a particular thinking style leads to a particular communication style in terms of both verbal communication and interpreting (perceiving) what is heard. For example, hierarchical and dichotomous thinking styles are likely to lead to *control talk* where the speaker exerts power through a one-up or one-down position. This type of verbal communication leads to *reactive listening,* and the reactive listener in turn discounts the speaker and twists and distorts information to fit it into dichotomous and hierarchical thinking, regardless of the speaker's communication style. Assessing thinking styles of all parties who are involved would aid creation of an effective treatment plan.

The presenting problem or conflict may have to do with entanglement between thinking styles of the client and his family members and their dominant identities. If the practitioner quantifies the multiple identities of each member of the family by using the Likert scale, it will give a clear picture of the conflict. For example, if a client's father's dominant identity is race and the client's dominant identity is sexual orientation, the practitioner may want to explore the dominant identity differences and how the father communicates his dominant identity to the client, how the client communicates his dominant identity to his father, or how the client chooses not to communicate it due to fear of rejection. If the father is a hierarchical and dichotomous thinker who has a control communication style, it may sound like he forces the client to abandon his dominant identity and to replace it with race (generalizing on the basis of $N = 1$, his dominant identity).

Thinking Style Rating

Issue:

Thinking Style	Client	Client's Mother	Client's Father	Client's Sister
Dichotomous	1——5——10	1——5——10	1——5——10	1——5——10
Hierarchical	1——5——10	1——5——10	1——5——10	1——5——10
Linear	1——5——10	1——5——10	1——5——10	1——5——10
Holistic	1——5——10	1——5——10	1——5——10	1——5——10

Some clients and family members may use one type of thinking style (e.g., dichotomous) most of the time while other clients and family members may vary their thinking styles according to an issue. The practitioner may want to have a thinking style rating sheet for each issue in order to assess the impact of thinking style differences and similarities on the presenting problem. It is important to record what the client and his family state (direct quote if possible) from an appropriate thinking style rather than just noting which particular thinking style is used without the direct quotes. If the practitioner writes down what they say and which thinking style they use, she can use these notes for clinical inquiry instead of using her own interpretation of the client and his family members' stories.

Multiple Identities and Dominant Identity Ratings

Identities	Client	Client's Father	Client's Mother	Client's Sister
Race	1——5——10	1——5——10	1——5——10	1——5——10
Gender	1——5——10	1——5——10	1——5——10	1——5——10
Ethnicity	1——5——10	1——5——10	1——5——10	1——5——10
Class	1——5——10	1——5——10	1——5——10	1——5——10
Sexual Orientation	1——5——10	1——5——10	1——5——10	1——5——10
Disability	1——5——10	1——5——10	1——5——10	1——5——10
Religion	1——5——10	1——5——10	1——5——10	1——5——10
Age	1——5——10	1——5——10	1——5——10	1——5——10
Region	1——5——10	1——5——10	1——5——10	1——5——10
Language	1——5——10	1——5——10	1——5——10	1——5——10
Dominant Identity				

〰 RATING SCALE FOR ACCULTURATION

As indicated in Chapter 11, reaching a balance of one's own culture with the dominant culture is a healthy sign of identity development. It is important to assess not only levels of acculturation but also models of acculturation of a client as well as his family members. There are two levels of acculturation: external process of acculturation when an individual moves to another country and internal process of acculturation when an individual moves from one region to another within a country (Casas & Pytluk, 1995; Cuellar, 2000). There are four models of acculturation: assimilation, separation, integration, and marginalization. Individuals in the *assimilation* model reject their culture of heritage and identify only with the dominant culture. Individuals in the *separation* model reject the dominant cultural values and identify only with their culture of heritage (traditional culture). Individuals in the *integration* model integrate the dominant cultural values with the cultural values of their heritage; they are bicultural. Individuals in the *marginalization* model reject both the cultural values of their heritage and the dominant cultural values (Cuellar; Kim-ju & Liem, 2003).

The client's difficulty or presenting problem may be related to conflicts due to different models and different degrees within models of acculturation between the client and his family members. Using a rating scale with specific examples of the client's and his family members' descriptions of their acculturation levels and models will assist the practitioner with evaluating family dynamics. The advantage of recording the client's and his family members' descriptions is that the practitioner can assist them with examining their own descriptions to evaluate whether the presenting issue is due to differences in levels, degrees, and models of acculturation.

Rating Scale for Levels and Models of Acculturation

Levels/Models	Client	Client's Father	Client's Mother	Client's Sister
External	1——5——10	1——5——10	1——5——10	1——5——10
Internal	1——5——10	1——5——10	1——5——10	1——5——10
Assimilation	1——5——10	1——5——10	1——5——10	1——5——10
Separation	1——5——10	1——5——10	1——5——10	1——5——10
Integration	1——5——10	1——5——10	1——5——10	1——5——10
Marginalization	1——5——10	1——5——10	1——5——10	1——5——10

THE *DIAGNOSTIC AND STATISTICAL MANUAL OF MENTAL DISORDERS (DSM-IV-TR)* AND ITS APPROPRIATENESS AS AN ASSESSMENT TOOL FOR MULTICULTURAL POPULATIONS

The *Diagnostic and Statistical Manual of Mental Disorders* is the most widely used assessment tool for diagnosing psychological disorders. It has been criticized for its inappropriateness for culturally different individuals due to its basic assumptions and underrepresentation of multicultural populations (Barney, 1994; Draguns, 1996, 1997; Fabrega, 1994; Gara, Rosenberg, & Goldberg, 1992; Jacobs, 1994; Leach & Sullivan, 2001; Lewis-Fernandez & Kleinman, 1994; Paniagua, 2005; Roysircar-Sodowsky & Kuo, 2001). The problems with the *DSM* can be divided into two categories. One is inherent problems with the *DSM*, and the other is the problems of practitioners. The inherent problems of the *DSM* include the fact that it is conceptualized on a medical model that assumes its categories and described symptoms are universal and that normality and abnormality lie within the self. At this level, it conceptualizes as if the self exists in isolation without being affected by interpersonal, institutional, sociocultural, and sociopolitical contexts. It is clear that these assumptions are based on an individualistic value orientation. However, the *DSM* contradicts its own assumptions at another level because its diagnoses are based on the dominant cultural norms as a result of political and social conventions instead of scientific studies (Leach & Sullivan, 2001). This is evidenced by disorders listed in the *DSM*. These disorders occur mostly due to relational and social factors of the dominant cultural values and have little biomedical basis (Draguns, 1996, 1997). An assumption that the dominant cultural norms are "intrinsic to all disorders and classification schemes" reflects the ethnocentric bias of psychiatrists and psychologists who contributed to the *DSM* (Leach & Sullivan, 2001, p. 356). Only the dominant sociocultural factors are considered important. As a result, individuals from multicultural backgrounds are assessed by the dominant culture's sociocultural factors. The *DSM-IV-TR*, the latest edition, adds that practitioners and practitioner-trainees need to increase their cultural sensitivity in assessment and diagnosis; however, it does not provide specific guidelines for how to be culturally appropriate (American

Psychiatric Association, 2000). This means it is up to practitioners to develop concrete strategies and guidelines for how to be culturally sensitive in assessment and diagnosis. As a result, the degree and level of multicultural competencies demonstrated by practitioners will determine how effectively they can use the *DSM* to the best interest of their clients.

The problems with practitioners are their inability to pay attention to detailed descriptions of criteria for each disorder and their lack of cultural competence. For example, many practitioners diagnose clients on the basis of only one behavior indicator, although the *DSM* describes specific criteria with multiple indicators for diagnosis (Lipton & Simon, 1985). Furthermore, the *DSM* describes in detail episode features; associated features and disorders; specific culture, age, and gender features; course; and differential diagnosis in addition to detailed criteria. Research also has shown that marginalized individuals (e.g., lower-class individuals, people of color, women) receive significantly more *DSM* diagnoses than individuals who are not marginalized (Bjorklund, 2006; Eubanks-Carter & Goldfried, 2006; Flanagan & Blashfield, 2005; Hunt, Matthews, Milsom, & Lammel, 2006; Kaschak, 1992; Landrine, 1989; Lucksted, 2004; Mirowsky, 1990) and that individuals whose worldviews are different from those of practitioners tend to be misdiagnosed (Parker, Georgaca, Harper, McLaughlin, & Stowell-Smith, 1995; Solomon, 1992). It is important for a practitioner to do her best to complete a culturally appropriate diagnosis since labeling will follow the client for the rest of his life. It is important that the practitioner knows detailed descriptions of each psychological disorder in the *DSM* and assesses the validity of the *DSM* for individuals from multicultural backgrounds. Practitioners need to think about the consequences and stigma attached to a person having a psychological disorder. Practitioners need to take an affective perspective position. They need to think about how they would feel if they were the ones who were diagnosed.

In order to implement transformative learning in relation to the *DSM* classification and its applicability to multicultural populations, the author uses case studies or seminar readings for students to practice diagnosing while considering multiple factors from a multilayered and multidimensional perspective. For seminar readings, students are asked to use the *DSM* to assess whether characters in the book being read meet criteria for certain disorders by showing evidence from reading. Then, in small groups, they compare their evidence and criteria before presenting their decision to the class. Most often students find it difficult to pay attention to detailed descriptions of a disorder and specified criteria in the *DSM*. As a result, they resort to only one or two behavior indicators, much like the practitioners who used a single behavior indicator (symptom) to determine a diagnosis in Lipton and Simon's (1985) study. For example, the *DSM-IV-TR* describes five criteria for a major depressive episode (A, B, C, D, and E), and criterion A has nine subcriteria.

CONCRETE STRATEGIES

Criterion A for a major depressive episode states:

A. Five (or more) of the following symptoms have been present during the same 2-week period and represent a change from previous functioning; at least one of the symptoms is either (1) depressed mood or (2) loss of interest or pleasure. (American Psychiatric Association, 2000, p. 356)

Criterion A is the first of five required criteria (A, B, C, D, and E), and students need to pick five of nine conditions from criterion A in addition to meeting criteria B, C, D, and E. It is hard for students to think about detailed information in each criterion and apply all criteria simultaneously. The students are encouraged to continue to deconstruct their dichotomous, hierarchical, and linear thinking styles in order to increase their ability to apply all criteria simultaneously. Their last task is examining applicability of diagnoses for culturally different clients. The importance of multilayered and multidimensional thinking in an accurate diagnosis and its impact on developing effective treatment for the client are emphasized.

Multiaxial Assessment

If practitioners are multiculturally competent, they will utilize the *DSM* multiaxial assessment from Axis I in a culturally sensitive manner. Practitioners reflect cultural appropriateness from Axis I, Clinical Disorders. Practitioners need to pay close attention to Axis IV, Psychosocial and Environmental Problems. For example, an ESL client may be having problems with his primary support group due to the role reversal between parents and child, in which the child assumes the parents' responsibilities due to the parents' poor English proficiency. The client's problems also could be due to differences between his acculturation level and that of his parents, or they may be due to institutional discrimination on the basis of the dominant cultural values and policies. Individuals from the lower socioeconomic class are marginalized by institutional policies that prevent them from having access to adequate education, jobs, housing, and health care. These are not the individuals' problems, and if practitioners pathologize them as such, they are not following their professional code of ethics (ACA, 2005; APA, 2002; NASW, 1999).

Practitioners also need to consider the sociocultural contexts of a client when assessing Axis V, Global Assessment of Functioning. Practitioners need to examine each sociocultural context on the Global Assessment of Functioning Scale with critical analysis to determine whether it is applicable to a particular client who has a history of nondominant value orientation in that particular sociocultural context. For example, a score of 91–100 on this scale says, "Superior functioning in a wide range of activities, life's problems never seem to get out of hand, is sought out by others because of his or her many positive qualities. No symptoms" (American Psychiatric Association, 2000, p. 34). This statement excludes individuals from nondominant cultures.

This book presents many narratives by various individuals who have been marginalized, oppressed, minimized, ridiculed, or discriminated against at individual, interpersonal, institutional, and cultural levels. For some, this type of experience happens on a daily basis. Is it ethical for practitioners to expect them to show "superior functioning" when normal responses to long-term systematic oppression are manifested as anger, depression, or rage? Is ignoring injustice and unequal treatment due to unearned privilege functioning healthy? Is this an indication of coping well with life?

Assessing Each Psychological Disorder Classification for Cultural Appropriateness

Practitioners need to evaluate each scale in a culturally sensitive manner in order to provide equal treatment to both the dominant and the nondominant cultural groups rather than assessing with an instrument that is biased against individuals from nondominant cultures. Equality is not based on using the same instrument. Equality is based on using an instrument that can equally assess both the dominant and the nondominant groups. It is important to find ways to assess all groups fairly. Practitioners need to read each classification carefully in order to diagnose an individual accurately.

The Welfare of Clients

An accurate assessment requires a practitioner to use a holistic thinking style and to have the ability to critically examine details from a multilayered and multidimensional perspective. After diagnosing a client, the practitioner needs to reflect on the decision by integrating her emotion. The practitioner needs to take time to complete an accurate assessment even when her organization pressures her for quick diagnosis in order to secure prompt reimbursement. Diagnosing is as important as not making an error during surgery. Once a client is diagnosed, it is in his permanent record. A quick diagnosis to receive prompt reimbursement not only is unethical but also is objectifying clients. The practitioner needs to apply the ethics code of her professional organization to assessment, diagnosis, and treatment of clients. Three helping professional association ethics codes reviewed in this book emphasize client welfare (ACA, 2005; APA, 2002; NASW, 1999).

☒ ACA, APA, AND NASW ETHICS CODES AND CULTURAL SENSITIVITY

The Helping Professional's Ethics Code

Implementing an ethics code that is culturally sensitive to assess clients from multicultural backgrounds is crucial for accurate assessment. Practitioners not only need to be competent in self-awareness and therapeutic skills but also need to be competent in helping professional ethics. The ethics codes of the American Counseling Association (2005), the American Psychological Association (2002), and the National Association of Social Workers (1999) state the need for practitioners' cultural sensitivity. As follows, the author has italicized sentences particularly relevant to cultural competency.

The ACA Code of Ethics (2005)

Preamble

The American Counseling Association is an educational, scientific, and professional organization whose members work in a variety of settings and serve in multiple capacities. ACA members are dedicated to the enhancement of human development throughout the life span. *Association members recognize diversity and embrace a cross-cultural approach in support of the worth, dignity, potential, and uniqueness of people within their social and cultural contexts.*

Professional values are an important way of living out an ethical commitment. Values inform principles. Inherently held values that guide our behaviors or exceed prescribed behaviors are deeply ingrained in the counselor and developed out of *personal dedication, rather than the mandatory requirement of an external organization.*

Section A. Counseling Relationship

Introduction: Counselors encourage client growth and development in ways that foster the interest and *welfare of clients* and promote formation of healthy relationships. Counselors actively attempt to understand the *diverse cultural backgrounds of the clients they serve.* Counselors also *explore their own cultural identities and how these affect their values and beliefs about the counseling process.*

Counselors are encouraged to contribute to society by devoting a portion of their professional activity to services for which there is little or no financial return (pro bono publico).

The APA Ethical Principles of Psychologists and Code of Conduct (2002)

Preamble

Psychologists are committed to increasing scientific and professional knowledge of behavior and people's understanding of themselves and others and to the use of such knowledge to improve the condition of individuals, organizations, and society. Psychologists respect and protect civil and human rights and the central importance of freedom of inquiry and expression in research, teaching, and publication. They strive to help the public in developing informed judgments and choices concerning human behavior. In doing so, they perform many roles, such as researcher, educator, diagnostician, therapist, supervisor, consultant, administrator, social interventionist, and expert witness. This Ethics Code provides a common set of principles and standards upon which psychologists build their professional and scientific work.

3. Human Relations

3.01 Unfair Discrimination. In their work-related activities, *psychologists do not engage in unfair discrimination based on age, gender, gender identity, race, ethnicity, culture, national origin, religion, sexual orientation, disability, socioeconomic status, or any basis proscribed by law.*

The NASW Code of Ethics (1999)

Mission Statement

The primary mission of the social work profession is to enhance human well-being and help meet the basic human needs of all people, *with particular attention to the needs and empowerment of people who are vulnerable, oppressed, and living in poverty. A historic and defining feature of social work is the profession's* focus on individual well-being in a social context *and the well-being of society. Fundamental to social work is attention to the environmental forces that create, contribute to, and address problems in living.*

Social workers promote social justice and social change with and on behalf of clients. "Clients" is used inclusively to refer to individuals, families, groups, organizations, and communities. Social workers are *sensitive to cultural and ethnic diversity and strive to end discrimination, oppression, poverty, and other forms of social injustice.* These activities may be in the form of direct practice, community organizing, supervision, consultation, administration, advocacy, social and political action, policy development and implementation, education, and research and evaluation. Social workers seek to enhance the capacity of people to address their own needs. Social workers also seek to promote the responsiveness of organizations, communities, and other social institutions to individuals' needs and social problems.

1. Social Workers' Ethical Responsibilities to Clients

Commitment to Clients: Social workers' primary responsibility is to *promote the well-being of clients.* In general, *clients' interests are primary.* However, social workers' responsibility to the larger society or specific legal obligations may on limited occasions supersede the loyalty owed clients, and clients should be so advised. (Examples include when a social worker is required by law to report that a client has abused a child or has threatened to harm self or others.)

The following learning activities are designed to raise a question about a practitioner's learning from the discrepancy between professional ethics codes and multicultural counseling research findings.

ACA, APA, the Association of Multicultural Counseling and Development, and the Council for Accreditation of Counseling and Related Educational Programs (CACREP) require multicultural competence in program accreditation standards (ACA, 2005; APA, 2003; CACREP, 2001; Roysircar et al., 2003), provider guidelines (APA, 1993), licensing, and

---

CONCRETE STRATEGIES

Experiential Learning Activities

After reading the above ethics codes of three professional associations, think and feel about the discrepancy between the ethics codes and research findings.

1. Why are marginalization, oppression, and minimization still occurring in the helping profession? Record your answer.

2. Share your answer with a small group of individuals (not more than four) who are in your class and who are reading this book and have participated in all of the experiential learning activities so far.

3. What do you think is your responsibility in reducing the discrepancy between the ethics codes and practitioners' conduct?

---

certification. If practitioners and practitioner-trainees took their association's ethics code and the above requirements seriously, they should have implemented multicultural competence in their practice. Yet numerous research findings show practitioners marginalizing clients because of their cultural differences (Bjorklund, 2006; Deegan, 2000; Eubanks-Carter & Goldfried, 2006; Flanagan & Blashfield, 2005; Hunt et al., 2006; Kaschak, 1992; Landrine, 1989; Lucksted, 2004; Mirowsky, 1990; Parker et al., 1995; Solomon, 1992). How do we explain the discrepancy between efforts put into increasing cultural competencies by professional associations and demonstrated cultural insensitivity by some practitioners?

Implications of Walking the Talk in Assessment

The reasons for these discrepancies may be diverse. They may be due to not focusing on the importance of ethics in practice. They may be due to intellectually understanding practitioners' professional ethics codes without emotional integration (transformative learning). They may be due to knowing other parts of the ethics codes but not the parts related to cultural sensitivity due to internalized privilege/oppression. Loyalty to dominant cultural values may be deeply ingrained in practitioners' psyche (unconscious and automatic activation of prejudice was discussed in earlier chapters). The cause of these discrepancies is not clear, but it is clear that the associations' efforts to increase cultural sensitivity have not been implemented in practice.

There are strategies to increase practitioners' ethical implementation for multicultural populations. One strategy is that programs for practitioner-trainees require trainees to gain knowledge on professional ethics through transformative learning. This can be accomplished through taking an ethics course that provides practitioner-trainees with an opportunity to integrate knowledge with emotion. When the author teaches multicultural counseling, students on a weekly basis are required to familiarize themselves with their state laws relating to psychologists and counselors in addition to studying APA's *Ethical Principles of Psychologists and Code of Conduct* (2002). The author uses the APA ethical principles because she is most familiar with them, but all three associations' guidelines focus on similar issues in terms of therapy and counseling practices. In order for transformative learning to occur, students examine ethics texts (APA ethics standards and state laws) on three different levels: (a) reading, (b) processing with other students through discussions, and (c) integrating knowledge with emotion through skill practice and internship experience. As students read weekly assigned sections of the texts, they are asked to evaluate which ethics principles and standards are Eurocentric or oriented to the dominant cultural values and which ones are culturally sensitive.

Then, students are asked to develop alternative models in place of Eurocentric ethics to increase cultural sensitivity. They are also asked to examine correlations between their inappropriate dichotomous, linear, and hierarchical thinking styles and their ability to evaluate ethics codes for cultural sensitivity. Students are asked to discuss their assignments with small groups and in whole-class group discussions. In order to implement theory into practice, students are asked to practice counseling skills by choosing ethical dilemmas as the presenting problems and to bring ethical issues from their internship settings to internship processing seminars. Students are asked to check their emotional reactions to ethical dilemmas during counseling practice and process them with their counseling skill practice group. For internship processing, students are asked to bring ethical dilemmas from their internship site and discuss culturally appropriate and ethical ways to handle the situation.

Through these three different levels of learning, students not only gradually develop concrete strategies to implement ethics codes into practice but also sort out the difference between their personal ethics and professional ethics. Examining a professional ethics code with critical reasoning and analytical skills in order to assess its overall cultural sensitivity leads them to evaluate their personal ethics code and assess whether it includes cultural sensitivity.

The power of transformative learning is that students are able to interact with texts and concepts as whole people without disconnecting emotion from academic learning. They are allowed to express their personal ethics and values, and they are listened to without judgment in the transformative learning process. Nonjudgmental discourse is necessary for students to critically evaluate their personal ethics. White students often face internal conflict when discussing racial equity because they are ethically bound to support equality for all people but afraid of losing their privilege if equality is practiced. In this case, these White students' honesty needs to be appreciated, and the class needs to have an honest and genuine discussion about benefits and losses of equality for all people. When all members of the class are able to participate from their perspective, participants' likelihood of examining the basis for their assumptions increases.

Cultural sensitivity statements written in helping professional associations' ethics codes and multicultural competency requirements in programs are substantial improvements in raising cultural sensitivity, but they are not sufficient for trainees and practitioners to implement ethical conduct in assessment and treatment of culturally different clients. Hunt and colleagues (2006) conclude, "Simply sharing cultural characteristics or even awareness of specific issues was not enough when the counselor did not practice in an ethical and professional manner" (p. 171). Transformative learning where emotional understanding is integrated with intellectual understanding of the ethics code and principles is necessary if practitioners and practitioner-trainees want to provide accurate assessment and adequate treatment for multicultural populations. The following experiential learning activities are designed for practitioner-trainees to practice how to apply professional ethics codes to counseling.

CONCRETE STRATEGIES

Experiential Learning Activities for Counseling Skill Practice on Ethical Dilemmas

1. Divide the class into groups of four. Pair up in your group.
    a. One pair will role-play, and the other pair will observe to give feedback. The first pair will decide who plays the counselor and who plays the client.
    b. Start regular counseling skill practice for 10 min for each pair. The student assuming the client role should talk about an ethical dilemma, and the student assuming the counselor role should apply various counseling skills to assist the client by using an ethics code.
    c. The student assuming the role of the client should observe his/her/zir feelings throughout the session.
    d. The other pair will give feedback about what they observed.
    e. The person playing the client should give feedback about his/her/zir feelings and thoughts about the counselor.
    f. Repeat the procedure until everyone has had the chance to be counselor, client, and observer.
    g. What have you learned about your personal ethics and professional ethics? Be specific.

CONCRETE STRATEGIES

Consciousness Practice

What are you conscious of now?

14

Culturally Appropriate Treatment/Healing

The previous chapters were steppingstones to this chapter. This chapter is about how to walk the talk of multicultural competencies and seeing the client from his worldview. It advocates culturally appropriate treatment designed for the client whose worldview is different from the dominant cultural worldview. With emphasis on a practitioner's preparedness in attitude, knowledge, emotion, inquiry skills, and listening skills for successful culturally appropriate treatment/healing, the chapter discusses the importance of a practitioner's accepting and open attitude and thorough knowledge not only in traditional personality theories but also in nontraditional healing techniques. The chapter also discusses the practitioner's ability to pay attention not only to her own affective process but also to that of the client in order to provide rapport, observant of transference and countertransference. Concrete strategies are incorporated into the chapter for transformative learning including case studies, other authors' excerpts, and the author's teaching and clinical experiences.

⊗ CULTURALLY APPROPRIATE TREATMENT

Culturally appropriate treatment relies on accurate assessment and requires a practitioner's willingness to develop treatment that (a) honors the client's worldview and the client's culture, (b) incorporates the client's cultural healing traditions, and (c) restores the client's dignity.

Honoring the Client's Worldview and the Client's Culture

In order to develop treatment that honors the client, a practitioner must view the client holistically as a person with emotion and intellect, multiple identities, rich sociocultural and familial history, a particular relationship to oppression and privilege, and particular thinking patterns. The treatment requires the practitioner to think and feel from a multilayered and multidimensional perspective. This means the practitioner examines a client from the client's multiple identities based on race, gender, class, sexual orientation, impairment/disability, age, language, religion, region, and so on. The practitioner assists the client in examining whether he is a member of the majority or the minority and whether he is privileged or oppressed in each area. If his particular identity belongs to the majority, it is likely that throughout socialization he has been benefiting from unearned privilege and has internalized that privilege. If his particular identity belongs to the minority, it is likely he has been suffering from oppression (systematic oppression) and has internalized that oppression. The client may have no discrimination experiences with class, gender, disability, age, sexual orientation, language, region, or religion but intense discrimination experience with race. The client's identities may change as a result of his negative and positive experiences with a particular sociocultural context, and the change may progress in diverse directions or his identities may stay the same despite external changes. His multiple identities may change with his thinking style (e.g., from linear, dichotomous, and hierarchical to holistic). Some parts of his thinking style may totally change, other parts of his thinking style may change somewhat, and still other parts may stay the same. Developing treatment that honors the client also requires the practitioner to listen attentively without judgment and be compassionate regardless of how different the client's culture is from her own. For example, extended family is as important as an immediate family for most clients from multicultural populations. Accepting the role of extended family from the client's cultural point of view without internal judgment is an example of seeing and understanding the client from his worldview. Understanding the client from his worldview requires the practitioner to understand her own worldview, which is based on her ability to be aware of her own values, beliefs, biases, prejudices, racial identity development, and thinking patterns and the impact of systematic privilege/oppression and internalized privilege/oppression on her worldview.

Incorporating the Client's Cultural Healing Traditions Into Treatment

If the practitioner is fluid and observes the dynamic processes of therapeutic relationships, she can utilize these processes to assist the client with understanding his internal as well as external experiences. These processes may lead the client to be in touch with his cultural and spiritual traditions that include but are not limited to indigenous healing. The practitioner explores the client's healing tradition with the client and finds ways to incorporate it if the client desires and/or if the practitioner assesses it may assist the client. The practitioner maintains her professional boundary of competence and makes sure she researches resources of the client's healing traditions with the client's assistance and respects all healers' expertise.

The client may not want to seek a healer from his cultural tradition but may want to tell the practitioner his story. He may think he does not have a problem. The problem may be identified as an authority figure who only values his/her/zir own beliefs (dominant) and labels the client as mentally ill because he does not fit into a particular mold. The practitioner needs to listen to the client's story attentively to evaluate the client as a whole person and to respect his cultural traditions, which may appear "odd" when compared with the dominant cultural perspective. Fadiman (1997) illustrates eloquently what happens when two cultures clash due to misunderstanding each other's traditions and cultural practices. She writes in her book, *The Spirit Catches You and You Fall Down:*

> Hmong epileptics often become shamans. Their seizures are thought to be evidence that they have the power to perceive things other people cannot see, as well as facilitating their entry into trances, a prerequisite for their journeys into the realm of the unseen (p. 21). . . . Dan had no way of knowing that Foua and Nao Kao had already diagnosed their daughter's problem as the illness where the spirit catches you and you fall down. Foua and Nao Kao had no way of knowing that Dan had diagnosed it as epilepsy, the most common of all neurological disorders. Each had accurately noted the same symptoms, but Dan would have been surprised to hear that they were caused by soul loss, and Lia's parents would have been surprised to hear that they were caused by an electrochemical storm inside their daughter's head that had been stirred up by the misfiring of aberrant brain cells. (p. 29)

Lia's case is an excellent example of how hard it is to walk the talk of multicultural competencies as discussed in Chapter 3. It is hard to walk the talk of multicultural competencies because helping professionals often are not able to be aware of the other culture's values, beliefs and traditions as a result of the role their cultural contexts played in shaping their values and beliefs. Both cultural helping professionals reflected their cultural values and beliefs in their diagnosis of Lia. Dan could not put equal importance to Hmong cultural values, beliefs, and meaning making because he was trained in modern medicine.

> To most of them, the Hmong taboos against blood tests, spinal taps, surgery, anesthesia, and autopsies—the basic tools of modern medicine—seemed like self-defeating ignorance. They had no way of knowing that a Hmong might regard these taboos as the sacred guardians of his identity, indeed, quite literally, of his very soul. What the doctors viewed as clinical efficiency the Hmong viewed as frosty arrogance. And no matter what the doctors did, even if it never trespassed on taboo territory, the Hmong, freighted as they were with negative expectations accumulated before they came to America, inevitably interpreted it in the worst possible light. (p. 61)

Helping professionals cared for Lia and they wanted to make sure that Lia's seizure was controlled through medication. They lacked understanding of Lia's culture. Lia's parents cared deeply for Lia and they did not understand the dominant culture. Lia's story reminds helping professionals how important it is to understand the client's culture and healing traditions. Due to the lack of understanding Hmong culture, Lia's doctor, Neil—who cared deeply about Lia—sent the following note to the Health Department and to Child Protective Services:

> Because of poor parental compliance regarding the medication this case obviously would come under the realm of child abuse, specifically child neglect. . . . Unless there could be some form of compliance with the medication regimen and control of the child's seizure disorder, this child is at risk for status epilepticus which could result in irreversible brain damage and also possibly death. It is my opinion that this child should be placed in foster home placement so that compliance with medication could be assured. (Fadiman, 1997, pp. 58–59)

The Superior Court of the State of California followed Lia's doctor's request in order to help Lia. As a result, Lia became a dependent child of the juvenile court. She was removed from the custody of her parents who showed love in their cultural way.

Lia's story demonstrates that caring deeply about a patient (client) is not enough if it does not extend to exploring the meaning of health, sickness, and healing from the patient's culture. The story reminds helping professionals that health, illness, and healing are interwoven with mind, body, spirit, and dynamic sociocultural and environmental factors. Health and healing are interdependent of cultural context.

Restoring the Client's Dignity

When a client is understood from his worldview, he feels he is accepted as who he is with his cultural beliefs, values, and traditions. He gains dignity for himself, his family, and his community. Counseling and psychotherapy rely heavily on the practitioner-client relationship, which is often determined by nonverbal communication. It relies on attitudes and emotions of the practitioner. When the practitioner says supportive words without a supportive attitude, the client can detect superficiality and the supportive words seem hollow. When the practitioner's words are from her heart, the client feels caring, genuineness, and compassion. Restoring the client's dignity does not depend on whether the problem is solved but depends on the practitioner's genuine and sincere attitude. The following reflection-based learning activities are designed to explore the role of verbal and nonverbal communication in evaluating attitudes.

CONCRETE STRATEGIES

Experiential Learning Activity

1. Name individuals who have liked or now like you. Write down how you know they like you.

2. Name individuals who were or are now not fond of you. Write down how you know they are not fond of you.

(Continued)

(Continued)

3. Review your responses to Questions 1 and 2.

   a. Identify which ones are based on nonverbal communication and which ones are based on verbal communication.

   b. When there was a discrepancy between the verbal and the nonverbal communication, which type did you use to evaluate how the person felt about you? For example, if the person's verbal expression was complimentary toward you but his/her/zir nonverbal expression was contradictory to such verbal expression, which type did you use?

4. What did you learn from this activity?

TO BE A MULTICULTURALLY COMPETENT PRACTITIONER

Definition of a Practitioner's Role and Success

How a practitioner defines the role of the practitioner in counseling and therapy influences the therapeutic process. If the practitioner defines her role as making sure a client reaches his goal, she is not going to be able to attend to the therapeutic process. She will be distracted by her own objective rather than fully engaged in where the client is in the process. One of the most challenging tasks for the author to teach students in multicultural counseling is how to be with the client during the therapeutic process. Students who are practicing the counselor role cannot stay in the therapeutic moment when they want to interrupt the client to make their point. They focus on not forgetting their point or waiting for the opportunity to make their point, which prevents them from listening to the client. Their nonverbal language communicates that they are not there for the client, and they are not aware of the fact the client can observe their nonverbal behavior. They are present physically but are not in the therapeutic moment when focusing their attention on making their point rather than on the client making his point. As students review their behavior on videotape during critique sessions, they often are really surprised to discover that they were not present. These students learn what it really means to be there for the client and what it means to be an attentive listener. Students learn the power of body language in addition to realizing how much they are the product of their own culture, which considers speaking more important than listening. They learn to be present for the client in the moment externally as well as internally.

If the practitioner defines her role as an expert, her way of dealing with the client is that she knows what is best. This attitude often leads to unintentional generalization and minimization of the client and difficulty in perceiving the client's worldview. The practitioner may be an expert in psychological theories, such as theories of personality, developmental psychology, abnormal psychology, learning theories, and various therapeutic techniques. However, being an expert in psychological theories does not lead to effective helping. The practitioner must listen attentively to the client's story in order to implement her expert knowledge for this particular client.

If the practitioner defines her role as a facilitator who focuses on the therapeutic process determined by collaborative work between the client and the practitioner, she will be focused on the moment. When the practitioner knows her responsibility is making sure she is present as a whole person, her inner and outer experiences are congruent.

How the practitioner defines therapeutic success also affects the therapeutic process. If the practitioner defines therapeutic success as how the client meets her expectation, she may be distracted from attending to the client's needs. A multiculturally competent practitioner defines therapeutic success by how attentive she is in the process and whether or not she utilizes all available therapeutic skills. She shows respect for the client and puts her maximum effort into viewing the client and his culture from the client's worldview during the therapeutic process.

The author had a female client who was working on a particular issue for about 6 months, and one day she said she was able to resolve her issue because she had gained insight as she was watching *The Oprah Winfrey Show*. The author was glad to hear she was finally able to resolve her issue, and it did not matter who the client thought helped her as long as the issue was resolved. The author was not there to be recognized by the client but to facilitate her journey to reach her therapeutic goals. Changing thoughts, feelings, and behaviors is a complex process and takes time. The client may intellectually understand the need for a change, but applying intellectual understanding to actual change requires not only emotional integration but also examining memories, beliefs (both implicit and explicit, conscious and unconscious), habits, and risks in existing interpersonal relationships.

The following reflection-based learning activities are designed for practitioners to reflect on their definition of some terms that affect the therapeutic process and outcome.

CONCRETE STRATEGIES

Reflection-Based Learning Activities on the Practitioner's Role

1. What was your definition of a practitioner's role in counseling or psychotherapy before reading this book?

2. What was your definition of a multiculturally competent practitioner before reading this book?

3. What is your definition of a practitioner's role in counseling or psychotherapy after reading this book and doing all the experiential learning activities?

4. How would you define therapeutic success?

Attitudinal Preparation Through Transformative Learning

Multicultural issues are emotionally intense because they are about socially constructed injustice and inequity created by the ethnocentric dominant group and embedded in Americans' psyche (Singer & Kimbles, 2004). Clients have been targets of injustice and inequity. If a practitioner wants to understand a client's worldview in order to provide effective treatment, she must understand the impact of internalized privilege and oppression and systematic privilege and oppression on the client with a nondominant background through transformative learning. Without transformative learning, the practitioner's implicit attitudes are likely to be communicated to the client during the therapeutic process. The difficulties of changing implicit attitudes were examined by cognitive information processing in Chapter 13. Transformative learning may transcend implicit attitudes of prejudice and stereotypes. As defined by O'Sullivan, Morrell, and O'Connor (2002),

> transformative learning involves experiencing a deep, structural shift in the basic premises of thought, feelings, and actions. It is a shift of consciousness that dramatically and permanently alters our

way of being in the world. Such a shift involves our understanding of ourselves and our self locations; our relationships with other humans and with the natural world; our understanding of relations of power in interlocking structures of class, race, and gender; our body-awareness; our visions of alternative approaches to living; and our sense of possibilities for social justice and peace and personal joy. (p. 11)

Intellectual understanding of concepts and theories of multicultural competencies is important, but it needs to be communicated to the client. The practitioner's attitude communicates her multicultural competencies to the client.

Attitudinal preparation has been built into the book through experiential and reflection-based learning activities in each chapter. If the practitioner-trainee has read each chapter and sincerely participated in every experiential learning activity from her heart and learned through transformative learning (integration of intellect and emotion), she is becoming a multiculturally competent practitioner. To be a multiculturally competent practitioner she needs to know herself. This means that she knows her values, beliefs, biases, inter- and intrapersonal communication styles/ patterns, and thinking styles (*dichotomous, hierarchical, linear, diunital*, or *holistic* from a *multilayered* and *multidimensional* perspective). She knows her internalized oppression/privilege, as well as her identity in relation to race, gender, sexual orientation, class, impairment/disability, age, language, religion, region, and other areas important to her. She knows whether she is using inappropriate dichotomous, hierarchical, or linear thinking styles in addition to knowing her dominant (salient or special) identity and the dynamics between her dominant identity and her family members' dominant identities. She understands the complexities involved in intersections of multiple identities. She practices unconventional methods such as journal writing, drawing, consciousness exercises, centering, yoga, or other body movement to be aware of her inner experience and external experience. She works on accepting who she is without judgment on a daily basis. She works on deconstructing inappropriate hierarchical, dichotomous, and linear thinking styles/ patterns. She is aware of the impact of systematic oppression on nondominant groups at individual, interpersonal, institutional, and cultural levels. If she is mindful of dismantling systematic privilege/oppression and internalized privilege/oppression, she knows she is both the oppressor and the oppressed. She works on not getting upset when she slips into being an unintentional oppressor but critically examines her behavior, thinks about what she has learned from reverting back to old habits, and considers steps she might take to prevent unintentional marginalization, minimization, or oppression. She defines her success on the process and not the product.

Knowledge Preparation Through Transformative Learning

In-Depth Knowledge in Conventional Therapeutic Techniques

It is important that a practitioner-trainee knows traditional personality theories in depth with both intellectual and emotional understanding in order to critically examine their applicability to multicultural populations. Critical examination requires an understanding of theories that are based on Eurocentric values, and gaining in-depth knowledge requires understanding these theories through transformative learning. The practitioner-trainee must know all major traditional (Western) therapeutic techniques and the theories behind each particular technique regardless of her preferences so she can utilize them as resources to develop the most effective treatment for clients if needed. Assessing the applicability of each theory to multicultural populations comes after knowing each theory thoroughly. Psychodynamic and humanistic theories are used as examples to illustrate how to assess the validity of a theory for multicultural populations. The major theoretical assumption of psychodynamic theory (Good & Beitman, 2006) is that personality develops in early childhood through interaction with parents. The practitioner who applies psychodynamic theory focuses on the parent-child relationship and the client's early childhood memories and experiences. The practitioner needs to evaluate the applicability of psychodynamic theory to individuals raised in a single-parent home, raised by an extended family, or raised according to nondominant cultural values since psychodynamic theory was not based on these types of families. The major theoretical assumption of Rogers's (1951, 1986) person-centered therapy is that individuals can figure out what is best for them if given unconditional positive regard. The practitioner who applies Rogers's theory focuses on providing a nonthreatening atmosphere by listening actively and paraphrasing so the client can utilize his organismic valuing tendency to figure out the solution to his presenting problem. The practitioner needs to evaluate the applicability of this theory to clients who are socialized with collectivism value orientation where self is undifferentiated from the family and interdependence is a core value. Examining each theory thoroughly for its validity for multicultural populations assists the practitioner in developing therapeutic techniques. Innovative therapeutic techniques will evolve as the practitioner examines each theory through transformative learning.

The following is an example of learning conventional personality theories through transformative learning, which the author implements in her multicultural counseling program. First, students read theories. Second, students are required to write about their personality development from the perspective of traditional theories of personality. Each week for 7 weeks, all students write about their personality development from a particular personality theory perspective. They are given prompt feedback to their personality development paper for accurate understanding of each theory. Most students find this task challenging because they have a difficult time staying focused on only one theoretical orientation. Third, students are asked to apply therapeutic techniques they have learned from that week's personality theory when they play a counselor's role. They are also given prompt feedback on their counseling skill practice both from their peers and from faculty. Lastly, they are asked to evaluate the applicability of the therapeutic technique to multicultural populations. The following are some students' evaluations of their self-achievement in regard to learning seven theories of personality through transformative learning.

STUDENT FEEDBACK

I had heard that this program is intense, but I had thought people mean the program workload is intense. Once in the program I realized the intensity is the challenge of emotional growth. Much of this growth has come from investigating myself from seven different personality theory perspectives: Psychoanalytic, cognitive, behavioral, humanistic, trait, family, and existential. I wrote a two page paper on myself from each of these perspectives, and got the opportunity to practice each of these theories (except existential) in a counseling setting with a partner. My skill practice for psychoanalytic, cognitive behavioral, behavioral, and humanistic were filmed so I had the chance to watch myself as

(Continued)

(Continued)

a counselor, observe my nonverbal communication and evaluate my performance. This has been an invaluable tool for me. Practicing each perspective as a counselor and as a client really let me experience each perspective to help me understand the uniqueness and assumptions that accompany the different perspectives.

—Joan, 2004

The program provided me with methods to take conceptual theories and apply them to my own experience. I explored my personality from seven different perspectives ... I discovered that it is one thing to understand the meaning of words on paper and another entirely to place oneself into the words and ideas being taught. The latter is a transforming act, which requires tremendous emotional and mental integrity. I believe I met this challenge with courage, honesty, humility, and a willingness to be molded by my discoveries. Through knowing myself deeper I am able to slowly deconstruct the isms and biases within my psyche that have led to the construction of an N =1 complex. My experience is not the only experience.

—Diane, 2005

I studied seven personality theories with the class. This study included reading about the theory, counseling a classmate with techniques of the theory, and writing my personality based on the theory. These three exercises gave me a solid understanding of the material; just as writing my personality development seven times gave me a deeper self-awareness. Within the study of personality development we explored how hierarchical, linear and dichotomous thinking impacts development. In practice, I am becoming aware of these thought patterns within my life and examining how they affect me.

—Susan, 2005

Evaluating the effectiveness of traditional counseling theories and therapeutic techniques can be achieved when students have learned traditional personality theories through transformative learning. Students are asked to evaluate the effectiveness of each theory for multicultural populations and to critically examine whether it is possible to modify the theory for multicultural populations and how to modify it. Simply being critical of existing theories does not provide tools to deal with multicultural populations. Transformative learning of personality theories not only allows students to understand each theory in depth through interaction but also gives them another opportunity to reflect on their values, beliefs, and biases.

Understanding the sociocultural context of theoretical assumptions with particular emphasis on therapeutic techniques to support these assumptions is important. Assessing the reasons for effectiveness/ineffectiveness of a particular therapeutic technique for a specific client in a particular period is also a crucial element in developing effective treatment. The most effective treatment may be integrating traditional (Western) therapeutic techniques with indigenous healing practices, or it may require modifying traditional therapeutic techniques to fit a particular client. Multiculturally competent practitioners should not generalize that all traditional therapeutic techniques are ineffective for clients with multicultural backgrounds or that indigenous healing methods are effective for all clients with multicultural backgrounds, because there are too many variations within groups as well as between groups. It is not about either/or (*dichotomous* or binary) thinking but developing a creative treatment on the basis of a holistic style, which includes appropriate dichotomous, linear, and hierarchical diunital, multilayered, and multidimensional thinking styles. There is no one effective therapeutic technique for one particular group because multiple factors determine the effectiveness of therapy. For example, Yau, Sue, and Hayden (1992) indicated that international students found both a nondirective, client-centered approach and a directive, problem-solving approach to be complementary and helpful while Essandoh (1995) indicated that Eurocentric therapeutic techniques were not effective for African international students.

Part of being aware of the client's worldview is finding out which methods work most effectively for that particular client at that particular time. Multicultural competencies require practitioners to be not only open and flexible but also creative. For example, when it is determined that indigenous healing is the most effective treatment for the client, the practitioner needs to refer the client to an indigenous healer or work with the healer if the client desires. The focus should be on the client and what is most helpful for him. This type of thinking requires deconstructing inappropriate dichotomous, hierarchical, and linear thinking styles.

Unconventional Creative Techniques

Counseling and psychotherapy are traditionally considered a verbal treatment, and this is based on Eurocentric values, which exclude other ways of healing by other cultures. Verbal treatment is one method of changing feelings, thoughts, and behaviors. A practitioner may not feel comfortable with the following therapeutic techniques mainly because she has not been exposed to them just like some clients from multicultural backgrounds are not comfortable with verbalizing their problems to a stranger (practitioner). If a practitioner wants to be multiculturally competent, she must learn the nondominant cultural group's way of healing and beliefs and values.

Drawing as a Therapeutic Process. Drawing could be a useful tool for clients who have difficulty articulating or connecting to emotion. The practitioner may ask, "Would you express what you are feeling right now through coloring or drawing?" Some clients will say that they do not draw well. The practitioner needs to assure the client that the purpose is not the quality of the drawing. The purpose is to have another medium to tell the client's story. The practitioner may say, "I don't know how to evaluate drawings since I am not trained in art. What I am interested in is hearing your story through drawing. Drawing is a right-brain (hemisphere) activity that deals with intuition and emotion." When the client is finished, the counselor may ask, "Would you explain your drawing to me?"

Drawing depicts an aspect of a problem the client may not be able to articulate or be consciously aware of. For example, one of the author's clients had been doing whatever her younger sister asked or demanded of her, even if she did not want to do it. The client recognized this pattern of enabling her younger sister but did not know how to stop. The author asked the client, "You said you know you are enabling her, but you don't know what makes you do that. Would you close your eyes for a moment and think and feel about your relationship with your younger sister?" Two minutes later, the author asked her, "Would you open your eyes and color or draw something to represent your relationship with your sister?" The author left the room for a couple of minutes so that the client could be free to explore without being distracted by the author's presence. When the author returned, the client had drawn a picture of two women. The client had drawn her younger sister twice as big as herself. The client was surprised to see the size differences in her own drawing. Tears rolled down her cheek, and she said, "You don't know how difficult it has been to live with a sister who is so huge. She is physically much stronger than me, and I've had to live with that all my life." Drawing opened up the aspect of her problem that she was not aware of. The author did not have to evaluate her drawing. The drawing opened another way to examine her relationship with her sister.

Narrative Movement. Individuals perceive only a part of the whole person if they do not consider body and mind as an integrated whole. Individuals' body communicates to them; however, some individuals have lost the capacity to listen to their body due to the socialization process, which focuses on Decartes's abandonment of body as an important source of understanding human beings. Decartes considered the body a machine with no connection to mind, emotion, or memory (Damasio, 1994; Radomsky, 1995). Narrative movement is telling the person's story through movement. Not all clients are able to articulate their story, but some of them can express it through their movement. Narrative movement and dance therapy are based on the assumption that body and mind are inseparable and are very effective in letting a client experience emotion. Halprin (2003), who is a pioneer in movement therapy, believes that everyone is a dancer, whether the person is trained formally or not. She uses untrained dancers in her performances. She moved dance from a theatrical art to simply movement that expresses a person's story. Halprin integrates metaphor, movement, and music as a healing art and has used this healing art to heal racial divisions and illness such as cancer and HIV/AIDS. People are transformed as they tell their stories through narrative movement. Her healing arts interconnect mind, body, emotion, and spirit (Halprin; Ross, 2007).

Narrative movement is particularly effective in dealing with ESL individuals, families, or groups. Using a translator may create problems since it is hard to translate exact meaning. Another problem is the client may not say exactly what he wants to through a translator. The author is often surprised by how meaning is lost in translation when one language is literally translated into another language. The literal translation of "You have good taste" from English to Korean is "You have a gracious hobby." If non-English-speaking Koreans heard "You have good taste" in place of "You have a gracious hobby," they would think the author had lost her mind. If the author said to North Americans "You have a gracious hobby" in place of "You have good taste," what meaning would they take from the statement? The author was asked to translate Korean into English for the host of an Asian scientists' conference in Seoul, South Korea, some years ago. The setting was beautiful, and each table was filled with various kinds of side dishes (at least 10 of them) in addition to main dishes like barbecued beef, chicken, port, stir-fried fish plus rice, and so on. It was a feast by North American or European standards. The first part of the speech by the host, the president of Korean Broadcasting System TV, was translated directly without losing meaning, but the second part of the speech was eloquent, humble, and intended to make guests feel welcome. The literal English translation was "I am really sorry for not preparing the best meal for you. I apologize from the bottom of my heart. I almost feel shamed since there are not that many things on the table to eat. I would sincerely appreciate you if you forgive me and eat even though you may not be satisfied with our preparation of the dinner." What the president meant was "Enjoy dinner."

The practitioner needs to be aware of the fact that not all translators are bicultural and meaning can be lost in translation from one culture to another. Fadiman (1997) depicts the confusion and frustration sometimes caused by using a translator in the following excerpt from *The Spirit Catches You and You Fall Down:*

> The history of the Hmong yields several lessons that anyone who deals with them might do well to remember. Among the most obvious of these are that the Hmong do not like to take orders; that they do not like to lose; that they would rather flee, fight, or die than surrender; that they are not intimidated by being outnumbered; that they are rarely persuaded that the customs of other cultures, even those more powerful than their own, are superior; and that they are capable of getting very angry. Whether you find these traits infuriating or admirable depends largely on whether or not you are trying to make a Hmong do something he or she would prefer not to do. Those who have tried to defeat, deceive, govern, regulate, constrain, assimilate, intimidate, or patronize the Hmong have, as a rule, disliked them intensely (p. 17). . . . Nonetheless, the Lees remained baffled by most of what was happening. And though Valley Children's was well known for its efforts to reach out to patients' families, Foua and Nao Kao did not realize that their "counseling" sessions, which usually left them confused and angry, were intended to reduce their stress. (p. 150)

The following experiential learning activities are designed to increase empathy and for experience with freestyle narrative movement.

CONCRETE STRATEGIES

1. Complete the following activities without screening (without judgment):

   a. For about 5 min, close your eyes and put yourself into the position of a helping professional who is assigned to deal with a Hmong individual. Then, write your thoughts and feelings without screening.

b. For about 5 min, close your eyes and put yourself into Foua and Nao's positions. Then, write your thoughts and feelings without screening. How would you communicate to them that the session was intended to reduce their stress?

c. What type of thinking styles (hierarchical, dichotomous, and/or linear) did you find in your writing?

d. Close your eyes to reflect. Stay still for 10 min and feel and think without screening.

2. For those of you in a class, complete the following additional activity: Divide the class into groups of four or five and read aloud what you wrote or express your feelings. Listen respectively to and validate each other, regardless of whether you agree with each other.

3. Students who do not feel comfortable sharing do not need to share but need to be aware of their feelings and thoughts internally.

4. As a small group of four or five, take the role of Foua, Nao, or a helping professional and express your feelings through body movement.

Instead of asking the client, his family, or groups to articulate, the practitioner can ask them to express their presenting problem or frustration, sadness, or anger through narrative movement. Narrative movement communicates emotions without verbal expression. Practitioners need training in narrative movement. Using narrative movement in a class setting is also helpful for practitioner-trainees to be in touch with their emotions as they participate. Creating a family sculpture as a small group and presenting it to the class is also a powerful experience with the effectiveness of narrative movement. Narrative movement leads to transformative learning since it is an expression of body, mind, and emotion. It integrates the cognitive (rational) transformative process and the affective (emotional) transformative process.

Poetry and Spoken Words. Expressing through spoken words or poetry is another medium for clients to articulate their internal world. The practitioner may ask the client to write poems or spoken words to express what he is feeling, thinking, and behaving and bring writings to the session and read them out loud. Often, clients feel various kinds of emotions and are surprised by their emotional reactions. The practitioner-trainee may ask clients to stay with their feelings and express them through spoken words, drawing, and/or movement. This may open another way of understanding the clients' inner world. The author has had several male clients who had difficulty articulating their inner experiences or were not able to identify their inner experiences. However, when the author expressed her appreciation for their honesty and encouraged them to reflect on the session and use whatever medium they could and bring back their reflections to the next session, these clients brought back poems they wrote. They were powerful in identifying their feelings and expressing their pain. They were surprised to find out their ability to express their inner experience through poetry. The author asked them questions by using their poem just like using clients' own words for inquiry. Also using the poem, these clients were able to articulate themselves much more clearly than in previous sessions.

Silence Is a Part of Communication. Traditionally, counseling or psychotherapy is a talking cure; however, not all people can freely express themselves verbally, especially individuals from collectivism-oriented cultural backgrounds (Covarrubias, 2007). The practitioner needs to be flexible in tailoring a treatment program that is receptive for specific clients. Awareness of the clients' worldviews includes how clients perceive the therapeutic sessions and the appropriate way to assist clients so they are healed and become peaceful, functional, and whole. After asking a question of a client, the practitioner needs to wait in silence if the client decides not to respond verbally. The practitioner needs to understand that sitting in silence is a part of the therapeutic process for some clients. She should not break the silence because she is uncomfortable. If the practitioner is uncomfortable with silence, she needs to examine herself to know the meaning of silence for her.

The following are reflection-based learning activities to raise awareness on silence.

CONCRETE STRATEGIES

Experiential Learning Activity

Close your eyes and breathe deeply, evenly, and slowly. As you breathe deeply and slowly, think and feel about your relationship to silence.

1. What did you discover about your relationship to silence?

2. When you are with other people (family, friends, discussion groups, or clients) and there is silence:

   a. How do you feel?

   b. What do you do, and why do you do it?

3. What are your assumptions about silence?

4. How does silence fit into your assumptions of therapy?

One of the most difficult tasks in training practitioner-trainees is teaching them to be still in silence with clients. During counseling skill practice, some practitioner-trainees who are role-playing the counselor get uncomfortable with silence, so they ask questions or make comments to the client. This breaks the client's internal processing. The client could be thinking actively or feeling intensely in silence about the question or questions. Practitioner-trainees who are not comfortable with silence need to examine their inner dialogue (intrapersonal communication) at the time of silence. They need to reflect on their own assumptions about the therapeutic process and silence. These practitioner-trainees need to remind themselves that counseling or psychotherapy is empowering clients through changing the clients' thoughts, feelings, and behavior. Thus, the practitioner's first priority is making an atmosphere possible for the client's empowerment. At the end of silence, the practitioner may say, "I am wondering what images came to your mind while you were in silence." Or the practitioner may ask, "What thoughts and feelings ran through your mind while you were sitting in silence?"

Dreams. Dreams can be traced all the way to ancient Mesopotamia, which was a central region of Iraq more than 5,000 years ago. Since then, the importance of dreams has been shown in beliefs of Hebrew, Egyptian, Chinese, Indian, Greek, and Roman cultures, up to the modern world (van de Castle, 1994). Various psychologists have interpreted dreams to understand the human psyche, and their dream interpretation heavily relied on their theories (Adler, 1936; Erikson, 1954; Freud, 1953, 1955; Jung, 1965; van de Castle). Scholars of consciousness have also studied dreams as altered states of consciousness. "Rabbi Hisda said, 'An uninterpreted dream is like an unread letter'" (van de Castle, p. 54). Jung and

Freud used dreams as a window to gaining access to the unconscious. Dreams are a rich source of understanding the client's worldview if the client believes that dreams are an important part of understanding who he is and his culture. Van de Castle's *Our Dreaming Mind* is the most comprehensive book about dream interpretation and research available.

The author once had a client who had difficulty articulating his thoughts and feelings but was able to keep a dream journal. He would read his dreams out loud and was able to articulate what the dreamer was feeling and thinking. Of course, he was the dreamer, and talking about himself as "he" was much easier than talking about himself as "I." After listening to his dreams, the author asked him what he thought was the main theme of each dream and the commonalities of all the dreams that he read. As he started to search for the main theme and commonalities, he was fascinated by his own discovery. He often expressed how the dreamer's conflict was similar to his own, and by exploring how the dreamer could approach his conflict to minimize pain and to maximize fulfillment the client was eagerly involved in the process. The author encouraged the client at times to apply some of his suggestions for the dreamer to himself. Often he would return to therapy with excitement about having made some progress by applying his suggestions. Another client told the author that he dreamed only in black and white and was surprised to hear other people see colors in dreams. As he was transcending his depression, he reported he was seeing some colors. Some clients said that they did not dream or remember dreaming. However, once they started to remember their dreams, they had much to say about them.

Knowing a Professional Ethics Code Through Transformative Learning

Implementing a culturally appropriate ethics code is crucial in treatment of clients from multicultural backgrounds. In order to do this, the practitioner needs to know the national as well as state professional ethics standards. The practitioner also needs to know about her values and personal ethics and figure out how to be professionally ethical if there is a contradiction between her personal and professional ethics. The practitioner needs to understand that knowing is not sufficient to implement ethics in her practice. As indicated in the previous chapter, there should not be marginalization of, minimization of, or discrimination against individuals who are culturally different by practitioners if practitioners have implemented their professional ethics standards in their practice. One of the author's former students wrote in his final synthesis paper about the importance of knowing ethics in multicultural counseling.

PERSONAL FEEDBACK ON LEARNING ETHICS

A major focus for spring quarter was examining APA ethics. I learned that ethical behavior and following ethical guidelines is essential to counseling. I also understood the importance of keeping good records. Ethics was also very essential in examining my internship site. CPS presented many unethical situations. Many social workers shared confidential information about clients for a laugh, carry too high of a number of caseloads to give clients the quality of service that they deserve, and did not respect the clients. If I had not studied ethics I do not believe I would have known how harmful this behavior was.

—Mel, 2005

All three professional organizations discussed in Chapter 13 state their best interest as the welfare of people they serve. The author will use American Psychological Association (2002) standards as an example. Human relations, under ethics standards, include no sexual harassment (3.02); no other harassment (3.03) based on factors such as those persons' age, gender, gender identity, race, ethnicity, culture, national origin, religion, sexual orientation, disability, language, or socioeconomic status; avoiding harm (3.04); only engaging in multiple relationships that would not impair or risk exploitation or harm (3.05); not being involved in issues, in organizations, and with persons which may lead to conflict of interest (3.06); and not exploiting persons over whom psychologists have supervisory, evaluative, or other authority such as clients/patients, students, supervisees, research participants, and employees (3.08).

It is up to the practitioner to study her professional ethical standards thoroughly and assess differences and similarities between her personal ethics and her professional ethics. If she is not able to modify her personal ethics to implement her professional ethics or modify the professional ethics to serve clients from multicultural populations, she needs to question whether it is ethical for her to work with clients from multicultural backgrounds. The following reflection-based learning activities are designed for practitioner-trainees to assess their understanding of ethics, values, and beliefs.

CONCRETE STRATEGIES

Experiential Learning Activities

Answer the following questions as honestly as possible.

1. Do you consider yourself an ethical person? From your personal experience, describe in detail the evidence for your answer.

2. Rate yourself from 1 (lowest) to 10 (highest) on the following.

   a. I like to be appreciated and recognized by others.
   b. I like to be able to fix others' problems.
   c. I believe a therapist must have had the same type of problem as the client to be an effective therapist.
   d. Whether I am a good therapist or not is determined by my client's behavior change.
   e. I may not insist on it but would like it if clients agreed with my values.
   f. When I assess myself as not being effective for the client, I am ethically bound to let the client know my limits.
   g. I do not think I can work with clients whose values are very different from mine.
   h. I say I am open to being challenged, but I really do not want to be challenged.
   i. I know my values and beliefs affect me as a person, but I am able to differentiate my professional life from my personal life.
   j. I have certain prejudices against people who are different from me in relation to (circle appropriate words) race, gender, class, sexual orientation, impairment/disability, age, language, religion, and region.

3. What did you learn about yourself?

4. How would you implement your learning to become a multiculturally competent practitioner?

Affect Preparation

As stated in the introduction, the goal of counseling and psychotherapy is for the client to change cognitive functions, affective functions, and/or behavioral functions in order to deal with the presenting problem. The efficacy of therapy partly depends on the practitioner's ability to provide rapport, which is based on affective relation between the therapist and the client. If the practitioner is going to facilitate the client's affective change, the practitioner needs to be aware of her own affective status. When the practitioner does not judge her emotions but just observes them and feels them, she begins to differentiate between real self and ideal self and starts to hear her voice within. She is able to differentiate between unscreened narratives and "shoulds." The practitioner is able to see how distracted she is from paying attention to the client when she is caught up in "shoulds." As she focuses on hearing her voice within without judgment, she begins to identify her own feelings. The key to awareness of her emotions is to observe her inner experience without judgment and to accept her emotions as they are.

The following is an experiential learning activity designed to increase empathy for clients through affective role-taking.

CONCRETE STRATEGIES

Experiential Learning Activity by Role-Taking

Read the following without screening (without judgment). Then close your eyes and put yourself into Mennis's parents' position for about 5 min. Then, write down your thoughts and feelings. Mennis (2000), who is Jewish and working class, wrote:

> *Lack of education and lack of money made for an insecurity and fear of doing almost anything, a fear tremendously compounded by anti-Semitism and World War II. My parents were afraid to take any risks—from both a conviction of their own incompetence and a fear that doing anything big, having any visibility, would place them in danger. From them I inherited a fear that if I touched something, did anything, I would make matters worse. There was an incredible nervousness in my home around fixing anything, buying anything big, filling out any forms. My mother still calls me to complete forms for her. When my father was sick, my parents needed me to translate everything the doctor said, not because they did not understand him, but because their fear stopped them from listening when anyone very educated or in authority spoke. (p. 189)*

Rapport

Establishing rapport is the foundation for how accepted the client feels by the practitioner. How much of his worldview the client will reveal is determined by the client's perception of the practitioner's trust and acceptance. Corsini and Wedding (2005) discuss "the whohowwhom factor" where they define what is important in psychotherapy: "who does it and how and to whom it is done" (p. 10). Rapport will be established easily if there is a match between *who* and *whom*. This is extremely important for clients from multicultural populations. Some individuals define match only by appearance factors such as gender, race, and sexual orientation, but there are differences within the same race, gender, and sexual orientation as discussed in this book. Matching criteria should be from qualities like the practitioner's ability to accept, value, and respect the client who has different cultural backgrounds. It is about the practitioner's attitude, which has emotional components. There is a difference between wanting to accept, respect, and value clients and accepting, respecting, and valuing clients. When there is an inconsistency between wanting to accept (intellect) and accepting (congruency between intellect and emotion), the client feels he is not accepted. The practitioner's thoughts, feelings, and behaviors and the client's thoughts, feelings, and behaviors are communicated verbally and nonverbally during the therapeutic process to both the practitioner and the client. Building rapport relies heavily on an affective component of this exchange. Both the practitioner and the client may assume that the other party does not know how he/she is feeling, but one's emotions are not necessarily communicated only through verbal language. They are also communicated through nonverbal language such as facial expression, body posture, eye contact/no eye contact, tone of voice, type of laughing, and so on.

Transference/Countertransference

Transference and countertransference provide effective treatment strategies if the practitioner is able to acknowledge and utilize them as therapeutic tools. They can also be barriers to therapeutic goals and building and maintaining rapport. Transference occurs when the client treats a practitioner as if the practitioner is a significant person in his life. For example, the client says, "My father controlled me all my life." When the practitioner simply paraphrases what the client said, the client screams at the therapist, "Who are you, telling me what to do?" or "Don't try to control me." If the practitioner does not react to the client and helps him become aware of what he said by asking questions like "Is it hard to hear what you said to me?" "Your scream says something, and I am not sure what it is. Would you like to tell me what's going on inside of you at this moment?" Or, the practitioner can just sit in silence for the client to process. When the practitioner does not react negatively to him, the client pays attention to his inner experience and may be able to understand the dynamics between his father and himself. However, if the practitioner becomes reactive, she loses the opportunity to assist the client on a deeper level of cognitive and affective transformative processing. Another kind of transference is easy to miss because the client is not externally reactive. For example, a client says what he thinks the practitioner wants to hear due to his cultural emphasis on obeying authority figures. The practitioner needs to gently confront the client. The practitioner may say, "I feel like I don't really know you yet. I would like to hear what you really think and feel. Would you tell me when was the first time you did what you wanted to do instead of doing what your parents or grandparents wanted you to do and what happened?" If the client says he has never disobeyed, the practitioner may want to explore his inner experience when he goes along with authority figures. Transference provides rich information about the client. It is up to the practitioner how to utilize the opportunity to learn more about the client's worldview.

Countertransference is when the practitioner treats a client as if the client is a significant person in her life. When the practitioner is not able to be aware of what is happening, it can be detrimental to the client. For example, a client comes to see the practitioner to resolve her work conflict. During a session, she tells the practitioner she was sexually molested by her brother 20 years ago. The practitioner, who was sexually abused by her father, focuses on this disclosure and encourages the client to report the sexual abuse. The client says she has resolved the issue and her main goal is how to resolve a work conflict. However, the practitioner brings back the sexual abuse case and insists that the client needs to deal with the sexual abuse issue before she can deal with her work issue.

Clients consider practitioners experts, and most clients do not confront practitioners. Some of them terminate therapy, and others continue without being aware of the extent of damage. It is crucial that practitioners reflect on their thoughts, feelings, and behaviors during each session to assess the presence and degree of countertransference. If the degree of countertransference is mild and fixable, the practitioner needs to fix it. But if the degree is more than mild and/or it is not fixable, the practitioner needs to consult with other colleagues about the issue or let the client know about the countertransference and do her best to find another therapist for the client. Countertransference is an ethical issue because it prevents the practitioner from applying her professional competence, following ethical standards, and caring for the client's welfare. Corey, Corey, and Callanan (1993) described countertransference as follows (italicized words have been added for clarification):

1. Being overprotective with clients can reflect a therapist's fears.

2. Treating clients in benign ways may stem from a counselor's fears of their [*clients'*] anger.

3. Rejection of clients may be based on perceiving them as needy and dependent.

4. [*Therapists'*] need for constant reinforcement and approval.

5. Therapists seeing themselves in their clients.

6. Development of sexual or romantic feelings *towards a client.*

7. Compulsively giving advice. (pp. 44–47)

Countertransference should not be a problem if practitioners know themselves in all the areas discussed in this book (values; beliefs; biases; thinking styles/patterns; identity development in relation to race, gender, class, sexual orientation, age, language, disability/impairment, religion, region, etc.; the impact of systematic oppression/privilege and internalized oppression/privilege on their identity development and intersections of multiple identities). It should not be a problem because the practitioner accepts herself as she is. Knowing who she is will assist her awareness of countertransference as it happens, and she will observe the process but not react to the client. After the session, she will utilize this information to know herself on a deeper level and work on the issue to grieve through or transcend it. If countertransference interferes with the therapeutic process, she will consult with her colleagues for assistance. Practitioners are multifaceted and multidimensional beings with conscious, preconscious, and unconscious components. Practitioners do not know what kind of sociocultural contexts will bring what type of information for them. What is important is being aware of transference/countertransference and accepting it, learning from it, and making an appropriate decision for the client.

Compassion and Resilience

When a practitioner becomes impatient because she feels the client is "dwelling on only one aspect of the self," she is not attentively listening to the client. When the practitioner thinks the client should move in some other direction, she is not listening to the client attentively. She needs to appreciate herself for being honest and create ways to return to attentive listening. One way to return to attentive listening is for the practitioner to go back to her own painful experiences and think and feel about what she wished others had said or done for her by taking an affective perspective. The practitioner needs to have an internal dialogue like "I don't really understand what the client is going through. But I do remember how painful it was for me with my experience. I am going to put myself in the client's situation by remembering my pain." This allows the practitioner to reexperience her own pain and imagine the client's pain as she listens to the client. For example, a Hispanic heterosexual male client is struggling with racism. After spending several grief sessions with him, the practitioner may say, "It must be very painful for you to face racism on a daily basis" and listen to his story attentively with compassion to understand his worldview. When the practitioner's inner experience and outer experience reflect her desire to provide empathy, the client can feel it and is able to tell his story. Remembering her own pain to understand the client's pain will assist the practitioner with providing empathy and compassion for the client (Mezirow, 2000b).

The following experiential learning activities are designed to increase compassion for others through taking an affective perspective.

CONCRETE STRATEGIES

Experiential Learning Activities

The following are stories from individuals representing various nondominant groups. As you read each story, pay attention to your affect.

1. One of my clients said:

   I used to wash myself until my skin peeled off because I thought my skin was dirty. I thought if I wash myself clean enough I will see my skin as white as my parents. (Brandy, 2000)

   (Continued)

(Continued)

Close your eyes and put yourself into Brandy's position for about 5 min. Then, record your thoughts and feelings without screening.

2. An Asian American male student who was adopted when he was 4 wrote:

To deal with racial paranoia, I went through regular channels of the student government and college president, and tried to handle the problem in a responsible way, but their attitudes were negative. What they told me basically was, "If you don't like it here, go somewhere else." So, I did, along with other Asian students. It was a big growing up year for me. As I recognized that there was racial hatred and bias in the society, I began to question, "Who am I." (Koh, 1993, pp. 47–48)

Close your eyes and put yourself into the student's position for about 5 min. Then, record your thoughts and feelings without screening.

3. Jennifer (Gaskins, 1999) wrote:

I never encountered outright prejudice from people, but I always knew that there was something different about me. There were just these comments here and there. There were things I experienced and knew about that they just didn't. I remember when I was ten and I had this friend and we were in this Chinese restaurant. She'd come with me and my parents, and we were having dinner. And she said in a really loud voice, "I think it's so sad that Chinese people don't have eyelashes." I remember thinking, "What? How can you say that? I have eyelashes. My dad has eyelashes." But she hadn't ever looked closely enough. She hadn't been around Chinese or Asian people enough to realize that they have eyelashes—they may be small, but they're there. She also didn't realize she was talking to Chinese people—she didn't think of me that way, and I guess she thought that my dad had been whitewashed by marrying my mom. (p. 33)

Close your eyes and put yourself in Jennifer's position for about 5 min. Then, record your thoughts and feelings without screening.

You have experienced what it would feel like being Brandy, an Asian American student, and Jennifer through taking their positions. How do you feel? How is it different from just reading their stories? You may want to discuss your feelings with others who completed the same experiential learning activities.

Sometimes the practitioner's heart may be aching as she puts herself into the other person's place. The author's heart ached so much when she was seeing sexually abused children during postdoctoral interning at the community mental health center. The author was not able to focus on therapeutic techniques because she was angry at the perpetrators and felt bad for the children. All the author wanted to do was just hold them and cry. The author was not able to listen attentively to the client because she was spending too much time with her inner battle. The author's supervisor listened attentively to the author's doubts about her qualification to become a psychologist and said that feeling sad for children was a good sign of becoming an empathetic psychologist. He encouraged the author to just feel the pain, and it would gradually transform into empathy. The pain was intense, and thinking about abused children still hurts but not to the same degree. Learning to be compassionate, genuine, and empathetic was achieved through experiencing feelings and not by intellectual understanding.

As the practitioner is compassionate and listens attentively to the client, the rapport builds, and the client starts to trust the practitioner. The practitioner may want to emphasize the client's strengths by guiding the client to discover his resilience. The practitioner may want to say, "You've come so far despite the pain. How did you manage?" and then wait to hear the client's story. Marginalized clients often do not recognize their resilience and strengths. To ask a client how he managed will help him focus on his strengths and resilience. Exploring consequences of perpetuating the victim perspective is important for the client to transcend the victim perspective to adopt an agent perspective. It needs to be explored after the client and/or his family has the opportunity to tell their stories and feel they are heard.

Inquiry Through the Client's Own Words

As indicated in Chapter 13, effective verbal and nonverbal communication styles of the practitioner, her ability to provide rapport, and her ability to understand silence as a part of communication are also important qualities for effective treatment. In addition, the practitioner's inquiry should be based on the client's own words and not on the practitioner's interpretation of the client's words. The inquiry based on the client's own words leads the client to feel that the practitioner is listening attentively and interested in his worldview and problems. As a result, the client may reveal more about his inner experience through both verbal and nonverbal language such as drawing, centering, and imagery. The practitioner-trainee may want to revisit Chapter 13 and its discussion on incorporating scientific inquiry with clinical inquiry. Due to the power differential relationship between practitioner and client and because the client usually considers the practitioner an expert, the client may assume the practitioner's interpretation is correct rather than honoring his own feelings and thoughts. When this happens, the therapy is about the client fitting his story to meet the standards set by the practitioner's worldview and not the client's worldview. Ruth's case discussed in Chapter 13 is revisited here.

Ruth: I know that being so afraid has closed in on my life in so many ways. I feel ready to take this on, but it would be too overwhelming to become so honest with myself and everybody else in lots of areas of my life all at once.

Therapist: So you would like to challenge fear and express yourself more openly, but you want to do so in small steps. Is that right?

Ruth: Sure. (Corey, 2005, p. 269)

The practitioner's inquiry through the client's own words might be, "What do you mean, it would be too overwhelming to become so honest with yourself?" or "What do you think would happen if you were so honest with yourself?" There are so many ways to gather information by using Ruth's words to find more about Ruth. Ruth was described as a person who wanted to please everyone, and a person who wants to please everyone is not capable of disagreeing with the therapist who says, "Is that right?" It will be difficult even for a client who is reasonably assertive to disagree with the therapist who says, "Is that right?" due to the power differential relationship between therapist and client and the client's assumption about the therapist being an "expert."

The practitioner's ability to inquire based on the client's words depends on her level of training in psychological research; her definition of her role as a practitioner; her thinking pattern/style (hierarchical, dichotomous, and linear); her awareness of her own biases, values, and beliefs; and the degree of her internalized oppression/privilege; the impact of systematic privilege/oppression on her identity construction; and her communication style. To paraphrase, the humanistic perspective technique values the person (client) rather than the practitioner first and is an excellent technique to stay focused on the inquiry derived from the client's words.

Attentive Listening

Many students state that it is difficult to clear their mind to listen attentively since their mind is "always" busy and racing with plans or worries about how to accomplish their multiple tasks in a limited time. In order to increase attentive listening, students are encouraged to think about what they are accomplishing by attending to their busy and racing mind when they are in class for counseling skill practice. When students are preoccupied with racing thoughts while in class, they cannot address what's on their mind. This affects their learning because while their body is in the classroom, their mind is not. One way to increase attentive listening is exploring existential reality. Practitioner-trainees live in a society that values the fast-paced life as the norm, and a fast pace is often equated to the road to success. Multitasking and completing some tasks with speed may be beneficial at times. However, generalizing this to all situations creates certain problems. If the practitioner-trainee's mind is busy with imposed cultural values, she needs to ask herself what the purpose is of sitting with the client in the room while her mind is not present with the client. The practitioner needs to reflect on her understanding of attentive listening and her implementation of attentive listening. The practitioner-trainee needs to ask herself about the different meanings of pretending to listen attentively and listening attentively. If her mind is busy focusing on speedy treatment, she needs to remind herself that emotional healing cannot be forced to be fast-paced or achieved through multitasking. Healing psychological and emotional wounds takes time. One does not know how long it will take since it is determined by multiple factors and their interrelated complex relationships. Degree, duration, intensity, frequency, and causes of emotional wounds; individuals involved in the sociocultural context; cultural values; availability of treatment; effort put into healing; support from family, community, and professionals, and so on determine how long it takes to heal. Healing runs the spectrum from linear and sequential to nonlinear and holistic.

Being preoccupied with other thoughts distracts the practitioner from being present for the client because the mind is not with the client. It creates superficiality from the onset. The client may perceive this as not caring. Being an attentive listener means the practitioner is present with her quiet mind and genuinely interested in the client and his worldview. Being an attentive listener means she has no preconceived expectations about the client but is interested in finding out about the client and his world as she listens to him attentively.

Balancing the Art and Knowledge Components of Therapy

The therapeutic relationship has two components: the art component and the knowledge component. For the knowledge component, the practitioner should have thorough knowledge of theories of personality, life-span developmental psychology in multicultural contexts, how to interpret both qualitative and quantitative research, differences and similarities among multiple identities (e.g., race, gender, class, sexual orientation, disability, ethnicity, age, religion, language, region), variations within and among these multiple identities, and intersections of them. The art component is the part that clients perceive as the affective domain such as rapport, supportiveness, empathy, active listening, trust, accepting and valuing clients, and so on. This component cannot be taught but evolves internally as practitioners understand their values, beliefs, and biases as they are without judgment. The knowledge component interacts with the art component dynamically. The practitioner is present with both heart (*art*) and mind (*knowledge*) during therapeutic sessions and processes information from both the right hemisphere (emotion and intuition to see holistically) and the left hemisphere (logic and sequence to see details) of the brain. Counseling and psychotherapy involve processing through both art (right hemisphere) and knowledge (left hemisphere) perspectives. It is an activity of both emotion and cognition. Embracing emotional understanding of the client's struggle with logical and rational understanding of the presenting problem is a beginning step toward understanding a client from the client's worldview. The practitioner provides empathy and compassion (art component, right-hemisphere function) while searching through traditional and nontraditional therapeutic techniques (knowledge) with the left hemisphere. The practitioner listens with empathy while figuring out which therapeutic technique is the most appropriate one for the client with this particular issue at the moment. If the practitioner is too involved in the art component of the therapy, she may not be able to ask specific questions that are important for understanding the client's problem and worldview. If the practitioner is too logical and rational and focuses on asking specific questions to assist the client with resolving the problem without providing empathy and compassion, the client may feel minimized and not be able to express his feelings and thoughts openly. Balancing the art component with the knowledge (scientific) component throughout the therapeutic process is crucial for effective treatment.

〢 EXPERIENTIAL LEARNING THROUGH CASE STUDIES

One of the foundations for effective treatment is the practitioner's ability to understand a specific client from his worldview. The practitioner's emotional as well as intellectual understanding of the client is an essential element of the therapeutic process. Emotional understanding cannot be taught through rational and logical information.

Five case studies are presented for practicing transformative learning. The practitioner-trainees are asked to read each case carefully and answer all the questions without screening or censoring. It is important that practitioner-trainees complete these experiential learning activities from where they are (real self) and not where they should be (ideal self). Answering questions from the ideal-self perspective distances the practitioner-trainee from the present self (real self). Practitioner-trainees need to feel without screening (without judgment) in order to be aware of how they really feel and think. Accepting self means not judging. Not judging requires thinking in nonhierarchical, nondichotomous, and nonlinear ways. When practitioner-trainees accept their real self without "shoulds," they are able to be aware of their inner experiences, which include but are not limited to their prejudices, biases, beliefs, and values. In other words, they are aware of who they are. Only then is there a possibility for them to view a client from the client's worldview.

CONCRETE STRATEGIES

Experiential Learning Activities Through Case Studies

Your task is answering questions at the end of each case description. There are 13 questions. You are required to answer the last two questions (12 and 13) and all other questions relevant to each case.

(Continued)

(Continued)

Case 1

A 24-year-old Korean female international student said:

> *I was so excited to go back home after 4 years. I missed my home so much, but I didn't want to go until I finished college. I didn't want my family to think I quit school because I got married. But I am so upset with my older sister. When I got home, I found out my sister threatened my parents that she would commit suicide if my parents told other people I was married to a White man. I guess she was ashamed of me or something like that. I was able to tolerate being laughed at by individuals in the United States because of the way I spoke English or because I didn't understand the U.S. culture. I was hurt by them, but they did not hurt me as much as my sister. I am so upset to a point I am hurting physically. I feel I am the same person regardless of who I married, and I don't understand why my sister is disturbed by my marriage. Why was she so excited about my visit? Why didn't she tell me not to come if she is so ashamed of me? I am so angry at her.*

Case 2

A 30-year-old Native American female student in a master's program came to a university counseling center because her friend thought it might help her sort out a problem. She said:

> *I received a B when I exceeded the 90th percentile in all my work while my class-mate received an A when he met the 75th percentile as his final work average. It is so unfair. I went to see the professor, and his response was that I lacked "cre-ativity." He told me the reason I received the B was because my answers were too precise. I don't know how he measured creativity, and measuring creativity was not included in the course syllabus. I cried until I could not see well because my eyes were so swollen. I felt injustice. I felt racially discriminated against by my professor. I knew he had his favorites in the class, and they often stayed after class. I did not want to receive a good grade because I was the teacher's pet. I wanted to earn a good grade but did not want to be given one because the teacher favored me. I feel deep pain in my heart and anger coming from each cell of my body. But I don't want to report the incident to the dean. You know I was taught to respect my elders. I don't know what to do.*

Case 3

A 50-year-old Afro American man seeking counseling for the first time says:

> *I don't know what to do. My boss is asking me to do things I don't think I should. If I don't, I will be fired, and I can't let that happen. If I do, I will eventually end up in jail. I don't think he would ask this if I were a White man. I need the job,*

and I don't think I can get another job at my age. It always happens to Black people. I don't know what to do.

Case 4

Pat, a 30-year-old White transgendered individual, said:

No one can help me because my problems are not solvable. I was born as a man and never felt comfortable within my body. I was always thinking about dying because life had no meaning for me. I felt trapped in my body, which I felt was not my body. After soul searching, I decided to have a sex change. My Christian family disowned me when they realized that I was going through hormonal treatment. Yes, I am a woman now and feel like I am comfortable within my body, but I am totally rejected by everybody. I have no family, no friends, and no community. They all laugh at me. I don't know which pain is worse, not being comfortable within my body or being disowned by my own family. My mom said I committed a big sin and my sin is too big for God to forgive. She said I shamed her too. I don't feel like living anymore.

Case 5

A 70-year-old woman says:

I have lived all my life doing what everybody told me to do. I cooked, cleaned, took care of children, and did what my husband wanted me to do. I served the church. I did everything that they wanted me to do. My husband never talks to me. If I don't say anything, the days go by in silence.

He won't talk to me. All he wants is for me to cook, clean, and be there for him to have sex when he wants. I asked him to talk to me; I withheld sex for years; I tried to accept him the way he was. . . . I guess I coped with him by focusing on my career and kids when we were younger. Now, it's just the two of us at home. He still doesn't talk, and I feel so empty and not valued. Yet, he orders me around. Instead of asking what I would like to fix, he says, "I want this and that for dinner." I stayed with him because of my church and hoped he would get better. I don't think he is going to get better. I wasted 50 years waiting for him to treat me like a human being. . . . My church doesn't want my service anymore because I am old. I am old, but I am healthy. I can do a lot of things I used to do for the church. But they assume I am too old to do them. They treat me like I am not a human being either. (She cries.) Here I am. I have no purpose and meaning in life. I feel guilty for saying this, but I feel trapped and lonely. It's so painful to just exist.

Read each case and answer all relevant questions as follows.

1. Identify the client's key experiences from each client's cultural perspective.

(Continued)

(Continued)

2. What feelings/emotions do these experiences generate for the client in each case?

3. What would be your key experiences from your cultural perspective if you were the client in each case?

4. What feelings/emotions do these experiences generate for you from your cultural perspective?

5. Assess the level of acculturation of the client, the client's family, the client's boss, the client's professor, and so on if you can. Then measure the degree of discrepancy or congruency between the client's level and that of the others (see Chapter 13).

6. Assess the level of racial identity of the client, the client's family, the client's boss, the client's professor, and so on if you can. Then measure the degree of discrepancy or congruency and the client's comfort level in relation to his racial identity and the others' comfort level in relation to theirs (see Chapter 13).

7. Could you assess the client's, family's, boss's, or professor's dominant identity? (See Chapter 13.)

8. Could you identify an intersection of race, gender, class, sexual orientation, or age from some of the cases?

9. Assess the client's, family's, boss's, or professor's thinking styles.

10. Could you identify behaviors that indicate internalized oppression/privilege from each case?

11. Which case(s) is (are) due to systematic oppression, and how do you go about treating systematic oppression?

12. Develop a treatment plan on the basis of information you gathered by answering the questions.

13. Would you use unconventional treatment methods with one or all of these clients? What would you do to prepare to use creative and unconventional methods?

Before the practitioner-trainee develops the treatment plan, she needs to ask herself what she knows about Korean, Native American, Afro American, and transgender and transsexual cultures as well as the culture of the elderly and how much having or not having knowledge about the culture will affect her ability to develop a treatment plan. What questions could she ask the client to assess how similar to and/or different from her cultural group the client is? How would she ask these questions? Is it ethical for the practitioner to encourage the client in Case 2 to report the professor to the dean?

Here is the author's analysis of Cases 1 and 2 as an example. Most practitioners who are socialized in the United States may suggest that the clients in Cases 1 and 2 confront the sister and parents (Case 1) or professor (Case 2). Confronting elders is not emphasized in typical Korean or Native American cultural values. Their typical cultural values emphasize respecting elders. If both females in Cases 1 and 2 are honoring their cultural values of respecting elders, they would have difficulty confronting them. It would be perceived as asking to be disloyal to their cultural values, which they were conditioned to cherish throughout their lives. Seeing the client from the client's worldview means understanding these types of values as being important for the client. If the client's acculturation level is such that the client would like to confront the sister and parents (Case 1) or professor (Case 2), the practitioner needs to be sensitive about what type of confrontation the client is interested in pursuing and the consequences of confronting an elder from a culture that does not accept such behavior as the norm. The practitioner needs to explore whether the client is ready to face consequences from her elders that may be severe. If the client still wants to confront her elders after weighing all the options, the practitioner can explore the dimensions and purposes of the confrontation from a multilayered perspective. For example, the purpose could be to hurt the other person, to be healed and not hurt anymore, to build a new relationship, or to have closure, to mention a few. After thorough exploration the client may not want to have the confrontation because she does not feel that it would heal her or help the other person. She may want to learn through therapy how to confront the other person without hurting that person or herself. Or, she may want to confront the other person and be ready to face the consequences.

The practitioner may ask the client in Case 1 about her parents' reaction to her sister's threat. It is important to know Korean culture and the parents' history before making any judgment. From a White middle-class

American mainstream value perspective, Korean people (and other cultures that emphasize collectivism) appear to be codependent. What Americans in the United States call codependent behaviors are the core of "caring behaviors" for the family (including extended family) in Korean culture. Instead of encouraging the client to confront her parents, the practitioner may ask, "Tell me about your parents. Do you know or guess what makes them so threatened by your sister?" The practitioner did ask that question, and the following is her answer.

CLIENT'S STORY

My parents could not take the chance of losing another child (my sister). My brother got killed in an automobile accident, and I came to the United States to go to school. My mom watched her mother suffering because the communists took her brother, my uncle, during the Korean War. He worked for an American agency and was captured because her neighbor, who was one of her brother's elementary schoolmates, told communists that my uncle worked for an American agency. My mom told me it was painful for her to watch her mother sighing and crying quietly at times when she was growing up. My mom told me that my grandmother went to the concentration camp and saw my uncle. My grandma wanted my uncle to escape, but he didn't want to because he felt the communists would let him go since he had not done anything wrong. My grandma felt it was her fault. She felt she did not persuade him enough to come home with her. My mom's recollection of my uncle was vague since she was a very young child when he was captured. But she felt pain through my grandma. My grandma carried her grief until her death. I do understand why my mom could not tell anyone about my marital status. I am positive that somehow my grandma's sadness affected my mom and her own pain about losing her son. I think she was scared about losing my sister. I feel bad that I left Korea to fulfill my dream. It had never occurred to me actually how much my parents would miss me when I was planning to come to the United States. I was only preoccupied with my own dreams. I guess I was selfish.

The practitioner gained a deeper understanding of the client's culture through the client's narrative of her family history just by encouraging the client to tell her story. It is important to ask the client to tell more stories (collecting data) before filling in the gaps or making assumptions about the client from the practitioner's worldview.

Assisting clients with sorting out family issues is one of the most diffi-cult tasks in the therapeutic process, especially for clients from collectivism-oriented cultures, because their beliefs, values, and worldviews are different from those of the dominant culture, which is based on individualism value orientation. The client is socialized to value family and cultural myths, but often this becomes a problem when the client's acculturation level is such that the client desires something different from family and cultural values and beliefs. As discussed in Chapter 11, identity development is a com-plicated process for people of color because of the dynamics between inter-nalized and systematic oppression, the intersection of multiple identities, and the level of acculturation. These complicated relationships are inter-woven through the practitioner's and the client's thinking styles. For example, if the Case 1 client's thinking style is dichotomous, the client interprets her sister's behavior only in two opposite ways. However, if the client is encouraged to think from multilayered and multidimensional per-spectives, she may learn to restructure her thinking styles to interpret her sister's behavior. In Case 1, the practitioner was able to assist the client with restructuring her thinking styles from dichotomous and hierarchical to multilayered and multidimensional. After learning to assess her thinking style by recording her intrapersonal communication each day for 3 months and applying behavior modification to restructure her thinking styles, the client said the following.

CLIENT'S STORY

Treatment Results:

I have come to the conclusion that my sister had no option but to think other Koreans at her status level would judge her if they found out that I was mar-ried to a White. The discrimination I felt was real to me, and it is still dis-crimination when I evaluate my sister's behavior from a multilayered and multidimensional perspective, but the difference is my internal reaction to her behavior. I don't have to feel the emotional, psychological, and physical pain from my sister's behavior. What she did and what my parents did were up to them, and I had no control over their own choices, thoughts, behaviors, feelings, and attitudes. I only have control over my own choices, thoughts, behaviors, feelings, and attitudes. I am the one who needs to set an appro-priate boundary that allows for the sister-sister relationship I want to have,

(Continued)

(Continued)

even knowing my sister's opinion about my marital status. The biological ties between us create social obligations not only for me but for others (i.e., my children, her children, our parents) who are linked to us by our relationship. I need to figure out how to manage my relationship with my sister in a way that does not hurt her relationship with others in the family. If I want to have some distance from my sister, I also need to accept the consequence of my choice. I am not good at that now. But as I think about the situation from multiple layers, rather than in an either/or fashion, I don't feel abandoned or rejected by her. I feel sorry for her that she has to be worried about how others think of her all the time.

The following experiential learning activities are designed to increase treatment plan skills through role-playing and small-group learning.

CONCRETE STRATEGIES

Experiential Learning Activities

After outlining the treatment plan and what to ask to know more about each client, complete the following.

1. Discuss your plans and reasons for them with a small group of 4 or 5.

    a. Use case studies as your counseling skill practice material. Trainees who play the counselor role should try to demonstrate their multicultural competency, and trainees who play the client should do their best to portray the client from their feelings when they took the client's perspective in experiential learning activities.

    b. Discuss what you have learned after counseling skill practice.

CONCRETE STRATEGIES

Consciousness Practice

What stands out to you as essentials of treatment now?

References

Aberson, C. L., Healy, M., & Romero, V. (2000). In-group bias and self-esteem: A meta-analysis. *Personality and Social Psychology Review, 4,* 157–173.

Aboud, F. E. (2003). The formation of in-group favoritism and out-group prejudice in young children: Are they distinct attitudes? *Developmental Psychology, 39,* 48–60.

Abrams, D., Rutland, A., & Cameron, L. (2004). The development of subjective group dynamics: Children's judgments of normative and deviant in-group and out-group individuals. *Child Development, 74,* 1840–1856.

Abrams, D., Rutland, A., Cameron, L., & Margues, J. M. (2003). The development of subjective group dynamics: When in-group bias gets specific. *British Journal of Developmental Psychology, 21,* 155–176.

Acevedo, A., Loewenstein, D. A., Agron, J., & Duara, R. (2007). Influence of sociodemographic variables on neuropsychological test performance in Spanish-speaking older adults. *Journal of Clinical and Experimental Neuropsychology, 29*(5), 530–544.

Acevedo, A., Loewenstein, D. A., Barker, W. W., Harwood, D. G., Luis, C., Bravo, M., et al. (2000). Category fluency test: Normative data for English and Spanish-speaking elderly. *International Journal of the International Neuropsychology Society, 6,* 760–769.

Adams, H. E., Wright, R. W., & Lohr, B. A. (1996). Is homophobia associated with homosexual arousal? *Journal of Abnormal Psychology, 105*(3), 440–445.

Adams, M. (2000). Classism. In M. Adams, W. J. Blumenfeld, R. Castaneda, H. W. Hackman, M. L. Peters, & X. Zuniga (Eds.), *Readings for diversity and social justice* (pp. 379–382). New York: Routledge.

Adams, M., Bell, L. A., & Griffin, P. (Eds.). (1997). *Teaching for diversity and social justice.* New York: Routledge.

Adams, M., Blumenfeld, W. J., Castaneda, R., Hackman, H. W. Peters, M. L., & Zuniga, X. (Eds.). (2000). *Readings for diversity and social justice.* New York: Routledge.

Adler, A. (1936). On the interpretation of dreams. *International Journal of Individual Psychology, 2,* 3–16.

Agars, M. (2004). Reconsidering the impact of gender stereotypes on the advancement of women in organizations. *Psychology of Women Quarterly, 28,* 103–111.

Allport, G. W. (1954). *The nature of prejudice.* Reading, MA: Addison-Wesley.

Almquist, E. M. (1987). Labor market gendered inequality in minority groups. *Gender and Society, 1,* 400–414.

Altemeyer, B. (2003). Why do religious fundamentalists tend to be prejudiced? *The International Journal for the Psychology of Religion, 13,* 17–28.

Altschul, I., Oyserman, D., & Bybee, D. (2006). Racial-ethnic identity in mid-adolescence: Content and change as predictors of academic achievement. *Child Development, 77,* 1155–1169.

Amadlume, I. (1987). *Male daughters, female husbands: Gender and sex in an African society.* London: Zed Books.

American Counseling Association. (2005). *Code of ethics.* Alexandria, VA: Author. Available at http://www.counseling.org/Resources/CodeOfEthics/TP/Home/CT2.aspx

American Psychiatric Association. (2000). *Diagnostic and statistical manual of mental disorders: DSM-IV-TR* (text rev.). Washington, DC: Author.

American Psychological Association. (1993). *Guidelines for the providers of psychological services to ethically, linguistically and culturally diverse populations.* Washington, DC: Author.

American Psychological Association. (2002). *Ethical principles of psychologists and code of conduct.* Washington, DC: Author. Available at http://www.apa.org/ethics/code2002.html

American Psychological Association. (2003). Guidelines on multicultural education, training, research, practice, and organizational change for psychologists. Retrieved February 19, 2009, from http://www.apa.org/pi/multiculturalguidelines/introduction.html

Amsterlaw, J., & Wellman, H. M. (2006). Theories of mind in transition: A microgenetic study of the development of false belief. *Journal of Cognition and Development, 7*(2), 139–172.

Andersen, L. E. (1994). A new look at an old construct: Cross-cultural adaptation. *International Journal of Intercultural Relations, 18,* 293–328.

Andersen, S. M. (1984). Self-knowledge and social inference: II. The diagnosticity of cognitive/affective and behavioral data. *Journal of Personality and Social Psychology, 46*(2), 294–307.

Andersen, S. M., & Ross, L. (1984). Self-knowledge and social inference: I. The impact of cognitive/affective and behavioral data. *Journal of Personality and Social Psychology, 46*(2), 280–293.

Anderson, J., Moeschberger, M., Chen, M. S., Jr., Kunn, P., Wewers, M. E., & Guthrie, R. (1993). An acculturation scale for Southeast Asians. *Social Psychiatry and Psychiatric Epidemiology, 28,* 134–141.

Arce, C. A. (1981). A reconsideration of Chicano culture and identity. *Daedalus, 110,* 177–192.

Ardila, A., Ostrosky-Solis, F., Rosselli, M., & Gomez, C. (2000). Age-related cognitive decline during normal aging: The complex effect of education. *Archives of Clinical Neuropsychology, 15,* 495–513.

Argyle, M. (1994). *Psychology of class.* New York: Routledge.

Arms, E., Bickett, J., & Graf, V. (2008). Gender bias and imbalance: Girls in U.S. special education programs. *Gender and Education, 20*(4), 349–359.

Asch, A. (1984). The experience of disability: A challenge for psychology. *American Psychologist, 39,* 529–536.

Atkinson, D. R., & Hackett, G. (Eds.). (2004). *Counseling diverse populations* (3rd ed.). New York: McGraw-Hill.

Atkinson, D. R., Morten, G., & Sue, D. W. (1989). A minority identity development model. In D. R. Atkinson, G. Morten, & D. W. Sue (Eds.), *Counseling American minorities* (3rd ed., pp. 35–52). Dubuque, IA: W. C. Brown.

Atkinson, D. R., Morten, G., & Sue, D. W. (1998). *Counseling American minorities* (5th ed.). Boston: McGraw-Hill.

Atkinson, R. L., Atkinson, R. C., Smith, E. E., Bem, D. J., & Nolen-Hoeksema, S. (2000). *Hilgard's introduction to psychology* (13th ed.). Fort Worth, TX: Harcourt Brace.

Attar, B. K., Guerra, N. G., & Tolan, P. H. (1994). Neighborhood disadvantage, stressful life events, and adjustments in urban elementary school children. *Journal of Clinical and Child Psychology, 23,* 391–400.

Aviram, R. B. (2007). Object relations and prejudice: From in-group favoritism to out-group hatred. *International Journal of Applied Psychoanalytic Studies, 4*(1), 4–14.

Axelson, J. A. (1999). *Counseling and development in a multicultural society* (3rd ed.). New York: Brooks/Cole.

Baldwin, C. (1991). *Life's companion: Journal writing as a spiritual quest.* New York: Bantam.

Banaji, M. R. (1997). Introductory comments. *Journal of Experimental Social Psychology, 33,* 449–450.

Banaji, M. R., & Bhaskar, R. (2001). Implicit stereotypes and memory: The bounded rationality of social beliefs. In D. L. Schacter & E. Scarry (Eds.), *Memory, brain, and belief* (pp. 139–175). Cambridge, MA: Harvard University Press.

Banaji, M. R., & Greenwald, A. G. (1994). Implicit stereotyping and unconscious prejudice. In M. P. Zanna & J. M. Olson (Eds.), *The psychology of prejudice: The Ontario symposium* (Vol. 7, pp. 55–76). Hillsdale, NJ: Erlbaum.

Banaji, M. R., & Greenwald, A. G. (1995). Implicit gender stereotyping in judgments of fame. *Journal of Personality and Social Psychology, 68,* 181–198.

Banaji, M. R., & Hardin, C. D. (1996). Automatic stereotyping. *Psychological Science, 7,* 136–141.

Bandura, A. (1977). *Social learning theory.* Englewood Cliffs, NJ: Prentice Hall.

Bandura, A., & Bussey, K. (2004). On broadening the cognitive, motivation, and sociostructural scope of theorizing about gender development and functioning: Comment of Martin, Ruble, and Szkrybalo (2002). *Psychological Bulletin, 130*(5), 691–701.

Barney, K. (1994). Limitations of the critique of the medical model. *Journal of Mind and Behavior, 15,* 19–34.

Barry, W. (1995). Health is membership. *Another turn of the crank: Essays* (pp. 86–109). Washington, DC: Counterpoint.

Baumeister, R. F. (1998). The self. In D. T. Gilbert & S. T. Fiske (Eds.), *The handbook of social psychology* (4th ed., pp. 680–740). New York: McGraw-Hill.

Beck, A. T., Rush, A., Shaw, B., & Emery, G. (1979). *Cognitive therapy of depression.* New York: Guilford.

Beck, A. T., & Weishaar, M. E. (2000). Cognitive therapy. In R. J. Corsini & D. Wedding (Eds.), *Current psychotherapies* (6th ed., pp. 238–268). Itasca, IL: F. E. Peacock.

Bemak, F., & Greenberg, B. (1994). Southeast Asian refugee adolescents: Implications for counseling. *Journal of Multicultural Counseling and Development, 22*(4), 115–124.

Bennett, M., Barrett, M., Karakozov, R., Kipiani, G., Lyons, E., Pavelnko, V., et al. (2004). Young children's evaluations of the ingroup and of outgroups: A multi-national study. *Social Development, 13,* 124–141.

Berry, J. O., & Jones, W. H. (1991). Situational and dispositional components of reactions toward persons with disabilities. *The Journal of Social Psychology, 131,* 673–684.

Berry, J. W., & Sam, D. L. (1997). Acculturation and adaptation. In J. Berry, M. Segall, & C. Kagitcibasi (Eds.), *Cross cultural psychology* (Vol. 3, pp. 291–326). Boston: Allyn & Bacon.

Bhatia, S., & Ram, A. (2001). Rethinking "acculturation" in relation to diasporic cultures and postcolonial identities. *Human Development, 44,* 1–18.

Bieschke, K. J., Croteau, J. M., Lark, J. S., & Vandiver, B. J. (2005). Toward a discourse of sexual orientation equity in the counseling professions. In J. M. Croteau, J. S. Lark, M. A. Lidderdale, & Y. B. Chung (Eds.), *Deconstructing heterosexism in the counseling professions* (pp. 189–209). Thousand Oaks, CA: Sage.

Birrell, P. J., & Freyd, J. J. (2006). Betrayal and trauma: Relational models of harm and healing. *Journal of Trauma Practice, 5,* 49–63.

Bizumic, B., & Duckitt, J. (2007). Varieties of group self-centeredness and dislike of the specific other. *Basic and Applied Social Psychology, 29*(2), 195–202.

Bjorklund, P. (2006). No man's land: Gender bias and social constructivism in the diagnosis of borderline personality disorder. *Issues in Mental Health Nursing, 27*(1), 3–23.

Black-Gutman, D., & Hickson, F. (1996). The relationship between racial attitudes and social-cognitive development in children: An Australian study. *Developmental Psychology, 32*, 448–456.

Blackmore, S. (2004). *Consciousness: Introduction.* New York: Oxford University Press.

Blackwood, E. (1984). Sexuality and gender in certain Native American tribes: The case of cross-gender females. *Signs: Journal of Women in Culture and Society, 10*, 27–42.

Blair, I., & Banaji, M. R. (1996). Automatic and controlled processes in stereotype priming. *Journal of Personality and Social Psychology, 70*, 1142–1163.

Blasi, A., & Loevinger, J. (1976). *Ego development: Conceptions and theories.* San Francisco: Jossey-Bass.

Blumenfeld, W. J. (2000a). Heterosexism. In M. Adams, W. J. Blumenfeld, R. Castaneda, H. W. Hackman, M. L. Peters, & X. Zuniga (Eds.), *Readings for diversity and social justice* (pp. 262–266). New York: Routledge.

Blumenfeld, W. J. (2000b). How homophobia hurts everyone. In M. Adams, W. J. Blumenfeld, R. Castaneda, H. W. Hackman, M. L. Peters, & X. Zuniga (Eds.), *Readings for diversity and social justice* (pp. 267–275). New York: Routledge.

Bolderson, H. (1991). *Social security, disability and rehabilitation: Conflicts in the development of social policy 1914–1946.* London: Jessica Kingsley.

Bolin, A. (1987). Transsexualism and the limits of traditional analysis. *American Behavioral Scientist, 31*, 41–65.

Bonham, V. L., Warshauer-Baker, E., & Collins, F. S. (2005). Race and ethnicity in the genome era: The complexity of the constructs. *American Psychologist, 60*, 9–15.

Boothby, N. (1994). Trauma and violence among refugee children. In A. J. Marsella, T. Bornemann, S. Ekblad, & J. Orley (Eds.), *Amidst peril and pain: The mental health and well-being of the world's refugees* (pp. 239–259). Washington, DC: American Psychological Association.

Bosma, H., van Boxtel, M. P., Ponds, R., Houx, P., & Jolles, J. (2003). Education and age related cognitive decline: The contribution of mental workload. *Educational Gerontology, 29*, 1–9.

Bosma, H. A., & Kunnen, E. S. (2001). Determinants and mechanisms in ego identity development: A review and synthesis. *Developmental Review, 21*, 39–66.

Boston, T. (1991). Race, class and political economy: Reflections on an unfinished agenda. In A. Zegeye, L. Harris, & J. Maxted (Eds.), *Exploitation and exclusion: Race and class in contemporary U.S. society* (pp. 142–157). New York: Hans Zell.

Boucouvalas, M. (1997, July). *An analysis and critique of transformation theory and adult learning: Contributions from consciousness studies.* Paper presented at Crossing Borders, Breaking Boundaries: Research in Education of Adults, 27th Annual SCUTREA Conference, Birkbeck College, University of London.

Bowman, S. (2003). A call to action in lesbian, gay and bisexual theory building and research. *The Counseling Psychologist, 31*(1), 63–69.

Braithwaite, C. (1990). Communicative silence: A cross-cultural study of Basso's hypothesis. In D. Carbaugh (Ed.), *Cultural communication and intercultural contact* (pp. 321–327). Hillsdale, NJ: Erlbaum.

Brewer, M. B. (2001). Ingroup identification and intergroup conflict: When does ingroup love become outgroup hate? In L. Jussim & R. D. Ashmore (Eds.), *Social identity, intergroup conflict, and conflict reduction* (pp. 17–41). London: Oxford University Press.

Brewer, M. B., & Brown, R. J. (1998). Intergroup relations. In D. T. Gilbert & S. T. Fiske (Eds.), *The handbook of social psychology* (4th ed., Vol. 2, pp. 554–594). New York: McGraw-Hill.

Brody, G., Chen, Y., Murry, V. M., Ge, X., Simons, R. L., Gibbons, F. X., et al. (2006). Perceived discrimination and the adjustment of African American youths: A five-year longitudinal analysis with contextual moderation effects. *Child Development, 77,* 1170–1189.

Brouwer, S. (2000). Sharing the pie. In M. Adams, W. J. Blumenfeld, R. Castaneda, H. W. Hackman, M. L. Peters, & X. Zuniga (Eds.), *Readings for diversity and social justice* (pp. 382–391). New York: Routledge.

Brown, C. S. (1995). The psychology of prejudice: Ingroup love or outgroup hate. *Journal of Social Issues, 55,* 429–444.

Brown, C. S., & Bigler, R. S. (2004). Children's perception of gender discrimination. *Developmental Psychology, 40,* 714–726.

Brown, C. S., & Bigler, R. S. (2005). Children's perceptions of discrimination: A developmental model. *Child Development, 76*(3), 533–553.

Brown, K. T., Ward, G. K., Lightbourn, T., & Jackson, J. S. (1999). Skin tone and racial identity among African Americans: A theoretical and research framework. In R. L. Jones (Ed.), *Advances in African American psychology: Theory, paradigms, and research* (pp. 191–215). Hampton, VA: Cobb & Henry.

Brown, S. E., Connors, D., & Stern, N. (2000). Invisible and on center stage: Who do we think we are, anyway? In M. Adams, W. J. Blumenfeld, R. Castaneda, H. W. Hackman, M. L. Peters, & X. Zuniga (Eds.), *Readings for diversity and social justice* (pp. 377–378). New York: Routledge.

Bryan, W. V. (2000). The disability rights movement. In M. Adams, W. J. Blumenfeld, R. Castaneda, H. W. Hackman, M. L. Peters, & X. Zuniga (Eds.), *Readings for diversity and social justice* (pp. 324–329). New York: Routledge.

Bufford, R. K. (1997). Consecrated counseling: Reflections on the distinctives of Christian counseling. *Journal of Psychology and Theology, 25,* 110–122.

Bufford, R. K. (2007). Philosophical foundations for clinical supervision within a Christian worldview. *Journal of Psychology and Christianity, 26*(4), 293–297.

Burbank, P. M. (Ed.). (2006). *Vulnerable older adults: Health care needs and interventions.* New York: Springer.

Burstow, B. (2003). Toward a radical understanding of trauma and trauma work. *Violence Against Women, 9*(1), 1293–1317.

Bush, D. M., & Simmons, R. G. (1992). Socialization over the life course: In M. Rosenberg & R. H. Turner (Eds.), *Social psychology: Sociological perspectives* (pp. 133–164). New Brunswick, NJ: Transaction.

Butler, R. (1969). Age-ism: Another form of bigotry. *The Gerontologist, 9,* 243–246.

Calasanti, T., Slevin, K. F., & King N. (2006). Ageism and feminism: From "et cetera" to center. *NWSA Journal, 18*(1), 13–30.

Cameron, J. (1992). *The artist's way: A spiritual path to higher creativity.* New York: Tarcher/Putnam.

Campbell, F. (2001). Inciting legal fictions: Disability's date with ontology and the ableist body of the law. *Griffith Law Review, 10,* 42–62.

Campbell, F. A. K. (2005). Legislating disability: Negative ontologies and the government of legal identities. In S. Tremanin (Ed.), *Foucault and the government disability* (pp. 108–130). Ann Arbor: University of Michigan Press.

Campbell, F. A. K. (2008). Exploring internalized ableism using critical race theory. *Disability & Society, 23*(2), 151–162.

Campbell, J. (Ed.). (1976). *The portable Jung* (R. F. C. Hull, Trans.). New York: Penguin.

Cappacchione, L. (1992). *The creative journal: The art of finding yourself.* North Hollywood, CA: Newcastle.

Carbaugh, D. (2001). "I can't do that!" but I "can actually see around corners": American Indian students and the study of public communication. In J. N. Martin, T. K. Nakayama, & L. A. Flores (Eds.), *Readings in intercultural communication: Experiences and contexts* (2nd ed., pp. 138–148). Columbus, OH: McGraw-Hill.

Caress, S. M., & Steinemann, A. D. (2004). Prevalence of multiple chemical sensitivities: A population-based study in the southeastern United States. *American Journal of Public Health, 4*(5), 746–747.

Carli, L. I. (1990). Gender, language and influence. *Journal of Personality and Social Psychology, 59,* 941–951.

Carli, L. I. (1999). Gender, interpersonal power, and social influence. *Journal of Social Issues, 55,* 81–99.

Carlson, N. (1999). *Psychology: The science of behavior.* Boston: Allyn & Bacon.

Carr, L. G. (1997). *Color-blind racism.* Thousand Oaks, CA: Sage.

Carter, C., & Steiner, L. (Eds.). (2004). *Critical readings: Media and gender.* Maidenhead, England: Open University Press.

Carter, R. T. (1990). The relationship between racism and racial identity among White Americans: An exploratory investigation. *Journal of Counseling & Development, 69,* 46–50.

Casas, J. M., & Pytluk, S. D. (1995). Hispanic identity development: Implications for research and practice. In J. G. Ponterotto, J. M. Casa, L. A. Suzuki, & C. M. Alexander (Eds.), *Handbook of multicultural counseling* (pp. 155–180). Thousand Oaks, CA: Sage.

Cass, V. C. (1979). Homosexual identity formation: Testing a theoretical model. *Journal of Sex Research, 20,* 143–167.

Castaneda, R., & Peters, M. L. (2000). Ableism: Introduction. In M. Adams, W. J. Blumenfeld, R. Castaneda, H. W. Hackman, M. L. Peters, & X. Zuniga (Eds.), *Readings for diversity and social justice* (pp. 319–323). New York: Routledge.

Castillo, L. G., Conoley, C. W., King, J., Rollins, D., Rivera, S., & Veve, M. (2006). Predictors of racial prejudice in White American counseling students. *Journal of Multicultural Counseling and Development, 34,* 15–26.

Caughy, M., Nettles, S. M., O'Campo, P. J., & Lohrfink, K. F. (2006). Racial socialization and African American child development: The importance of neighborhood context. *Child Development, 77,* 1220–1236.

Cecchi, M., Khoshbouei, H., Javors, M., & Morilak, D. (2002). Modulatory effects of norepinephrine in the lateral bed nucleus of the stria terminalis on behavioral and neuroendocrine responses to acute stress. *Neuroscience, 112,* 13–21.

Chen, M., & Bargh, J. A. (1997). Nonconscious behavioral confirmation processes: The self-fulfilling consequences of automatic stereotype activation. *Journal of Experimental Social Psychology, 33,* 541–560.

Chernik, A. F. (2000). The body politic. In M. Adams, W. J. Blumenfeld, R. Castaneda, H. W. Hackman, M. L. Peters, & X. Zuniga (Eds.), *Readings for diversity and social justice* (pp. 243–246). New York: Routledge.

Chiu, M. L. (1995). The influence of anticipatory fear on foreign student adjustment: An exploratory study. *International Journal of Intercultural Relations, 19,* 1–44.

Chung, R. C. Y. (2001). Psychosocial adjustment of Cambodian refugee women: Implications for mental health counseling. *Journal of Mental Health Counseling, 23,* 115–126.

Clair, R. P. (1998). *Organizing silence.* Albany: State University of New York.

Clement, W., & Myles, J. (1994). Relations of ruling: Class and gender in postindustrial societies. Quebec, Canada: McGill-Queen's University Press.

Coffey, D. M., Marmol, L., Schock, L., & Adams, W. (2005). The influence of acculturation on the Wisconsin Card Sorting Test by Mexican Americans. *Archives of Clinical Neuropsychology, 20,* 795–803.

Coie, J. D., & Dodge, K. A. (1998). Aggression and antisocial behavior. In W. Damon (Series Ed.) & N. Eisenberg (Vol. Ed.), *Handbook of child psychology: Social, emotional, and personality development* (pp. 779–862). New York: Wiley.

Collins, N. M., & Pieterse, A. L. (2007). Critical incident analysis based on training: An approach for developing active racial/cultural awareness. *Journal of Counseling & Development, 85,* 14–23.

Collins, P. H. (1991). *Black feminist thought: Knowledge, consciousness, and the politics of empowerment.* New York: Routledge & Kegan Paul.

Comstock, D. L., Hammer, T. R., Strentzsch, J., Cannon, K., Parsons, J., & Salazar, G., II (2008). Relational-cultural theory: A framework for bridging relational, multicultural and social justice competencies. *Journal of Counseling & Development, 86,* 279–287.

Comstock, G. (1993). The medium and society: The role of television in American life. In G. L. Berry & J. K. Asamen (Eds.), *Children and television: Images in a changing sociocultural world* (pp. 117–131). Thousand Oaks, CA: Sage.

Connell, R. W. (1987). *Gender and power: Society, the person, and sexual politics.* Stanford, CA: Stanford University Press.

Constantine, M. G., Hage, S. M., Kindaichi, M. M., & Bryant, R. M. (2007). Social justice and multicultural issues: Implications for the practice and training of counselors and counseling psychologists. *Journal of Counseling & Development, 85,* 24–29.

Constantine, M. G., Kindaichi, M., Okazaki, S., Gainor, K. A., & Baden, A. L. (2005). A qualitative investigation of the cultural adjustment experiences of Asian international college women. *Cultural Diversity and Ethnic Minority Psychology, 11,* 162–175.

Constantine, M. G., & Sue, D. W. (Eds.). (2005). *Strategies for building multicultural competence in mental health and educational settings.* Hoboken, NJ: Wiley.

Cook-Daniels, L. (1995). Lesbian, gay male, bisexual and transgendered elders: Elder abuse and neglect issues. Retrieved April 1, 2008, from http://www.forge-forward.org/handouts/tgelderabuse-neglect.html

Cooley-Quile, M. R., Turner, S. M., & Beidel, D. C. (1995a). Assessing community violence: The children's report of exposure to violence. *Journal of the American Academy of Child and Adolescent Psychiatry, 34,* 201–208.

Cooley-Quile, M. R., Turner, S. M., & Beidel, D. C. (1995b). Emotional impact of children's exposure to community violence. *Journal of the American Academy of Child and Adolescent Psychiatry, 34,* 1362–1368.

Corey, G. (2001). *Case approach to counseling and psychotherapy* (5th ed.). Belmont, CA: Thomson Brooks/Cole.

Corey, G. (2005). *Case approach to counseling and psychotherapy* (6th ed.). Belmont, CA: Thomson Brooks/Cole.

Corey, G., Corey, M., & Callanan, P. (1993). Issues and ethics in the helping professions. Pacific Grove, CA: Brooks/Cole.

Corsini, R. J., & Wedding, D. (Eds.). (2005). *Current psychotherapies* (7th ed.). Belmont, CA: Brooks/Cole-Thomson Learning.

Cortes, D. E., Rogler, L. H., & Malgady, R. H. (1994). Biculturation scale for Mexican American normal and clinical populations. *Hispanic Journal of Behavioral Sciences, 2*(3), 199–217.

Council for Accreditation of Counseling and Related Educational Programs. (2001). *2001 standards.* Alexandria, VA: Author.

Covarrubias, P. (2007). (Un)Biased in Western theory: Generative silence in American Indian communication. *Communication Monographs, 74*(2), 265–271.

Coward, H. (1986). Intolerance in the world's religions. *Studies in Religion, 15*, 419–431.

Cox, S. S. (Ed.). (1999). *Voices from another place: A collection of works from a generation born in Korea and adopted to other countries.* St. Paul, MN: Yeong & Yeong.

Cranton, P., & Roy, M. (2003). When the bottom falls out of the bucket: Toward a holistic perspective on transformative education. *Journal of Transformative Education, 1*(2), 86–98.

Crethar, H. D., Rivera, E. T., & Nash, S. (2008). In search of common threads: Linking multicultural, feminist, and social justice counseling paradigms. *Journal of Counseling & Development, 86*, 269–278.

Crick, N. R. (1996). The role of overt aggression, relational aggression, and prosocial behavior in the prediction of children's future social adjustment. *Child Development, 67*, 2317–2327.

Crompton, R. (2001). The gendered restructuring of the middle classes. In M. Western & J. Baxter (Eds.), *Reconfigurations of class and gender* (pp. 39–54). Stanford, CA: Stanford University Press.

Cross, W. E. (1995). The psychology of nigrescence: Revising the Cross model. In J. G. Ponterotto, J. M. Dasa, L. A. Suzuki, & M. Alesander (Eds.), *Handbook of multicultural counseling* (pp. 93–122). Thousand Oaks, CA: Sage.

Cross, W. E., Jr. (1971). The Negro-to-Black conversion experience: Toward a psychology of Black liberation. *Black World, 20*, 13–27.

Cross, W. E., Jr., & Vandiver, B. J. (2001). Nigrescence theory and measurement: Introducing the Cross Racial Identity Scale (CRIS). In J. G. Ponterotto, J. M. Casas, L. A. Suzuki, & C. M. Alexander (Eds.), *Handbook of multicultural counseling* (2nd ed., pp. 371–393). Thousand Oaks, CA: Sage.

Croteau, J. M., & Constantine, M. G. (2005). Race and sexual orientation in multicultural counseling: Navigating rough waters. In J. M. Croteau, J. S. Lark, M. A. Lidderdale, & Y. B. Chung (Eds.), *Deconstructing heterosexism in the counseling professions* (pp. 159–185). Thousand Oaks, CA: Sage.

Croteau, J. M., Lark, J. S., & Lance, T. S. (2005). Our stories will be told: Deconstructing the heterosexist discourse in the counseling profession. In J. M. Croteau, J. S. Lark, M. A. Lidderdale, & Y. B. Chung (Eds.), *Deconstructing heterosexism in the counseling professions* (pp. 1–15). Thousand Oaks, CA: Sage.

Croteau, J. M., Lark, J. S., Lidderdale, M. A., & Chung, Y. B. (Eds.). (2005). *Deconstructing heterosexism in the counseling professions.* Thousand Oaks, CA: Sage.

Cuddy, A. J. C., Norton, M. I., & Fiske, S. T. (2005). This old stereotype: The pervasiveness and persistence of the elderly stereotype. *Journal of Social Issues, 61*(2), 267–285.

Cuellar, I. (2000). Acculturation and mental health: Ecological transactional relations of adjustment. In I. Cuellar & F. A. Paniagua (Eds.), *Handbook of multicultural mental health: Assessment and treatment of diverse populations* (pp. 45–62). New York: Academic Press.

Currie, D. (1997). Decoding femininity: Advertisements and their teenage readers. *Gender & Society, 11*, 453–477.

Daloz, L. (1999). *Mentor: Guiding the journey of adult learners.* San Francisco: Jossey-Bass.

Damasio, A. (1994). *Descartes' error: Emotion, reason and the human brain.* New York: Putnam.

Dana, R. H. (1993). Examining the usefulness of DSM-IV. In K. Kurasaki, S. Okasaki, & S. Sue (Eds.), *Asian American mental health: Assessment theories and methods* (pp. 29–46). New York: Kluwer.

Dana, R. H. (1998). *Understanding cultural identity in intervention and assessment.* Thousand Oaks, CA: Sage.

D'Andrea, M., & Heckman, E. F. (2008). A 40-year review of multicultural counseling outcome research: Outlining a future research agenda for the multicultural counseling movement. *Journal of Counseling & Development, 86,* 356–363.

Daniels, J. (2007). The fourth force in counseling and therapy: Multicultural and feminist perspectives. In A. E. Ivey, M. D'Andrea, M. B. Ivey, & L. Simek-Morgan (Eds.), *Theories of counseling and psychotherapy: A multicultural perspective* (6th ed., pp. 319–358). Boston: Pearson Education.

Dawson, E. J., Crano, W. D., & Burgoon, M. (1996). Refining the meaning and measurement of acculturation: Revisiting a novel methodological approach. *International Journal of Intercultural Relations, 29*(1), 97–114.

Deater-Deckard, K., Dodge, K., & Sorbring, E. (2005). Cultural differences in the effects of physical punishment. In M. Rutter & M. Tienda (Eds.), *Ethnicity and causal mechanisms* (pp. 204–226). Cambridge, England: Cambridge University Press.

DeCoster, J., Banner, M. J., Smith, E. R., & Semin, G. R. (2006). On the inexplicability of the implicit: Differences in the information provided by implicit and explicit tests. *Social Cognition, 24,* 5–21.

Deegan, P. E. (2000). Recovering our sense of value after being labeled mentally ill. In M. Adams, W. J. Blumenfeld, R. Castaneda, H. W. Hackman, M. L. Peters, & X. Zuniga (Eds.), *Readings for diversity and social justice* (pp. 359–363). New York: Routledge.

Deihl, M., & Ochs, R. (2000). Biphobia. In M. Adams, W. J. Blumenfeld, R. Castaneda, H. W. Hackman, M. L. Peters, & X. Zuniga (Eds.), *Readings for diversity and social justice* (pp. 276–280). New York: Routledge.

DeJong, G. (1982). Independent living. In M. G. Elsenberg, C. Giggins, & R. J. Duval (Eds.), *Disabled people as second-class citizens.* New York: Springer.

Delphin, M. E., & Rowe, M. (2008). Continuing education in cultural competence for community mental health practitioners. *Professional Psychology: Research and Practice, 39*(2), 182–191.

Dempsey, M. (2002). Negative coping as mediator in the relation between violence and outcomes: Inner-city African American youth. *American Journal of Orthopsychiatry, 72,* 102–109.

Dennett, D. C. (1976). Are dreams experiences? *Philosophical Review, 73,* 151–171.

Deutsch, R., Gawronski, B., & Strack, F. (2006). At the boundaries of automaticity: Negation as reflective operation. *Journal of Personality and Social Psychology, 91,* 319–326.

Devine, P. G. (1989). Stereotypes and prejudice: Their automatic and controlled components. *Journal of Personality and Social Psychology, 60,* 817–830.

Devine, P. G., & Monteith, M. J. (1999). Automaticity and control in stereotyping. In S. Chaiken & Y. Trope (Eds.), *Dual process theories in social psychology* (pp. 339–360). New York: Guilford.

Dewey, J. (2004). *Democracy and education.* Mineola, NY: Dover.

Donaldson, E. J. (2002). The corpus of the madwoman: Toward a feminist disability studies theory of embodiment and mental illness. *NWSA Journal, 4*(3), 99–119.

Douce, L. A. (1998). Can a cutting edge last twenty-five years? *The Counseling Psychologist, 26,* 777–785.

Douce, L. A. (2005). Coming out on the wave of feminism, coming to age on the ocean of multiculturalism. In J. M. Croteau, J. S. Lark, M. A. Lidderdale, & Y. B. Chung (Eds.), *Deconstructing heterosexism in the counseling professions: A narrative approach* (pp. 59–64). Thousand Oaks, CA: Sage.

Dovidio, J. F., Evans, N., & Tyler, R. B. (1986). Racial stereotypes: The contents of their cognitive representations. *Journal of Experimental Social Psychology, 22,* 22–37.

Dovidio, J. F., & Gaertner, S. L. (1998). On the nature of contemporary prejudice: The causes, consequences, and challenges of aversive racism. In J. Eberhardt & S. T. Fiske (Eds.), *Confronting racism: The problem and the response* (pp. 3–32). Newbury Park, CA: Sage.

Dovidio, J. F., & Gaertner, S. L. (2000). Aversive racism and selection decisions: 1989 and 1999. *Psychological Science, 11,* 319–323.

Dovidio, J. F., & Gaertner, S. L. (2004). Aversive racism. In M. P. Zanna (Ed.), *Advances in experimental social psychology* (Vol. 36, pp. 1–51). San Diego, CA: Academic Press.

Dovidio, J. F., & Gaertner, S. L. (2005). Understanding and addressing contemporary racism: From aversive racism to the common ingroup identity model. *Journal of Social Issues, 61*(3), 615–639.

Dovidio, J. F., Gaertner, S. L., Kawakami, K., & Hodson, G. (2002). Why can't we just get along? Interpersonal biases and interracial distrust. *Cultural Diversity & Ethnic Minority Psychology, 8,* 88–102.

Dovidio, J. F., Kawakami, K., & Gaertner, S. L. (2002). Implicit and explicit prejudice and interracial interaction. *Journal of Personality and Social Psychology, 82,* 62–68.

Dovidio, J. F., Kawakami, K., Johnson, C., Johnson, B., & Howard, A. (1997). The nature of prejudice: Automatic and controlled processes. *Journal of Experimental Social Psychology, 33,* 510–540.

Downey, G., Khouri, H., & Feldman, S. (1998). Early interpersonal trauma and later adjustment: The mediational role of rejection sensitivity. In D. Cicchetti & S. Toth (Eds.), *Developmental perspectives on trauma: Theory, research, and intervention.* Rochester Symposium on Developmental Psychology (Vol. 8, pp. 85–114). Rochester, NY: University of Rochester Press.

Draguns. J. G. (1996). Humanly universal and culturally distinctive: Charting the course of cultural counseling. In P. B. Pedersen, J. G. Draguns, W. J. Lonner, & J. E. Trimble (Eds.), *Counseling across cultures* (pp. 1–20). Thousand Oaks, CA: Sage.

Draguns. J. G. (1997). Abnormal behavioral patterns across cultures: Implications for counseling and psychotherapy. *International Journal of Intercultural Relations, 21*(2), 213–248.

Dudek, S. (2008, February). Becoming inclusive communities of faith: Biblical reflection and effective frameworks. *New Theology Review,* 40–51.

Dufrene, P., & Herring, R. (Eds.). (1994). Guest editorial comment for this special issue on Native American Indians: Native American Indians [Special issue]. *Journal of Multicultural Counseling and Development, 22*(3), 131–133.

Dunning, D., Meyerowits, J. A., & Holzber, A. D. (1989). Ambiguity and self-evaluation: The role of idiosyncratic trait definitions in self-serving appraisals of ability. *Journal of Personality and Social Psychology, 57,* 1082–1090.

Egeland, G., Carlson, E., & Sroufe, L. (1993). Resilience as process. *Development and Psychopathology, 5,* 517–528.

Ehlers, A., & Clark, D. M. (2000). A cognitive model of posttraumatic stress disorder. *Behaviour Research and Therapy, 38,* 319–334.

Eisenberg, N. (1988). The development of prosocial and aggressive behavior. In M. Borstein & M. Lamb (Eds.), *Developmental psychology: An advanced textbook* (2nd ed.). Hillsdale, NJ: Erlbaum.

Elias, S. M. (2004). Means of assessing ordinal interactions in social psychology: The case of sexism in judgments of social power. *Journal of Applied Social Psychology, 34,* 1857–1877.

Elias, S. M., & Cropanzano, R. (2006). Gender discrimination may be worse than you think: Testing ordinal interactions in power research. *The Journal of General Psychology, 133*(2), 117–130.

El-Sarraj, E. R., Tawahina, A. A., & Heine, F. A. (1994). The Palestinians: An uprooted people. In A. J. Marsella, T. Bornemann, S. Ekblad, & J. Orley (Eds.), *Amidst peril and pain: The mental health and well-being of the world's refugees.* (pp. 141–152). Washington, DC: American Psychological Association.

Elwood, P. C., Pickering, J., & Gallacher, J. E. (2001). Cognitive function and blood rheology: Results from the Caerphilly cohort of older men. *Age and Ageing, 30,* 135–139.

Epley, N., & Dunning, D. (2000). Feeling "holier than thou": Are self-serving assessments produced by errors in self- or social predictions? *Journal of Personality and Social Psychology, 79,* 861–875.

Erikson, E. (1950). *Childhood and society.* New York: Norton.

Erikson, E. (1954). The dream specimen of psychoanalysis. *Journal of the American Psychoanalytic Association, 2,* 5–56.

Erikson, E. (1964). *Childhood and society* (2nd ed.). New York: Norton.

Erikson, E. (1968). *Identity, youth, and crisis.* New York: Norton.

Essandoh, P. K. (1995). Counseling issues with African college students in U.S. colleges and universities. *Counseling Psychologist, 23,* 348–360.

Eubanks-Carter, C., & Goldfried, M. (2006). The impact of client sexual orientation and gender on clinical judgments and diagnosis of borderline personality disorder. *Journal of Clinical Psychology, 62*(6), 751–770.

Fabrega, H. (1994). International system of diagnosis in psychiatry. *Journal of Nervous and Mental Disease, 182,* 356–363.

Fadiman, A. (1997). *The spirit catches you and you fall down: A Hmong child, her American doctors, and the collision of two cultures.* New York: Noonday.

Fairbairn, W. R. D. (1952). *Psychoanalytic studies of the personality.* New York: Routledge.

Falicov, C. J. (1995). Training to think culturally: A multidimensional comparative framework. *Family Process, 34,* 373–388.

Farver, J. M., Kim, Y. K., & Lee, Y. (1995). Cultural differences in Korean- and Anglo-American preschoolers' social interaction and play behaviors. *Child Development, 66,* 1088–1099.

Fassinger, R. E. (1998). Lesbian, gay, and bisexual identity and student development theory. In R. L. Sanlo (Ed.), *Working with lesbian, gay, bisexual, and transgender college students: A handbook for faculty and administrators* (pp. 13–22). Westport, CT: Greenwood.

Fassinger, R. E., & Miller, B. A. (1997). Validation of an inclusive model of homosexual identity formation in a sample of gay men. *Journal of Homosexuality, 32,* 53–78.

Fausto-Sterling, A. (2000). *Sexing the body.* New York: Basic Books.

Fazio, R. H. (1995). Attitudes as object-evaluation associations: Determinants, consequences, and correlates of attitude accessibility. In R. E. Petty & J. A. Kronsnick (Eds.), *Attitude strength: Antecedents and consequences* (pp. 247–283). Hillsdale, NJ: Erlbaum.

Fazio, R. H., Jackson, J. R., Dunton, B. C., & Williams, C. J. (1995). Variability in automatic activation as an unobtrusive measure of racial attitude: A bona fide pipeline? *Journal of Personality and Social Psychology, 69,* 1013–1027.

Fernandez, M. S. (1988). Issues in counseling Southeast Asian students. *Journal of Multicultural Counseling and Development, 16,* 157–166.

Ferrer, J., Romero, M., & Albareda, R. (2005). Integral transformative education [Electronic version]. *Journal of Transformation Education, 3*(4), 306–330.

Festinger, L. (1954). A theory of social comparison process. *Human Relations, 7,* 117–140.

Fine, M., & Asch, A. (Eds.). (1981). *Women with disabilities: Essays in psychology, culture and politics.* Philadelphia: Temple University Press.

Fine, M., & Asch, A. (2000). Disability beyond stigma: Social interaction, discrimination, and activism. In M. Adams, W. J. Blumenfeld, R. Castaneda, H. W. Hackman, M. L. Peters, & X. Zuniga (Eds.), *Readings for diversity and social justice* (pp. 330–339). New York: Routledge.

Fishbein, H. D. (1996). *Peer prejudice and discrimination: Evolutionary, cultural, and developmental dynamics.* Boulder, CO: Westview Press.

Fiske, S. T. (1998). Stereotyping, prejudice, and discrimination. In D. T. Gilbert, S. T. Fiske, & G. Lindzey (Eds.), *The handbook of social psychology* (4th ed., Vol. 2, pp. 357–411). New York: McGraw-Hill.

Fiske, S. T., & Neuberg, S. L. (1990). A continuum of impression formation, from category-based to individuating processes: Influences of information and motivation on attention and interpretation. In M. P. Zanna (Ed.), *Advances in experimental social psychology* (Vol. 23, pp. 1074). New York: Academic Press.

Flanagan, E., & Blashfield, R. (2005). Gender acts as a context for interpreting diagnostic criteria. *Journal of Clinical Psychology, 61*(12), 1485–1498.

Flaskerud, J. H., & Liu, P. Y. (1991). Effects of an Asian client-therapist language, ethnicity and gender match on utilization and outcome of therapy. *Community Mental Health Journal, 27,* 31–42.

Floyd, M. F., & Shinew, K. J. (1999). Convergence and divergence in leisure style among Whites and African Americans: Toward an interracial contact hypothesis. *Journal of Leisure Research, 31*(4), 359–384.

Flumerfelt, S., Ingram, I., Brockberg, K., & Smith, J. (2007). A study of higher education student achievement based on transformative and lifelong learning processes [Electronic version]. *Mentoring & Tutoring, 15*(1), 107–118.

Foa, E. B., & Rothbaum, B. O. (1998). *Treating the trauma of rape: Cognitive-behaviour therapy for PTSD.* New York: Guilford.

Foucault, M. (1990). *The use of pleasure: The history of sexuality.* New York: Vintage Books.

Frankenberg, R. (1993). *White women, race matters: The social construction of Whiteness.* Minneapolis: University of Minnesota Press.

Frederick, J., & Goddard, C. (2007). Exploring the relationship between poverty, childhood adversity and child abuse from the perspective of adulthood. *Child Abuse Review, 16,* 323–341.

Fredrickson, G. M. (1999). Models of American ethnic relations: A historical perspective. In D. A. Prentice & D. T. Miller (Eds.), *Cultural divides: Understanding and overcoming group conflict* (pp. 161–171). New York: Russell Sage Foundation.

Freedman, V. A., Martin, L. G., & Schoeni, R. F. (2004). Disability in America. *Population Bulletin, 59,* 3–33.

French, S. (2000). Equal opportunities—yes, please. In M. Adams, W. J. Blumenfeld, R. Castaneda, H. W. Hackman, M. L. Peters, & X. Zuniga (Eds.), *Readings for diversity and social justice* (pp. 364–366). New York: Routledge.

Freud, S. (1953). *The interpretation of dreams.* New York: Basic Books.

Freud, S. (1955). *The interpretation of dreams.* London: Hogarth Press.

Frieden, L., & Cole, J. A. (1985). Independence: The ultimate goal of rehabilitation for spinal cord-injured persons. *American Journal of Occupational Therapy, 39*(11), 734–739.

Friedlmeier, W., & Trommsdorff, G. (1999). Emotion regulation in early childhood: A cross-cultural comparison between German and Japanese toddlers. *Journal of Cross-Cultural Psychology, 30*(6), 684–711.

Frisby, C. (2004). Does race matter? Effects of idealized images on African American women. *Journal of Black Studies, 34*, 323–347.

Frith, K., Cheung, H., & Shaw, P. (2004). Race and beauty: A comparison of Asian and Western models in women's magazine advertisements. *Sex Roles, 50*, 53–61.

Fukuyama, M. A., & Ferguson, A. D. (2000). Lesbian, gay, and bisexual people of color: Understanding cultural complexity and managing multiple oppressions. In R. Perez, K. DeBord, & K. Bieschke (Eds.), *Handbook of counseling and psychotherapy with lesbian, gay, and bisexual clients* (pp. 81–106). Washington, DC: American Psychological Association.

Fukuyama, M. A., & Sevig, T. (1999). *Integrating spirituality into multicultural counseling.* Thousand Oaks, CA: Sage.

Fulton, A. S., Gorsuch, R. L., & Maynard, E. A. (1999). Religious orientation, antihomosexual sentiment, and fundamentalism among Christians. *Journal for the Scientific Study of Religion, 38*, 14–22.

Gaertner, S. L. (1973). Helping behavior and racial discrimination among liberals and conservatives. *Journal of Personality and Social Psychology, 25*, 335–341.

Gaertner, S. L., & Dovidio, J. F. (1977). The subtlety of White racism, arousal, and helping behavior. *Journal of Personality and Social Psychology, 35*, 691–707.

Gaertner, S. L., & Dovidio, J. F. (1986). The aversive form of racism. In J. F. Dovidio & S. L. Gaertner (Eds.), *Prejudice, discrimination, and racism* (pp. 61–89). Orlando, FL: Academic Press.

Gaertner, S. L., & McLaughlin, J. P. (1983). Racial stereotypes: Associations and ascriptions of positive and negative characteristics. *Social Psychology Quarterly, 46*, 23–30.

Gallagher, M. (2005). *Who makes the news: Global media monitoring project 2005.* London: WACC.

Gallor, S. M. (2005). Becoming visible: A balance of challenge and support. In J. M. Croteau, J. S. Lark, M. A. Lidderdale, & Y. B. Chung (Eds.), *Deconstructing heterosexism in the counseling professions: A narrative approach* (pp. 71–76). Thousand Oaks, CA: Sage.

Gara, M. A., Rosenberg, S., & Goldberg, L. (1992). DSM-III-R as a taxonomy: A cluster analysis of diagnosis and symptoms. *Journal of Nervous and Mental Disease, 180*, 11–19.

Garcia Coll, C., Crnic, K., Lamberty, G., & Wasik, B. (1996). An integrative model for the study of developmental competencies in minority children. *Child Development, 67*, 1891–1914.

Garofalo, R., Wolf, R. C., Wissow, L. S., Woods, E. R., & Goodman, E. (1999, May). Sexual orientation and risk of suicide attempts among a representative sample of youth. *Archives of Pediatrics and Adolescent Medicine, 153*(5), 487–493.

Garrett, J. T., & Garrett, M. W. (1994). The path of good medicine: Understanding and counseling Native American Indians. *Journal of Multicultural Counseling and Development, 11*, 134–144.

Gaskins, P. F. (1999). *What are you? Voices of mixed-race people.* New York: Henry Holt.

Gecas, V. (1992). Contexts of socialization. In M. Rosenberg & R. H. Turner (Eds.), *Social psychology: Sociological perspectives* (pp. 165–199). New Brunswick, NJ: Transaction.

Gee, G. C., Spencer, M. S., Chen, J., & Takeuchi, D. (2007). A nationwide study of discrimination and chronic health conditions among Asian Americans. *American Journal of Public Health, 97*(7), 1275–1282.

Geoghehan, T. (1997, June 3). Overeducated and underpaid. *The New York Times*, p. A25.

Gibbs, J. (1997). African-American suicide: A cultural paradox. *Suicide and Life Threatening Behavior, 27*(1), 68–79.

Gibran, K. (1978). *The prophet.* New York: Knopf. (Original work published 1923)

Gibson, M. S. (2001). Immigrant adaptation and patterns of acculturation. *Human Development, 44,* 19–23.

Gilbert, D. T. (1998). Ordinary personality. In D. T. Gilbert & S. T. Fiske (Eds.), *The handbook of social psychology* (4th ed., Vol. 2, pp. 89–150). New York: McGraw-Hill.

Gilbert, D. T., & Hixon, J. G. (1991). The trouble of thinking: Activation and application of stereotypic beliefs. *Journal of Personality and Social Psychology, 60,* 509–517.

Giles, J. W., & Heyman, G. D. (2005). Young children's beliefs about the relationship between gender and aggressive behavior. *Child Development, 76*(1), 107–121.

Gill, C. (1995). Comment. *The Disability Rag & ReSource, 16*(5), 5.

Gilligan, M. (1997). *Reflections on a national epidemic violence.* New York: Vintage Books.

Gladding, S. T. (2006). *Counseling: A comprehensive profession* (6th ed.). New York: Prentice Hall.

Gloria, A. M., & Peregoy, J. J. (1995). Counseling Latino alcohol and other substance users/abusers: Cultural considerations for counselors. *Journal of Substance Abuse Treatment, 13,* 1–8.

Goggin, G., & Newell, C. (2000). Crippling paralympics? Media, disability and Olympism. *Media International Australia, 97,* 71–83.

Good, G. E., & Beitman, B. D. (2006). *Counseling and psychotherapy essentials: Integrating theories, skills, and practices.* New York: Norton.

Goulet, J. A. (2006). The "berdache"/"two-spirit": A comparison of anthropological and native construction of gendered identities among the Northern Athapaskans. *Journal of Royal Anthropological Institute, 2*(4), 683.

Green, A. I. (2007). On the horns of a dilemma: Institutional dimensions of the sexual career in a sample of middle-class, urban, Black, gay men. *Journal of Black Studies, 37*(5), 753–774.

Greene, B. (1994). African American women. In L. Comas-Diaz & B. Greene (Eds.), *Women of color: Integrating ethnic and gender identities in psychotherapy* (pp. 10–29). New York: Guilford.

Greene, B. (2000). Beyond heterosexism and across the cultural divide: Developing an inclusive lesbian, gay, and bisexual psychology: A look to the future. In B. Greene (Ed.), *Education research, and practice in lesbian, gay, bisexual, and transgendered psychology* (pp. 1–45). Thousand Oaks, CA: Sage.

Greene, M. G., Adelman, R. D., Charon, R., & Friedmann, R. (1989). Concordance between physicians and their older and younger patients in primary care medical encounters. *Gerontologist, 29,* 808–813.

Greenwald, A. G., & Banaji, M. R. (1995). Implicit social cognition: Attitudes, self-esteem, and stereotypes. *Psychological Review, 102,* 4–27.

Greenwald, A. G., McGhee, D. E., & Schwartz, J. L. (1998). Measuring individual differences in implicit cognition: The implicit association test. *Journal of Personality and Social Psychology, 74,* 1464–1480.

Gross, L. (2005). The past and the future of gay, lesbian, bisexual, and transgender studies. *Journal of Communication, 58*(3), 508–528.

Groves, B., & Zuckerman, B. (1997). Interventions with parents and caregivers of children who are exposed to violence. In J. D. Osofsky (Ed.), *Children in a violent society* (pp. 183–201). New York: Guilford.

Guimond, S., Chatard, A., Martinot, D., Crisp, R., & Redersdoff, S. (2006). Social comparison, self-stereotyping, and gender differences in self-construals. *Journal of Personality and Social Psychology, 90*(2), 221–242.

Gunn Allen, P. (1994). Who is your mother? Red roots of White feminism. In R. Takaki (Ed.), *From different shores: Perspectives on race and ethnicity in America* (2nd ed., pp. 192–198). New York: Oxford University Press.

Guthrie, R. V. (1998). *Even the rat was white: A historical view of psychology* (2nd ed.). Boston: Allyn & Bacon.

Gutierrez-Jones, C. (1998). Injury by design. *Cultural Critique, 40,* 73–102.

Hacker, A. (1997). *Money: Who has how much and why.* New York: Scribner.

Hagestad, G. O., & Uhlenberg, P. (2005). The social separation of old and young: A root of ageism. *Journal of Social Issues, 61*(2), 343–360.

Halprin, D. (2003). *The expressive body in life, art and therapy: Working with movement, metaphor and meaning.* Philadelphia: Jessica Kingsley.

Hamilton, D. L., & Sherman, J. W. (1994). Stereotypes. In R. S. Wyer & T. K. Srull (Eds.), *Handbook of social cognition* (Vol. 2, pp. 1–68). Hillsdale, NJ: Erlbaum.

Hardiman, R. (1982). White identity development: A process oriented model for describing the racial consciousness of White Americans. *Dissertation Abstracts International, 43,* 104A. (University Microfilms No. 82–10330)

Harper, F. D., & McFadden, J. (Eds.). (2003). *Culture and counseling: New approaches.* Boston: Allyn & Bacon.

Hart, S. N., Binggeli, M. J., & Brassard, M. R. (1998). Evidence for the effects of psychological maltreatment. *Journal of Emotional Abuse, 1,* 27–58.

Harvey, M. R., Liang, B., Harney, P. A., Koenen, K., Tumamal-Narra, P., & Lebowitz, L. (2003). A multidimensional approach to the assessment of trauma impact, recovery and resilience: Initial psychometric findings. *Journal of Aggression, Maltreatment & Trauma, 6*(2), 87–109.

Harvey, M. R., Mishler, E. G., Koenen, K. C., & Harney, P. A. (2000). In the aftermath of sexual abuse: Making and remaking meaning in narratives of trauma and recovery. *Narrative Inquiry, 19*(2), 291–311.

Haubegger, C. (2000). I'm not fat, I'm Latina. In M. Adams, W. J. Blumenfeld, R. Castaneda, H. W. Hackman, M. L. Peters, & X. Zuniga (Eds.), *Readings for diversity and social justice* (pp. 242–243). New York: Routledge.

Hays, D. G. (2008). Assessing multicultural competence in counselor trainees: A review of instrumentation and future directions. *Journal of Counseling & Development, 86,* 95–101.

Hays, P. A. (2001). *Addressing complexities in practice: A framework for clinicians and counselors.* Washington, DC: American Psychological Association.

Heath, C. (1999). On the social psychology of agency relationships: Lay theories of motivation overemphasize extrinsic incentives. *Organizational Behavior and Human Decision Processes, 78,* 25–62.

Hehir, T. (2002). Eliminating ableism in education. *Harvard Educational Review, 72,* 1–32.

Heintz, J. S., & Folbre, N. (2000). Who owns how much. In M. Adams, W. J. Blumenfeld, R. Castaneda, H. W. Hackman, M. L. Peters, & X. Zuniga (Eds.), *Readings for diversity and social justice* (pp. 391–396). New York: Routledge.

Helms, J. E. (1984). Toward a theoretical explanation of the effects of race on counseling: A Black and White model. *Counseling Psychologist, 12,* 153–165.

Helms, J. E. (Ed.). (1990). *Black and White racial identity: Theory, research, and practice.* Westport, CT: Greenwood.

Helms, J. E. (1994a). The conceptualization of racial identity and other "racial" constructs. In E. J. Trickett, R. J. Watts, & D. Birman (Eds.), *Human diversity: Perspectives on people in context* (pp. 285–311). San Francisco: Jossey-Bass.

Helms, J. E. (1994b). How multiculturalism obscures racial factors in the psychotherapy process. *Journal of Counseling Psychology, 41,* 162–165.

Helms, J. E. (1995). An update of Helms's White and people of color racial identity models. In J. Ponterotto, M. Casas, L. Suzuki, & C. Alexander (Eds.), *Handbook of multicultural counseling* (pp. 181–198). Thousand Oaks, CA: Sage.

Helms, J. E., & Carter, R. T. (1991). Relationships of White and Black racial identity attitudes and demographic similarity to counselor preferences. *Journal of Counseling Psychology, 38,* 446–457.

Helms, J. E., & Cook, D. A. (1999). *Using race and culture in counseling and psychotherapy.* Boston: Allyn & Bacon.

Helms, J. E., Jernigan, M., & Mascher, J. (2005). The meaning of race in psychology and how to change it: A methodological perspective. *American Psychologist, 60*(1), 27–36.

Helms, J. E., Malone, L. T. S., Henze, K., Satiani, A., Perry, J., & Warren, A. (2003). First annual Diversity Challenge: "How to survive teaching courses on race and culture." *Journal of Multicultural Counseling and Development, 31,* 3–11.

Henderson, G., & Bryan, W. V. (1984). *Psychosocial aspects of disability.* Springfield, IL: Charles C. Thomas.

Henderson-King, E. L., & Nisbett, R. E. (1996). Anti-Black prejudice as a function of exposure to the negative behavior of a single Black person. *Journal of Personality and Social Psychology, 71,* 654–664.

Hendry, L. B., Kloep, M., & Olsson, S. (1998). Youth, lifestyles and society: Class issue? *Childhood: A Global Journal of Child Research, 5*(2), 133–150.

Heppner, P. P., Leong, F. T. L., & Chiao, H. (2008). The growing internationalization of counseling psychology. In S. D. Brown & R. W. Lent (Eds.), *Handbook of counseling psychology* (4th ed., pp. 68–85). New York: Wiley.

Herek, G. M. (2000). Internalized homophobia among gay men, lesbians, and bisexuals. In M. Adams, W. J. Blumenfeld, R. Castaneda, H. W. Hackman, M. L. Peters, & X. Zuniga (Eds.), *Readings for diversity and social justice* (pp. 281–283). New York: Routledge.

Herek, G. M. (2004). Beyond "homophobia": Thinking about sexual prejudice and stigma in the twenty-first century. *Sexuality Research & Social Policy, 1*(2), 2–24.

Herman, M. (2004). Forced to choose: Some determinants of racial identification in multiracial adolescents. *Child Development, 75*(3), 730–748.

Herrnstein, R., & Murray, C. (1994). *The bell curve: Intelligence and class structure in American life:* New York: Free Press.

Hewstone, M., Rubin, M., & Willis, H. (2002). Intergroup bias. *Annual Review of Psychology, 53,* 575–604.

Hickson, J., & Phelps, A. (1997). Women's spirituality: A proposed practice model. *Journal of Family Social Work, 2,* 43–57.

Hill, R. J. (1992). Attitudes and behaviors. In M. Rosenberg & R. H. Turner (Eds.), *Social psychology: Sociological perspectives* (pp. 347–377). New Brunswick, NJ: Transaction.

Hinnant, J. B., & O'Brien, M. (2007). Cognitive and emotional control and perspective taking and their relations to empathy in 5-year-old children. *The Journal of Genetic Psychology, 168*(3), 301–322.

Hirsch, R. D., & Vollhardt, B. R. (2002). Elder maltreatment. In R. Jacoby & C. Oppenheimer (Eds.), *Handbook of social cognition* (Vol. 2, pp. 1–68). New York: Oxford University Press.

Hobson, J. A. (1999). *Dreaming as delirium: How the brain goes out of its mind.* Cambridge, MA: MIT Press.

Hodson, G., Dovidio, J. F., & Gaertner, S. L. (2002). Processes in racial discrimination: Differential weighting of conflicting information. *Personality and Social Psychology Bulletin, 28,* 460–471.

Holcomb-McCoy, C. C., & Myers, J. E. (1999). Multicultural competence and counselor training: A national survey. *Journal of Counseling & Development, 77,* 294–302.

hooks, b. (2000). Homophobia in Black communities. In M. Adams, W. J. Blumenfeld, R. Castaneda, H. W. Hackman, M. L. Peters, & X. Zuniga (Eds.), *Readings for diversity and social justice* (pp. 283–287). New York: Routledge.

Hornsey, M. J., & Hogg, M. A. (2000). Assimilation and diversity: An integrative model of subgroup relations. *Personality and Social Psychology Review, 4,* 143–156.

Hovland, R., McMahan, C., Lee, G., Hwang, J., & Kim, J. (2005). Gender role portrayals in American and Korean advertisements. *Sex Roles, 53,* 887–899.

Hu, S. M. (1988). The Chinese family: Continuity and change. In B. Birns & D. F. Hay (Eds.), *The different faces of motherhood* (pp. 119–135). New York: Plenum.

Hudley, C., Britschi, B., Wakefield, W., Smith, T., DeMorat, M., & Cho, S. (1998). An attribution retraining program to reduce aggression in elementary school students. *Psychology in the Schools, 35,* 271–282.

Hudley, C., & Novac, A. (2007). Environmental influences, the developing brain, and aggressive behavior. *Theory Into Practice, 46*(2), 121–129.

Huesmann, L. R. (1998). The role of social information processing and cognitive schema in the acquisition and maintenance of habitual aggressive behavior. In R. Gree & E. Donnerstein (Eds.), *Human aggression: Theories, research, and implications for social policy* (pp. 73–109). San Diego, CA: Academic Press.

Huesmann, L. R., Lagerspetz, K., & Eron, L. D. (1984). Intervening variables in the TV violence-aggression relations: Evidence from two countries. *Developmental Psychology, 20,* 746–775.

Hunsberger, B., & Jackson, L. M. (2005). Religion, meaning, and prejudice. *Journal of Social Issues, 61*(4), 807–826.

Hunt, B., Matthews, C., Milsom, A., & Lammel, J. A. (2006). Lesbians with physical disabilities: A qualitative study of their experiences with counseling. *Journal of Counseling & Development, 84,* 163–173.

Huston, A. C., Watkins, B. A., & Kunkel, D. (1989). Public policy and children's television. *American Psychologists, 44,* 424–433.

Inhelder, B., & Piaget, J. (1958). *The growth of logical thinking: From childhood to adolescence.* New York: Basic Books.

Interstate School Leaders Licensure Consortium. (1996). *ISLLC standards for school leaders.* Available at http://www.ccsso.org/content/pdfs/isllcstd.pdf

Ivey, A. E., D'Andrea, M., Ivery, M. B., & Simek-Morgan, L. (Eds.). (2007). *Theories of counseling and psychotherapy: A multicultural perspective.* Boston: Pearson Education.

Ivey, D. C., Wieling, E., & Harris, S. M. (2000). Save the young—the elderly have lived their lives: Ageism in marriage and family therapy. *Family Process, 39*(2), 163–175.

Jackson, J. C. (2001). Women middle managers' perception of the glass ceiling. *Women in Management Review, 16*(1), 30–41.

Jackson, L. C. (1999). Ethnocultural resistance to multicultural training: Students and faculty. *Cultural Diversity and Ethnic Minority Psychology, 5,* 27–36.

Jackson, M., Barth, J. M., Powell, N., & Lochman, J. E. (2006). Classroom contextual effects of race on children's peer nominations. *Child Development, 77,* 1325–1337.

Jacobs, C. (2006). Transformation and kaleidoscope memories. *Smith College Studies in Social Work, 76*(4), 113–123.

Jacobs, D. H. (1994). Environmental failure—oppression is the only cause of psychopathology. *Journal of Mind and Behavior, 15,* 1–18.

Jacobs, J. H. (1977). Black/White interracial families: Marital process and identity development in young children. *Dissertation Abstracts International, 38,* 10-B. (University Microfilms No. 78–31730)

Jacobs, J. H. (1992). Identity development in biracial children. In M. P. Root (Ed.), *Racially mixed people in America* (pp. 190–206). Thousand Oaks, CA: Sage.

Jahoda, G. (1999). *Images of savages: Ancient roots of modern prejudice in Western culture.* New York: Routledge.

James, J., & Haley, W. (1995). Age and health bias in practicing clinical psychologists. *Psychology and Aging, 10*(4), 610–616.

Jay, N. (1981). Gender and dichotomy. *Feminist Studies, 7,* 38–56.

Jenkins, E. J., & Bell, C. C. (1997). Exposure and response to community violence among children and adolescents. In J. D. Osofsky (Ed.), *Children in a violent society.* New York: Guilford.

Jensen, A. R. (1969). How much can we boost IQ and scholastic achievement? *Harvard Educational Review, 39,* 1–123.

Johnson, A. (2006). *Privilege, power and difference.* New York: McGraw-Hill.

Johnson, L., & Moxon, E. (1998). In whose service? Technology, care and disabled people: The case for a disability politics perspective. *Disability and Society, 13,* 241–258.

Jones, J. S., Veenstra, T. R., Seamon, J. P., & Krohmer, J. (1997). Elder mistreatment: National survey of emergency physicians. *Annals of Emergency Medicine, 30,* 473–479.

Jons, N. A., & Smith, A. S. (2001). The two or more races population: 2000: Census 2000 brief. Washington, DC: U.S. Census Bureau. Retrieved August 18, 2003, from http://www.census.gov/prod/2001pubs/c2kbr01–6.pdf

Juergensmeyer, M. (2000). *Terror in the mind of God: The global rise of religious violence.* Berkeley: University of California Press.

Jung, C. G. (1965). *Memories, dreams, reflections.* New York: Vantage Books.

Jung, C. G. (Ed.). (1985). *The practice of psychotherapy.* New York: First Princeton.

Kabat-Zinn, J. (1999). Indra's net at work: The mainstreaming of dharma practice in society. In G. Warson, S. Batchelor, & G. Claxton (Eds.), *The psychology of awakening: Buddhism, science and our day-to-day lives* (pp. 225–249). London: Rider.

Kapleau, R. P. (1980). *The three pillars of Zen: Teaching, practice, and enlightenment.* New York: Doubleday.

Karp, T. (2005). An action theory of transformative process [Electronic version]. *Journal of Change Management, 5*(2), 153–175.

Kaschak, E. (1992). *Engendered lives.* Boston: Basic Books.

Kast, V. (1993). *Imagination as space of freedom: Dialogue between the ego and the unconscious.* New York: Fromm International.

Katz-Gerro, T. (2006). Comparative evidence of inequality in cultural preferences: Gender, class, and family status. *Sociological Spectrum, 26,* 63–83.

Kenny, M., & Gallagher, L. A. (2000). Service-learning as a vehicle in training psychologists for revised professional roles. In F. T. Sherman & W. R. Torbert (Eds.), *Transforming social inquiry, transforming social action: New paradigms for crossing the theory/practice/practice divide in universities and communities: Volume 18. Outreach scholarship series* (pp. 189–205). Boston: Kluwer Academic.

Kidd, J. D., & Witten, T. M. (2008). Transgender and transsexual identities: The next strange fruit—hate crimes, violence and genocide against the global trans-communities. *Journal of Hate Studies, 6*(31), 31–63.

Kilborn, P. T. (2001, April 15). Doing without the extras amid a flagging economy. *The New York Times*, p. A13.

Killen, M. (2007). Children's social and moral reasoning about exclusion. *Current Directions in Psychological Science, 16*(1), 32–36.

Killen, M., Richardson, C., Kelly, M. C., Crystal, D., & Ruck, M. (2006). *European-American students' evaluations of interracial social exchanges in relation to the ethnic diversity of school environments*. Paper presented at the annual convention of the Association for Psychological Science, New York City.

Kim-ju, G. M., & Liem, R. (2003). Ethnic self-awareness as a function of ethnic group status, group composition, and ethnic identity orientation. *Cultural Diversity and Ethnic Minority Psychology, 9*, 289–302.

Kimmel, M. S. (2000). Masculinity as homophobia: Fear, shame, and silence in the construction of gender identity. In M. Adams, W. J. Blumenfeld, R. Castaneda, H. W. Hackman, M. L. Peters, & X. Zuniga (Eds.), *Readings for diversity and social justice* (pp. 213–219). New York: Routledge.

Kindlon, D., & Thompson, M. (2000). *Raising Cain: Protecting the emotional life of boys*. New York: Ballantine.

Kinney, A. (2005, September 1). "Looting" or "finding"? *Salon*. Retrieved February 19, 2009, from http://dir.salon.com/story/news/feature/2005/09/01/photo_controversy/index.html

Knobloch, S., Callison, C., Chen, L., Fritzsche, A., & Zillmann, D. (2005). Children's sex-stereotyped self-socialization through selective exposure to entertainment: Cross-cultural experiments in Germany, China, and the United States. *Journal of Communication, 55*(1), 122–138.

Knowles, E. D., & Peng, K. (2005). White selves: Conceptualizing and measuring a dominant-group identity. *Journal of Personality and Social Psychology, 89*(2), 223–241.

Koh, F. M. (1993). *Adopted from Asia: How it feels to grow up in America*. Minneapolis, MN: East West Press.

Kohlberg, L. (1987). The development of moral judgment and moral action. In L. Kohlberg (Ed.), *Child psychology and childhood education: A cognitive-developmental view* (pp. 259–328). New York: Longman.

Kohut, H. (1971). *The analysis of the self*. New York: International Universities Press.

Kovan, J. T., & Dirkx, J. M. (2003). "Being called awake": The role of transformative learning in the lives of environmental activists. *Adult Education Quarterly, 53*(2), 99–115.

Kovel, J. (1970). *White racism: A psychohistory*. New York: Pantheon.

Kowalski, K. (2003). The emergence of ethnic and racial attitudes in preschool-aged children. *Journal of Social Psychology, 143*, 677–690.

Kowalski, K., & Kanitkar, K. (2003, April). *Ethnicity and gender in the kindergarten classroom: A naturalistic study*. Poster presented at the meeting of the Society for Research in Child Development, Tampa, FL.

Kozaric-Korvacic, D., Folnegovic-Smale, V., Skringjaric, J., Szajnberg, N., & Marusic, A. (1995). Rape, torture and traumatization of Bosnian and Croatian women: Psychological sequelae. *American Journal of Ortho-Psychiatry, 65*, 428–433.

Kruger, J., & Gilovich, T. (1999). "Naïve cynicism" in everyday theories of responsibility assessment: On biased assumptions of bias. *Journal of Personality and Social Psychology, 76*, 743–753.

Landrine, H. (1989). The politics of personality disorder. *Psychology of Women Quarterly, 13*, 325–340.

Langston, D. (2000). Tired of playing monopoly? In M. Adams, W. J. Blumenfeld, R. Castaneda, H. W. Hackman, M. L. Peters, & X. Zuniga (Eds.), *Readings for diversity and social justice* (pp. 397–400). New York: Routledge.

Laythe, B., Finkel, D. G., Bringler, R. B., & Kirkpatrick, L. A. (2002). Religious fundamentalism as a predictor of prejudice: A two-component model. *Journal for the Scientific Study of Religion, 41,* 623–635.

Laythe, B., Finkel, D. G., & Kirkpatrick, L. A. (2001). Predicting prejudice from religious fundamentalism and right-wing authoritarianism: A multiple-regression approach. *Journal for the Scientific Study of Religion, 40,* 1–10.

Lazarus, R. S. (1982). Thoughts on the relations between emotion and cognition. *American Psychologist, 37,* 1019–1024.

Leach, M. M., & Sullivan, A. (2001). The intersection of race, class, and gender on diagnosis. In D. B. Pope-Davis & J. L. K. Coleman (Eds.), *The intersection of race, class, and gender in multicultural counseling* (pp. 353–383). Thousand Oaks, CA: Sage.

Leak, G. K. (2006). An empirical assessment of the relationship between social interest and spirituality. *The Journal of Individual Psychology, 62*(1), 59–69.

Leaper, C. (Ed.). (1994). *Childhood gender segregation: Causes and consequences* (New Directions for Child Development No. 65). San Francisco: Jossey-Bass.

Lee, S. J. (1997). The road to college: Hmong American women's pursuit of higher education. *Harvard Educational Review, 67,* 803–831.

Lee, S. J. (2006). Additional complexities: Social class, ethnicity, generation, and gender in Asian American student experiences. *Race Ethnicity and Education, 9*(1), 17–28.

Levy, G. D., Sadovsky, A. L., & Troseth, G. L. (2000). Aspects of young children's perceptions of gender-typed occupations. *Sex Roles, 42,* 993–1006.

Lewis-Fernandez, R., & Kleinman, A. (1994). Culture, personality, and psychopathology. *Journal of Abnormal Psychology, 103*(1), 67–71.

Lewthwaite, M. (1996). A study of international students' perspectives on cross-cultural adaptations. *International Journal for the Advancement of Counseling, 19,* 167–185.

Liben, L. S., Bigler, R. S., & Krogh, H. R. (2001). Pink and blue collar jobs: Children's judgment of job status and job aspirations in relation to sex of worker. *Journal of Experimental Child Psychology, 79,* 346–363.

Liben, L. S., & Signorella, M. L. (1993). Gender-schematic processing in children: The role of initial interpretations of stimuli. *Developmental Psychology, 29,* 141–149.

Lim-Hing, S. (2000). Dragon ladies, snow queens, and Asian-American dykes: Reflections on race and sexuality. In M. Adams, W. J. Blumenfeld, R. Castaneda, H. W. Hackman, M. L. Peters, & X. Zuniga (Eds.), *Readings for diversity and social justice* (pp. 296–299). New York: Routledge.

Linton, S. (1998). *Claiming disability: Knowledge and identity.* New York: New York University Press.

Linville, P. W., Fischer, G. W., & Salovey, P. (1989). Perceived distributions of the characteristics of in-group and out-group members: Empirical evidence and a computer simulation. *Journal of Personality and Social Psychology, 57,* 165–188.

Lipton, A. A., & Simon, F. S. (1985). Psychiatric diagnosis in a state hospital: Manhattan State revisited. *Hospital and Community Psychiatry, 36,* 368–373.

Liu, W. M. (2001). Expanding our understanding of multiculturalism: Developing a social class worldview model. In D. B. Pope-Davis & H. L. K. Coleman (Eds.), *The intersection of race, class, and gender in multicultural counseling* (pp. 127–170). Thousand Oaks, CA: Sage.

Liu, W. M., & Pope-Davis, D. B. (2003). Understanding classism to effect personal change. In T. B. Smith (Ed.), *Practicing multiculturalism: Internalizing and affirming diversity in counseling and psychology* (pp. 294–310). New York: Allyn & Bacon.

Liu, W. M., Soleck, G., Hopps, J., Dunston, K., & Pickett, T., Jr. (2004). A new framework to understand social class in counseling: The social class worldview model and modern classism theory. *Journal of Multicultural Counseling and Development, 32,* 95–122.

Livingston, R. W., & Brewer, M. B. (2002). What are we really priming? Cue-based versus category-based processing of facial stimuli. *Journal of Personality and Social Psychology, 82,* 5–18.

Loevinger, J. (1976). *Ego development.* San Francisco: Jossey-Bass.

Loevinger, J. (1983). On ego development and the structure of personality. *Developmental Review, 3,* 339–350.

Longmore, P. K. (1995). The second phase: From disability rights to disability culture. *Disability Rag & Resource, 16*(5), 4–11.

Lorber, J., & Moore, L. J. (2002). *Gender and the social construction of illness* (2nd ed.). Walnut Creek, CA: Altamira Press.

Lucksted, A. (2004). Lesbian, gay, bisexual, and transgender people receive services in the public mental health system: Raising issues. *Journal of Gay & Lesbian Psychotherapy, 8*(3/4), 25–42.

Luschen, K. V., & Bogad, L. (2003). Bodies that matter: Transgenderism, innocence and the politics of "unprofessional" pedagogy. *Sex Education, 3*(2), 145–155.

Maccoby, E. E. (1998). *The two sexes: Growing up apart, coming together.* Cambridge, MA: Belknap Press.

Maccoby, E. E. (2002). Gender and group process: A developmental perspective. *Current Directions in Psychological Science, 11,* 54–58.

MacPhee, D., Kreutzer, J. C., & Fritz, J. J. (1994). Infusing a diversity perspective into human development courses. *Child Development, 65,* 699–715.

Macrae, C. N., Bodenhausen, G. V., Milne, A. B., & Jetten, J. (1994). Out of mind but back in sight: Stereotypes on the rebound. *Journal of Personality and Social Psychology, 67,* 808–817.

Macrae, C. N., Hewstone, M., & Griffiths, R. J. (1993). Processing load and memory for stereotype-based information. *European Journal of Social Psychology, 23,* 77–87.

Maddox, K. B. (2004). Perspectives on racial phenotypicality bias. *Personality and Social Psychology Review, 8*(4), 383–401.

Mantsios, G. (2004). Class in America—2003. In P. S. Rothenberg (Ed.), *Race, class, and gender in the United States* (6th ed., pp. 193–207). New York: Worth.

Marable, M. (2000). *How capitalism underdeveloped Black America.* Cambridge, MA: South End Press.

Marans, S., & Adelman, A. (1997). Experiencing violence in a developmental context. In J. D. Osofsky (Ed.), *Children in a violent society* (pp. 202–222). New York: Guilford.

Marcia, J. (1966). Development and validation of ego-identity. *Journal of Personality and Social Psychology, 3,* 551–558.

Marcia, J. (1980). Identity in adolescence. In J. Adelson (Ed.), *Handbook of adolescent psychology* (pp. 159–187). New York: Wiley.

Marin, G., & Gamba, R. J. (1996). A new measurement of acculturation for Hispanics: The Bidimensional Acculturation Scale for Hispanics (BAS). *Hispanic Journal of Behavioral Sciences, 18*(3), 297–316.

Markus, H. (1977). Self-schemata and processing information about the self. *Journal of Personality and Social Psychology, 35,* 63–78.

Markus, H., Kitayama, S., & Heiman, R. J. (1996). Culture and basic psychological principles. In E. T. Higgins & A. W. Kruglanski (Eds.), *Social psychology handbook of basic principles* (pp. 857–913). New York: Guilford.

Markus, H. R., Steele, C. M., & Steele, D. M. (2000). Colorblindness as a barrier to inclusion: Assimilation and non-immigrant minorities. *Daedalus, 129,* 233–259.

Marotta, T. (1981). *The politics of homosexuality.* Boston: Houghton Mifflin.

Mayer, K. U., & Schopflin, U. (1989). The state and the life course. *Annual Review of Sociology, 15,* 187–209.

McDonald, K. E., Keys, C. B., & Balcazar, F. E. (2007). Disability, race/ethnicity and gender: Themes of cultural oppression, acts of individual resistance. *American Journal of Community Psychology, 39,* 145–161.

McGoldrick, M., Giordiano, J., & Pearce, J. (1996). *Ethnicity and family therapy.* New York: Guilford.

McHale, S. M., Crouter, A. C., Kim, J., Burton, L. M., Davis, K. D., Dotterer, A. M., et al. (2006). Mothers' and fathers' racial socialization in African American families: Implications for youth. *Child Development, 77,* 1387–1402.

McIntosh, P. (1989, July/August). White privilege: Unpacking the invisible knapsack. *Peace and Freedom,* 10–12.

McIntyre, A. (1997). *Making meaning of Whiteness: Exploring racial identity with White teachers.* Albany: State University of New York.

McKown, C., & Weinstein, R. S. (2004). The development and consequences of stereotype consciousness in middle childhood. *Child Development, 74,* 498–515.

McLoyd, V. (2006). The legacy of child development's 1990 special issue on minority children: An editorial retrospective. *Child Development, 77,* 1142–1148.

Meador, B. (2004). Light the seven fires—seize the seven desires. In T. Singer & S. L. Kimbles, (Eds.), *The cultural complex* (pp. 171–195). New York: Brunner-Routledge.

Mennis, B. (2000). Jewish and working class. In M. Adams, W. J. Blumenfeld, R. Castaneda, H. W. Hackman, M. L. Peters, & X. Zuniga (Eds.), *Readings for diversity and social justice* (pp. 188–190). New York: Routledge.

Merikel, P. M., Smilek, D., & Eastwood, J. D. (2001). Perception without awareness: Perspectives from cognitive psychology. *Cognition, 79,* 115–134.

Metzinger, T. (Ed.). (2003). *Being no one: The self-model theory of subjectivity.* Cambridge, MA: MIT Press.

Mezirow, J. (2000a). Learning to think like an adult. In J. Mezirow & Associates (Ed.), *Learning as transformation: Critical perspectives on a theory in progress* (pp. 3–33). San Francisco: Jossey-Bass.

Mezirow, J. (2000b). Theory building and the search for the common ground. In J. Mezirow & Associates (Ed.), *Learning as transformation: Critical perspectives on a theory in progress* (pp. 285–328). San Francisco: Jossey-Bass.

Middleton, R. A., Stadler, H. A., Simpson, C., Guo, Y., Brown, M. J., Crow, G., et al. (2005). Mental health practitioners: The relationship between White racial identity attitudes and self-reported multicultural counseling competencies. *Journal of Counseling & Development, 33,* 444–456.

Miike, Y. (2003). Toward an alternative metatheory of human communication: An Asiacentric vision. *Intercultural Communication Studies, 12*(4), 39–63.

Miike, Y. (2007). An Asiacentric reflection on Eurocentric bias in communication theory. *Communication Monographs, 74*(2), 272–278.

Miller, S., & Miller, P. A. (1997). *Core communication: Skills and processes.* Evergreen, CO: Interpersonal Communication Programs.

Mio, J. S., & Awakuni, G. I. (2000). *Resistance to multiculturalism: Issues and interventions.* Philadelphia: Brunner/Mazel.

Mirowsky, J. (1990). Subjective boundaries and combinations in psychiatric diagnosis. *Journal of Mind and Behavior, 11,* 407–424.

Mobley, M. (1998). Lesbian, gay, and bisexual issues in counseling psychology training: Acceptance in the millennium. *The Counseling Psychologist, 26,* 784–794.

Monette, P. (with a foreword by Harrison, K.). (2004). *Becoming a man: Half a life story.* New York: Perennial Classics.

Moore, M. (2005). The transtheoretical model of the stages of change and the phases of transformative learning [Electronic version]. *Journal of Transformative Education, 6*(3), 394–415.

Morrow, S. L. (2003). Can the master's tools ever dismantle the master's house? Answering silences with alternative paradigms and silences. *The Counseling Psychologist, 31*(1), 70–99.

Mulvey, A., Terenzio, M., Hill, J., Bond, M. S., Huygens, I., Hamerton, H. R., et al. (2000). Stories of relative privilege: Power and social change in feminist community psychology. *American Journal of Community Psychology, 28,* 883–911.

Murray, S. O., & Roscoe, W. (1997). *Islamic homosexualities: Culture, history, and literature.* New York: New York University Press.

Nash, P. T. (1992). Multicultural identity and the death of stereotypes. In M. P. P. Root (Ed.), *Racially mixed people in America* (pp. 330–332). Thousand Oaks, CA: Sage.

National Association of Social Workers. (1999). *Code of ethics* (Rev. ed.). Available at http://www.socialworkers.org/pubs/code/default.asp

Nelson, T. D. (Ed.). (2002a). *Ageism: Stereotyping and prejudice against older adults.* Cambridge, MA: MIT Press.

Nelson, T. D. (2002b). *The psychology of prejudice.* New York: Allyn & Bacon.

Nelson, T. D. (2005). Ageism: Prejudice against our feared future self. *Journal of Social Issues, 61*(2), 207–221.

Nesdale, D., & Brown, K. (2004). Children's attitudes towards an atypical member of an ethnic in-group. *International Journal of Behavioral Development, 28,* 328–335.

Nesdale, D., Durkin, K., Maass, A., & Griffiths, J. (2005a). Group norms, threat, and children's racial prejudice. *Child Development, 76*(3), 652–663.

Nesdale, D., Durkin, K., Maass, A., & Griffiths, J. (2005b). Threat, group identification and children's ethnic prejudice. *Social Development, 14,* 189–205.

Nguyen, H. H., Messe, L. A., & Stollak, G. E. (1999). Toward a more complex understanding of acculturation and adjustment: Cultural involvement and psychological functioning in Vietnamese youth. *Journal of Cross-Cultural Psychology, 30*(1), 5–31.

Novac, A. (2003). Trauma: Global and social considerations. *The Psychiatric Times, 20,* 33.

Nugent, J. K. (1994). Cross-cultural studies of child development: Implications for clinicians. *Zero to Three, 15*(2), 1–8.

O'Connor, A. (2001). *Poverty knowledge: Social science, social policy, and the poor in twentieth-century U.S. history.* Princeton, NJ: Princeton University Press.

Ogbu, J. U. (1988). Class stratification, racial stratification, and schooling. In L. Weis (Ed.), *Class, race, and gender in American education* (pp. 163–182). Albany: State University of New York.

Oldmeadow, J., & Fiske, S. (2007). System-justifying ideologies moderate status-competence stereotypes: Roles for belief in a just world and social dominance orientation. *European Journal of Social Psychology, 37,* 1135–1148.

Olkin, R., & Pledger, C. (2003). Can disability studies and psychology join hands? *American Psychologist, 58,* 296–304.

Olsen, A. (1998). *BodyStories: A guide to experiential anatomy.* New York: Barrytown.

Omi, M. A. (2001). The changing meaning of race. In N. J. Smelser, W. J. Wilson, & F. Mitchell (Eds.), *America, becoming: Racial trends and their consequences* (Vol. 1, pp. 243–263). Washington, DC: National Academies Press.

Onorato, R. S., & Turner, J. C. (2001). The "I," the "me," and the "us": The psychological group and self-concept maintenance and change. In C. Seidkides & M. B. Brewer (Eds.), *Individual self, relational self, collective self* (pp. 147–170). Philadelphia: Psychology Press.

Onorato, R. S., & Turner, J. C. (2004). Fluidity in the self-concept: The shift from personal to social identity. *European Journal of Social Psychology, 34,* 257–278.

Oropeza, B. A., Fitzgibbon, M., & Baron, A., Jr. (1991). Managing mental health crises of foreign college students. *Journal of Counseling and Development, 69,* 280–284.

Ortega, S., Beauchemin, A., & Kaniskan, R. B. (2008). Building resiliency in families with young children exposed to violence: The Safe Start Initiative pilot study. *Best Practices in Mental Health, 4*(1), 48–64.

O'Sullivan, E. V., Morrell, A., & O'Connor, M. A. (Eds.). (2002). *Expanding the boundaries of transformative learning.* New York: Palgrave.

Ottavi, T., Pope-Davis, D., & Dings, J. (1994). Relationship between White racial identity attitudes and self-reported multicultural counseling competencies. *Journal of Counseling Psychology, 41,* 149–154.

Overboe, J. (1999). Difference in itself: Validating disabled people's lived experience. *Body and Society, 5,* 17–29.

Oyserman, D., & Markus, H. R. (1993). The sociocultural self. In J. Suls (Ed.), *Psychological perspectives on the self: The self in social perspective* (Vol. 4, pp. 1216–1232). Hillsdale, NJ: Erlbaum.

Pack-Brown, S. P. (1999). Racism and White counselor training: Influence of White racial identity theory and research. *Journal of Counseling & Development, 77,* 87–92.

Padulla, A. M., & Perez, W. (2003). Acculturation, social identity, and social cognition: A new perspective. *Hispanic Journal of Behavioral Sciences, 25,* 35–55.

Pahl, K., & Way, N. (2006). Longitudinal trajectories of ethnic identity among urban low-income Black and Latino adolescents. *Child Development, 77,* 1403–1415.

Paniagua, F. A. (2005). *Assessing and treating culturally diverse clients: A practical guide* (3rd ed.). Thousand Oaks, CA: Sage.

Park, B., & Judd, C. M. (2005). Rethinking the link between categorization and prejudice within the social cognition perspective. *Personality and Social Psychology Review, 9*(2), 108–130.

Park, B., & Rothbart, M. (1982). Perception of out-group homogeneity and levels of social categorization: Memory of the subordinate attributes of in-group and out-group members. *Journal of Personality and Social Psychology, 42,* 1051–1068.

Parker, L., Georgaca, E., Harper, D., McLaughlin, T., & Stowell-Smith, M. (1995). *Deconstructing psychopathology.* London: Sage.

Passalacqua, S., & Cervantes, J. M. (2008). Understanding gender and culture within the context of spirituality: Implications for counselors. *Counseling and Values, 52,* 224–239.

Pasupathi, M., & Lockenhoff, C. E. (2002). Ageist behavior. In T. Nelson (Ed.), *Ageism: Stereotyping and prejudice against older persons* (pp. 201–246). Cambridge, MA: MIT Press.

Pedersen, P. B., Lonner, W. J., Draguns, J. G., & Trimble, J. E (Eds.). (2007). *Counseling across cultures* (6th ed.). Thousand Oaks, CA: Sage.

Perdue, C., & Gurtman, M. (1990). Evidence for the automaticity of ageism. *Journal of Experimental Social Psychology, 26,* 199–216.

Peregoy, J. J. (1993). Transcultural counseling with American Indians and Alaskan Natives: Contemporary issues for consideration. In J. McFadden (Ed.), *Transcultural counseling: Bilateral and international perspectives* (pp. 163–191). Alexandria, VA: American Counseling Association.

Perry, P. (2002). *Shades of white: White kids and racial identities in high school.* Durham, NC: Duke University Press.

Peterson, T. (2007). Another level: Friendship transcending geography and race. *The Journal of Men's Studies, 15*(1), 71–82.

Pettigrew, T. F. (1979). The ultimate attribution error: Extending Allport's cognitive analysis of prejudice. *Personality and Social Psychology Bulletin, 5,* 461–476.

Pettigrew, T. F., & Tropp, L. R. (2006). A meta-analytic test of intergroup contact theory. *Journal of Personality and Social Psychology, 90,* 751–783.

Petty, R. E., Brinol, P., & DeMarree, K. (2007). The meta-cognitive model (MCM) of attitudes: Implications for attitude measurement, change and strength. *Social Cognition, 25*(5), 657–686.

Phillimore, P. (1991). Unmarried women of the Dhaula Dhar: Celibacy and social control in Northwest India. *Journal of Anthropological Research, 47*(3), 331–350.

Phillips, D. A., Voran, M., Kisker, E., & Howes, C. (1994). Child care for children in poverty: Opportunity or inequity? *Child Development, 65,* 472–492.

Phillips, J. C., Ingram, K. M., Grant Smith, N., & Mindes, E. (2003). Methodological and content review of lesbian-, gay-, and bisexual-related articles in counseling journals: 1990–1999. *The Counseling Psychologist, 31*(1), 25–62.

Phinney, J. S. (1989). Stages of ethnic identity in minority group adolescence. *Journal of Early Adolescence, 9,* 34–49.

Phinney, J. S. (1990). Ethnic identity in adolescents and adults: Review of research. *Psychological Bulletin, 108,* 499–514.

Phinney, J. S. (1992). The multigroup ethnic identity measure: A new scale for use with diverse groups. *Journal of Adolescent Research, 7,* 156–176.

Phinney, J. S., & Alipuria, L. (1990). Ethnic identity in older adolescents from four ethnic groups. *Journal of Adolescence, 13,* 171–183.

Phinney, J. S., Horenczyk, G., Liebkind, K., & Vedder, P. (2001). Ethnic identity, immigration, and well-being: An interactional perspective. *Journal of Social Issues, 57,* 493–510.

Phinney, J. S., & Rotheram, M. J. (Eds.). (1987a). *Children's ethnic socialization: Pluralism and development.* Newbury Park, CA: Sage.

Phinney, J. S., & Rotheram, M. J. (1987b). Children's ethnic socialization: Themes and implications. In J. S. Phinney & M. J. Rotheram (Eds.), *Children's ethnic socialization: Pluralism and development* (pp. 274–292). Newbury Park, CA: Sage.

Phinney, J. S., & Tarver, S. (1988). Ethnic identity search and commitment in Black and White eighth graders. *Journal of Early Adolescence, 8,* 265–277.

Piaget, J. (1969). *The child's conception of physical causality.* Totowa, NJ: Littlefield, Adams.

Piaget, J. (1972). *The psychology of intelligence.* Totowa, NJ: Littlefield, Adams.

Plutchik, R. (1980). *Emotion: A psychoevolutionary synthesis.* New York: Harper & Row.

Ponterotto, J. G. (1988). Racial consciousness development among White counselor trainees: A stage model. *Journal of Multicultural Counseling and Development, 16,* 146–156.

Ponterotto, J. G. (1998). Charting a course for research in multicultural counseling training. *Counseling Psychologist, 26,* 43–68.

Ponterotto, J. G., & Austin, R. (2005). Emerging approaches to training psychologists to be culturally competent. In R. T. Carter (Ed.), *Handbook of racial-cultural psychology and counseling: Training and practice* (Vol. 2, pp. 19–35). New York: Wiley.

Ponterotto, J. G., Casas, J. M., Suzuki, L. A., & Alexander, C. M. (Eds.). (2001). *Handbook of multicultural counseling* (2nd ed.). Thousand Oaks, CA: Sage.

Ponterotto, J. G., Utsey, S. O., & Pedersen, P. B. (2006). *Preventing prejudice: A guide for counselors, educators, and parents.* Thousand Oaks, CA: Sage.

Pope-Davis, D. B., & Coleman, H. L. K. (Eds.). (1997). *Multicultural counseling competencies: Assessment, education and training, and supervision.* Thousand Oaks, CA: Sage.

Pope-Davis, D. B., & Coleman, J. L. K. (Eds.). (2001). *The intersection of race, class, and gender in multicultural counseling.* Thousand Oaks, CA: Sage.

Pope-Davis, D. B., & Ottavi, T. M. (1994). The relationship between racism and racial identity among White Americans: A replication and extension. *Journal of Counseling & Development, 72,* 293–297.

Poran, M. (2002). Denying diversity: Perceptions of beauty and social comparison processes among Latina, Black, and White women. *Sex Roles, 47,* 65–81.

Poston, W. S. C. (1990). The biracial identity development model: A needed addition. *Journal of Multicultural Counseling and Development, 18,* 152–155.

Power, M., & Dalgleish, T. (1997). *Cognition and emotion: From order to disorder.* Hove, United Kingdom: Erlbaum.

Powlishta, K. (1995). Intergroup processes in childhood: Social categorization and sex role development. *Developmental Psychology, 31,* 781–788.

Powlishta, K., Serbin, L. A., Doyle, A., & White, D. R. (1994). Gender, ethnic, and body type biases: The generality of prejudice in childhood. *Developmental Psychology, 30,* 526–536.

Poyrazli, S., & Lopez, M. D. (2007). An exploratory study of perceived discrimination and homesickness: A comparison of international students and American students. *The Journal of Psychology, 14*(3), 263–280.

Progoff, I. (1992). *At a journal workshop: Writing to access the power of the unconscious and evoke creative ability.* New York: Tarcher/Putnam.

Pronin, E., Gilovich, T., & Ross, L. (2004). Theoretical note: Objectivity in the eye of the beholder: Divergent perceptions of bias in self versus others. *Psychological Review, 111*(3), 781–799.

Pronin, E., Kruger, J., Savitsky, K., & Ross, L. (2001). You don't know me, but I know you: The illusion of asymmetric insight. *Journal of Personality and Social Psychology, 81,* 639–656.

Pronin, E., Lin, D. Y., & Ross, L. (2002). The bias blind spot: Perceptions of bias in self- versus others. *Personality and Social Psychology Bulletin, 28,* 369–381.

Prossor, J. (1998). *Second skins: The body narratives of transsexuality.* New York: Columbia University Press.

Pugh, K. J., & Bergin, D. A. (2005). The effect of schooling on students' out-of-school experience. *Educational Researcher, 34*(9), 15–23.

Quinn, M. J., & Tomita, S. K. (1986). *Elder abuse and neglect: Causes, diagnosis, and intervention strategies.* New York: Springer.

Radomsky, T. R. (1995). *Lost voices: Women, chronic pain, and abuse.* Philadelphia: Haworth Press.

Rapley, M. (2004). *The social construction of intellectual disability.* Cambridge, England: Cambridge University Press.

Rauscher, L., & McClintock, M. (1997). Ableism curriculum design. In M. Adams, L. A. Bell, & P. Griffin (Eds.), *Teaching for diversity and social justice: A sourcebook* (pp. 198–299). New York: Routledge.

Regents of the University of Michigan. (2006). *Poverty in the United States: Frequently asked questions.* Retrieved December 15, 2007, from http://www.npc.umich.edu/poverty/

Reid, D. K., & Knight, M. G. (2006). Disability justifies exclusion of minority students: A critical history grounded in disability students. *Educational Researcher, 35,* 18–23.

Reid, P. T. (1984). Feminism versus minority group identity: Not for Black women only. *Sex Roles, 10*(3/4), 247–255.

Remafedi, G., Farrow, J., & Deisher, R. (1991). Risk factors for attempted suicide in gay and lesbian youth. *In Pediatrics, 87*(6), 869–876.

Reyes-Ortiz, C. (1997). Physicians must confront ageism. *Academic Medicine, 72*(10), 831.

Reyna, C., Henry, P. J., Korfmacher, W., & Tucker, A. (2005). Examining the principles in principled conservatism: The role of responsibility stereotypes as cues for deservingness in racial policy decision. *Journal of Personality and Social Psychology, 90*(1), 109–128.

Reynolds, A. L. (1995). Challenges and strategies for teaching multicultural counseling courses. In I. G. Ponterotto, J. M. Casa, L. A. Suzuki, & C. M. Alexander (Eds.), *Handbook of multicultural counseling* (pp. 312–330). Thousand Oaks, CA: Sage.

Rich, A. (1990). Compulsory heterosexuality and lesbian existence. *Signs, 5,* 631–660.

Riddle, D. (1985). Homophobia scale. In K. Obear & A. Reynolds (Eds.), *Opening doors to understanding and acceptance* (p. 14). Boston: Unpublished essay.

Ridley, C. R. (2005). *Overcoming unintentional racism in counseling and therapy: A practitioner's guide* (2nd ed.). Thousand Oaks, CA: Sage.

Ridley, C. R., Hill, C. L., Thompson, C. E., & Ormerod, A. J. (2001). Clinical practice guidelines in assessment. In D. B. Pope-Davis & H. L. K. Coleman (Eds.), *The intersection of race, class, and gender in multicultural counseling* (pp. 191–211). Thousand Oaks, CA: Sage.

Robb, C. (2006). *This changes everything: The relational revolution in psychology.* New York: Farrar, Straus & Giroux.

Robbins, J. M., & Krueger, J. I. (2005). Social projection of ingroups and outgroups: A review and meta-analysis. *Personality and Social Psychology Review, 9*(1), 32–47.

Robinson, T. L. (1999). The intersections of dominant discourses across race, gender, and other identities. *Journal of Counseling and Development, 77,* 73–79.

Robinson, T. L. (2005). *The convergence of race, ethnicity and gender: Multiple identities in counseling* (2nd ed.). Upper Saddle River, NJ: Pearson.

Robinson, T. L., & Howard-Hamilton, M. F. (2000). *The convergence of race, ethnicity, and gender.* Upper Saddle River, NJ: Prentice Hall.

Robinson-Wood, T. L. (2008). *The convergence of race, ethnicity and gender: Multiple identities in counseling* (3rd ed.). Upper Saddle River, NJ: Pearson.

Roediger, D. R. (1999). *The wages of Whiteness: Race and the making of the American working class* (Rev. ed.). New York: Verso Books.

Rogers, C. (1951). *Client-centered therapy.* Boston: Houghton Mifflin.

Rogers, C. (1986). Carl Rogers on the development of the person-centered approach. *Person-Centered Review, 1*(3), 257–259.

Root, M. P. (1990). Resolving "other" status: Identity development of biracial individuals. In L. Brown & M. P. P. Root (Eds.), *Complexity and diversity in feminist theory and therapy* (pp. 185–205). New York: Haworth Press.

Root, M. P. (1992). *Racially mixed people in America.* Thousand Oaks, CA: Sage.

Root, M. P. (1998). Experiences and processes affecting racial identity development: Preliminary results from the Biracial Sibling Project. *Cultural Diversity and Mental Health, 4,* 237–247.

Root, M. P. (1999). The biracial baby boom: Understanding ecological constructions of racial identity in the 21st century. In R. Hernandez-Sheets & E. R. Hollins (Eds.), *Racial and ethnic identity in school practices: Aspects of human development* (pp. 67–90). Mahwah, NJ: Erlbaum.

Roscoe, W. (2000). *Changing ones: Third and fourth genders in native North America.* New York: Palgrave Macmillian

Rosenwasser, P. (2000). *Tool for transformation: Co-operative inquiry as a process for healing from internalized oppression.* Paper presented at the Adult Education Research Conference (AERC), June 2–4, in British Columbia, Canada. Retrieved February 25, 2009, from http://www.edst.educ.ubc.ca/aerc/2000/rosenwasserp1-web.htm

Ross, J. (2007). *Anna Halprin: Experience as dance.* Berkeley: University of California Press.

Rothenberg, P. S. (Ed.). (2005). *White privilege: Essential readings on the other side of racism* (2nd ed.). New York: Worth.

Roughgarden, J. (2004). *Evolution's rainbow: Diversity, gender, and sexuality in nature and people.* Berkeley: University of California Press.

Rowe, W., Behrens, J. T., & Leach, M. M. (1995). Racial/ethnic identity and racial consciousness: Looking back and looking forward. In J. G. Ponterotto, J. M. Casa, L. A. Suzuki, & C. M. Alexander (Eds.), *Handbook of multicultural counseling* (pp. 218–235). Thousand Oaks, CA: Sage.

Rowe, W., Bennett, S. K., & Atkinson, D. R. (1994). White racial identity models: A critique and alternate proposal. *Counseling Psychologist, 22,* 129–146.

Roysircar, G., Arredondo, P., Fuertes, J. N., Ponterotto, J. G., & Toporek, R. L. (Eds.). (2003). *Multicultural counseling competencies.* Alexandria, VA: Association of Multicultural Counseling and Development.

Roysircar-Sodowsky, G., & Kuo, P. Y. (2001). Determining cultural validity of personality assessment: Some guidelines. In D. B. Pope-Davis & J. L. K. Coleman (Eds.), *The intersection of race, class, and gender in multicultural counseling* (pp. 213–239). Thousand Oaks, CA: Sage.

Rubin, M., & Hewstone, M. (1998). Social identity theory's self-esteem hypothesis: A review and some suggestions for clarification. *Personality and Social Psychology Review, 2,* 40–62.

Ruble, D. N., & Martin, C. L. (1998). Gender development. In N. Eisenberg (Ed.), *Handbook of child psychology: Social emotional and personality development* (pp. 933–1016). New York: Wiley.

Rudman, L. A. (2004). Social justice in our minds, homes, and society: The nature, causes, and consequences of implicit bias. *Social Justice Research, 17,* 129–142.

Ruesch, J., & Bateson, G. (1987). *Communication: The social matrix of psychiatry.* New York: Norton.

Ruiz, A. S. (1990). Ethnic identity: Crisis and resolution. *Journal of Multicultural Counseling and Development, 18,* 29–40.

Rutland, A. (2004). The development of self-regulation of intergroup attitudes in children. In M. Bennett & F. Sani (Eds.), *The development of the social self* (pp. 247–265). New York: Psychology Press.

Rydell, R. J., McConnell, A. R., Mackie, D. M., & Strain, L. M. (2006). Of two minds: Forming and changing valence-inconsistent implicit and explicit attitudes. *Psychological Science, 17,* 954–958.

Rydell, R. J., McConnell, A. R., Strain, L. M., Claypool, H. M., & Hugenberg, K. (2007). Implicit and explicit attitudes respond differently to increasing amounts of counterattitudinal information. *European Journal of Social Psychology, 37,* 867–878.

Sabnani, H. B., Ponterotto, J. G., & Borodovsky, L. G. (1991). White racial identity development and cross-cultural counselor training. *The Counseling Psychologist, 19,* 76–102.

Salk, J. (1973). *Survival of the wisest.* New York: Harper & Row.

Salomon, G., & Perkins, D. N. (1989). Rocky roads to transfer: Rethinking mechanisms of a neglected phenomenon [Electronic version]. *Educational Psychologists, 24*(2), 113–142.

Sanchez-Hucles, J. V. (1998). Racism: Emotional abusiveness and psychological trauma for ethnic minorities. *Journal of Emotional Abuse, 1*(2), 69–87.

Sandhu, D. S. (Ed.). (1997a). Introduction: Asian and Pacific Islander Americans [Special issue]. *Journal of Multicultural Counseling and Development, 25*(1), 4–6.

Sandhu, D. S. (1997b). Psychocultural profiles of Asian and Pacific Islander Americans: Implications for counseling and psychotherapy [Special issue]. *Journal of Multicultural Counseling and Development, 25*(1), 7–22.

Sandoz, J. (2005). *Bodies of knowledge at Evergreen: Teaching, learning, impairments and social disablement* [Position paper]. Retrieved August 15, 2007, from Evergreen State College, Office for Diversity Affairs and Equal Opportunity Web site, at http://www.evergreen.edu/diversity/articles

Santiago-Rivera, A. L., Arredondo, P., & Gallardo-Cooper, M. (2002). *Counseling Latinos and la familiar: A practical guide.* Thousand Oaks, CA: Sage.

Schacter, D. L. (1987). Implicit memory: History and current status. *Journal of Experimental Psychology: Learning, Memory, and Cognition, 13,* 501–518.

Schacter, D. L., & Scarry, E. (2001). *Memory, brain, and belief.* Cambridge, MA: Harvard University Press.

Schneider, D. J. (2004). *The psychology of stereotyping.* New York: Guilford.

Schultz, R., & Decker, S. (1985). Long-term adjustment to physical disability: The role of social support, perceived control, and self-blame. *Journal of Personality and Social Psychology, 48,* 1162–1172.

Schure, M. B., Christopher, J., & Christopher, S. (2008). Mind-body medicine and the art of self-care: Teaching mindfulness to counseling students through yoga, meditation, and qigong. *Journal of Counseling & Development, 86,* 47–56.

Schwartz, S. J., Montgomery, M. J., & Briones, E. (2006). The role of identity in acculturation among immigrant people: Theoretical propositions, empirical questions, and applied recommendations. *Human Development, 49,* 1–30.

Searle, J. (Ed.). (1997). *The mystery of consciousness.* New York: New York Review of Books.

Seidman, S. (1993). Identity and politics in a "postmodern" gay culture. In M. Warner (Ed.), *Fear of a queer planet* (pp. 105–142). Minneapolis: University of Minnesota Press.

Sengupta, R. (2006). Reading representations of Black, East Asian, and White women in magazines for adolescent girls. *Sex Roles, 54,* 799–808.

Shaley, A. Y. (2002). Treating survivors in the immediate aftermath of traumatic events. In R. Yehuda (Ed.), *Treating trauma survivors with PTSD* (pp. 157–188). Arlington, VA: American Psychiatric Publishing.

Shapiro, J. P. (2000). A separate and unequal education for minorities with learning disabilities. In M. Adams, W. J. Blumenfeld, R. Castaneda, H. W. Hackman, M. L. Peters, & X. Zuniga (Eds.), *Readings for diversity and social justice* (pp. 340–342). New York: Routledge.

Sheng-Yen, C., Crook, J., Child, S., Kalin, M., & Andricevic, Z. (2002). *Chan comes West.* Elmhurst, NY: Dharma Drum.

Shotter, J. (1989). Social accountability and the social construction of "you." In J. Shotter & K. J. Gergen (Eds.), *Texts of identity* (pp. 133–151). London: Sage.

Sidis, B. (1898). *The psychology of suggestion.* New York: Appleton.

Simon, B., & Brown, R. (1987). Perceived intragroup homogeneity in minority/majority contexts. *Journal of Personality and Social Psychology, 53,* 703–711.

Simon, R. J., & Lynch, J. P. (1999). A comparative assessment of public opinion towards immigrants and immigration policies. *International Migration Review, 33,* 455–467.

Singer, T., & Kimbles, S. L. (Eds.). (2004). *The cultural complex.* New York: Brunner-Routledge.

Smedley, A., & Smedley, B. D. (2005). Race as biology is fiction, racism as a social problem is real: Anthropological and historical perspectives on the social construction of race. *American Psychologist, 60*(1), 16–26.

Smith, L. (2005). Psychotherapy, classism, and the poor: Conspicuous by their absence. *American Psychologist, 60,* 687–696.

Smith, L. Foley, P. F., & Chaney, M. P. (2008). Addressing classism, ableism, and heterosexism in counselor education. *Journal of Counseling & Development, 86,* 303–309.

Sodowsky, G. R., & Lai, E. W. M. (1997). Asian immigrant variables and structural models of cross-cultural distress. In A. Booth, A. C. Crouter, & N. Landale (Eds.), *Immigration and the family: Research and policy on U.S. immigrants* (pp. 211–237). Thousand Oaks, CA: Sage.

Sodowskly, G. R., Lai, E. W. M., & Plake, B. (1991). Moderating effects of sociocultural variables on acculturation attitudes of Hispanics and Asian Americans. *Journal of Counseling and Development, 70,* 194–204.

Solomon, A. (1992). Clinical diagnosis among diverse populations: A multicultural perspective. *Journal of Contemporary Human Services, 73,* 371–377.

Solso, R. L. (2001). *Cognitive psychology* (6th ed.). Needham Heights, MA: Allyn & Bacon.

Sorsoli, L. (2007). Where the whole thing fell apart: Race, resilience, and the complexity of trauma. *Journal of Aggression, Maltreatment & Trauma, 14*(1/2), 99–121.

Stainton, T. (1994). *Autonomy and social policy: Rights, mental handicap and community care.* Aldershot, United Kingdom: Avebury.

Steele, C. M. (1988). The psychology of self-affirmation: Sustaining the integrity of the self. In L. Berkowitz (Ed.), *Advances in experimental social psychology* (Vol. 21, pp. 261–302). New York: Academic Press.

Stetsenko, A., Little, T. D., Gordeeva, T., Grasshof, M., & Oettingen, G. (2000). Gender effects in children's beliefs about school performance: A cross-cultural study. *Child Development, 71*(2), 517–527.

Steward, R. J., Wright, D. J., Jackson, J. D., & Jo, H. (1998). The relationship between multicultural counseling training and the evaluation of culturally sensitive and culturally insensitive counselors. *Journal of Multicultural Counseling and Development, 3,* 205–217.

Stier, A., & Hinshaw, S. P. (2007). Explicit and implicit stigma against individuals with mental illness. *Australian Psychologist, 42*(2), 106–117.

Storey, K. (2007). Combating ableism in schools. *Preventing School Failure, 52*(1), 56–58.

Stott, R. (2007). When head and heart do not agree: A theoretical and clinical analysis of rational-emotional dissociation (RED) in cognitive therapy. *Journal of Cognitive Psychotherapy: An International Quarterly, 21*(1), 37–50.

Strassberg, Z., Dodge, K. A., Pettit, G. S., & Bates, J. E. (1994). Spanking in the home and children's subsequent aggression toward kindergarten peers. *Development and Psychopathology, 6,* 445–461.

Stubblefield, A. (2007). "Beyond the pale": Tainted Whiteness, cognitive disability, and eugenic sterilization. *Hypatia, 22*(2), 162–181.

Sue, D. W., Arredondo, P., & McDavis, R. J. (1992). Multicultural counseling competencies and standards: A call to the profession. *Journal of Counseling and Development, 70,* 477–483.

Sue, D. W., Carter, R.T., Casas, J. M., Fouad, N. A., Ivey, A. E., Jensen, M., et al. (1998). *Multicultural counseling competencies: Individual and organizational development.* Thousand Oaks, CA: Sage.

Sue, D. W., & Sue, D. (1990). *Counseling the culturally different: Theory and practice* (2nd ed.). New York: Wiley.

Sue, D. W., & Sue, D. (1999). *Counseling the culturally different: Theory and practice* (3rd ed.). New York: Wiley.

Sue, D. W., & Sue, D. (2003). *Counseling the culturally diverse: Theory and practice* (4th ed.). Hoboken, NJ: Wiley.

Sue, D. W., & Sue, D. (2007). *Counseling the culturally diverse: Theory and practice* (5th ed.). New York: Wiley.

Susskind, J. E. (2003). Children's perception of gender-based illusory correlations: Enhancing preexisting relationships between gender and behavior. *Sex Roles, 48,* 483–494.

Susskind, J. E., & Hodges, C. (2007). Decoupling children's gender-based in-group positivity from out-group negativity. *Sex Roles, 56,* 707–716.

Swann, W. B., Langlois, J. H., & Gilbert, L. A. (Eds.). (1999). *Sexism and stereotypes in modern society.* Washington, DC: American Psychological Association.

Swartz-Kulstad, J. L., & Martin, W. E. (1999). Impact of culture and context on psychosocial adaptation: The cultural and contextual guide process. *Journal of Counseling & Development, 77,* 281–293.

Swim, J. K., Hyers, L. L., Cohen, L. L., Fitzgerald, D. C., & Bylsma, W. H. (2003). African American college students' experiences with everyday racism: Characteristics and responses to these incidents. *Journal of Black Psychology, 29,* 38–67.

Tajfel, H. (1981). *Human groups and social categories.* Cambridge, England: Cambridge University Press.

Tajfel, H., & Turner, J. C. (1979). An integrative theory of intergroup conflict. In W. G. Austin & S. Worchel (Eds.), *The social psychology of intergroup relations* (pp. 33–47). Monterey, CA: Brooks/Cole.

Tajfel, H., & Turner, J. C. (1986). The social identity theory of intergroup behavior. In S. Worchel & W. G. Austin (Eds.), *Psychology of intergroup relations* (pp. 7–24). Chicago: Nelson-Hall.

Takaki, R. (1993). *A different mirror: A history of multicultural America.* Boston: Little, Brown and Company.

Tatum, B. D. (2000). Defining racism: "Can we talk?" In M. Adams, W. J. Blumenfeld, R. Castaneda, H. W. Hackman, M. L. Peters, & X. Zuniga (Eds.), *Readings for diversity and social justice* (pp. 78–82). New York: Routledge.

Taylor, S. E., & Brown, J. D. (1988). Illusions and well-being: A social psychological perspective on mental health. *Psychology Bulletin, 103*, 193–210.

Teasdale, A., & Barnard, P. (1993). *Affect, cognition and change.* Hove, United Kingdom: Erlbaum.

Teitelbaum, S. (1990, April 1). Making everything perfectly fuzzy. *Los Angeles Times Magazine,* pp. 24–42.

Thomas, A., & Sillen, S. (1972). *Racism and psychiatry.* New York: Citadel Press.

Thomas, A. J., & Schwarzbaum, S. (2006). *Culture and identity: Life stories of counselors and therapists.* Thousand Oaks, CA: Sage.

Thompson, A. O. (1977). Race and color prejudice and the origin of the trans-Atlantic slave trade. *Caribbean Studies, 16,* 29–59.

Thompson, C., & Zoloth, B. (1989). *Homophobia* [Pamphlet]. Cambridge, MA: Campaign to End Homophobia.

Thompson, M. S., & Keith, V. M. (2001). The blacker the berry: Gender, skin tone, self-esteem and self-efficacy. *Gender & Society, 15,* 336–357.

Thompson, S. A. (2007). De/centering straight talk: Queerly informed inclusive pedagogy for gay and bisexual students with intellectual disabilities. *Journal of LGBT, 5*(1), 37–56.

Tropp, L. R., Erkut, S., Garcia Coll, C., Alarcon, O., & Garcia, H. A. (1999). Psychological acculturation: Development of a new measure of Puerto Ricans on the U.S. mainland. *Educational and Psychological Measurement, 59*(2), 351–367.

Tu, W. (1996). Global community as lived reality: Exploring spiritual resources for social development. *Social Policy and Social Progress, 1*(1), 39–51.

Turner, J. C., & Onorato, R. S. (1999). Social identity personality and the self-concept: A self-categorization perspective. In T. R. Tyler, R. M. Kramer, & O. P. Hon (Eds.), *The psychology of the social self* (pp. 11–46). Mahwah, NJ: Erlbaum.

Uba, L. (1994). *Asian Americans: Personality patterns, identity, and mental health.* New York: Guilford.

United Nations. (1995). Notes for speakers: Social development. New York: Author.

United Nations High Commissioner for Refugees, Statistical Unit. (1998). *Refugees and others of concern to UNHCR: 1997 statistical overview.* Retrieved February 25, 2009, from http://www.unhcr.org/cgi-bin/texis/vtx/home?id

United States Census Bureau. (2003). National population estimates: Characteristics. Retrieved August 18, 2004, from http://www.census.gov/popest/archives/2000s

United States Census Bureau. (2004). National population estimates: Characteristics. Retrieved August 15, 2005, from http://www.census.gov/popest/archives/2000s

Updegrave, W. L. (1989, December 1). Race and money. *Money, 18*(12), 152–172.

U.S. Department of Justice, U.S. Equal Employment Opportunity Commission. (2002, August 23; 2005, February 2). Americans with Disabilities Act: Questions and answers. Available at http://www.usdoj.gov/crt/ada/q%26aeng02.htm

U.S. Equal Employment Opportunity Commission. (2008). The Civil Rights Act of 1991. Retrieved July 18, 2008 from http://www.eeoc.gov/policy

Utsey, S. O., Ponterotto, G., & Porter, J. (2008). Prejudice and racism, year 2008—still going strong: Research on reducing prejudice with recommended methodological advances. *Journal of Counseling & Development, 86,* 339–347.

Valian, V. (2004). Beyond gender schemas: Improving the advancement of women in academia. *NWSA Journal, 16*(1), 207–220.

van Boven, L., Dunning, D., & Loewenstein, G. (2000). Egocentric empathy gaps between owners and buyers: Misperceptions of the endowment effect. *Journal of Personality and Social Psychology, 79*, 66–76.

van de Castle, R. (1994). *Our dreaming mind.* New York: Ballantine.

van der Kolk, B. A. (2002). The assessment and treatment of complex P.T.S.D. In R. Yehuda (Ed.), *Treating trauma survivors with PTSD* (pp. 127–156). Washington, DC: American Psychiatric Publishing.

Vandiver, B. J., Cross, W. E., Jr., Worrell, F. C., & Fhagen-Smith, P. (2002). Validating the Cross Racial Identity Scale. *Journal of Counseling Psychology, 49*, 71–85.

Velasquez, R. J. (Ed.). (1997). Guest editor: Counseling Mexican Americans/Chicanos [Special issue]. *Journal of Multicultural Counseling and Development, 25*(2), 92–93.

Verkuyten, M. (2007). Ethnic in-group favoritism among minority and majority groups: Testing the self-esteem hypothesis among preadolescents. *Journal of Applied Social Psychology, 37*(3), 486–500.

Vinson, T. S., & Neimeyer, G. J. (2000). The relationship between racial identity development and multicultural counseling competency. *Journal of Multicultural Counseling and Development, 28*, 177–192.

Vohs, K. D., & Finkel, E. J. (Eds.). (2006). *Self & relationships: Connecting intrapersonal and interpersonal process.* New York: Guilford.

von Hooren, S. A. H., Valentun, A. M., Bosma, H., Ponds, R. W. H., van Boxtel, M. P. J., & Jolles, J. (2007). Cognitive functioning in healthy older adults aged 64–81: A cohort study into the effects of age, sex, and education. *Aging, Neuropsychology, and Cognition, 14*, 40–54.

Waldman, I. (1996). Aggressive boys' hostile perceptual and response biases: The role of attention and impulsivity. *Child Development, 67*, 1015–1033.

Warwick, L. L. (2002). Self-in-relation theory and women's religious identity in therapy. *Women and Therapy, 24*, 121–131.

Wegener, D. T., Clark, J. K., & Petty, R. E. (2006). Not all stereotyping is created equal: Differential consequences of thoughtful versus nonthoughtful stereotyping. *Journal of Personality and Social Psychology, 90*(1), 42–59.

Weinstein, L., & D'Amico, F. (1999). Introduction. In F. D'Amico & L. Weinstein (Eds.), *Gender camouflage: Women and the U.S. military* (pp. 1–9). New York: New York University Press.

Wellman, H. M. (1990). *The child's theory of mind.* Cambridge, MA: MIT Press.

Wellman, H. M., & Cross, D. (2001). Theory of mind and conceptual change. *Child Development, 72*(3), 702–707.

Wellman, H. M., Cross, D., & Watson, J. (2001). Meta-analysis of theory-of-mind development: The truth about false beliefs. *Child Development, 72*(3), 655–684.

Wikan, U. (1991). The Xanith: A third gender role? In *Behind the veil in Arabia: Women in Oman* (pp. 168–186). Chicago: University of Chicago Press.

Williams, W. L. (1986). *The spirit and the flesh: Sexual diversity in American Indian culture.* Boston: Beacon Press.

Wilson, W. J. (1987). *The truly disadvantaged: The inner city, the underclass, and public policy.* Chicago: University of Chicago Press.

Wise, T. (2005). Membership has its privileges: Thoughts on acknowledging and challenging whiteness. In P. S. Rothenberg (Ed.), *White privilege: Essential readings on the other side of racism* (2nd ed., pp. 119–122). New York: Worth.

Woolley, J. D., & Wellman, H. M. (1992). Children's conceptions of dreams. *Cognitive Development, 73*, 365–380.

Woolley, J. D., & Wellman, H. M. (1993). Origin and truth: Young children's understanding of imaginary mental representations. *Child Development, 64*(1), 1–17.

Wright, E. O. (2001). A conceptual menu for studying the interconnections of class and gender. In J. Baxter & M. Western (Eds.), *Reconfigurations of class and gender* (pp. 28–38). Stanford, CA: Stanford University Press.

Yamada, A., Marsella, A. J., & Yamada, S. Y. (1998). The development of the ethnocultural identity behavior index: Psychometric properties and validation with Asian American and Pacific Islanders. *Asian American and Pacific Islander Journal of Health, 6*(1), 35–45.

Yau, T. Y., Sue, D., & Hayden, D. (1992). Counseling style preference of international students. *Journal of Counseling Psychology, 39*, 100–104.

Yeh, C. J., & Inose, M. (2003). International students' reported English fluency, social support satisfaction, and social connectedness as predictors of acculturative stress. *Counseling Psychology Quarterly, 16*, 15–28.

Ying, Y. (2002). The conception of depression in Chinese Americans. In K. Kurasaki, S. Okasaki, & S. Sue (Eds.), *Asian American mental health: Assessment theories and methods* (pp. 173–184). New York: Kluwer Academic.

Yorks, L., & Kasl, E. (2002). Toward a theory and practice for whole-person learning: Reconceptualizing experience and the role of affect. *Adult Education Quarterly, 52*(3), 176–192.

Young, I. M. (2000). Five faces of oppression. In M. Adams, W. J. Blumenfeld, R. Castaneda, H. W. Hackman, M. L. Peters, & X. Zuniga (Eds.), *Readings for diversity and social justice* (pp. 35–49). New York: Routledge.

Zhang, W., Lingin, G., Zhang, Q., Wang, Y., & Chen, X. (2003). A longitudinal study on the development of 3- to 4-year-old children's aggressive behavior. *Psychological Science, 26*, 49–52.

Zweig, C., & Abrams, J. (1991). *Meeting the shadow: The hidden power of the dark side of human nature.* New York: Penguin Putnam.

Zweig, M. (2000). *The working class majority: America's best kept secret.* Ithaca, NY: Cornell University Press.

Index

About the Author

Dr. Heesoon Jun has a master's degree in psychology from Radford University in Virginia and a doctorate in psychology from the University of Washington. Currently she resides in Washington state where she is a licensed psychologist with a part-time private practice and teaches psychology, including multicultural counseling, at Evergreen State College.

Dr. Jun was born into and raised by a religiously tolerant but race- and class-biased family in Seoul, South Korea. She came to the United States alone to study psychology as an undergraduate where she experienced a status change from the majority to the minority and privileged to oppressed. Dr. Jun's bicultural and bilingual experiences have been instrumental in facilitating an interest in the impact of sociocultural contexts on one's own values, beliefs, and automatic thoughts and how to implement social justice and equity for diversified populations.